THE IMPORTANCE OF THE
COMMUNITY RABBI

Leading with Compassionate Halachah

Daniel Sperber

Foreword by
Rabbi Dov Linzer
and Chaim Trachtman MD

מכון לינדנבאום
ללימוד הלכה
LINDENBAUM CENTER
FOR HALAKHIC STUDIES

URIM PUBLICATIONS
Jerusalem • New York

The Importance of the Community Rabbi:
Leading with Compassionate Halachah
by Daniel Sperber
Foreword by Rabbi Dov Linzer and Chaim Trachtman MD
Index by Marc I. Sherman

Copyright © 2020 Daniel Sperber

Typeset by Ariel Walden

Printed in Israel

First Edition
ISBN 978-965-524-238-6

Lindenbaum Center for Halakhic Studies
3700 Henry Hudson Parkway, Bronx, NY 10463 USA
www.YCTorah.org

Urim Publications
P.O. Box 52287, Jerusalem 9152102, Israel
www.UrimPublications.com

Cover art by Andi Arnovitz

This piece, part of the "Women of the Book" project (see: womenofthebook.org) features *Parshat Re'eh* which is full of compassionate guidance regarding *tzedakah* (charity) towards members of the community. I worked in layers in this piece, symbolizing the many levels of understanding and interpretation that exist in the Torah. I have used the image of the hamsa, so prevalent here in Jerusalem, to represent the open hand in giving. Hanging from these hands are all the categories of obligation to which an individual is required to give charity, as enumerated in the *Kitzur Shulhan Aruch*. A rabbi deeply connected to his community knows who is in need and sensitively directs his congregants to the optimal ways of helping one another.

Library of Congress Cataloging-in-Publication Data

Names: Sperber, Daniel, author.
Title: The importance of the community rabbi : leading with compassionate halachah / Daniel Sperber.
Description: First edition. | Brooklyn, N.Y. : Urim Publications, [2020] | Includes index.
Identifiers: LCCN 2017057642 | ISBN 9789655242386 (hardcover : alk. paper)
Subjects: LCSH: Rabbis—Training of—United States. | Rabbis—Ordination—United States. | Orthodox Judaism—United States.
Classification: LCC BM75 .S64 2020 | DDC 296.6/1—dc23
LC record available at https://lccn.loc.gov/2017057642

This book is dedicated to
all of YCT's *musmakhim* (currently 133 and growing!)
in the U.S., Israel and throughout the world
who dedicate their lives each day to serving Klal Yisrael,
giving halakhic guidance that is humane and sensitive
and embodying a Torah and religious leadership
that welcomes, engages and inspires.

*D*edicated to

Rabbi MOSHE *zt"l* and SARAH RAKOWITZ

In tribute to their many years of devoted
service to the rabbinate
and their generosity and vision
in support of TORAH education in Israel
and especially for the
Jesselson Institute for Advanced Torah Studies
at Bar-Ilan University

CONTENTS

FOREWORD
By Rabbi Dov Linzer and Chaim Trachtman MD

Countless books have been written on halachah. This vast literature focuses not just on substantive halachah, which has been going on for millennia, but also, more recently, on "meta" topics – history of halachah, the nature of the halachic process, values and halachah, and even halachah as a theology. Far too few books have been written on the halachist or the *posek*. What – besides the foundation of mastery of the halachic material and strong analytic abilities – should be the traits that make for the ideal *posek*, the one that communities should be looking to hire, and that rabbinical schools and *yeshivot* should be looking to train? What should be his (and now also her!) character, his orientation towards halachah, his relationship to the larger world, and most importantly his relationship to his community and to the individuals who come to ask him questions and for whom he serves as a religious and moral guide?

Rabbi Dr. Daniel Sperber has done us all a great service by writing what we believe to be one of the first books on this topic. With his enormous erudition and scope of knowledge, he has gathered and organized the wealth of Talmudic and Rabbinic material on this topic, and presented it in a clear and highly readable style. Even more significant than the Rabbinic sources cited are the *stories* of rabbis that appear throughout the book, both in the body of the work and in the footnotes. If one wants to understand what being a rabbi of the people, an empathic and responsive *posek*, and a spiritual role model is truly about, there is no better source material than the *posek* himself.

In the book's preface Rabbi Sperber reminds us that in the past, ordination was a *personal* granting of authority by rabbi to student, and that the testing of a student was not only, or even primarily, to judge his knowledge and mastery of halachah and his halachic thinking, but also to assess his "spirit and character – whether he was able to discern the nature of the questioner, to listen and feel not just his questions but also his inner requirements." In real life, the rabbi's ability to empathize, to hear the question behind the question, allows for true spiritual guidance to take place and for real *pesak* to occur. Rav Moshe Feinstein was known to say that he *paskens* the *shoel*, the questioner and her specific realities, and not the *she'eila*, the question in the abstract. It is this spirit that drives the entire book.

As co-authors of this Foreword, we suggest there are parallels between the friendly *posek* and the competent physician. Throughout his works, Rambam frequently highlighted aspects of how doctors care for their patients to provide insight into the content or purpose of specific halachot. As a physician and halachist, Rambam seems to have viewed doctors and rabbis as partners in fostering people's well-being, one physical and the other spiritual. His description of dose escalation of medications to minimize the risk of adverse events and resorting to drastic interventions such as amputation of gangrenous limbs to protect against systemic complications and greater harm, served as models for specific mitzvot and rabbinic ordinances. In addition to understanding actual practices, the profession of medicine and the ideal "friendly" doctor may shed light on what it means to be a fully qualified *posek*, beyond the details of specific procedures and interventions.

Similar to the rabbinic student confronting the huge corpus of halachah, medical students are asked to learn a huge, rapidly growing body of knowledge. However, in parallel with the pressing need to convey increasing amounts of complex information in a limited amount of time, there is recognition that imparting a sense of professionalism is a critical element in training physicians and maintenance of certification. There is much discussion about what exactly is meant by professionalism, but there is an emerging consensus that professionalism encompasses more than a mastery of the facts. It involves those aspects of care that involve interpersonal relationships and interactions with other components of the patient's sphere of living.

This emphasis on professionalism intersects with Rabbi Sperber's "friendly" *posek*. Each of the features he describes has a parallel in medicine. On the most basic level, the issue of "friendly *posek*" is a question of whether a rabbi will decide, as a matter of black-letter law, in favor of a stricter position or a more lenient reading of the sources whenever feasible in halachic decision-making. The tendency to be stringent in religious practice stems from a fear of the spiritual consequences of transgressing the law. But taken as a standard approach, it can impose hardships on congregants and communities. Similarly in medicine, one can always recommend more intensive or invasive treatments to patients out of concern that any compromise in therapy will result in inadequate control of disease. But leniency, or adoption of more tolerable regimens, is more humane and professional if the data are supportive and account for the patient's overall state of health. Recognition of disadvantaged populations and the urgent need to enhance their access to comprehensive health care are analogous to Rabbi Sperber's admonition to show "sensitivity to the have-nots" and know "the needs of others." In medicine, inadequate care can arise from financial, social, or biological factors. Rabbi Sperber underscores the need for the thoughtful community rabbi to be aware and responsive to each of them – the poor, the *agunah*, the LGBT congregant, the physically disabled – as he guides his community. A friendly rabbi is engaged with the larger community and recognizes that her service is embedded in a larger social matrix. By taking these large-scale issues into account, he ensures that his decisions and guidance are not in conflict with the more global concerns of his congregants. Physicians too are being trained to be aware that their patient's illnesses occur in a wider context that extends far beyond the confines of the doctor's office. Engagement with these external factors ensures that the physician is more attuned to where her patients "live" and that her therapeutic recommendations are more likely to be accepted and implemented. Finally, Rabbi Sperber urges the good rabbi to be independent and steadfast in his opinions. Similarly, physicians must ensure that their recommendations are consistent and not unduly influenced by extraneous factors, conflicts of interest of all types, which are not relevant to the patient. The Sperberesque good rabbi and professional physician can be superimposed on one another. A rabbi or doctor should not be trained solely as a jurist of Jewish law or an expert in pathophysiology. Both must be attentive and aware of the whole person(s) in front of them so they can both guide and heal.

In the world of halachah, Rabbi Sperber probes more deeply and examines the mechanisms that are embedded in the system itself, that permit or even demand a more lenient ruling in a specific case than what may be dictated by the black-letter law. This includes well-known principles such as monetary loss, physical or emotional distress, human dignity, and ways of peace, as well as lesser-known strategies such as casting a blind eye, or special override legislation like *takkanat ha'shavim*.

Of great importance is the recurring theme that the ideal being discussed is not just a *pesak* that is lenient, but rather one that emerges from the deep values of the Torah. Halachah and *pesak* care about the human being just as much as they care about ritual concerns. This idea is embodied in the famous line by Rabbi Chaim Soloveitchik, who was extremely lenient when any health issue arose on Shabbat – "Do not say that I am lenient about Shabbat. I am very strict about protecting human life." This theme is underscored by some of the humane stories, which show how rabbis modeled this type of caring ethical life in all areas, not just as a factor in *pesak*.

In this regard, it is worth emphasizing that Rabbi Sperber includes in his list of principles for the "friendly *posek*" standards of behavior that may make *greater* demands on the individual than the letter of the law, such as *lifnim mi'shurat ha'din*, which might call on a person to return a lost object to the owner even if not technically obligated to do so. This principle is not so "friendly" to the person who found the object, but – beyond being the right thing to do – it shows the need for concern for the person who lost the object. This example points to the fact that being "friendly" is not always the same as being lenient, and it requires a broader sense of, and responsibility towards who is being impacted and the well-being of the whole community. Returning to the world of medicine, the competent doctor may also be required on occasion to provide care that exceeds the normal standards of practice but will act accordingly based on the overall needs of the patient, family, and community.

After reading the opening chapter, many readers will be convinced that the principle of leniency and the mechanisms to implement it are part of the very fabric of the halachic system but at the same time will wonder, "What are the limits?" This question must be addressed, not just because a full, nuanced understanding of the topic demands it, but because responsible *pesak* is always a balancing act between fidelity to black-letter, consensus law and responsiveness to the individual standing before the rabbi. To not rule leniently when warranted is to forget your halachically-mandated obligation to the *shoel;* to rule leniently when it is not warranted is to forget your obligation to the limits and ethos of the halachah in question.

The key word here is "warranted." For example, not every case of illness is a *choleh kol ha'guf,* a full-body illness which overrides certain Rabbinic restrictions on Shabbat; some are *meichush be'alma,* a slight discomfort. Not every issue can be raised to the level of a compromise of human dignity or of emotional distress, and not every difficult situation is a *she'at ha'dechak.* While one may certainly argue that we should, as a rule, adopt more expansive definitions of these criteria, there are limits. Even when a case falls into one of these categories, one must be cognizant of the counterbalancing weight of the halachah in question. Specifically, we almost never use these mechanisms when we are dealing with a biblical violation (almost never, but not never: there is an important debate whether a minority opinion can be relied upon for biblical matters in exigent cases). Even when dealing with Rabbinic prohibitions, there are areas – such as Shabbat – where the Sages allowed for many leniencies, and other areas where the Rabbis were much stricter. Admittedly, these points are not the focus of the book, and they emerge between the lines in some of the stories that Rabbi Sperber recounts. Nevertheless, it is important to underscore that all *pesak* is a balancing act, and that there are limits within which even "friendly" *poskim* must operate.

There is no educational formula for training "friendly *poskim*" or teaching professionalism in medicine. At best, medical school faculty can point to key elements and processes that allow a foundation to be created in training in the hope that a competent "friendly" physician will emerge over time with experience. Rabbi Sperber's objective and program is similar – it defines the key features of the halachic system and elements of the ideal community rabbi as a person and provides narrative examples of its emergence over time in varied settings throughout history and around the world.

This vision of an empathic, responsive, and professionally-trained rabbi, who has both mastery of halachah and a deep understanding of how to apply it to the people and communities who turn to him for guidance, is one that – as Rabbi Sperber tells us in his preface – has shaped the curriculum and approach of the newly founded "Moshe and

Sarah Rakowitz Rabbinic Training Program" at *Machon ha-Gavoah le-Torah*. It is also the vision that has guided YCT Rabbinical School since its inception nearly 20 years ago. Our training begins with a rigorous foundation in all the relevant halachic material, from the Talmud through the Rishonim, Shulhan Aruch, and *poskim*. This is then complemented by practicum within the yeshiva and outside its four walls, and by importing seasoned rabbis to engage students around challenging cases that they have confronted during their careers. Throughout, an ethos of empathy and responsiveness shapes the teaching and discussions. Students' tests consist not of "spit-back" questions that test mere knowledge, but of dozens of practical real-world cases which test their ability to analyze and assess the different aspects of the case, and to use good judgment in determining the best *pesak* for the individual person in her unique circumstance. In our Teshuva Workshops, students write *teshuvot* to real questions drawn from a database of hundreds that have been collected from our rabbis in the field. In addition to matters of technical halachah, their *teshuvot* must address pastoral, communal, and policy issues, and must display throughout a deep understanding of what it means to be both a *posek* and a religious guide. Our weekly process groups and world-class pastoral training program, with classes, role-plays, and over 400 hours of fieldwork, has a profound impact on students, the results of which can be seen not only in their explicitly pastoral work, but in every interaction they have with a congregant and student, and in their roles as *poskim*.

This ethos is also fundamental to The Lindenbaum Center for Halakhic Studies at YCT, which is proud to be the co-publisher of this book. The Lindenbaum Center promotes advanced Torah scholarship dedicated to enriching the discourse of halachah in the Modern Orthodox community and addressing contemporary issues with scholarship, sophistication, and sensitivity. Activities of the Center include the composition and dissemination of *teshuvot*, as well as producing podcasts, source sheets, and halachic writings to make this discourse accessible to a wide audience. In 2017, the Center also inaugurated the Lindenbaum Scholars, a cohort of prominent *poskim* from the Modern Orthodox and *dati leumi* community who learn, discuss, debate, and write on some of the most important topics facing our communities. The Lindenbaum Center for Halakhic Studies was established through a generous grant from Belda and Marcel Lindenbaum z"l. The Linden-baum family's generosity continues to fund the Center.

Educating future rabbis, like teaching medical students, is a time-con-suming, laborious process. There is always a danger that the importance of values, becoming a "friendly rabbi" or a professional "physician of the spirit," will be lost in the vast amount of knowledge to be mastered. At least for rabbis, there is a reliable guide to help students reach the desired destination. Hopefully, Rabbi Sperber's book will find a prom-inent place on the bookshelf of every rabbinical student and practicing rabbi, and may even serve as inspiration for the healing professional.

THE LUDWIG AND ERICA JESSELSON
INSTITUTE FOR ADVANCED TORAH STUDIES
AT BAR-ILAN UNIVERSITY

T HE *MACHON GAVOAH LETORAH*, ALSO KNOWN AS THE LUDWIG and Erica Jesselson Institute for Advanced Torah Studies at Bar-Ilan University, has provided for over forty years a *Bet Midrash* for men and *Midrasha* for women, offering students the opportunity to engage in intensive text-oriented Torah study while simultaneously pursuing their academic studies in the university in the faculties of their choice.

It further encourages their commitment to Torah study by providing qualified students both full and partial tuition scholarships and living stipends, based on their weekly hours of study. The faculty is made up of first-rate *talmidei chachamim* who number amongst the finest in Israel, along with instructors, both men and women, who are renowned scholars and charismatic teachers.

One can find all types of students in the *Machon*, even students who have little or no background in Jewish life or traditional texts. For these students, the *Johann and Norman Sternthal Reshit Torah Program* offers small classes, dynamic young teachers drawn from the ranks of the University's most gifted doctoral students, and a unique introduction to Jewish literature and life. The *Reshit* program gives its participants an intensive, authentic, and personalized Jewish learning experience, starts them on the path to independent Jewish learning, and empowers them to make life decisions informed by their Jewish identity in a non-coercive and non-judgmental environment.

The Bet Midrash is also the home to a variety of Torah activities. They include the Israel Experience for Overseas Students; classes for all students sponsored by the Campus Rabbi's Office; the Wengrovsky Family *Kollel Yom Shishi* for retirees; and the Rabbi Moshe and Sarah

Rakowitz Program in Practical Rabbinics, which trains community rabbis and their wives, and organizes placement and financial support in independent communities all over Israel. And here we must also acknowledge the generosity of the late Marcel Lindenbaum, without whose help successful placement of our "graduates" would not have been possible.

One of the Machon's most innovative new programs is *Nitzotzot, the President's Doctoral Forum for Torah and Science. Tochnit Nitzotzot* brings together scientists and Torah scholars, each without previous background in the other's field. The Torah scholar defines the challenge which is posed by the scientific discovery, and thus confronts new phenomena in the spirit of the rabbinic dictum that "there is no Torah study that does not reveal new insights." Similarly, the scientist is exposed to profound Torah concepts which can inform his findings and provide ongoing stimulation. The ground-breaking findings of the latest scientific research present an array of conceptual, cognitive, ethical and legal challenges to previously accepted notions; similarly, they may challenge conventional Torah perspectives. Yet at its core, the Torah has within it the power to provide intuitive and novel approaches to the complexities of today's cutting-edge issues in the world of science. There have been over fifty *Nitzotzot* seminars since their inception in 2009.

R. Shimon Altshul

PREFACE

WHEN MY SAINTLY GRANDFATHER FELT THAT MY FATHER, both of blessed memory, was ready to be called a rabbi – at a very young age - he sent him off on a journey to be examined by the leading rabbis in Romania in order to receive his rabbinic ordination, his *semichah*. He packed up his belongings and off he went to the various *gedolim*, and stayed with each of them for a couple of weeks. In those days, the examination consisted of a sort of dialogue between the rabbi and his pupils about the different halachic questions that were posed to him by the members of his community, which were discussed on the spot. The examinee, in this case my father, would be requested to express his opinion on each specific question that came up before the rabbi. At times they might agree on the answer, alternatively the rabbi would have to decide between different possible answers. The aim of the rabbi was not to test my father's "knowledge of the material" as it was assumed he had thoroughly mastered it. The aim was rather to reveal his spirit and character – whether he was able to discern the nature of the questioner, to listen and feel not just his questions but also his inner requirements. I should point out that my father, in his youth, studied everything with his father by heart, because in those years he was almost blind and could not read books. Hence, his knowledge of Torah was all from memory.

Nowadays, had my father sought to be examined for the Israeli Rabbinate, he would have found himself in a very different and somewhat strange situation. He, and several hundred of his fellow examinees, would enter anxiously into a large hall, be seated, and have to respond in writing to a single "silent" sheet of questions on a specific pre-determined section of the *Shulhan Aruch*. After several hours, he would silently get up, and submit his answers to the supervisor. Then, after half a year or so, if he was lucky, he would receive the results of the examination from an anonymous examiner upon whom he had never set eyes in his life.

This dramatic change in the nature of rabbinic ordination is by no means a hidden mystery. For just as in other areas, the procedure for granting ordination has been standardized. Try to imagine a thousand young students sitting in the salon of the *Gedol ha-Dor* – the leading rabbinic authority – for a personal examination! And even more paradoxically, most of the examinees in this huge crowd might have no intention whatsoever of actually serving in the rabbinate. For some see ordination as a part of learning Torah *li-shma* – for the sake of pure learning. Others regard the ordination as a sort of "academic diploma" which may grant them financial advantages, such as increases to their salary, as well as satisfying the requirements of the education authorities. Only a small handful truly dream of entering into the communal rabbinate as their life's vocation.

It is clear that such a vast *production-line* approach cannot possibly serve as an adequate framework for developing an understanding of the functions of community leadership and cultivating a personality with both knowledge and empathy. The creation of an active and successful community rabbinate requires an innovative and creative training program that is radically different from the formal preparations for the examinations of Israel's Chief Rabbinate.

What then is the alternative? We in the *Machon ha-Gavoah le-Torah*, known as the Ludwig and Erica Jesselson Institute for Advanced Torah Studies, in cooperation with *Likrat Shlichut*, seek to renew the face of the rabbinate, and introduce a new understanding of the nature and requirements of communal rabbinic leadership.

As a result, over the past several years we have trained and successfully placed some sixty rabbis across a large spectrum of communities throughout Israel.

To this end, and through the generosity of Rabbi Moshe Rakowitz and his dear wife Sarah, we developed the "Moshe and Sarah Rakowitz Rabbinic Training Program," and we also owe our thanks to Rabbi Carpel Bender for his success in broadening this initiative. As a result, the aforesaid renewal begins with our training program, which stresses the communal characteristics demanded of the rabbi in addition to his halachic functions.

The emphasis on community, and the attention given by the rabbi to every man and woman, boy and girl, had also led to new directions in teaching *pesikah*, the methodology of rendering halachic rulings. Our program integrates a broad knowledge of a variety of halachic approaches combined with an awareness of the implications of the ruling upon the individual, his family and even upon the rabbi's reputation and his standing in his congregation. This is accomplished through a series of complex "case studies" in which the young rabbi-to-be learns to identify the hidden aspects of the questions thrown out at him lurking beneath the more obvious stratum, and the complex and sometimes unintended effects that may result from his rulings.

Nowadays, more than ever before, the transformation of the face of the communal rabbinate is crucial. It has always been the case that the congregational rabbi would concern himself with the welfare of every member of his congregation and attend to the needs of each poor person, helping him from the communal fund, and in many other ways as well. I remember how my grandfather of blessed memory, before Yom Kippur would go to each member of his community, inquiring as to his state of health, and giving him detailed directives as to how to deal with the fast. This tradition was passed on to me by my father zt"l, and my practice to the present day. He knew personally each and every member, and any person in distress knew that he could approach the rabbi, and would find an open ear and an open heart, and would usually also get some sort of help from him. These individual needs are still with us, but there is a more comprehensive need today. If he is properly and professionally prepared, the rabbi, with a broad acquaintance with the world of Torah and with a deep and open feeling for the tremendous changes that are taking place in our society, will be able to offer to both the individual and the congregation the direction they seek in the complex and ever-challenging reality in which we live.

As already mentioned above, the way to move forward towards a greater participation of the rabbi in the social life of the community begins with a true realization of the functions of the young rabbi, his professional training and an emphasis upon his need to be open, sensitive and empathetic to a broad spectrum of individuals. He must be motivated to forge a real community out of what is often merely a group of regular "visitors" to the synagogue.

In the following study, I shall try to describe and articulate my vision of what the effective rabbi should be, what are his characteristics and his basic requirements. They are many and challenging, but I believe necessary, if we wish to work towards a more effective rabbinate whose aim is truly *tikun olam*.

*

And here I feel duty-bound to express my deep feelings of gratitude to my colleagues in the *Machon ha-Gavoah le-Tora*, both in the *beit midrash*, headed so brilliantly by Rabbi Shabtai Hacohen Rapaport and in the *Midrashah* so ably run by Dr. Tova Ganzel. I am also indebted to my loyal secretary, Mrs. Esther Dranger, who is one of the few people who can read my handwriting both in Hebrew and in English, and tirelessly always manages to put reasonable shape to my very messy manuscripts.

As will be evident from a perusal of this study, I owe much of my style in Torah learning to my father zt"l, Rabbi Samuel Sperber zt"l, and *pesikah* to my grandfather, Rabbi David Sperber zt"l. My traditional learning methodology has been blended with an academic flavor, which owes much to my association with that great Torah scholar, the late Prof. Saul Lieberman. Many close colleagues from the Talmud department and at Bar-Ilan have enhanced my knowledge and analytic abilities, and to all of them my debt of gratitude is expressed.

But above all else, my deep-felt thanks to my wife Chana, whose love and forebearance only match those of my beloved mother zt"l.

שלי משלך, ושלי משלכם.

Daniel Sperber

INTRODUCTION

I N THIS STUDY I WILL TRY TO DEMONSTRATE THE NEED FOR contemporary halachic authorities to rethink their methods of issuing halachic rulings, and my vision of the future cadre of "good rabbis." In an article that I published in 2002, I tried to show that the contemporary trend in halachic ruling is toward greater stringency and exaggerated conservatism.[1] I brought examples to support this position, and

---

1. This began as an updated translation of an article published in Hebrew in Y. Z. Stern and S. Friedman (eds.), *Rabbanut: ha-Etgar, Rabbis and Rabbinate: The Challenge*, Jerusalem, 2011, vol. 2, pp.747–784. I am deeply grateful to Shmuel Peerless for his excellent translation. However, this version has been very considerably expanded, so that the similarity to the original is almost incidental.

Daniel Sperber. "Paralysis in Contemporary Halakhah?" *Tradition* 36:3 (Fall 2002), pp. 1–13.

See also my article "Modern Orthodoxy: A Crisis in Leadership," *Conversations* 3, 2007, pp.1–11; and "How Not to Make Halakhic Rulings," ibid. 5, 2009, pp. 60–73.

See also Haym Soloveitchik's seminal essay, "Rupture and Reconstruction: The Transformation of Contemporary Orthodoxy," *Tradition* 28/4, 1994, pp. 64–130, and note, for example, his comment in note 22:

The impetus to *humra* is so strong and widespread that the principle of *le-hotzi la'az al rishonim*, has, for all practical purposes, fallen into desuetude (*Le-hotzi la'az* states that any new stringency implicitly casts aspersion on the conduct of past generations, and hence, is to be frowned upon.)

(On this principle see the summarizing article by Eliav Shochetman, "*Ha-Hashash le-Hotzaat Laaz al ha-Rishonim ke-Shikul be-Pesikat Halachah*," *Bar-Ilan* 18–19, 1981, pp. 170–195.)

Much of what I wrote in the *Tradition* article had already been brilliantly articulated in Soloveitchik's article, albeit within a different contextual framework.

There is currently a very strong tendency in both lay and rabbinic circles towards stringency (*humra*). No doubt this inclination is partly due to any group's need for self-differentiation, nor would I gainsay the existence of religious one-upsmanship. It would be unwise, however, to view this development simply as a posture towards outsiders. The development is also immanent . . .

It is one thing to fine-tune an existing practice on the basis of "newly" read books;

suggested explanations for this phenomenon: The Hatam Sofer exerted tremendous influence when, in his battle against the Reform movement in the beginning of the 19th century, he coined the oft repeated phrase "anything new is prohibited by the Torah" (*"hadash assur min ha-Torah"*), meaning that one should not introduce any innovations because innovation (*hidushim*) is the method of the reformers (*ha-mehadshim*). The Hafetz Hayyim continued on this path in his very well-received halachic work, the *Mishnah Berurah* (on the *Orah Hayyim* section of the *Shulhan Aruch*). The Hazon Ish advanced the process even more by developing a theory that certain periods are characterized by consolidation of the halachah. That which was consolidated in the *Shulhan Aruch*, he posited, is the will of God, which should not be changed even if circumstances change. Similarly, the desire to "fulfill the demands of all opinions" that is prevalent in many halachic works suggests that the stringent opinions be taken into account and included when issuing halachic rulings. Furthermore, in our times, a "fear of issuing a ruling"

---

it is wholly another to construct practice anew on the exclusive basis of books. One confronts in Jewish law, as in any other legal system, a wide variety of differing positions on any given issue. If one seeks to do things properly (and these "things" are, after all, God's will), the only course is to attempt to comply simultaneously with as many opinions as possible. Otherwise one risks invalidation. Hence the policy of "maximum position compliance," so characteristic of contemporary jurisprudence, which in turn leads to yet further stringency.

This reconstruction of practice is further complicated by the ingrained limitations of language. Words are good for description, even better for analysis, but pathetically inadequate for teaching how to do something. (Try learning, for example, how to tie shoe laces from written instructions.) One learns best by being shown, that is to say, mimetically. When conduct *is* learned from texts, conflicting views about its performance proliferate, and the simplest gesture becomes acutely complicated.

Fundamentally, all the above-stringency, "maximum position compliance," and the proliferation of complications and demands – simply reflect the essential change in the nature of religious performance that occurs in a text culture. Books cannot demonstrate conduct; they can only state its requirements. One then seeks to act in a way that meets those demands. Performance is no longer, as in a traditional society, replication of what one has seen, but implementation of what one knows. Seeking to mirror the norm, religious observance is subordinated to it. In a text culture, behavior becomes, inevitably, a function of the ideas it consciously seeks to realize . . .

Soloveitchik demonstrates that there was a caesura (rupture) in mimetic tradition – due to historical upheavals etc., and ever-more dependence on textual book sources, which led, inter alia, to accentuated *humra*. For an example of the extremes to which *humrot* can reach, see what I wrote in *Minhagei Yisrael*, vol. 2, Jerusalem, 1991, pp.147–149, on the *kitniyot* (legumes) issue on Pesach. And see also my brief article in the *Jerusalem Post Magazine*, March 23, 2013, p. 37, entitled "A plea for 'kitniyot'."

prevails because information is so quickly distributed that there is no privacy in halachic rulings. The halachic authority therefore fears the reaction of the rabbis of the "establishment" to which he belongs. This problem has been exacerbated by the politicization of the process for appointing rabbis and rabbinic judges, which ties every rabbinic appointee to a particular professional organization that determines his policies and limits his independent halachic thought and worldview.

The result of this trend is that contemporary halachic rulings are all too often not sufficiently sensitive to questions that are posed. The well-known trend to adopt the stringent opinion is the path of least resistance that minimizes complications and errors in halachic rulings. The examples that I brought to demonstrate this assertion in an article in 2004 included some exceptions that prove the rule.[2]

More importantly, I have tried to demonstrate in my previous articles and books that this trend is not consistent with the traditional method of halachic decision-making. Throughout the generations – from the tannaitic period onward – the great rabbis dealt with new problems and tried to the best of their ability to solve them in a manner that would allow the community to live, because the Torah is a "Torah of life" and "its ways are ways of pleasantness" (Proverbs 3:17).

After all, who does not look in a mirror nowadays? (though according to *Tosefta Avodah Zarah* 3:6, *B. Avodah Zarah* 29a, and *B. Shabbat* 94b this is forbidden). When the Tosafist, R. Shimshon of Sens had to look in a mirror in order to examine his sore eye, he covered the whole of his face with the exception of a slit for his eye (*Tashbetz* no. 546). Later R. Moshe of Coucy in his *Smag, Sefer Mitzvot Gadol*, chapter 45, stated that if looking in a mirror strengthens one's eyesight, then it is permitted. He adds that "God searches the hearts to know whether it is for improving one's eyes or improving one's appearance." (See further *Shulhan Aruch, Yoreh Deah* 156:2.) What about rabbis receiving a salary, which is likewise prohibited by Talmudic Law? See, for example, the story in *B. Nedarim* 62a, when R. Tarfon grieved all

---

2. Daniel Sperber, "On Sensitivity and Compassion in Psak," *JOFA Journal* 5:2 (2004), pp. 1–3. See also my books: *Darka shel Halacha* (*The Path of Halacha*), Jerusalem, 2007 (Hebrew); *Netivot Pesika* (*Modes of Halakhic Decision Making*), Jerusalem, 2008. See Appendix I.

his life because on one occasion he had received material benefit from his Torah. However, the Rosh to *Bechorot* 4:6 writes:

> At the present day, teachers are paid, and it is to be permitted if they have no other means of gaining a livelihood. And even if they have alternative sources of income, it is nonetheless to be tolerated, provided they abandon all other persuits.

So nowadays most Rabbis receive their salaries from their congregations, and often also have additional sources of income. (See on the above in greater detail, Solomon Zucrow, *Adjustment of Law to Life in Rabbinic Literature*, Boston, Mass, 1928, pp. 51–53, 59–62; and see my *Darkah shel Halachah*, Jerusalem, 2007, for many additional examples. In my essay "Congregational Dignity and Human Dignity: Women and Public Torah Reading," apud *Women and Men in Communal Prayer: Halakhic Perspectives*, ed. C. Trachtman, Jersey City, N.J., 2010, pp. 140–149, I bring eight somewhat random examples where contemporary normative halachah is not in accordance with the *Shulhan Aruch*.) The examples are too numerous to be presented, but recognizing them makes it preeminently clear that our halachic practices are in a constant state of change, adaptability, and flux, while remaining within the framework of classical Jewish legal thinking. Indeed, in contrast to what we see all too often in the rulings of many prominent decisors (*poskim*) who strongly resist all manner of innovations, declaring that "*hadash assur min ha-Torah*, innovation is forbidden by the Torah," and warning us of the pernicious "slippery slope," one of the great characteristics of halachah is that it has always been able to adapt itself to ever-changing circumstances, remaining within the normative parameter of *kelalei ha-psak* – the rules of rabbinic adjudication.

Dynamism in Halachah

There is a basic point of great significance, namely that the halachah is dynamic and not static, and has to deal with changing circumstances as it always had. This was very clearly articulated by Rabbi Hayim David Halevi, in his essay "On the Flexibility of Halachah" [Hebrew], published in *Shanah Be-Shanah* 5749 (1988), pp. 182–186, where he wrote:

As it is extremely clear that no law or edict can maintain its position over a long period of time due to changes in the conditions of life, and that laws which were good in their time are no longer suitable after a generation or more but require correction or change, how is it that our Holy Torah gave us righteous and upright laws and edicts thousands of years ago and we continue to act in accordance with them to this very day (and will even continue to do so until the end of all generations)? How is it that these same laws were good in their time and are good in this very day as well? . . . Such a thing was only possible because the Sages of Israel were given permission in every generation to innovate in matters of halachah in accordance with the changing times and situations. And it is only by virtue of this that the existence of the Torah has been possible in Israel, and that they were able to follow the Torah and mitzvot. . . . Anybody who thinks that the halachah is frozen and that one is not permitted to deviate from it right or left is very much mistaken. On the contrary, there is nothing as flexible as the halachah, for a teacher of halachah can rule regarding the very same question and at the very same time to two different enquirers, declaring something treif to the one and kosher to the other – a thing that is well known to those who give rulings on what is permitted and forbidden. . . . This is only by virtue of the flexibility of the halachah that the Jewish people have been able, by virtue of the numerous and useful innovations that were introduced by Jewish Sages over the generations, to follow in the way of the Torah and mitzvot for thousands of years.[3]

---

3. See what I wrote in my study "Congregational Dignity and Human Dignity," in C. Trachtman (ed.), *Women and Men in Communal Prayer: Halakhic Perspectives*, Jersey City, NJ, 2010, pp. 92–93. For an expanded analysis of Rabbi Halevi's theory of halachah, see Avi Sagi, *Halakhic Loyalty: Between Openness and Closure* [Hebrew], Ramat Gan, 2012, pp. 188–202, and especially 197–199, a chapter that was first published in *Iyunim Be-Yetzirato Ha-Hagutit Hilchatit Shel Harav Hayim David Halevi*, Jerusalem: Machon Hartman, 2007, pp. 311–330. And see the sugya in *B. Baba Kama* 117a for an example of repeated changes in halachic perception of a given issue.

We find it difficult to accept R. Joseph B. Soloveitchik's position on "halachic formalism," according to which the "halachic man" is like a scientist "who exists in an ideal world of a priori concepts, a world unimpaired by any sort of historical or psychological contingencies." Thus he writes:

The halachah has no need to reflect the character of the halachist, and neither changes in circumstances nor historical events contribute to shaping it . . . Psychologization or sociologization of the halachah are an assault on its soul . . . If halachic thought depends on psychological factors, it loses all its objectivity and deteriorates to a level of subjectivity lacking all substance.

Similarly, Rabbi Benzion Meir Hai Uziel, in the introduction to his *Mishpatei Uziel* (Part 1, Tel Aviv, 1935, pp. ix–x) wrote:

> In each generation, the conditions of life, the changes in values, [and] the discoveries of technology and science bring about new questions and problems that require solutions. We cannot close our eyes to these questions and say that "innovation is forbidden by the Torah"; that is, that anything not explicitly mentioned by our forbears is to be considered as prohibited.[4]

This is similar to the position enunciated somewhat earlier by R. Eliyahu Hazan (1847–1908), in his *Zichron Yerushalayim*, Livorno, 1874, p. 57:

> Being as the Torah was given to human beings [i.e., people limited by the human nature] who are subject to all sorts of vicissitudes, such as changes in time and periodization, rulings and edicts, difference of nature and temperament, various states [i.e., political entities], and differing climates, therefore all statements in the Torah came to us with wonderous wisdom in a undisclosed form – *setumim* [i.e., unclear as to their precise meaning.], and, hence, are able to accommodate any true interpretation at any time.

Indeed, I believe this is the deeper meaning of the statement in *Mishnat R. Eliezer*, ed. H. Enelow, New York, 1933, p. 266. For when comparing the differences between the first and the second tablets of the Law, it states that:

(J.B. Soloveitchik, *Philosophical Essays* (*Divrei Hagut ve-Haarachah*, Jerusalem, 1982, pp.76–78).

See also J.B. Soloveitchik, *Halakhic Man*, Philadelphia, 1983; idem, *The Halakhic Mind: An Essay on Jewish Tradition and Modern Thought*, New York, 1986. For a brief critique on this position, see, most recently, Ronit Irshai, *Fertility and Jewish Law*, Waltham, Mass., 2012, pp. 12–14, referring also to the writings of M. Halbertal, *Interpretative Revolutions in the Making: Values as Interpretative Considerations in Midreshei Halakhah*, [Hebrew], Jerusalem, 1997; A. Sagi, *Judaism: Between Religion and Morality* [Hebrew], Tel-Aviv, 1998.

This, of course, by no means exhausts the subject, but will lead the reader on to additional literature, and further discussion.

4. See my "Congregational Dignity," ibid., p. 92 and continuation cited ibid. note 72.

> The first tablets did not have the countenance of Moses shining within them, but the last tablets had the countenance of Moses shining within them.

In other words the human element was somehow taken into account in the latter tablets of the Law. This is peresumably why some sources point to yet another difference, namely that the earlier ones did not have the words relating to goodness, but the latter do, as is it written "that it may go well with you" (Deuteronomy 5:16).

Furthermore *Mishnat R. Eliezer* notes that concerning the first ones, there was no order to build them a container, but for the latter ones it is said, "And I made an ark of shittim wood, and two hewed tablets of stone like the first . . ." (Deuteronomy 10:3). In other words, it was clear that the first ones could not survive and thus did not require a protective container, precisely because they did not take into account the human element and promised no manner of reward – a naturally required human incentive. This is homiletically expressed in *Exodus Rabba* 46:1 in the following matter: After explaining that Moses was greatly regretful that he had broken the tablets of the Law, he is comforted by God who says to him

> Do not despair, for the first tablets contained only the ten commandments; but in the second ones that I give you there will be in them *halachot, midrash ve-aggadot* . . .

And in another source, cited by Enelow (in his *Mishnat R. Eliezer*, p. 265, note to line 7) we read of additional differences between the two sets of tablets, namely that the second set include "the thirteen hermenentic rules . . . they were given for all generations, and they were given from heaven and earth" (i.e., by a grant of partnership, as it were, between God and Moses).

All these statements express homiletically that a rigid and intractable legal system cannot survive; hence, the first tablets had to be broken. It is therefore inherent that there be in it possibilities of interpretation – hermeneutic rules – which enable it to take into account the dynamic human element: in all its fragility, the countenance of Moses, and the component of mercy and reward – "that it may go well with you." Only with this in-built developmental dynamism can the system survive the vicissitudes of time "for all generations."

Indeed, this principle that the Torah was given to human beings, or in Talmudic terms, "the Torah was not given to angels" (*B. Berachot* 25b, *B. Yoma* 30a, *B. Kiddushin* 54a, *B. Meilah* 14b, and similarly in *Midrashim, Sechel Tov,* ed. Buber, Exodus 13, *Yalkut Shimoni, Ki-Tisa* sect. 386) forms a central element in the halachic philosophy of Eliezer Berkovitz, as has been so ably and extensively expounded by Meir Roth, in his recent *Orthodoxiah Humanit: Mahshevet ha-Halachah Shel ha-Rav Professor Eliezer Berkovitz,* Tel-Aviv, 2013, pp. 74–96. We shall not duplicate his analysis of numerous examples illustrating his premises, but, as indicated above, this is reflected, I believe, in the rabbinic homilies cited above. Thus, laws engraved in stone must paradoxically embody interpretative flexibility. (Cf. *B. Eruvin* 54a, the word-play on *harut* in Exodus 32:16 and *herut*.)

But perhaps the next remarkable articulation of this theme is to be found in R. Mosheh Shmuel Glasner's introduction to his *Dor Revi'i* (*Hiddushin* to *Hulin,* Klausenberg 1921), which is remarkable for its contents, but also because he was the great grandson of the Hatam Sofer (1856–1924)! There he writes – I follow Yaakov Elman's translation in his article in *Tradition* 25 (3), 1991, pp. 66–67:

> Thus you see clearly that although the Oral Torah was given over to Moses at Sinai, since it was not given word for word but only the contents [were given], and it was not permitted to be written down, *this indicates that the will of the One Who commanded, may He be blessed, was not to make the interpretation of Torah unchanging, in order that there should not appear an open contradiction between life and the Torah.* This is what the Talmud answers regarding the question – if there is substance to the Oral Torah, why was it not written down? The answer given is because of the verse "of making books there is no end," (Ecclesiastes 12:12) viz., it would then be necessary to write a new and different interpretation for every time, according to the needs of the time and place, and that is why the Oral Torah is called "new" (*B. Berachot* 40a), for the Oral Torah is not absolute truth but rather conventional. Only that which the sages of the generation agree upon is true [in this sense]. When they contradict that which was [accepted as true until then], their new interpretation becomes the true one [for their generation]; so have

we been commanded by Him, may He be blessed, that we "should not depart from the thing (the sages of that generation) tell us either to the right or left" (Deuteronomy 17:11) – *even if they uproot that which was agreed upon until now.* This too is what they intended when they said "Both these and these are the word of the Living God . . ." (*B. Eruvin* 13b) (My emphasis – D.S.)

[On the obligations to accept rabbinic decisions "either to the right or left," see *Sifrei Deuteronomy* 17:1, sect. 154, ed. Finkelstein, p. 207, and the apparent contradictory parallel in *Y. Horayot* 1:1; and see S.Z. Mavlin's summarizing discussion in his *Masoret ha-Torah she-Baal-Peh*, Jerusalem, 2002, pp. 224–240.]

We may also take note of R. Tzvi Pesach Frank's statement in his *Har Tzvi, Yoreh Deah*, Jerusalem, 1926, no. 113, p. 103, with regards the law of *stam yeinano* (wine touched by a non-Jew):

Furthermore, it is clarified there [in *Imrei Baruch* 124, to *Shach Yoreh Deah* 124:71] that he derived from the formulation of Rabbenu Peretz that in his time he would be more lenient than during the period of Rabbenu Tam, because from day to day they [i.e., the gentiles] are forgetting the nature of idolatry. . . . By the same token one could argue that for that reason the Rema was more lenient than the Maharil, since more than one hundred and forty years had passed since the decease of the Rivash, which was in the year 1423, and the annotations of the Rema were completed in the year 1571. It is known that in his time more and more was the nature of libation forgotten by the gentiles then for his words. It has become clear that the passing of time leads to [the use of] leniency, and hence, since from the Shach till now close to three hundred years have passed, one may assume that the Shach too would agree to rule leniently in accordance with the view of Rabbenu Peretz.[5]

It is especially interesting to read the Hatam Sofer to *B. Hulin* 6b–7a – the *Hatam Sofer*, who usually appears to be the ultra-conservative

---

5. For the sources on this view see Tur, *Yoreh Deah* 123 in the name of the Rashbam, Rema, *Darkei Moshe* ibid., in the name of the Ran; cf. R. Ovadiah Yosef, *Yabia Omer*, vol. 9, Jerusalem, 2002, *Yoreah Deah* 5, p. 276. And see below sect. 17, "Adaptability of Halachah to Changing Circumstances."

authority, see e.g., the introduction to his response on *Yoreh Deah*, entitled *Pituhei Hotam* – where he is, as it were, forced to explain how the brazen serpent which was created by Moses (Numbers 21:9) was destroyed by King Hezekiah (2 Kings 18:4):

> . . . The fact that the Holy One blessed be He revealed certain things only to the ancient ones – from this we may deduce that from the Heavens space was left, concealing things from the *Rishonim* so that the *Aharonim* would be able to make excellent use of them (*le-hitgader*). And this is what is written in Proverbs 2:7, "He layeth up (*yitzpon*) sound wisdom for the righteous . . .", the Holy One blessed be he conceals and hides (*matzpin*) sound, wisdom, and Torah from the eyes of the righteous until he brings forth someone who is destined that this [hidden element] fall into his portion. And it is for this that we pray, "Give us our portion in Your Torah," so that in any case each person should merit his hidden portion so that we not struggle [in our learning] in vain . . .

In a rather different formulation, but adding up to much the same upshot, we read in R. Moshe Feinstein's *Igrot Moshe Yoreh Deah* 1, New York, 1960, no. 101, p. 186:

> Let me now respond to your question as to how we can rely in practice on new ideas like those I explained, especially when they are in conflict with the opinions of some *Aharonim*. I say – has the Torah come to a stop and an end, God forbid, so that we decide solely on the basis of what is found in books? And if we are presented with problems which are not found in books we will not decide them, even if we are able to do so? Certainly, in my opinion, it is prohibited to say any such thing! For certainly the Torah will grow even now, in our day. So anyone who is capable of deciding any question that comes before him by thorough investigation in the Talmud and *Poskim* with common sense and accurate proofs is obliged to do so even if it is a new issue which was not discussed in books. Even on a question which is found in books the rabbi must understand the issue and be able to decide it in his own mind and be able to rule on in, and not merely decide according to what is found [in a book]. . . .
>
> Even if his decision contradicts that of some distinguished *Aharonim* – so what? We are authorized to disagree with the *Aharonim*, and some-times even with *Rishonim* when there are good proofs, and especially

with straightforward reasoning. It is in reference to this type of situation that they said "The judge can act only on what is before their eyes . . ." [*B. Baba Batra* 131a; *B. Sandhedrin* 6b; *B. Nidah* 20b].

The Ritba to *B. Eruvin* 13b, on the statement of R. Aba in the name of Shmuel, that a heavenly voice (*bat kol*) came down from heaven declaring that "Both these [i.e., the opinions of Beit Shamai and of Beit Hillel] are both the words of the living God (even though they are in conflict with each other), wrote that:

> The Holy One blessed be His Name [when asked how this could be] replied, that if [the rulings] would be granted to the Wise Ones of Israel in every generation and the final decision would be theirs.

Upon which R. Hayyim Friedlander, in his *Siftei Hayyim* (*Emunah ve-Hashgahah* part 2, *Pardes ha-Torah*, p. 276), commented:

> Granted to the Wise Ones of Israel in every generation" is because things can change from one generation to another, so that what the majority of the rabbis of that time decide to be forbidden can in another generation be decided by the majority of rabbis to be permissible, and so indeed will be the halachah in that generation, because the final decision is granted to the rabbis of each generation.[6]

Very recently R. Moshe Lichtenstein in a public speech formulated this basic idea in a very eloquent manner:

> . . . We must be aware that the halachah is a system which evolves and develops over a long duration. Halachah is both a living system which is influenced by changing circumstances and a legal system in which precedent, continuity and endurance are meaningful. We like the halachah in the present, not in the past nor in the future. Our life of mitzvot reflects

---

6. Cited by Michael David Bush, in his *Kevod Hachamim*, Kiryat Sefer, 2006, p. 109. On the statement (cited above) that "both are the words of the living God, i.e., the notion of multiple truths in rabbinic thought, see my discussion in my forthcoming book on *Nostra Aetate*, chapter 3.

human relationship with the Divine and the people of Israel with their maker these relationships are here and now . . .

He then went on very properly to distinguish between "legitimate evolutionary change" and "improper radical revision," admitting that at times it is difficult to clearly distinguish between the two.

We may finally point to the writings of the great Hassidic master, R. Tzadok ha-Cohen mi-Lublin Rabinowitz (1823–1900), who in a number of places in his writings speaks of the great virtue of halachic change, so that "in sync with humanity's mutation from generation to generation so too must the Torah change, so much so that what may be prohibited today may be some permissible tomorrow."[7]

And, of course, we should always keep in mind Rav Kook's beautifully formulated statement, which is both poetic and almost prophetic:

Ha-Yashan Yithadesh ve-ha-Hadash Yitkadesh . . .
The old will be renewed and the new will be sanctified, and together they will serve as torches illuminating Zion (*Igrot ha-Reiyah*, vol. 1, Jerusalem, 1962, p. 214).[8]

---

7. See also his lengthy responsum in his *Orah Mishpat*, Jerusalem, 1979, no. 126, on the legitimacy of new adjudication and revision of earlier rulings in the wake of changing circumstances. See his *Resisei Leilah*, Lublin, 1903, sect. 53, p.160, 162, and *Tzidkat ha-Tzaddik ha-Shalem*, Jerusalem, 1968, sect. 90, p. 56, cited by Joshua Berman, in his essay "What is This Thing Called Law?" *Mozaic*, December 3, 2013, p. 10.

8. And see R. Yehuda Amital, *Jewish Values in a Changing World*, Alon Shvut, Israel and Jersey City, N.J., 2005, pass.; Moshe Higger, "*Tzedek u-Mishpat: Erko shel 'Lifnim mi-Shurat ha-Din' ba-Mishpat ha-Ivri*" *Nezir Ehav* vol. 3, Jerusalem, 1978, p. 153 pass. And see also what I wrote in my article entitled "Congregational Dignity and Human Dignity: Women and Public Torah Reading," apud *Women and Men in Communal Prayer: Halachic Perspectives*, ed. C. Trachtman, Jersey City, N.J., 2010, p.88–106, section entitled "The Halachic Process: Static or Dynamic?"; Solomon Zucrow, *Adjustment of Law to Life in Rabbinic Literature*, Boston, Mass., 1928.

Note that Rav Kook did not say that the old will be nullified (*yitbatel*), but that it would be renewed (*yithadesh*). Because ultimately the new derives from the old, giving it new meaning and relevance. And that is the meaning of the passage in Y. *Peah* 2:6, that what "a distinguished scholar will write in the future . . . was already said to Moses at Sinai," as explained by R.Barach Halevi Epstein, in his *Torah Temimah* to *Exodus* 24:12, note 28, pp. 179–180.

Halachah and Modernity

It is true that in the area of technology, great and important strides have been taken to accommodate the halachah to modern life – or perhaps more precisely to adapt modern life to halachah – using normative halachic principles and precedents found in traditional rulings. Examples of this are the widespread use of the "kosher clock", the reliance on the principle of secondary actions (*grama* – lit. cause) to solve issues relating to medical care on Shabbat and festivals, etc. (This study is too brief to go into all of the details. See, however, Alan Dundes' somewhat unbalanced criticism in his *The Sabbath Elevator and Other Sabbath Subterfuges*, Lanham, Maryland, 2003.)

And in areas of *Hoshen Mishpat* the challenges are enormous, challenges to which we cannot close our eyes. So writes, for example, Prof. Haym Soloveitchik, in his article in *The Torah u-Madda Journal* 14, 2006–07, p. 194:

> Suppose religious Jews were to insist on having all their business litigation adjudicated by rabbinic courts, or that the State of Israel were to hand civil litigation over to rabbinic courts; [Should we] not think that efforts would be made to justify the existence in Halakhah of corporations, of the stock markets, of credit cards? What would he say of a decisor or respondent (*dayyan* or *meshiv*) who upon being asked to adjudicate the inheritance of Walter Annenberg, were to rule that Mr. Annenberg had all the while been a pauper, and that there were precious few assets to be divided among his heirs? Most of Annenberg's famous business acquisitions were exercises of the purest *asmakhta*; the bulk of his assets were in stocks and securities – intangible goods (*davar she-ein bo mammash* or *davar shelo ba laollam*) which are not subject to acquisition; and as for his famous art collection, almost all of it had been acquired from Gentiles, and the proper modes of acquisition (*kinyan*) had never been employed.

He goes on to say (p. 195):

> The world of affairs is not under Jewish control; corporations exist as does the stock market, and they will not disappear because Halakhah refuses to recognize them. The sages of the Talmud (*Hazal*) realized this and grappled with these problems, as did the Geonim and medieval Tal-

mudists (*rishonim*). If Halakhah is to regulate the office no less then the home, it must come to grips with an alien reality and give it recognizance in its thinking. Both Modern Orthodox and most *haredi* communities have no need for any work on *Hoshen Mishpat* similar to the *Mishnah Berurah* on *Orah Hayyim*, for Halakhah stops at the office door. In their personal life they live lives of scrupulous religiosity; in their business affairs they live like pagans, by the law of the Gentiles. That they do so is understandable; less understandable are those who take their paganism as a mark of purity. Seder Nezikin exists for them as a beautiful world of theory, not as a regulative system. One does not sully this pure world with dross of daily affairs . . .

He continues to say that "in an open society in a modern democratic state, such a bifurcation between the public and private sphere is possible, and the binding form of *Hoshen Mishpat* is entirely optimal." In pragmatic terms, this may be so, but is this an ideal situation? Should we not ask ourselves how this should interplay with Jewish law and values? (Again this is a vast area, some of which has been grappled with in the various writings of Prof. Nahum Rakover, Menachem Elon, and others, an area with which we cannot deal in the context of this study.)

Similarly, in areas relating to relations between people, such as matters relating to marriage and divorce, – the *Agunah* issue, i.e., the status of the enchained partner due to the recalcitrant partner – illegitimate children (*mumzerut*), birth control, and modest dress, we do not generally find the same open thinking. We see in this treatment of technology little sensitivity to the petitioner, nor even the pleasant disposition characteristic of former generations, with some notable exceptions.

It is possible that modernity, with its permissiveness and its acceptance of alternative lifestyles, is threatening and intimidating for many contemporary rabbis, and the fear of "the slippery slope" rings constantly in their minds. This concern drives them to protect their community behind the ramparts of the religion, and to fortify it against any breach. Yet, in my opinion, this approach hardly protects hardly the community; it distances a large number of its members from the Torah world or pushes them to other movements which these very rabbis denounce and from which they distance themselves.

This, therefore, leads me to the suggestion that we return the world of halachah to its former glory and struggle to raise the consciousness that indeed "the power of leniency is preferable" (see below Appendix 2). Let us strengthen sensitivity to those who come to us with a question of importance in their personal lives. This must be done, of course, within the traditional parameters of normative halachah as they have been transmitted to us from the mouths and writings of the great sages throughout the generations.

It is clear that there are situations in which we will not be able to find a halachic solution that will satisfy the petitioner, and that we will not be able to address his/her needs. Indeed, there will be cases in which the distress, the pain, and the personal tragedy will break our hearts, and we can do no more than empathize with these unfortunate individuals. Such situations exist in every legal system. But my hope is that we can minimize their scope through the proper and sophisticated use of the wealth of halachic tools at our disposal, and find an equitable response to the distress of those who seek the pleasant path of the halachah.

In the first part of this study, I will attempt to present what I believe are the fundamental values of the halachah that serve as markers to guide the rabbi in his decision-making process on halachic rulings. In the second section of this study, I will describe the personal qualities that are needed for a rabbi to properly fulfill his role as a halachic authority in the Jewish community.

I. THE "FRIENDLY" *PESAK*

Fundamental Values in Halachah

I have often tried to demonstrate that the halachah is based on fundamental values that afford the *posek* the requisite flexibility to relate to
every problem or situation in a manner that is unique to the specific
time, place, and circumstances.[1] These values find expression in our

---

1. See my article "*Ol Mitzvot Noam Mitzvot: Mavo le- 'Halachah Hevratit'*" *Akdamot* 15 (2005), pp. 129–140. The topic of the article in *Akdamot* is brought here in
a different and expanded version. See also my article in the *JOFA Journal, supra* note
2. The relationship between law, halachah, and ethics is discussed at length. We make
note here of Moshe Zilberg, *Kach Darko Shel Talmud*, Jerusalem: Akademon, 1962,
pp. 69–96 (published also in *Hok u-Mussar be-Mishpat ha-Ivri*, Jerusalem, 1952);
Menachem Elon, *Ha-Mishpat ha-Ivri: Toldotav, Mekorotav, Ekronotav*, Jerusalem:
Magnes, 1973, pp. 171–180; Rabbi Aharon Lichtenstein, "*Mussar Ve-Halachah
Be-Messoret Ha-Yehudit*," *De'ot* 46 (1976), pp. 5–25. See also, Zeev Falk, *Erchai
Mishpat ve-Yahadut*, Jerusalem, 2000; Zeev Falk, *Religion, Law, and Ethics*, Jeru-
salem, 1991; Eliezer Berkowitz, *Ha-Halachah Kohah ve-Tafkidah*, Jerusalem, 2001,
pp. 84–117. On the relationship between values and commandments, see the chapter
"*Mashma'utam Shel Arachim ba-Torah*" in the book of Rabbi Yehudah Amital, *Ve-
Ha'aretz Natan Livnei Adam: Pirkei Hagut ve-Hinuch*, Alon Shevut, 2005, pp. 76–81.
I will add that already many years ago there were attempts (in my opinion, not so
successful) to study this area. As an example, we point out the book by Maurice
Fleugel, *The Humanity, Benevolence, and Charity Legislation of the Pentateuch and
the Talmud*, Baltimore, 1908.
Here, I would like to give another example of this phenomenon. In Exodus 28:1-5
we read how all the "wise hearted" shall make the "holy garments for Aaron," etc.
And verse 5 states: "And they shall take gold, and blue, and purple, and scarlet, and
fine linen." The "they" presumably refers to the "wise hearted," (see *Lekah Tov* ad loc);
Torah Shelemah of R. M.M. Kasher, vol. 20, Jerusalem, 1961, pp. 159–160, note 34).
On this verse the *Yerushalmi Shekalim* 5:2 comments:
And one does not appoint authority over the community in money matters less
than two. Rav Nahman in the name of R. Mana: "From, 'And *they* shall take gold,
and blue, and purple, and scarlet . . .'"

halachic literature, and though they are scattered among a variety of sections, their significance and influence go well beyond the subject of those sections and impact on all branches of the halachah. The sages throughout the generations have linked these values to earlier sources, although the connection may appear to be more of an *asmachta* (a verse that is used retroactively to support an existing concept) rather than the source from which it is derived. Thus, for example, from the verse

---

And since the minimum of plural is two, therefore the "they" who "take" these valuable commodities must number at least two. So too in B. *Baba Batra* 8b we read: We have learned that the charity box should be collected by two [persons] . . . for one does not appoint authority over the community less than two . . . From where do we know this? Said Rav Nahman: "The Scripture says, 'And *they* shall take . . .'" Cf. parallels in *Midrash ha-Gadol* etc.; cited in *Torah Shelemah* ibid., p.160, note 25.

Now this halachic interpretation of the verse is by no means straightforward. If "they" in verse 5 refers to "*all* the wise hearted" of verse 3, then one would expect the simple meaning of "they" to mean many more than "two," indeed "all" of them. Furthermore, if the materials for priestly garments come from the donations of the people, as would appear to be the case from the plain reading of Exodus 35:21, "And they come, every one whose heart stirred him up, and every one whom his spirit made willing, and they brought the Lord's offering to the work of the tabernacle of the congregation, and for all his service, *and for the holy garments*" (see *Torah Shelemah* ibid. for other views), there is no clear indication that this verse refers to "authority over the community", i.e., collecting dues against the will of the people, since these were voluntary donations (as already noted by the *Reshash* to Baba Batra ibid.; *Torah Shelemah* ibid.). Indeed, the same plural form is already found in Exodus 25:2, "and they shall bring me an offering," albeit there too the offering is "of every man that giveth it willingly with his heart." But the rabbis did not learn from here that one must accept willingly offered donations by at least two persons. We may further add that the changes from singular to plural in these verses require further understanding. It is true that "And they shall take" (*ve-hem yikhu*) is someone more definite than "that they bring me" (*ve-yikhu li*), but this still does not fully justify the rabbinic interpretation.

Hence, it would clearly appear that the rabbis felt that when authority is given over to individuals to collect command dues or taxes, there is a natural tendency to some sort of dishonesty or corruption, or, at least, a suspicion on the part of some members of that community that not all was above order. Indeed, this is the reason that according to M. *Shekalim* 3:2 those who dealt with the half-shekels were not permitted to wear "a sleeved cloak" etc., lest he be suspected of having pilfered the Shekel-chamber. And the Ralbag (to Exodus 28:5) adds "that people do not regard it as a serious sin to take for themselves public money." (Also see *Exodus Rabba* 51:1, that Moses himself was careful to act in a manner that allayed any sort of suspicion in himself.) It is for this reason they sought out a verse upon which, as it were, to hang the halachic ruling required to counter any kind of possible breach of the community's trust (a kind of *asmachta*). It was then the primal ethical value that served as a trigger to the halachah and its "derivation."

"and if the household be too small for a lamb" (Exodus 12:4), referring to the paschal lamb, they learned the general principle that the Torah is concerned about the assets of Jewish people. In other words, if the number of people in a household is too small to eat an entire lamb, and since the leftover meat would have to be discarded, then "he and his neighbor next to his house shall take one according to the number of the souls" (ibid.). Because the leftover meat from the paschal lamb must be burned, the Torah provided a solution out of concern for the assets of the participants in the pascal meal by stating preemptively that "he and his neighbor next to his house shall take one," so that they not suffer a monetary loss. Similarly, the same principle was learned from the verse dealing with a house in which a blemish is seen: "And the priest shall command that they empty the house, before the priest go in to see the plague, all that is in the house be not made unclean; and afterward the priest shall go in to see the house" (Leviticus 14:36). Emptying the house protects the contents from impurity and preempts the loss of fabrics that might be ruined if they require laundering and of ceramic utensils that can only be purified by breaking them. The Torah therefore prescribes "that they empty the house" out of concern for the assets of the household (see Rabbenu Bahya on Shemot 12:4).

An interesting example of the application of this principle is to be found in a responsum of R. David Tzvi Hoffmann (1843–1921), in his *Melamed le-Hoil*, Frankfurt a-Main, 1926, part 1, no. 91, pp. 108–111. (For convenience I here quote Jonathan M. Brown's translation in *Modern Challenges to Halakhah*, Chicago, 1969, pp. 75–76):

> The situation indicated in the responsum is as follows: A group of a few Christians and one Jew owned a restaurant, with each member of the group owning a few shares in the business, and having the power to sell his shares to whomever he pleased. For each share which he held, the owner would receive a certain sum each month. The question then was: What should the Jewish owner do with his shares during *Pesah*, since the restaurant would undoubtedly continue to stock and sell *hamez* during that period. The questioner felt that the Jew should sell his shares to a Christian prior to the Passover.
>
> Hoffmann begins his reply with the statement that, in his opinion, there is no need to sell the stock, if that would mean a financial loss to the Jew, *since Scripture has consideration for the money of Jews*. [My

emphasis - D.S.] Furthermore, the prohibitions against benefitting from *hamez* do not apply in this case.

He bases his permission on a related examination question prepared by his predecessor, R. Azriel Hildesheimer (1820–1899). Hildesheimer had asked the students about a brewery owned by a joint-stock company, most of whose owners were Jewish, while the operator of the plant was a Christian. All the students agreed to permit the Jews to take their usual profit during Passover, and Hildesheimer accepted their answers, some of which Hoffmann quotes.

Hoffmann also mentions another responsum [*Responsa Mahari ha-Levi* 2:124] about a real estate company which owned, among other properties, a brewery. The rabbinical authority appealed to in that instance decided to permit the Jewish owners to retain their stock over the Passover. Based on these precedents, then, Hoffmann finds no reason to force the Jewish owner to sell his stock in the restaurant.

And similar such examples could be greatly multiplied.[2]

---

2. The principle is "*Ha-Torah Hassah al Memonam shel Yisrael.*" Cf. R. Akiva's statement, in B. *Bechorot* 40a, where he ruled leniently in a certain case, in opposition to the ruling of R. Yohanan ben Nuri. And R. Akiva said to him, "Till when are you going to waste the assets of [the people of] Israel?" To which R. Yohan ben Nuri replied, "Till when are you going to feed *neveilot* to [the people of] Israel?" See further Y.Y. Bronstein, *Avnei Gazit*, Jerusalem, 2002, p. 183, quoting the view of Maharatz Chajes, to B. *Hulin* 49b, that this principle does not apply to *issurei Torah,* things forbidden by biblical law. Here is the place to comment on that which is found in the book *Minhah Belulah* (cited by M.M. Kasher, *Torah Shleimah*, vol. 9, p. 90, note 56) on the verse from Exodus 9:19: "'Now therefore send, hasten in your cattle and all that you have in the field; for every man and beast that shall be found in the field, and shall not be brought home, the hail shall come down upon them, and they shall die.' The rabbis were wont to say that the Torah takes pity on the finances of the Jewish people, and here it is proven that it also takes pity on the finances of the nations of the world." (Rabbi Avraham Menahem ha-Cohen Rappaport, *Minhah Belulah*, Verona, 1594.) See *Hulin* 49b where Rava declared it proper to use impure fat to stop up a hole because the Torah takes pity on the finances of the Jewish people. And Rav Papa asked him: "This is a Torah prohibition, and you say that the Torah takes pity on the finances of the Jewish people?" Tosafot writes there: "The law is in accordance with Rav Papa that in a Torah prohibition, it is not relevant to say that the Torah takes pity on the finances of the Jewish people, that in a Torah prohibition we do not permit for that reason, and even Rava revoked his opinion." Also see the comment of Maharatz Chajes (in his gloss on *Hulin* 49), where he makes a distinction between positive and negative commandments in this regard: "that it is not relevant to say that the Torah takes pity on the finances of the Jewish people with regard to a negative commandment, because we have established in accordance with the Rema (*Orah Hayyim* 656) that for

a negative commandment a person must use up all of his money rather than transgress, which is not the case for a positive commandment, in which he does not have to use up his money." See also Rabbi Shimon Leib Eckstein, *Toldot ha-Habif* (Rabbi Hayyim Palache), Jerusalem, 1999, p. 201, note 91.

In this connection we may relate a very moving story told of R. Yisrael Salanter when he went to visit the Rebbe of Ger, R. Yitzhak Meir Alter. The Rebbe exhibited great respect for the founder of the *Musar* movement, and at the end of his visit he accompanied him on the way. In short, the Gerer Hasidim heard that a great visitor had arrived, and so when R. Yisrael came to the nearby synagogue to pray *Minhah*, the place was immediately filled with people who came to pay him their respect. The Hasidim noted carefully how R. Yisrael prayed, and were most surprised to see that he prayed briefly, like a simple person, and did not pray lengthily as they would have expected. At the end of the service, R. Yisrael became aware of the feeling of surprise that permeated the synagogue, and so he explained to the Hasidim as follows:

I saw that on my account people had interrupted their work: the tailor his sewing, the cobbler his last, the blacksmith his anvil. They all left their work to see me. Had I prayed lengthily I would have been causing them a loss of income. Hence, I prayed briefly.

We learn here of the need for extreme sensitivity on the part of the rabbi for the fortunes of his constituents.

This principle finds expression in many different halachic contexts. (See my *Netivot Pesikah*, 2nd edition, Jerusalem, 2008, pp.136–139, for a number of examples.) See, for example, *Mishnah Keritot* 1:7 (Danby transl. p. 564):

Once in Jerusalem a pair of doves cost a golden *denar*. Rabban Simeon b. Gamliel said: By this Temple! I will not suffer the night to pass by before they cost but a [silver] *denar*. He went into the court and taught: If a woman suffered five miscarriages that were not in doubt or five issues that were not in doubt, she need bring but one offering, and she may then eat of the animal-offerings; and she is not bound to offer the other offerings. And the same day the price of a pair of doves stood at a quarter-*denar* each.

Similarly, though it is thought to be mandatory to eat fish on Shabbat, the *Mishnah Berurah* (*Orah Hayyim* 222:2) ruled that if the price of fish is raised by the vendors to an unreasonable level, he would forbid the purchase of fish for Shabbat, in order to cover the price.

See also responsa *Tirosh ve-Yitzhar*, by R. Tzvi Yehezkel Michelsohn, Bilgurai, 1937, sect. 88, who urged all the rabbis of Poland, after the Second World War to forbid the eating of fish, the price of which had risen beyond what he thought to be reasonable, in order to bring down the prices. (His suggestion was not accepted.) In R. Yaakov Hayyim Sofer's *Kaf ha-Hayyim*, *Orah Hayyim* ibid. sect. 12, he relates this issue to the *Mishnah* in *Keritot* cited above.

And yet another example is the case that was brought before R. Aaron Levine, the Rabbi of Sombar in Galitzia, (responsa *Avnei Hefetz*, Bilgurai, 1934, sect. 95). In 1921 there was a dearth of *schach* to cover the *Sukkot*, and the merchants raised the price very considerably, so that the local inhabitants, who were generally poor, could not afford to buy it. The locals approached the Rabbi asking whether they could cut down branches growing in the cemetery. According to the plain understanding of the law, one may gain no benefit from all that grows in a cemetery (*Shulhan Aruch, Yoreh Deah* 368:1, based on *Semag* [*Sefer Mitzvot Gadol*], *Hilchot Evel* 245c; *Mordechai*

Megilah 830; *Rosh Megilah* sect.9; and cf. *Shach* in the name of the *Bah, Shulhan Aruch* ibid. sect.6; *Gesher ha-Hayyim* vol.1, chapter 27 sect.5). But the Rabbi allowed it, for the benefit of the poor, arguing, inter alia, that this prohibition is in order to accord respect to the dead (Rema ibid.); but in this case the dead would surely agree that people cover their *sukkot* in order to perform the mitzvah as required.

Of course, he could also base his permission on additional sources, such as what we read in *B. Sanhedrin* 47b:

It was the practice of people to take earth from Rav's grave and apply it on the first day of an attack of fever. When Samuel was told of it [that people were using an object belonging to the dead, which is forbidden] he said, "They do well; it is natural soil, and natural soil does not become forbidden, for it is written, *And he cast the dust thereof upon the graves of the common people* (2 Kings 23:6), thus he compares the graves of the common people to idols. Just as idols [are] not forbidden when they are 'attached' [to the earth], for it is written, *Ye shall utterly destroy all the places … upon the high mountains* (Deut. 12:2). i.e., their gods, which are *upon* the high mountains, but not the *mountains* which themselves are their gods' so here too, what is 'attached' is not forbidden."

But his clearly expressed avowed purpose was to break the monopoly for the good of his poor constituents. (See below section on "Beyond the Letter of the Law," on Shmuel's bringing down the price of myrtle branches.)

See also *Igrot Moshe Yoreh Deah*, vol. 3, sect. 134, where R. Moshe was told of a *Hevrah Kaddisha* who had raised the prices of their services inordinately, against the rulings of the local rabbis. They asked R. Moshe if they were permitted to direct their constituents to other *Hevrat Kaddisha*, who had more reasonable prices, or whether this would constitute *hasagat gevul* (encroachment on the rights of the *Hevrah Kaddisha*). He replied that actually they were duty-bound to do so, to save the poor families from extortion. On the other hand, the *Aruch ha-Shulhan, Hoshen Mishpat* 231:20, is at pains to point out that one may not permit a shopkeeper to lower his prices so much as to prevent other merchants from making any sort of profit, and thus severely damaging their businesses.

An issue tangentially related to *Ha-Torah Hasah al Memonam shel Yisrael* is the principle of *ba'al tashhit*. It is too complex a subject to be dealt with here. I have touched upon it in a number of essays, e.g.: "Jewish Environmental Ethics," *The Edah Journal* 21:2002; "*Baal Tashit*: Waste Not Want Not," *Milin Havivin: Beloved Words* 5, 2010–2011, pp. 85–92. See N. Rakover, *A Bibliography of Jewish Law*, vol.1, Jerusalem, 1975, pp. 285–286 (no. 7034–7044), vol. 2, Jerusalem, 1990, p. 278 (no. 4660–4669). [Hebrew]; idem, *Eichut ha-Sevivah: Hebeitim Raayoniim u-Mishpatiim bi-Mekorot ha Yehudim*, Jerusalem, 1993, pp. 32–41; Daniel Farbstein, "*Be-Gidrei Issur de-Baal Tashit*," *Moriah* 28, 2006, pp. 126–131; Manfred Gerstenfeld, *Judaism Environmentalism and the Environment: Mapping and Analysis*, Jerusalem, 1998, pp. 138–141, 149. This is but a sampling of the studies on this subject.

Additional discussions may be found in passing in *Be'er Moshe* by R. Moshe Stern, Jerusalem, 1984, vol. 3, no. 22, p. 26, on the extravagant spending in festive halls for banquets:

"I was asked by a very learned scholar, [concerning the fact] that many times people make weddings … here in New York in large hotels … (but, much to our distress,

Applications of These Values: Halachic Adjudication

The significance of this principle – that the Torah is concerned about the assets of Jewish people – goes well beyond the sacrifice of the paschal lamb, the treatment of the blemished house, or any other particular law in which it is mentioned (e.g., improperly slaughtered meat – *neveilah*, forbidden fats – *heilev*, etc.). Rather, it is the foundation of a very great and important principle in halachic decision-making (*hefsed merubeh*), i.e., that in making halachic decisions, we must take severe financial

what will they answer when they are called to order on the waste of money without any earthly benefit?) . . .

And see further vol. 4, no. 147, section 31, pp. 236–237:

"Furthermore, I wish to alert people to a bitter phenomenon, that takes place here, namely, the waste of Jewish money in organizing weddings and other festivities. Lunacy has seized hold of almost every woman, whose husband has an extra dollar in his purse, that for every such event she needs a new dress, and that it is shameful unbecoming to appear twice in the same garment. In this way they impoverish their husbands with additional stupidities . . . which is a criminal act. . . . Just the other day I was at a wedding which was full of flowers, and the experts said that the flowers cost thousands of dollars, may Heavens be shocked! – on the next day all these flowers are thrown into the garbage. . . . It is the duty of the rabbis to gather together and to decide to announce a prohibition against the excessive use of flowers, and costly garments for a wedding . . . And without doubt it is within the power of the rabbis to protest, and all will hearken [unto them], for many are awaiting this, and they will all listen to their decisions and prohibitions."

Would that it were so.

And finally, two additional examples:

R. Yosef Hayyim, in his *Responsa Torah le-Shmah*, Jerusalem, 1973, no. 76 (2nd edition, Jerusalem, 2013, p. 94), writes:

And I ruled for those whose custom it is to leave a candle with two wicks every weekday night to have some light in the house, and they leave the candlelight also while they sleep until the morning . . . that they should take out the wick while they sleep, and leave only one wick burning, since they do not need so much light while they are asleep . . . the two wicks [burning] together . . . uses up [more] oil wastefully, and this constitutes *ba'al tashhit* . . .

And in *Sefer Kedosh Yisrael*, Reb Yisrael of Vishnitz, Natan Eli Roth, Bnei Brak, 1976, pp. 228–229, describes the extent to which the Vishnitze Rebbe was sensitive to *ba'al tashhit*. He relates (ibid. p. 228) that he would light his cigarette from a lit candle, rather than use a match, because specially lighting a match would be wasteful and constitute a transgression of the command, *ba'al tashhit*.

As to the apparent contradiction between the principle of *Ha-Torah Hasah al Memonam shel Yisrael*, on the one hand, and *Ain Aniyut bi-Mekom Ashirut*, on the other, see the analysis of R. Hayyim Uri Lifshitz, in his *Pri Hayyim*, vol. 1, Jerusalem, 1980, pp. 105–113.

loss into account.[3] A practical application of this principle is that if two

---

3. See *Entziklopedia Talmudit* 11, p. 245; Daniel Sperber, *Minhagei Yisrael* 3, Jerusalem, 1994, pp. 53–55, on the approach of the Rema in cases of severe financial loss idem, vol. 8, p. 263; and the entry on *"hefsed merubeh"* in *Entziklopedia Talmudit* 10, pp. 32–48; and also the Shach to *Yoreh Deah Hanhagot Issur Ve-Heter.*

And see further the Rema's own statement in his introduction to his *Torat Hatat*: And he who studies [my writings] should not doubt me . . . Because at times I ruled leniently where there is serious monetary loss [*hefsed merubeh*], or to a poor man concerning something important or in order to pay respect to the Shabbat and that is because in those places [i.e., cases] it would appear to me absolutely permitted [*heter gamur*] according to the halachah, and it is only that latter-day authorities were stringent in this matter. I therefore wrote that in cases of stress and need one should rule according to the law. And, indeed, we have found both early and late authorities that ruled thus.

(See further Asher Ziv, *Rabbenu Moshe Isserles* (Rema), New York, 1972, p. 211.) See also the lengthy discussion in my article in *Akdamot, supra* note 9, pp. 131–132, note 7; *Shut ha-Maharshal* (R. Shlomo Luria), sect. 46. As a general example, we note the opinion of Yavetz (vol. 2, 139) who permitted writing performed by a non-Jew on the second day of a festival in the Diaspora in cases of severe loss (in opposition to the *Noda bi-Yehudah, Tinyana* [2nd] edition, *Orah Hayyim* 33, who prohibited it). See also ibid., *Teshuvot Nosafot*, in Machon Yerushalayim ed., Jerusalem, 1994, sect. 10, pp. 306–307, on *"Ha-Torah Hasah Al Memonam Shel Yisrael,"* and the apparently opposing principle of *"Ain Aniyut bi-Mekom Ashirut."*

Yossi Tzurel, wrote a brief article in *Alon Shvut* 91, Kislev, 1982, pp. 40–49, entitled *"Ain Aniyut bi-Mekom Ashirut leumat Ha-Torah Ha-Torah Hasah al Memonam shel Yisrael,"* in which he suggested the different categories in which these two apparently contradictory principles function. Let us see the extent of the power of this principle. According to the *Responsa of the Rashba*, vol. I, 253, "In extenuating circumstances when there is a severe economic loss, or the like," one can rely on a minority opinion rather than following the majority, even in Torah prohibitions. The Shach was surprised by his opinion from a strict legal standpoint, (242, practices in prohibitions and permits), holding that this approach would only be utilized regarding rabbinic prohibitions. The Rema (ibid.) establishes that to do so requires both extenuating circumstances and severe financial loss, while the Bah contends that severe financial loss alone is sufficient (and see the comment of the editor of the *Responsa of the Rashba* , Machon Yerushalayim edition, Jerusalem, 1997, p. 107, note 150). This is not the place for a lengthy discussion on this issue. See further *B. Shabbat* 154b; *Pesahim* 26b; *Ketubot* 60a; *Nidah* 6b, 9b; *Kaf ha-Hayyim Yoreh Deah* 30, *Dinei Hefsed Merubeh; Maharsham* (R. Shalom Mordechai ha-Cohen), *Daat Torah*, Lvov, 1891, introduction to *Hilchot Tereifot;* and, most recently, R. Asher Weiss, *Minhat Asher*, vol. 2, Jerusalem, 2014, sect. 50, pp. 179–189, for a discussion on the parameters for the application of this principle.

Economic considerations of a national nature and the danger of great financial loss are crucial considerations in some of R. Uziel's halachic rulings. See Marc C. Angel, *Loving Truth & Peace: The Grand Religious Worldview of Rabbi Benzion Uziel*, Northvale, N.J. and Jerusalem, 1999, pp. 102–104, thus:

Over the generations, rabbinic sages debated whether grafted etrogim were accept-

people, one rich and one poor, come to a halachic authority with the

---

able for the fulfillment of the mitzvah of the four species on Succoth. After reviewing arguments for and against the use of such etrogim, Rabbi Uziel concluded that "all who buy etrogim grown in Israel, even if it is known that they were grafted, may rely on the opinion of those who permit them." His reasoning to justify this decision included his concern for the needs of the Jews of Israel.

Even though halachically there is no law to give precedence to the fruits of Israel, nevertheless because of the love of the land and the mitzvah of settling the land of Israel, it is a mitzvah to seek out etrogim grown in Israel. This is in order to aid those who exert effort to develop the land among the Jewish people. Anyone who prefers etrogim grown in the diaspora sins against his people and his land, since he weakens the position of his brethren who dwell in the land of Israel and who wish to support themselves by their labor. [*Mishpetei Uziel, Orah Hayyim* and *Yoreh Deah*, Tel-Aviv, 5695, no. 24].

In this decision, Rabbi Uziel recognized the need to consider the condition of the Jewish etrog growers in the land of Israel. He believed that it was a moral obligation of world Jewry *to support the Israeli economy*. Although halachic arguments could be marshaled for and against permitting grafted etrogim, Rabbi Uziel introduced the moral and practical issues relating to strengthening Jewish labor in the land of Israel; these considerations led him to permit – and even encourage – the use of Israeli etrogim, even if grafted.

Another issue arose relating to the newly developing dairy industry in the land of Israel. Cattle sometimes suffered from an ailment which was treated by means of an injection into the stomach. The perforation in the stomach created by the injection soon healed completely. The halachic question arose: Is such an animal rendered *tereifah* (unkosher) by having had a hole pierced into its stomach? If it is, then its milk is forbidden during its lifetime, and its meat is forbidden even after the animal is slaughtered. The only alternative would be to sell such animals to non-Jews for their use. *But to do this would cripple the dairy industry of the Jews of Israel.*

Following a thorough halachic analysis, Rabbi Uziel offered an additional point which shaped his final decision: The situation demands [that we not prohibit such animals] because if we do prohibit them, we will preclude the possibility of Jewish involvement in the milk industry, and we will remove an important economic enterprise which supports purveyors of drink and food to the entire public. In such an instance, certainly we are allowed to say that "Rabbi Shimon is worthy enough that we may follow his opinion in a crisis situation" [i.e., we may rely on a minority opinion in an emergency]. So we will rely on the opinion of those who declare the animal to be kasher, even when an incision has been made in its stomach. . . . [*Mishpetei Uziel, Yoreh Deah, Mahadura Tinyana*, Jerusalem 5710, no. 3].

Rabbi Uziel sent this decision to his colleague, Rabbi Yitzhak Herzog, for his comments. Rabbi Herzog, who was also deeply concerned about the need to develop the economy of Israel, agreed with Rabbi Uziel's ruling, a fact which pleased Rabbi Uziel very much. Responding to Rabbi Herzog, Rabbi Uziel wrote:

I read your letter with great joy . . . may your mind be at ease as you have eased my mind. From the time I faced this question, I suffered greatly in order to resolve it. I saw in it an essential problem which *affects our entire settlement and our dairy industry in particular.* Therefore, I sought arguments to be lenient and I sent them to you . . . I was much gladdened by your important conclusion utilizing the power of lenience [Ibid. no. 9]. [My emphasis – D.S.]

(See also Appendix 2.)

Another very fascinating example of how economic circumstances may be a vital consideration in *pesikah* can be found in the rulings of Rabbi David ben Zimra and described by Israel M. Goldman in his *The Life and Times of Rabbi David Ibn Abi Zimra*, New York, 1970.: On the one hand the Radbaz was extremely concerned with women's modesty as is evident in his responsa. So writes Goldman on p. 142:

As a moral safeguard, it was considered improper for a man to walk directly behind a woman. For even though women wore clothing which covered their bodies from head to foot, yet the man would notice the movements of her body and this might lead to immoral thoughts. It was therefore proper for the man to walk slightly in front of the woman. It was forbidden to walk within four paces of a prostitute, in any direction. R. David admonishes that men should not walk behind a prostitute even at a distance greater than four paces . . . [Responsa vol. 3, Fürth, 1781, no. 481].

(On the subject of a man walking behind a woman, this was explicitly forbidden in B. *Berachot* 61a, but the *Terumat ha-Deshen* is quoted in *Leket Yosher, Yoreh Deah* p. 37, as permitting it, as "nowadays we are not that prohibited *(ain anu muzharim kol koch)*" . . . see R. Yehuda Henkin, *Understanding Tzniut: Modern Controversies in the Jewish Community*, Jerusalem/New York, 2008, pp. 52–58, and his chapter 2, ibid. (pp. 74–84), entitled "The Significant Role of Habituation in Halachah." See also what I wrote in the *JOFA Journal* VI/4, 2007, pp. 7–9, article entitled "The Human Element in the Commandments: The Effect of Charging Community Norms on Halakhic Decisions." See note 83.)

Furthermore, in a different responsum (vol. 1, no. 121) dealing with the issue of *yihud*, he rules according to the custom of modesty, which is beyond the requirements of the law.

Nonetheless, when it came to questions of livelihood, he showed great understanding and ruled with surprising leniency, even against earlier rulings of prominent authorities. And so writes Goldman (ibid.):

In Egypt, Jewish women were employed in weaving factories owned by Gentiles. The Jewish women would at times remain for several days and nights in these places of occupation. This condition of long standing, which went back to the days of the Nagidate, was objected to on moral grounds. The *Negidim* issued decrees against it but it was of no avail, since these women were extremely poor, as were their husbands. In most instances women went with the consent of their husbands. R. David informs us that in his own day, rules were issued permitting these women to work on condition that they shall not sit at the same work-table with men, and that only women of forty years of age and over should be allowed to work [Responsa vol. 1, Venice, 1749, no. 67].

See further the analysis of Samuel Morell in his *Studies in the Judicial Methodology of Rabbi David Ibn Abi Zimra*, New York and Oxford, 2004, pp. 89–80.

Further on the detailed categories of *hefsed merubeh*, see the summarizing comments of Moshe Mendel Shklarsh, *Hayyei Moshe*, Bnei Brak, 2001, pp. 266–272, including the notions of *tzorech gaddol*, great need (ibid., p. 269); so too Maharatz Chajes, *Darkei Horaah*, chapter 4, apud *Kol Sifrei Maharatz Chajes*, vol. 1, Jerusalem, 1958, p. 231.

Here, I cannot resist retelling a remarkable tale related by R. Eliyahu Goldberg, a disciple of R. Hayyim of Volozin, to R. Yechiel Michel Epstein, the author of the *Aruch ha-Shulhan*. The tale is told by R. Epstein's son, R. Baruch Halevi Epstein, in his *Mekor Baruch*, vol. 3, Vilna, 1928, pp. 1165–1170, who heard it from his father. (I am presenting it in a shortened form.)

Once, R. Hayyim was sitting at the table surrounded by his disciples when a woman came in with a halachic question. She had prepared radishes with (animal) fat, and later on realized that she had cut it with a milky knife. R. Hayyim pondered a moment, and then asked, as to the colour of the outside of the radishes – black or white. The woman answered that they were white. "In that case," replied R. Hayyim, "the radishes are kosher," and the woman went home.

The students were amazed, casting questioning looks to one another as if to say, "What is this? What difference does the colour of the radishes make in this context, and where did our master find a source for this strange innovative reply?" [Their astonishment was clear, since the taste of sharp foods is not cancelled even in a mixture of 1 to 60, so that in this case there was an admixture of milk and meat (fat) which rendered the food non-kosher.]

R. Hayyim, seeing their astonishment, explained his ruling as follows:

"Know, my sons, that I have received a tradition from my teacher, the Gra [the Gaon R. Eliyahu of Vilna], that I should always follow my own understanding of the law. . . . Yet, together with that, I must always take care not to rule counter to the *Shulhan Aruch*. And so, if I come across a situation where my opinion seems to contradict the ruling of the *Shulhan Aruch*, I should search hard to find some kind of way, even if it be weak, to argue that this case was not what the *Shulhan Aruch* had in mind. And had this case come up before R. Yosef Karo, he would have ruled as I do now.

"Now you know," continued R. Hayyim, "that author of the *Shulhan Aruch* was of the opinion that radishes are of the 'sharp' category, and, hence, in our case one should have ruled that they were forbidden. [And this is the opinion of the *Pri Hadash* to *Yoreh Deah* 116, basing himself on R. Shmuel Ashkenazi's *Yefei Mareh*, also cited in the *Aruch ha-Shulhan, Yoreh Deah* 116 note 11, and cited in Y.Y. Lerner, *Shmirat ha-Guf ve-ha-Nefesh*, Jerusalem 1996, p. 657. I am grateful to Prof. Zohar Amar for this latter reference.] But my opinion is with those who hold that radishes are not of this category. (See *Shulhan Aruch, Yoreh Deah* 96.) And therefore I should rule permissively. However, I could not do so contrary to the ruling of the *Shulhan Aruch*, so I searched for a pretext (*amatla*) to create a means of ruling permissively without going against the *Shulhan Aruch*.

Now I have seen in the literature describing the geographic qualities of different lands that in the Land of Israel the radishes are only of the blackish [perhaps purplish] hue, and, as is well known, this type has a sharper flavour than the whitish radishes. Since R. Yosef Karo lived in the Land of Israel, in the city of Safed, and it is there that he wrote his *Shulhan Aruch*, it is for this reason that he regarded radishes as being of the sharp category. I, therefore, asked the lady, 'What colour were your radishes, black or white?' And when she replied that they were white, I felt that in this case I could follow my own opinion on the halachic status of radishes, ruling permissively, without contradicting the *Shulhan Aruch*."

R. Eliyahu Goldberg added:

"And from that event onwards we follow the methodology of R. Hayyim, and

same ritual question, they may not receive the same response, since the wealthy petitioner may not feel the monetary loss sustained as the result of a more stringent decision, while for the poor person the consequence of a stringent decision may constitute a meaningful loss. This principle guides the posek to search for a leniency within the normative halachic context so that the poor person will not endure great suffering. Thus, we may note that the Rema, in *Torat Hatat* introduction, citing *Sheelot u-Teshuvot Mahari Minz* 15, writes that a poor person during the week and a wealthy one on the eve of Shabbat have the same status vis-à-vis the application of the principle of *hefsed merubeh*. This is also recorded in the Shach, *Kitzur Hanhagot Horaot Issur ve-Heteir*, in *Yoreh Deah* 242:3. The relative nature of the principle of *hefsed merubeh* is beautifully illustrated in the following tale told by R. Tzvi Pesach Frank. Once, a young girl came to Rabbi Frank with a question concerning an egg. The Rabbi asked her where she lived, and then permitted to eat the egg on the basis of the principle of *hefsed merubeh*. He noticed that the rabbis who were sitting with him were astounded that he should apply this principle an egg! He then explained the matter to them, saying "If parents send a young girl from Shaarei Hesed, a district which is a long way away, for just an egg, then apparently for them this is a question of serious loss – *hefsed merubeh*." (See Lior Silber, *Milei de-Hassiduta* second edition, Jerusalem c. 2004, p. 75.) Of related interest is Rav Frank's responsum in *Har Tzvi, Yoreh Deah*, Jerusalem, 1976, no. 113, p. 103, where he permits the use of wine which had been examined by

do not gainsay our own opinions, and certainly not to accept new muddled (*gibuvei*) stringencies that have appeared after the *Shulhan Aruch*, and he who does so is not caring about the [loss of] the money of Israel (אינו חס על ממונם של ישראל), and may I have no part in their lot."

R. Baruch Halevi Epstein, himself, added in a note and loc. (pp. 1168–1169, note 1) that this difference between dark and light coloured radishes is already indicated in B. *Pesahim* 39a, which states: All bitter herbs have a dark hue, (*machsifin*, literally, silverish or black, Rashi *Shabbat* 36b). R. Baruch brings further evidence to support R. Hayyim's assumption. Not being a botanist I cannot give an opinion on this issue, but R. Hayyim's approach is deeply instructive.

Finally, Prof. Zohar Amar referred me to R. Yosef Schwarz, *Tevuot ha-Aretz*, Jerusalem, 1900, p. 395, when he speaks of the types of radishes, the *nafotz*, which is long and thin, and the other kind which is round and broad, called in Arabic *Al-trof*, which is sharp and has a reddish skin. The other kind, he writes, is not sharp and its skin is whitish. So it would appear that R. Hayyim's conjecture was correct.

And see further ibid., pp. 1174–1183 for additional examples of his father's striving after leniencies.

a non-Jew, though without actually touching it, only using a special measuring cup, since "nowadays it is exceedingly difficult to make a living, and one should rule that [in this case] there is a situation of *hefsed merubeh*." (See also Moshe Walter, *The Making of a Halachic Decision*, Brooklyn, 2013, pp. 157–159, notes 22–32.) There are a number of comparable principles in halachah such as "in order to provide sustenance" (*mi-shum hayei adam*) that permits one to work in order to earn a living during the three weeks of mourning between the 17th of Tammuz and the 9th of Av,[4] on the intermediate days of the festivals,[5] and even for mourners during their seven days of mourning after the

---

4. See my *Minhagei Yisrael*, vol. 3, Jerusalem, 1994, pp. 50–51, and compare to p. 57. See *Entziklopediah Talmudit* 3, p. 117, and compare to 10, 1962, p. 179, on the issue of taking *hallah* from the dough of a common person, based on *Gittin* 62 a.

5. And to give just two somewhat random examples of how the great *poskim* (decisors), when faced with serious economic challenges to their communities, sought to find viable solutions to these challenges.

The *Mishnah* at the end of *Ta'anit*, (4:7) states that when the month of Av begins one reduces joyful activities.

The *Gemara* in *Yevamot* 43a further brings a *beraita* that states:

Before this time (i.e., the week in which *Tisha be-Av* falls, i.e., from the first of Av) one reduces one's business activities, and also building and planting . . .

The Tosafot at loc. explain as follows:

In the last chapter of [Yerushalmi] *Ta'anit* they limit [the building etc.] to the "building of joy" . . . And some explain that also in business activities we are talking of those related to joyful activities, such as the requirements for a marriage. But this does not seem convincing, for there was no prohibition of dealing with the requirements of the banquet. And therefore it would appear that we are speaking of not increasing our business activities, but rather somewhat reducing them from our normal activities.

The Tur (*Orah Hayyim* 551) writes:

And some say that since our *Gemara* forbids undefined building (*setam*), it refers to any type of building, (and not necessary that which is related to joyful activities), in the same way that all kinds of business dealings are proscribed . . .

The *Beit Yosef* expands this issue further as follows:

From the words of the Tosafot . . . it would appear that from the beginning of Av until the fast one may only not involve oneself in building and planting of joy. And so too here (i.e., with regard to business activities), nowadays most people are not accustomed to reducing their business activities in any manner from the first of Av . . . And they interpret (the sources as referring specifically to building and planting (and business deals) of joy, as was the view which the Tosafot rejected. And, as a consequence, they conduct their business as normal, and without hesitation or doubt. . . .

And it is possible to say that the majority (*ha-olam*) is of the opinion that one need not reduce one's business activities in any way, even if they relate to marriage, and hence, [this ruling] was omitted by the Rif, and the Rosh, and the Rambam. And I have seen that the community of Budin adopted the custom to stop any business activities after the beginning of Av, and it would appear that they have nothing which to base this view . . . and it is an unnecessary stringency. However, those who do have such a custom, require that their vows be annuled (*heter nedarim*).

The Bah (*Bayit Hadash*) rules:

As to the halachah, it would appear . . . that only business related to marriage is proscribed. And see the Maharil . . . according to whom all business, which is not related to "joy" is permitted. And so ruled R. Shlomo Luria (*Maharshal*). Nowadays it is our practice to rule leniently, and we do not have doubts as to continue practicing our business. And perhaps this is because in our days everything (i.e., all business activities) is for our basic livelihood (*kedei hayyim*).

The *Shulhan Aruch, Orah Hayyim* notes:

From the first of Av until the Fast one reduces one's business activities . . .

On this the *Mishnah Berurah* comments (ibid., sect. 11):

There are those authorities who are of the opinion that one should not involve oneself in any sort of business activities that are "of joy," such as buying silver utensils for a wedding, and such like, but regular business activities need not be reduced. And there are those who were of the opinion that one must reduce all one's business activities, and only deal as to receive one's basic needs (*kedei parnasato*). . . . However, in our days it is practice to rule leniently in this matter, because everything is regarded as for our basic needs (*kedei parnasato*).

And see also *Taz* (*Turei Zahav* to *Orah Hayyim* 559:2).

In a like manner the *Shulhan Aruch, Orah Hayyim* 551:9 relates that there are varying customs as to the length of time that eating meat and drinking wine is forbidden within the framework of the "three weeks." To this the Rema (ad loc.) adds that the *shochtim* (slaughterers) hide their knives used for *shehitah* from the beginning of Av onwards . . . for one does not slaughter other than for the purpose of a mitzvah, such as for a sick person, or for the Shabbat, or a circumcision, and so forth.

To this the *Mishnah Berurah* (sect. 60) adds the following:

[They hide their knives] up to the tenth of Av, and at times of need (*sha'at ha-dehak*) one may rule leniently and slaughter on *Tisha be-Av* after midday. Similarly, if *Tisha be-Av* falls on a Thursday, everyone agrees that one may slaughter after midday to honour the Shabbat. And the Magen Avraham (sect. 28) and the Eliya Rabba (sect.29) write that in our communities it is the practice of [our neighbors] the non-Jews not to eat meat on Fridays and Saturdays. And if the slaughtered animal be found to be *tareif*, and one will not be able to find a non-Jewish purchaser for this non-kosher meat, it is permitted to slaughter also on a Wednesday (for otherwise they would desist from slaughtering), and [in this way] if the meat is found to be *tareif* they will have enough time to sell it [to a non-Jew] by Thursday [i.e., before Friday].

(See, however, the dissenting view of R. Shalom Mordechai Schwadron in his notes to R. Nahman Kahana, *Orhot Hayyim*, vol. 2, Siget 1898, sect. 651:30, who was unwilling to permit the *shochtim* to slaughter during this period, even though the result might be that non-observant Jews would go to buy meat from non-Jews, and consequently would be eating non-Jewish meat. R. Ovadiah Yosef brings this ruling, and additional supporting opinions, in *Yabia Omer*, vol. 1, *Orah Hayyim* sect. 30:15, p. 106, and again ibid., vol. 8, *Yoreh Deah* 12:3, p. 289; and on *sha'at ha-dehak*, see Shach, *Kitzur be-Hanhagot Horaot Issur ve-Heter* 3; Taz, *Yoreh Deah* 9:2; *Shulhan Aruch, Yoreh Deah* 108:3, with *Beur ha-Gra* 26, etc.)

These are, of course, merely two out of the numerous examples that demonstrate

loss of a close relative.[6] Similarly, just as the halachah permits one to
engage in work on the intermediate days of the festivals or on the eve
of Passover in order to prevent an irreparable loss (*davar ha'aved*),
because the Torah is concerned for the people's financial status, so too,
we find that at times it even overrules rabbinic prohibitions because of
financial loss (*Eruvin* 55b).

An additional example from the area of finances is the well known
prozbul enacted by Hillel that circumvented the cancellation of loans in
the sabbatical year in order to maintain the possibility of poor people
borrowing money, i.e., to enable poor people to access loans during
times of personal financial crisis. Subsequently, the rabbis developed the
"permit to do business" (*heter iska*) that was also designed to maintain
loan opportunities for poor people by circumventing the prohibition
of charging interest in order to motivate lenders to extend credit. *Sefer
Meir Einayim* wrote the following on these enactments: "These things
seem to be strange and fictitious, but they should nevertheless not be
prohibited in order to give our coreligionists sustenance at times of
need."

And in a related issue Prof. Haym Soloveitchik, in his "Pawn brok-
ing: A Study in Usury and Halakhah in Exile," apud his *Collected
Essays*, vol. 1, Oxford, 2013, pp. 130–136 (first published in *PAAJR*
38, 1970–1971), has demonstrated how due to intense pressure to
allow intra-Jewish usury in 12 cent. France, despite its being biblically

---

how the *poskim* were keenly aware of economic problems and offered their solutions.
Such examples are legion, and are to be found throughout the whole range of halachic
literature.

And even though I have, of necessity, somewhat simplified the issues by not citing
all the authorities, what emerges clearly, even from this brief note, is how the leading
halachic authorities – seeing the difficulties involved for their constituents reducing (in
a somewhat undefined manner) their business activities for well over a week, or the
potential loss of income to the *shochtim* which would also effect "Sabbath joyfulness"
– sought to limit the various restrictions, taking into account the local socio-religious
and economic conditions, but doing so within the parameters of normative halachic
thinking, and basing themselves on the opinions of classical authorities which constituted their halachic precedents. This, of course, is a vast field requiring much further
research. (On not eating meat or drinking wine during the three weeks, see what I
wrote in *Minhagei Yisrael*, vol. 1, pp. 138–153.)

See *Minhagei Yisrael*, ibid., pp. 54–56.

6. See Rabbi Hayyim Binyamin Goldberg, *Pnei Baruch: Aveilut ba-Halachah*
(Mourning in Jewish Law), published by the author, 1986, pp. 149–150 (Hebrew).

prohibited, Rabbenu Tam (c. 1100–1171) advocated the *a priori* use of Christian intermediaries, self-consciously asserting that he did so "in order to give substenance to the children of the covenant" (*latet mihye li-vnei berit*). (See *Sefer Or Zarua* no. 202. My thanks to Prof. Jeffrey R. Woolf for this reference, found in his recent book, *The Fabric of Religious Life in Mediaeval Ashkenaz (1000–1300); Creating Sacred Communities*, Leiden and Boston, 2015, pp. 10–11.)

Most instructive is the statement of R. Yishmael, in *Mechilta, Masechta de-Kaspa* 1, (ed. Lauterbach, vol. 3, Philadelphia, 1955, p. 147, ed. Horowitz-Rabin, Jerusalem 1960, p. 315; on the verse in Exodus 22:24):

> "If thou lend money to any of my people": R. Yishmael says: Every "if" in the Torah refers to a voluntary act except this (and two others) . . .

That is to say, the Torah does not give us the choice to help the poor, but commands us to do so.

Its Ways Are the Ways of Pleasantness

We see from these examples how the halachah beams a ray of kindness toward the poor and disadvantaged. As we stated, the formal sources relate to unique and specific instances while the generic implications covers the entire halachic system. This is expressed in the section of *Massechet Sukkah* (32a) dealing with the identification of the four species of the *lulav*. The *Gemara* there rejects two possible identifications, the oleander tree as the "boughs of thick trees (*anaf etz avot*)" (Leviticus 23:40) and the *kufra* plant as the "palm tree (*kapot temarim*)" (ibid.). This is because these plants are thorny and it is inconceivable that the Torah would require us to take species that would prick and scratch one's hands, since "its ways are ways of pleasantness, and all of its paths are peace" (Proverbs 3:17), as the *Gemara* explains there.[7]

---

7. See also *B. Yevamot* 15a, 87b; *B. Gittin* 59b; *Tosafot* to *Yevamot* 2a, s.v. *Ve-Ahot*. See Maharashdam's (Rabbi Shmuel de Medina, 1506–1584) use of this in his responsa, *Hoshen Mishpat* 259: "The agreement of the majority constitutes that 'its ways are ways of pleasantness and all of its paths are peace.' They therefore stated that their words are upheld when all are in agreement and united as one unit, and one of them cannot retract and destroy its quality of truth and peace . . ." In this regard, he

follows in the footsteps of Rabbi Eliyahu ben Binyamin Halevi (first half of the 16th century) in his book *Zekan Aharon*, Constantinople, 1534, 143, where he writes: "The minority must follow in the direction taken by the majority, for if not, the absolute truth of the law will never emerge, and that is why the Torah warned to 'follow the majority,' whose ways are ways of pleasantness and whose paths are paths of peace." (See Appendix 2.) See Eliezer Bashan, *"Deracheha Darkei Noam"* Deot 48 (1966), pp. 171–176, and particularly 172–173. See also, *supra* note 9. Aaron Kirschenbaum, in his article "Subjectivity in Rabbinic Decision-Making," apud *Rabbinic Authority and Personal Autonomy*, ed. Moshe Sokol, Northdale, N.J. and London, 1992, pp.78–82, gave further examples of the application of this principle. We may add from a totally different area of halachah that the rules of neighborly relations (*hilchot shecheinim*) may be understood according to the Rosh's statement (*Shut ha-Rosh, Kelal* 108:10) that the rules dictating distance between neighbors is also based on the principle of *darkei noam*. See now Yitzhak Rones, *"Ha-Hovah le-Afsher Hangashat Binyan Megurin le-Neichim" Le-Shichno Tidreshenu: Kovetz Maamarim be-Hilchot Shecheinim*, Ha-Machon ha-Gavoah le-Torah: Bar-Ilan University, 2013, pp. 116–117. See also the responsa of the Radbaz, 1052 and 1079, on the principle "in order to promote peace" (*mipnei darkei shalom*). See Rabbi Yehuda Unterman, *"Darkei Shalom ve-Hagdarotav"* Or Mizrah 15 (1965-1966), pp. 27–32, and in *Kol Torah* 2, pamphlet 6 (1966), pp. 3–7, as well as in *Morashah* 1 (1971), pp. 5–10, in which he asserts that this principle is implemented *a priori* and not just *ex post facto*, and that its existence derives from the deep study of Torah ethics as a fundamental obligation. See also the critique of Rabbi Hayyim David Halevy, *Aseh Lecha Rav,* Tel Aviv: Ha-Va'adah le-Hotza'at Sifrei ha-Gaon ha-Rav Hayyim David Halevy, 1978–1989, Section 33, pp. 83–87, where he asserts that it is only implemented *ex post facto*, as he does as well in his article, *"Darkei Shalom be-Yahasim Bein Yehudim le-She'einam Yehudim"* Tehumin 9 (1988), pp. 71–81. On this issue of supporting gentiles economically, visiting the gentile sick, and burial of gentiles – *mi-pnei darkei shalom* – see *Shulhan Aruch, Yoreh Deah* 335:9, ibid., 380:5, based on *B. Gittin* 61a. See B. Goldberg, *Penei Baruch: Bikur Holim ke-Hilchato*, Jerusalem, 1985, pp. 8–9, note 37; H. B. Goldberg, *Bein Yisrael la-Nochri: Yoreah Deah*, Jerusalem, 1994, pp. 452–453, note 1, 456, etc. But this is a slightly different application of these principles. For more on this issue, see Aryeh Carlin, *"Darchhei Noam Ve-Darkei Shalom"* Divrei Sefer, Tel Aviv: Mahberot Le-Sifrut, 1952, pp. 125–134; Eliezer Bograd, *"Mi-Pnei Darkei Shalom"* Doctoral Thesis, Tel Aviv University, 1977; Alter Hilvitz, *"Le-Biur ha-Sugya 'Mi-Pnei Darkei Shalom' be-Yahas la-Goyim"* Sinai 100 (1987), pp. 328–358; Hayyim Pardes, *"Mi-Pnei Darkei Shalom"* in *Sefer Hagai: Zikaron le-Arba'a mi-Talmidei Yeshivat Nir Kiryat Arba*, Hevron, 1985, pp. 467–474; Shmuel Tanhum Rubinstein, *"Takanot she-Hitkinu Hazal mi-Pnei Darkei Shalom"* Torah Sheba'al Peh 21 (2000), pp. 60–66; and *Entziklopedia Talmudit* 7, Jerusalem, 1956, 715–724. (And see below p. 97 note 61.) See further the illuminating remarks of Daniel Z. Feldman, *The Right and the Good: Halakhah and Human Relations*, 2nd edition, New York, 2005, pp. 73–95, and in my essay in *"Women and Men in Communal Prayer: Halachic Perspectives,"* Jersey City, N.J., 2010, pp. 150–153.

Yehuda Copperman, in his *Kedushat Pshuto shel Mikra*, vol.2, Jerusalem, 2009, pp. 235–237, shows how Rabbenu Bahya uses this principle in a number of different halachic contexts. See his commentary to Leviticus 14:44–46, where he explains the

On the basis of the above, R. Kook used this principle as an element in his advice and ruling that one should not use raw *hazeret* as *maror* (bitter herbs) in the seder night meal, because of its extreme sharpness, but rather "grate it up and leave it awhile to weaken its extreme sharpness, until there remains only a slight bitter taste, and then it will be easier to eat." See his responsum in *Orah Mishpat*, Jerusalem, 1985, no. 124.[8]

This notion expresses itself in a slightly different form in the writings of R. Meir Simchah ha-Cohen of Dvinsk, both in his *Or Sameah* and his *Meshech Hochmah*. Thus, in *Or Sameah* to Rambam, *Hilchot Evel* 3:8, he explains why the Torah permitted an ordinary *Kohen* to become impure to his deceased brother:

. . . Because a person's soul is in pain [at the death of a close relative], and

---

order in which the bible lists the different forms of leprosy in accordance with this principle, and he refers us further to his commentary to Genesis 7:11; ibid., 1:6; and on pp. 336–339, and to his commentary to Numbers 16:1, and to Leviticus 16:6.

A fine example of the use of this notion of "its ways are the ways of pleasantness and all of its paths are peace," is to be found in *Rambam Hilchot Megillah ve-Hannukah* 4:14. There he rules (basing himself on B. *Shabbat* 23b) that:

If he had before him [the choice of] *ner beito*, literally his "house candle," i.e., the Shabbat candle, and the Hannukah candle, the Shabbat candle has precedence, for the name of God may be erased to make peace between husband and wife [see Numbers 5:23]. Great is peace, for the whole Torah was given to bring peace to the world, as it is said "its ways are the ways of pleasantness and all its paths are peace," (Proverbs 3:17).

The Talmudic source only gives the reason of *shlom beito*, that the Shabbat candle banishes the stress or discomfort of sitting together during the Shabbat meal in darkness (Rashi ad loc., based on B. *Shabbat* 25b). The Rambam adds the quotation from Proverbs to emphasize the requirement of individual comfort, and also uses this verse as a fitting means to end *Seder Zemanim*. However, Feldman, ibid., pp. 52–53, refers us to R. Menachem Mendel Schneerson, the seventh Lubavitcher Rebbe, who explains that Rambam is not claiming that the Shabbat candles are more important than Hannukah candles or than *Kiddush*. For he argues that their rabbinic origins would place them on an equal, or even a lesser, footing then the latter mitzvot. "Rather, the result of the fulfillment of this mitzvah, shalom, is more all-encompassing than the others. This is evidenced by the Rambam's concluding his words by noting that 'the entire Torah is given to make peace . . .' As this is the case, showing precedence to the cause of peace is consistent with the goals of all mitzvot, and thus is the course of action that will reap the most spiritual benefit" (*Ha-Maor* 50, no. 6:311).

8.   This responsum was analyzed by Y. Zoldan, in an article entitled "'*Derachebah Darkei Noam'- Ke-Nimuk. le-Hafagat Merirut ha-Maror be-Pesach*" apud *Birurim be-Hilchot ha-Rayah*, eds. M. Tzvi Neriah, A. Stern and N. Gotel, Jerusalem, 1992, pp. 263–269.

if he (i.e., the *Kohen*) would not be permitted to deal with [his relative's] burial, there could be no greater anguish for him than that. And therefore the Torah did not prohibit the *Kohen* from acting against man's natural temperament.

And in the *Meshech Hochmah* to Genesis 9:7, he explains why women are exempt from the mitzvah of procreation thus:

> It would appear to me most likely that the Torah exempted women from the mitzvah of procreation, and obligated only men, because God's commandments and His ways are "ways of pleasantness and pathways of peace," and He did not burden Israel with that which the body cannot support . . . [i.e., because of the pains of birth-pangs].

And in a number of places he supports his conjecture by referring to the case of the *lulav* mentioned above.[9]

Samuel Morell, in his *Studies in the Judicial Methodology of Rabbi David Ibn Abi Zimra*, New York and Oxford, 2004, p. 112, gives a number of examples where Radbaz's rulings are in accordance with the guiding principle of this verse that "Its ways are ways of pleasentness."

Indeed, "this principle – that the halachah must provide ways of pleasantness – appears in many places in the Talmud, in different and varied halachic discussions, and each is like a detail that is removed from the general principle in order to teach the specific rule."[10] Subse-

---

9. On this passage see the comments of R. Yaakov Hayyim Sofer, in his *Menuhat Shalom* 12, Jerusalem, 2003, p. 170. On the halachic implications of the pain during birth, see Rambam to Leviticus 12:7, referring to *B. Niddah* 31b. See further Yitzhak Cohen, *Or Sameah-Halachah u-Mishpat,* Beer Sheva, 2013, p. 269, and see also his discussion ibid. pp. 262–265; Yehuda Copperman, *Kedushat Pshuto shel Mikra*, vol. 2, Jerusalem, 2009, pp. 236–238. See further *B. Yevamot* 65b, on the wife of R. Hiyya, on the basis of which the Maharshal, R. Shlomo Luria, in *Yam Shel Shlomo* to *Yevamot* 6:44, ruled that a woman who suffers greatly in childbearing may make use of birth control methods. Cf. ibid. 1:8, for his position on contraception. See Bah to *Even ha-Ezer* 5. catchword *Ve-ha-Ishah*; similarly this was used as an element in the permissive ruling of R. Shalom Messas, in his *Tevuot Shemesh*, Jerusalem, 1981, no. 151, p. 306; and see the extensive discussion in David M. Feldman, *Birth Control in Jewish Law*, New York and London, 1968, p. 211 et seq. See also below section entitled "Leniency to Prevent Stress and Suffering."

10. See Eliezer Berkowitz, *supra* p. 31 note 1, and *Entziklopediah Talmudit* 3. See also, Rabbi Baruch Halevi Epstein, *Torah Temimah*, Exodus 20:24, note 171, on "an

quently, the Radbaz (1480–1573) wrote in a responsum (*Orah Hayyim* 37, Salonika, 1595) that "most of the enactments of the Rabbis were in the spirit of mercy and concern for the welfare of the community, which they derived from the verse 'its ways are ways of pleasantness.'" This principle plays a prominent role in the ruling of R. Uziel. See Marc C. Angel, *Loving Truth and Peace: The Grand Religious Worldview of Rabbi Benzion Uziel*, Northvale, N.J., Jerusalem, 1989, pp. 108–109. Thus, for instance:

> When the Jewish man acknowledged that he is the father of a child from a non-Jewish mother, Rabbi Uziel stated that the man had a humanitarian obligation to support the child. If he had married the non-Jewish woman, then he had accepted the civil responsibilities of child support; he could not resort to halacha to help him find a way out of this obligation. Rabbi Uziel concluded by saying that "the Torah and the sages did not exempt the father from child support, since in the final analysis the child is a product of this father. He caused [the child] to be brought into the world. He is obligated to raise and sustain him, at least to the same extent of sustenance he owes to other dependents for whom he is responsible; indeed his responsibility [to the child] takes priority. "*This is the way of Torah whose ways are ways of pleasantness and all its paths are peace*" (*Mishpetei Uziel, Even ha-Ezer*, Jerusalem, 5724, no. 4). It would be unconscionable to exempt a Jewish man from financial support for his children born of a non-Jewish woman. Because the Torah's ways are pleasant and peace loving, it could not sanction such a morally repugnant situation.[11]
>
> Another case dealt with a man who was suffering, apparently, from prostate problems. He was informed that his illness could only be cured through an operation that would leave him impotent. Since halakhah generally forbids acts of sterilization, was this man permitted to undergo this medical procedure?
>
> After a discussion of the relevant texts, Rabbi Uziel concluded that the operation was permitted in this case. "And this should be done without

---

eye for an eye, etc." (I found Dan Seter's book, entitled *Darkhei Noam*, 2nd edition, 2000, somewhat disappointing.)

11. And cf. Nahum Stepansky, *Ve-Aleihu Lo Tibol: Mi-Hanhagotav ve-Hadrachotav shel R. Shlomo Zalman Auerbach*, vol. 2, Jerusalem, 2013, pp. 67–68, on helping a non-Jew.

delay since there is no other cure . . . It is preferable to advance [the date of the procedure] to save and free him from pains which distract him from Torah, and which [cause him] a life of anguish and suffering, so as to return him to a life of quiet and peace in the ways of Torah and mitzvot, whose *ways are ways of pleasantness and all its paths are peace"* (*Mishpetei Uziel*, ibid., no. 6). It was a moral obligation to heal the man from his illness as soon as possible, even though the act of sterilization was generally forbidden. The Torah wants us to live by its words, not to suffer unnecessarily by them.

A related question concerned a man who underwent necessary surgery which left his sterile. Was he allowed to continue his marriage with his wife? The Torah forbids the marriage of a castrated man or one whose genitals are damaged so that he is impotent. Rabbi Uziel asserted that the prohibition refers only to one who willingly mutilated himself or had himself mutilated; it does not refer to one born sterile nor to one who had to undergo surgery for health reasons. Therefore, the man in question was allowed to continue his marriage with his wife, "and this is what the dictates of the law and truth teach, about which it is written that her ways [i.e., the ways of Torah] are ways of pleasantness" (*Mishpehtei Uziel*, ibid., no. 7). (My emphasis – D.S.)

Sensitivity to Personal Feelings

It is clear from the above that personal comfort and the prevention of suffering must be central factors in halachic thought and *pesak*.

Indeed, the definition of suffering is in itself a subject of halachic discussion. Thus, R. Yehiel Weinberg, in his *Seridei Aish*, vol. 2, no. 158, when discussing the case of a person who claims *matzah* harms him, and the doctor says it does not, asserts that we follow the doctor's opinion. He argues that the principle "the heart knoweth his own bitterness" (Proverbs 14:10, and cf. *B. Yoma* 83a, *Exodus Rabba* 19:1), namely that a person knows best what harms him, only applies to situations of hunger and not to others. R. Eliezer Yehuda Waldenberg, in his *Tzitz Eliezer*, vol. 15, 2nd edition, Jerusalem, 1985, no. 32:8, pp. 77–78, rejects this argument (and its suggested sources) stating explicitly that this principle is not based on intellectual understanding (*meivinut*), but on "the deep *feelings* that a person has been granted to preserve his body (i.e., health)." He cites R. Shlomo Kluger's responsum (*Orah Hayyim* no. 328) who likewise explains that "the heart's knowledge . . . is only because his heart is telling him [what is harmful to him]." He bolsters his argument by referring to R. Shlomo of Vilna's *Binyan Shlomo* no. 47, who writes that it is simple and straightforward to him that we rely on the feelings of a sick person – if he suspects that something will be harmful to him, be it eating a *ke-zayit* of *matzah* or *maror*, or sitting in a *Sukkah* – and in all such cases he may not rule stringently in his own case. Thus, the halachah relies on the personal subjective feelings of the unwell, even if this would appear to be irrational over the objective and rational opinion of an expert doctor. In other words, the personal feelings of the individual in such cases take halachic precedence. (Cf. his responsum in vol. 14, 2nd edition, 1985, no. 27, p. 48.)

This sensitivity to the state of the individual expresses itself in numerous halachic contexts. Thus R. Waldenberg, in that same volume no.43:3 p.101, gives an example concerning a woman who gave birth to two children with serious genetic ailments, and who, out of fear for yet another such child, wishes to practice birth control for a while until her fears are allayed. This he rules to be permissible, declaring the permissibility of temporary birth control in case of the pain of birthing (*tzaar leidah*). Weakness, or indeed any kind of great distress, even if it is not the direct result of sexual intercourse, including the distress of giving birth to deformed children, can change a halachic ruling, "for there cannot be greater emotional distress than this . . ."

And for a different kind of example, one of the great scholars from the period of the *Aharonim* ruled that the person leading the prayers in the synagogue should not recite the blessing "that he did not make me a woman" out loud so as not to possibly offend women.[12] Already

---

12. See Rabbi Aharon ben Avreli Wermes [Worms], *Meorei Or* 4, Beer Sheva: Metz, 1819, p. 20, cited by Rabbi Yehuda Herzl Henkin, responsa *Bnai Banim* 4, Jerusalem: Y. Henkin, 2005, Section 1, p. 11; see also my *On Changes in Jewish Liturgy: Options and Limitations*, Jerusalem, 2010, pp. 33–38. Rabbi Hayyim Hirschenson also saw this declaration as an affront to women, although he did not come to the same conclusions as Rabbi Wermes. See Rabbi Hayyim Hirschenson, *Malki ba-Kodesh* 4, St. Louis: Moinester Printing, 1923, p. 104, where he wrote as follows:

This is all to justify the blessing, while in truth I would say to you that all of the early and later poskim were not sensitive to this issue. Only the early cantors in their prayerbooks demonstrated even the trace of knowledge of this, which is that the Babylonian Talmud already opposed this blessing. . . . And in this section of the Talmud itself (*Menahot* 47b), there is opposition to the blessing "that He did not make me a woman" even if a man does not sense it, but give me some time, and I will tell you. . . .

during the times of the Second Temple, the rabbis permitted women to perform *semichah* (placing their hands) on sacrifices that they brought – a practice that was apparently forbidden – in order to give them a sense of satisfaction.[13]

This principle appears in a variety of different halachic contexts, and its meaning has been significantly extended. Thus, for example, a responsum of R. Joseph b. Lev (Maharival, 16th century, a contemporary of R. Yosef Karo) describes a case in which a man whose wife was barren took another wife and fathered several children. He then wished to divorce the second wife but keep the children for himself. Maharival wrote (*Teshuvot Maharival,* part 1, sect. 40):

> Such an affair is cause for great chagrin. It is not proper to demean Jewish women in such a manner, to send off the mother and take the children.

Yet, it is clear to me that both Rav Aha and his son opposed the blessing "that He did not make me a woman," even if the blessing is based on the fact that women are not obligated to perform certain commandments, as we have explained, these perfect individuals nevertheless sensed a feeling of insulting women, and Rav Aha bar Yaakov did not want to recite the blessing. His son went and recited a different blessing in its place – "that He did not make me an imbecile," but his father indicated that this was also not proper since it insults the dignity of the regular people, who are obligated to fulfill the commandments, and who have the possibility of improvement. . . . And on this, his son asked him what he should recite to complete these three instead of "that He did not make me a woman," and his father told him to recite "that He did not make me a slave." . . . Even so, after all of this, I still recite the blessing "that He did not make me a woman" daily, for it is not my approach to change the custom of the earlier and later posqim, even if my opinion is at times not the same as theirs on the level of theoretical study, but not practice. But my intent when saying this blessing is in accordance with the Tosefta, to express my happiness at being obligated to sustain my wife faithfully in the custom of Jewish men and for the positive commandments that are time bound that I am commanded to perform and a woman is not commanded to perform.

(From David Zohar, *Mehuyavut Yehudit be-Olam Moderni: Harav Hayyim Hirschenson ve-Yahaso La-Modernah,* Jerusalem, 2003, p. 371, note 10.) And see my *On Changes in Jewish Liturgy: Options and Limitations,* Jerusalem, 2010, pp. 33–40, for an extended discussion of this issue. See also Joel Wolowelsky, "A Quiet Berakha," *Tradition* 29/4, 1995, pp. 61–68; and E. Feldman, "An Articulate Berakha," ibid., pp. 69–74.

13. *B. Hagigah* 16b. The prohibition is a *shvut de-mitzvah.* See *Y. Hagigah* 2:2, and cf. *Alei Tamar* by Yisachar Tamar, to *Y. Hagigah,* ibid., Alon Shvut, 1991, p. 259. I discussed this issue in my essay "Congregational Dignity and Human Dignity: Women and Public Torah Reading," apud *Women and Men in Communal Prayer: Halakhic Perspectives,* ed. C. Trachman, Jersey City, N.J., 2010, p. 74.

[This is a play on the verse in Deuteronomy 11:7: "You shall surely send away the mother and take the chicks to yourself."] And great is *kevod ha-beri'ot*, which supplants a negative commandment in the Torah.

His remarks imply that, even though such a thing is permissible and acceptable from a halachic point of view, it would nevertheless be a source of grief and pain to the second wife. Hence, considerations of "human dignity" – the sensitivity that anyone ought to feel for the distress and anguish that the second wife might experience – overcome even a negative commandment in the Torah.

On this basis, the sages of Ashkenaz in the Middle Ages permitted women in a state of impurity (*niddah*) to enter the synagogue on festivals and the high holidays – a practice that was not permitted throughout the rest of the year – because it would cause them great distress to be unable to participate in the prayer service with the rest of the community.[14]

---

14. See also R. Ovadia Yosef, *Hazon Ovadiah: Yamim Noraim*, Jerusalem, 2005, p. 130, note 10, citing the Raviah, to *Rosh ha-Shanah* sect.534, p. 215. And see my "Women and Public Torah Reading: A Halakhic Study," apud *Women and Men in Communal Prayer: Halakhic Perspectives*, Jersey City, N.J., 2010, p. 76, with additional references.

See further on this issue in Y.A. Dinari's articles in *Tarbiz* 49; pp. 3–4, 1980, pp. 302–324; idem. *Teudah*, 1983, pp. 17–37; idem. *Hachmei Ashkenaz be-Shilhei Yemei-ha-Benayim, Darkeihem ve-Kitveiheim be-Halachah*, Jerusalem, 1984, pp. 81–82. The authority who permitted this was R. Yisrael Isserlein (1390–1460), in his *Terumat ha-Deshen, Psakim u-Ketavim* no.132, ed. Warsaw, 1882, p. 26, who writes as follows: Concerning women at the time of their menstruation, it is true I permitted them [to enter the synagogue] during the high holy days and similar occasions, when many of them gather together to the synagogue to have the prayers and the reading [of the Torah] . . . , and I relied on Rashi who permitted women during their period of menstruation in order to give them satisfaction (*nahat ruah*), for [otherwise] they have sadness and heartache, when everyone [else] gather to be [in] the congregation and they stand outside . . .

And then he refers us to the aforementioned passage in B. *Hagigah* 16b. Dinari (*Hachmei Ashkenaz* p. 82) remarks that Isserlein saw the Talmud's ruling on women's *semichah* – laying hands on a sacrificial animal – not as a *heiter* for this single issue alone, but as if a general nature referring to a variety of cases where women's distress could be alleviated. His ruling was accepted by the later poskim (e.g., *Leket Yosher* by R. Yosef be R. Yehudah c. 1460, ed. Y. Freimann, Berlin, 1903, part 1, p. 131, part 2, p. 23, etc.). And on the basis of Isserlein's ruling the Rema, in his responsum no. 98, ed. Asher Ziv, Jerusalem, 1971, pp. 428–429, permitted "a man who suffered from the illness of kidney stones, . . . , because of which urine was constantly dripping from him uncontrollably, to enter the synagogue wearing *tefillin*."

The *Torah Temimah*, by R. Baruch Halevi Epstein, in his comment to Genesis 18:9, p. 167, note 30, gives several additional examples of this sensitivity towards the feelings of women, and their innate desire to preserve their modesty. Referring to M. *Baba Batra* 8:1, B. *Baba Batra* 139b, B. *Ketubot* 188b, 140a, *Shulhan Aruch, Even ha-Ezer* 112:11, regarding orphan girls as opposed to boys; *Shulhan Aruch, Hoshen Mishpat* 124, that women are not called to the *beit din*, but the court-scribes come to them (cf. ibid. 86:6, B. *Yevamot* 101a); and relatedly *Even ha-Ezer* 103:1, M. *Ketubot* 11:2, B. *Ketubot* 97a, that a widow does not sell property before the court, etc.

And we may further note that the Ba'al ha-Tanya in his *Shulhan Arukh ha-Rav, Hilchot Rosh ha-Shanah*, sect. 586, subsect. 2, writes as follows:

> Even though women are free of the obligation of hearing the *shofar* on Rosh Hashanah, nonetheless, if they wish to blow it themselves, they are permitted to do so. And even though blowing it on Yom Tov is forbidden by Rabbinic law (*mi-divrei sofrim*), nevertheless, in order to give women a sense of satisfaction (*nahat ruah*), they permitted this slight prohibition (*issur qal*), which is not even a real *shevut* but merely [forbidden] because it is like a secular activity (*uvdin de-hol*).[15]

Similarly, R. Benzion Meir Hai Uziel writes as follows regarding "participation of women in elections for public institutions":

> As I have not found so much as a hint of such a prohibition, I see no reason to oppose or even to refuse to deal with this question . . . Moreover, they [our Sages] said: "Women [are allowed to] lay their hands on it [the sacrificial animal] in order to please the women [*Hagigah* 1b], even though it seemed like a prohibition." All the more so in our case, in which there is no aspect of prohibition in the matter, *and preventing them from participating would be an insult and an act of oppression* – certainly in such a case we need to give them their rights.[16] (My emphasis - D.S.)

---

15. On the halachic concept of *uvdin de-hol*, see Admiel Kosman's study in *Mishpat ve-Historiah*, ed. D. Gotvein and M. Mountner, Jerusalem, 1999, pp. 75–101.

16. *Piskei Uziel be-she'elot ha-Zeman*, Jerusalem, 1977, sect. 44, pp. 229–230. And cf. his remarks in *Mishpetei Uziel*, vol. IV, sect. 5–6, esp. ibid., p. 37.

But regarding the matter of alleviating the community's pain, Nachum Rakover writes (op cit., 143) as follows:

> An interesting extension of the principle of human dignity, including enabling a community to recite the blessing over the etrog during Sukkot, thereby saving them from a sense of great distress, appears in a responsum of R. David Pardo of Italy [Venice 1718 – Jerusalem 1790; he came to Jerusalem in 1780 and served in the rabbinate in various cities of the Balkans: Ragusa, Espalatro, and Sarajevo. His works include *Hasdei David* on the Tosefta and *Shoshanim le-David* on the *Mishnah*]. R. David Pardo was confronted by the question [*Teshuvot Mikhtam le-David, Orah Hayyim*, sect.6], asked by the community of Ragusa, who wished during *Hol ha-Moed* to forgo the one *etrog* they had in their possession in order to enable the inhabitants of Sarei to recite the blessing on it during the remaining days of Sukkot. The respondent first considered the question of whether it is permissible to forsake a less important *mitzvah* in order to enable others to have a greater *mitzvah*. Thereafter, he relied upon the principle of human dignity and stated that, since on the other days of the festival the mitzvah of taking the Four Species is only based upon Rabbinate enactment, this mitzvah may be put aside by considerations of human dignity, for "there is no greater example of [affront to] human dignity than that there should be a large community completely unable to perform such a great mitzvah at all, for it is obvious that in this case every inhabitant in Israel dwells in pain and trouble, [an elaborate word-play on Leviticus 23:42 and Psalms 116:3]. And they are pained because they are unable to even see the mitzvah of our God all the days of the holiday, as if this mitzvah had been denied them completely. . . . And since they sent a special messenger, who ran here because of their great desire, and they looked [to this *etrog*] when will they merit to fulfill this mitzvah – certainly if this emissary were to return empty-handed, such a thing would cause them great anguish to their heart and enhance their suffering. There is thus no greater [case of] human dignity than this" (*Teshuvot Michtam le-David*, ibid. 12a, s.v. *Hadran*).

From all these examples we see the extent to which the Sages of all generations took human dignity into account, in matters of both the individual and the public.

For yet another example of the use of this rule to alleviate individual distress, see R. Yosef Hayyim's *Teshuvot Rav Pealim*, vol. I, Jerusalem, 1901, *Even ha-Ezer*, sect.1:

> And I said hastily that in all cases such as this [of suspicion of adultery] there is a blemish that becomes attached to the family, *and there is a great issue of human dignity involved* [my emphasis - D.S.]; also, perhaps he will not believe it and will not separate [from his wife]. [Therefore,] one needs to find a ground for permissive ruling, both for the adulterer and for the sage to whom he confessed, that they not reveal the matter [so that the woman not be forced to be divorced from her husband]. And I saw the following in the name of the Gaon Maharish [R. Joseph Saul Halevi Nathanson], in *Sho'el u-Meishiv Kamma*, Pt. I (Lvov, 1869), sect. 262, p. 101 [b], that there were those among the *Rishonim* who think that if the woman did not commit adultery in the presence of witnesses, she is not forbidden to her husband, and her [subsequent] relations with him are not considered as forbidden. [And he noted there *Sefer Benei Ahuvah*, in chap. 24 of *Hilkhot Ishut*, of the Gaon Mahari (R. Jonathan Eybeshuetz, Prague, 1819) who wrote extensively on this issue.] According to this, regarding the question of R. Nathanson, in which the husband himself does not know of his wife's unfaithfulness, and she committed adultery without any witnesses, the adulterer is not required to inform the husband, for he may rely upon the approach of those *Gedolim* that there is no prohibition for the husband so long as there are no witnesses. All the more so if we add to it all the above-mentioned reasons: that it entails a blemish to the family, *and there is a great issue of human dignity*; and, moreover, that he, i.e., the *Poseq*, does not see with his own eyes that the husband has relations with his wife, for perhaps there is some reason that he is unable to have relations with her subsequently, nor is it clear to him that he will believe her and separate from her.

This rule served not only to prevent individual or public suffering, but also to increase public joy, as we learn from a responsum of R. Isaiah di Trani the Elder (Italy, 13th century):

> Regarding what you wrote to me about lighting candles in the synagogue on festival days, it seems to me that there is no prohibition or even a hint of transgression in this. . . . For all those labors which are permitted for purposes of preparing food to be eaten [on the festival] were also

permitted for non-food purposes (*Beitzah* 12a). And according to Torah law, even though there is no need for those labors at all, they are allowed as if it were a weekday, and it was the rabbis who made an edict regarding those things for which there is no need whatsoever . . . But a candle on a festival day is something that is needed. And this is so, even if there is no need for its light, for it also involves an element of *human dignity and augmenting joy*, for in general people are not accustomed to light candles during daylight hours were it not for honor and something that rejoices man's heart . . . (*Teshuvot ha-Rid*, ed. A. Y. Wertheimer, Jerusalem, 1967, sect. 21, p. 119).

And, in a fuller version,

People would not be accustomed to lighting candles in a house where there is joy were it not considered a matter of human dignity. For in order to increase people's joy and to broaden their hearts, the Sages were lenient regarding their edict in this matter, because they saw this as a matter of human dignity (*Shibolei ha-Leket*, sect. 242.)

In my essay on "Congregational Dignity and Human Dignity: Women and Public Reading," apud *Women and Men in Communal Prayer: Halachic Perspectives*, ed. C. Trachtman, Jersey City, N.J., 2010, pp. 74–83, and ibid. Appendix V, pp. 154–161, I brought many additional examples. Admittedly some of them can be interpreted slightly differently. Nonetheless, they all demonstrate a level of sensitivity to the special needs of women, which can be generally subsumed under the generic category of *kevod ha-briyot*.

Human Dignity

And clearly this principle is intimately intertwined with the prohibition against embarrassing and shaming people, a prohibition discussed in detail in the following section. Thus, for example, the *sugya* in the *Yerushalmi* (*Kilaim* 9:1) discusses the case of someone walking in a public place who suddenly realizes that he is wearing clothes which are woven with *kilaim* (a weave of a forbidden mix of fibres). One opinion states that he should remove his clothing immediately, since the prohibition is of biblical authority (cf. *B. Berachot* 19b–20a), and the other states that he need not do so, because of his dignity, the dignity of the individual, *kevod ha-briyot*. For it would greatly embarrass him to bare his body in public. Similarly, the Talmud in *B. Shabbat* 50b, cites a *beraita* that rules that, under certain circumstances, a person may on Shabbat scrape off his body scabby encrushments of scabs of wound, because of his discomfort (*mi-shum tzaaro*). To which the *Tosafot* ad loc. write:

> And if he has no other discomfort other than that he is ashamed to walk among people [with those dirty spots on his body], he may do so [i.e., scrape them off], for there is no greater discomfort than this.

(And see below section on "Leniency to Prevent Distress and Suffering," from which we can clearly see the interdependence of all those principles, and their common ethical foundation, so much so that in many cases these different elements are interchanged or syncretized.)

Indeed, the sages enacted a number of great leniencies based on this principle of *kevod ha-briyot*, i.e., not to degrade the dignity of human beings.[17]

---

17. It should be noted that *kevod ha-briyot* is a generic, all-encompassing principle under which fall many sub-categories, such as not shaming others, preserving marital integrity, respecting the less learned, etc., many of which are discussed throughout this study. There is much literature on this subject. But for the basic and fullest study of this principle see N. Rakover, *Gadol Kevod ha-Briyot: Kevod ha-Adam Ke-Erech Al (Human Dignity in Jewish Law)*, Jerusalem, 1998, and the important article of Rabbi Aharon Lichtenstein, "*Kevod ha-Briyot*" *Machanayim* 5 (Iyar, 5753), pp. 8–15. On page 14, he writes: "Several decades ago, I wrote . . . about the limited use in actual practice of this rule by the scholars of the *halachah*." He continues to analyze why this halachic concept is under-utilized, and concludes as follows (p. 15): "The need to internalize the value of *kevod ha-briyot* faces us, and it is forbidden to evade it. We should not adopt other, more delicate formulations of secular humanism, but we should stand firm on its clear form – on our approach to *kavod ha-briyot* from all of its perspectives." He also treated this subject in his essay "'*Mah Enosh*': Reflections on the Relation between Judaism and Humanism" *The Torah u-Madda Journal* 14, 2006–2007, pp. 33–49. See Benyamin Lau, apud *Rabbanut: Ha-Etgar*, Jerusalem, 2011, vol.1, eds. Y. Stern, S. Friedman. See also my article on this issue "Congregational Dignity and Human Dignity: Women and Public Torah Reading," *The Edah Journal*, 3(20), (Elul, 5763/2002), pp. 1–14, and my book *Darkah shel Halachah, supra* note 2, in which I expanded on this issue. See also Eliezer Berkowitz, *supra* note 1, where he brings many examples of the use of this concept. (Recently, Meir Roth, in his *Orthodoxiah Humanit: Mahshevet ha-Halachah shel ha-Rav Professor Eliezer Berkovitz*, Jerusalem, 2013, pp. 102–114, summarized very lucidly Berkovitz's views on this

We may also point to another expression of this basic concept of the

---

subject.) Of related interest is Menachem Elon, *Kevod ha-Adam ve-Heruto be-Darkei ha-Hotzaah le-Poal (Human Dignity and Freedom in the Methods of Enforcement of Judgements: The Values of a Jewish and Democratic State)*, Jerusalem, 2000. So too in my *On the Relationship of Mitzvot between Man and his Neighbor and Man and his Maker*, Jerusalem and New York, 2014, pp. 106–114.

For a further expansion of this principle, see *Kuntres Kevod ha-Torah*, Anonymous, Bnei Brak, 2013, which contains *Kuntres Kevod ha-Briyot*, pp. 1–60, 7, relating this concept to the prohibition of "*lo tonu*" (ye shall not oppress) Leviticus 25:17.

Interestingly enough, this principle on occasions was applied to non-Jews too. Thus, for example, R. Yekutiel Yehuda Teitelbaum, in his response *Avnei Tzedek*, Lvov, 1885–1886, *Yoreh Deah*, sect. 105, ruled that a non-Jewish woman who wishes to have a ritual ablution in order to convert to Judaism, but is ashamed to shave all her body, is permitted to immerse without shaving, despite the fact that the Rema and the Levush, in *Yoreh Deah* 268:2, and in *Orah Hayyim* 156, wrote that there are those that say he/she should shave. (See also supercommentaries to the *Shulhan Aruch* ibid. that ex posteriori such conversion is valid.) R. Teitelbaum explains that shaving is mandatory only for those who are converting from being idolators. But since nowadays most Christians – he is referring specifically to Christians – are not considered idolators according to the Rema and the Levush themselves (*Orah Hayyim* 156), shaving is not mandatory, and if such would shame a woman it may be bypassed.

I will cite here two examples that Berkowitz brings (*Ha-Halakhah Kohah ve-Tafkidah*, supra note 9, p. 108): Also in other contexts the rabbis were concerned about the dignity of other human beings. Regarding the verse "she that is sick with her impurity" (Leviticus 15:33), the early scholars interpreted it as follows: "It means that she must not rouge nor paint nor adorn herself in dyed garments." This rule remained in force until Rabbi Akiva came and taught: "If so, you make her repulsive to her husband, with the result that he will divorce her! But what [then] is taught by, 'and she that is sick with her impurity'? She shall remain in her impurity until she enters into water" (*Shabbat* 64b). Here, the simple ethical logic that you should not cause a woman to become repulsive to her husband is what drives the intent of the verse. More than that is what is stated in the *Mishnah* in the beginning of chapter "*Yom ha-Kippurim*," that even though the prohibition of washing is one of the hardships of Yom Kippur, a bride is permitted to wash her face. The reason given for this law by Rabbi Hananyah ben Taradyon is "that she not become repulsive to her husband." So too, "one must not withhold jewelry from a bride for a full thirty days after her wedding" (*Yoma* 73a and 78b). The innovative element of the permission for a bride to wash on Yom Kippur is that some of the *Rishonim* hold that washing on Yom Kippur is a Torah prohibition. (This was the position of the Ran on this *Gemara*, and Maimonides in *Mishneh Torah, Hilchot Shvitat Asor* 1:5 also tends toward this approach. See also the *Kessef Mishnah* there, and the *Beit Yosef* in *Orah Hayyim* on this commandment. This, however, is not the opinion of the *Maggid Mishnah*. See also the explanation of his comments in the *Lehem Mishnah* there.)

For a very full discussion of *kevod ha-briyot*, see Nahum Rakover, *Gadol Kevod ha-Briyot: Kevod ha-Adam ke-Erech Al (Human Dignity in Jewish Law)*, Jerusalem, 1998; David Z. Feldman, *The Right and the Good: Halachah and Human Relations* 2nd edition, Brooklyn, N.Y., 2005, pp. 197–215, and my treatment in *Women and*

concern for the dignity of the individual, as it is reflected in rabbinic and post-rabbinic exegesis. The last verse of *Parshat Yitro* (Exodus 20:26) is, "Neither shalt thou go by steps unto mine altar, that thy nakedness be not discovered thereon." This verse is clearly speaking of the need for great respect and modesty when approaching the Temple – or Tabernacle – altar. The following verse, at the beginning of *Parshat Mishpatim* (21:1) is, "Now these are the judgments which thou shalt set before them." The verses, in the next two chapters, list commandments relating to the relationship between man and his neighbor. But the rabbis of the Tannaitic period linked the last and the first verse of these two consecutive chapters. Thus in *B. Sanhedrin* 75 Bar-Kappara asks from where do we learn that judges have to be careful, or considerate and patient, in judgment (*M. Avot* 1:1)? His reply is from the proximity of these two verses, the first reinterpreted as meaning do not go up in haughtiness (*v'lo ta'aleh bma'alot*), when dealing with judgments (*mishpatim*) of the following verse. Thus a verse already referring to a need for *ritual* respect is reinterpreted homiletically to refer to the requirement for *interpersonal* respect – a midrashic transfer from the realm of the ritual to that of the socio-ethical.

So too, in yet another such Tannaitic statement on the same couplet of verses, for in *B. Sanhedrin* 7b, R. Eliezer inquires:

> From whence do we know that a judge must not step over the heads of the holy people (*shelo yifseh al roshi am kodesh*)?[18]

Men in Communal Prayer: Halakhic Perspectives, Jersey City, N.J., 2010, pp. 74–87, 154–161.

A deep and complex analysis of this concept is to be found in R. Meir Teomim (author of the *Pri Megadim) Shoshanat ha-Amakim*, new ed. Israel and New York, 2005, pp. 62–82, pointing out that the shame or humiliation need not be great, but even when slight this principle comes into effect.

See also the comment of A.Y. Heschel, in his *Torah min ha-Shamayim be-Aspa-clariah shel ha-Dorot*, vol. 3, Jerusalem, 1970, pp. 167–168. Indeed, it is on this note his magnum opus ends.

See also most recently, David Novak, *Natural Law and Revealed Law*, eds. H. Tirosh-Samuelson, Aaron W. Hughes, Leiden and Boston, 2014, pp. 71–88, chapter entitled "On Human Dignity."

18. But cf. *B. Bechorot* 13b. See on this A. Büchler's classic essay in *Dissertatione in honorem Dr. Eduardi Mahler*, Budapest, 1937, pp. 370–405; and see the related discussion beginning with *B. Kiddushin* 32b, the statement of R. Shimon ben Eleazar, ibid. 33a, *Shulhan Aruch, Yoreh Deah* 244:6; *Birkei Yosef* to *Yoreh Deah* ibid., and

the analysis of R. Shimon Levi, in his article *"Kibud Talmid Hacham, Rav ve-Zaken"* *Shematin* 28/104–105, pp. 52–53; and R. Yaakov Hayyim Sofer *Brit Yaakov*, Jerusalem 1985, pp. 232–237. [Incidentally, on his note on פוסע – פוסס, on p. 236, cf. Tzvi Moshe Kahn, *He-Akov le-Mishor*, Brooklyn, Jerusalem, 1992, p. 11, on this consonantal change.] The basic source for this subject is in B. *Kiddushin* 31b, Rambam, *Hilchot Talmud Torah*, chapter 5.

A related ruling is that which we find in *Shulhan Aruch, Hoshen Mishpat* 124: The defendant cannot appoint an appointee to come before the court and reply on his behalf to the claimant, while he [the dependant] sits at home. [But] our precioius women, for whom it is not dignified to come to the court, we send them clerks of the court, and they can make their claims before them. And we act similarly for a *Talmid Hacham* who studies (*Torah*) in his profession, and for him it is demeaning (*ve-zila bei milta*) to go to the court and to argue with a ignorant person.

The reason "precious women" are permitted to make their claims at home before the court clerks is based on the verse in *Psalms* 45:14, "The king's daughter (i.e., daughters of Israel) is all glorious within," that is to say: they do not go out in public (see B. *Shevuot* 30a). See *Derishah, Hoshen Mishpat* ad loc., citing the Rosh, Ramban, Ri Halevi and Rif (Alfasi) to *Shevout* ibid. And the *Beit Yosef* ibid. wrote:

And a woman, who is not wont to come before a court, because "all her dignity is within" (*Psalms* ibid.), we do not hear her claims through her agent, but the court sends her clerks to hear her claims directly from her mouth, and afterwards the agent stands before the court . . .

And the same is true of the Sage.

However, the *Beit Yosef* (*Bedek ha-Bayit* to *Hoshen Mishpat* 96 ad fin.) cites a Gaon that this is the ruling, despite the fact that it would seem to him contrary to another ruling found in B. *Sanhedrin* 7b:

Hear the causes between your brethren, and judge [righteously between every man and his brother . . .]" (*Deuteronomy* 1:16) – Said R. Haninah: This is a warning to the court not to hear the words of the claimant before his fellow defendant.

Rashi (ad loc.) explains that they must both be present together before the court, and not that the court hear the one without the other [being present]. And cf. B. *Sotah* 21b: What is an example of a crafty evil doer? Said R. Yohanan: This is one who makes his case before the judge before the other plaintiff arrives. (And cf. *Tanhuma Mishpatim* 6; *Sheiltot, Mishpatim*, 66, ed. S.K. Mirsky, vol. 3, Jerusalem, 1964, p. 178.) The Hida, in his *Birkei Yosef* to *Hoshen Mishpat* 17:4 claims that this rule is of biblical authority (*mi-de-Oraita*). (See also, *Zohar Genesis* 179b close in formulation to B. *Sotah* ibid., R. Reuven Margaliot, *Margaliot ha-Yam* to *Sanhedrin* ibid., vol. 1, Jerusalem 1958, p. 36; M. Spielman, *Tiferet Tzvi*, vol. 3, New York, 1989, pp. 191–192.) And, nonetheless, writes the *Beit Yosef*: In order to allow this virtuous behavior (*middah zu*, i.e., the virtue of modesty) one makes a great amendment [to the basic law], *takanah gedolah*.

See the detailed discussion of this issue in Meir Shoresh, *Kol Kvudah Bat Melech Pnimah: Yesodotav Mashmauto ve-Tokfo*, Jerusalem, 1943, pp. 10–11. (This booklet first appeared as a series of articles in *Shmatin* 60, 64–68.)

We see, then, that in certain given situations it was necessary to devise the legal means to protect the modesty of the "precious" women, and the dignity of the learned Sage, even at the expense of the (biblical?) code of judicial legislation.

However, at least with regards to women, nowadays this discussion is largely

And again the reply is from the proximity of these two verses, namely that he, the judge of *Mishpatim*, should not haughtily step over the heads of the litigants. The author of *Torah Temimah* (R. Baruch Halevi Epstein, p. 223, note 3) further explains this verse (in contradistinction to Rashi's explanation ad loc.):

> That the rabbi or judge should not look disparagingly upon the common folk as though they are not considered worth anything in his eyes, so that he brushes them aside from his thoughts as unworthy of his consideration, and does not treat them with any form of respect.

Here we find a total interpretative transferal from the simple plain meaning of the ritual requirement in the Temple to that of the area of decency and respect even to people who one might regard as being of a lower class.

Similarly, the *Mechilta* (*de-ha-Hodesh II*) to this verse, ed. Horovitz – Rabin, second edition, Jerusalem, 1960, p. 245, writes:

> Now, this is a *fortiori* matter. If, with respect to stones which have no sense for better or for worse, the Holy One blessed be He, said "Do not treat them disdainfully" – your fellow, who is in the image of He who spoke and the world came into being, certainly you should not treat him with disdain.

Rabbi Aharon Lichtenstein, in his article "'*Mah Enosh*': Reflections of the Relation between Judaism and Humanism," *The Torah u-Madda Journal* 14, 2006–2007, p. 33, connects this to the laws prohibiting the disgrace of inanimate object, such as covering the hallah while making Kiddush over wine, "so as not to shame the bread" (according to the Mordechai, *Pesachim* 100b), explaining that this is:

> Not, of course because of some primitive animation, but because the

---

irrelevant, because even the most stringently modest women in our days go regularly out of the house for a variety of public activities. See Yehuda Henkin, in his book, *Understanding Tzniut: Modern Controversies in the Jewish Community*, Jerusalem, 2009, pp. 73–91, and what I wrote in a brief article in the *JOFA Journal* 7/2, 2007, pp. 7–9, entitled "The Human Element in the Commandments: The Effect of Changing Norms on Halakhic Decisions."

Halakhah's concern for respect and dignity has been so wide-ranging. People concerned about shaming bread have a reminder not to insult their fellows.

We can add numerous examples of this halachic phenomenon, such as not placing a *siddur* upon a *humash*, because the *humash* being holier would be, as it were, offended having a book of lesser sanctity placed upon it. So too one does not use one book to prop up another, for much the same reason, (e.g., *Sefer Hasidim*, no. 141, 902, 915, etc.; see ed. Shimon Gutman, Brooklyn, 2014, index vol. 2, p. 61, s.v. *Sefarim – Kevod Sefarim*, and his notes ad loc.; also Eliyahu Yohanan Gurarie, *Ha-Sefer be-Halachah*, Kfar Habad, 1990, chapter 9, pp. 75–84). Likewise, the edge of the *tallit* with the *atarah* must always be on top, so not to shame it (*Magen Avraham* to *Orah Hayyim* 8:6; see also Josef Lewy *Minhag Yisrael Torah*, vol. 1, Brooklyn, 1984, p. 72.) These somewhat random examples amply exemplify the degree of sensitivity the halachah demands vis-à-vis inanimate objects, to sensitize, and to be no less sensitive to their fellow humans.

Perhaps, conversely, we learn from the Rambam, *Hilchot Sanhedrin* 15:9, that:

> The gallows on which a person was hung should be buried with him, so that there be no negative memory of him, so that [people will not be able to see the gallows] and say, "These are the gallows upon which so-and-so was hung." And likewise, the stone[s] with which he was stoned [to death] and the sword with which he was executed and the scarf with which he was strangled – all of these should be buried close to the grave of the executed, but not actually in his own grave.

We see here that the halachah counsels hiding these inanimate objects to minimize the shame of the deceased, even though he was justly executed by a legitimate court of law (*beit din*). In this case, the sensitivity to the object is a function of our ultimate compassion for the deceased.[19]

And returning to the subject of human dignity, and how a rabbi should treat his students, we read in *Numbers Rabba* 15:17, that R.

---

19. And cf. Responsa *Sheilat Yaavetz*, by R. Yaakov Ashkenazi, part 2, no. 158, and *Pithei Teshuvah* to *Yoreh Deah* 8:1.

Aba ha-Cohen bar Papa, when he saw a group of people, would take a different route in order not to trouble them, since if they would see him, they would stand up before him our of respect. However, the Midrash continues, that when he related this to R. Yossi be R. Zevida he chastised him, arguing that in doing so he was preventing them from carrying out the mitzvah of rising up before a Sage (Leviticus 19:31), which leads one to the fear of Heavens. This too was the opinion of R. Hiyya bar Aba in B. Ketubot 96a.

However, in B. Kiddushin 33a we are specifically told that a Sage should avoid troubling people who would otherwise rise up before him. Abbaye adds that it is his tradition that one who circumvents people in order to avoid troubling them will be granted long life. In B. Menahot 33a it is related that R. Yehudah HaNasi would enter the Academy through a small entrance specially prepared for him so as not to disturb the public.

Though there appears to be a contradiction between these two sets of tradition, a number of solutions have been offered, such as that there is a difference if the public is seated on the ground, since for them it would be difficult to rise, and those who are seated on benches, for whom there would be little difficulty to rise, (see Shach to Shulhan Aruch, Yoreh Deah 244, sect. 4). Other solutions have been offered.[20]

In this discussion we see the apparent clash between the dignity of the rabbi and the dignity of the public. Both have to be accorded respect, and in accordance with different situations the priorities may change.

Care Not to Shame or Embarrass

Let us now see the degree to which this level of sensitivity developed. There is a commandment of the Torah to rebuke one's neighbor's improper practice, as it states: "You shall surely rebuke your neighbor, and not bear sin because of him." (Leviticus 19:17).[21] Furthermore, the Gemara (Erachin 16b) brings the following beraita:

---

20. See Meorot ha-Daf ha-Yomi, vol. 3, Bnei Brak, 2006, pp. 98–99.
21. On this commandment, see the book of Rabbi Meir ha-Cohen Kaplan, Sefer Mitzvat ha-Tocheha Jerusalem,1951, which is accompanied at the end of the book by a special essay entitled "Meor Ha-Tocheha" – see especially chapter 4 (pp. 13–30): "Shiyurei Tocheha . . .". See also Rabbi Benzion Meir Hai Uziel, Mishpatei Uziel 4, Jerusalem, 2000 (2nd edition), "Inyanim Klaliyim," section 3, pp. 245–250; and also

From where do we know that if a man sees something unseemly in his friend he is obligated to rebuke him? Because it is said: "You shall surely rebuke." If he rebuked him and he did not accept it, from where do we know that he must rebuke him again? The text states: "surely rebuke" – in all ways. . . . How far shall reproof be administered? Rav said: "Until he [the rebuker] be beaten." Shmuel said: "Until he be cursed." Rav Yohanan said: "Until he be rebuked."

Similarly, the *Gemara* in *Baba Metzia* 31a states that one can rebuke a sinner, "even up to 100 times," and that it is also an obligation for a student to rebuke his teacher. In addition, in *Sanhedrin* 27b, the verse in Leviticus 26:37 is interpreted as follows: "'And they stumble one upon the other,' meaning that one [stumbles] through the sin of the other, which teaches that they are all responsible one for another. . . . There it refers to those who had the power to restrain and did not." The *Gemara* in *Avodah Zarah* 18a recounts the story that when Rabbi Hananya ben Taradyon was taken out to be burned and his wife to be executed, he said that his fate had been decreed because he thought about the ineffable name with its letters, and his wife had not restrained him. The rabbis added there: "From here we learn that anyone who has the opportunity to restrain and does not do so is punished for it" (compare *B. Shabbat* 54b).

Rabbi Aharon Lichtenstein, "The Parameters of Tolerance" in Moshe Sokol (ed.), *Tolerance, Dissent, and Democracy: Philosophical, Historical, and Halakhic Perspectives,* Northvale, 2002, pp. 137–174; Yehuda Amital, "Rebuking a Fellow Jew: Theory and Practice" apud *Jewish Tradition and the non-traditional Jew,* ed J.J. Schacter, Northvale, New Jersey and London, 1992, pp. 119–138. And on the subject of shaming, see R. Shmuel Sperber, *Maamarot,* Jerusalem, 1978, pp. 197–205. See also *Mishnah Berurah* to *Orah Hayyim* one, in his *Beur Halachah* 6, s.v. *Ve-Lo Yitbayesh,* and R. Rami Berachyahu's article, "*Tochechah ba-Kehilah*" in *Ha-Rav ba-Kehilah: Assufat Maamarim,* ed. R. Benayahu Broner, (Jerusalem n.d.), pp. 62–70; R. Ovadiah Yosef, "*Be-Inyan Mitzvat ha-Tochehah*" in his *Masa Ovadiah,* Jerusalem, 2007, pp. 188–195 (reprinted from *Torah she-Baal-Peh,* 1994). See further the Anonymous *Kuntres Kevod ha-Torah,* in the section entitled *Kuntres Kevod ha-Briyot,* Bnei Brak, 2013, pp. 39–49. In *B. Eruvin* 16b R. Tarfon is cited as saying: I am dubious (*timhani*) if there is in this generation anyone who can be rebuked, for by saying "Remove the splinter from between your teeth" he will be answered, "Remove the plank from between your eyes" . . . meaning, a person cannot rebuke his neighbor, for as soon as he remarks to him on a minor transgression, his neighbor will respond, that he is guilty of a greater transgression. Hence, adds Rashi, ibid., no one can rebuke for we are all sinners. In other words only one who knows he is truly free of sin can rebuke. (See Malbim's commentary to *Leviticus* 19:7, based on *B. Baba Batra* 60b, referring to *Zefaniah* 2:1.)

Nevertheless, the sages established (*Torat Kohanim* on Leviticus, ibid. *Erachin*, ibid.): "One might think [that it is obligatory to rebuke] even if his face blanches. Therefore, the text states: 'and not bear sin because of him.'" In other words, he should not speak to him harshly to the point that he be humiliated. Thus, even though there is a commandment in the Torah to rebuke, it is prohibited to do so if the rebuke will lead to embarrassment (see *Sefer Mitzvot Gadol,* Negative Commandments 6; *Sefer Yere'im ha-Shalem*, end of section 195). While the *Gemara* in *Yevamot* 65b finds textual support for this rule, the verse utilized is from the Writings (*Ketuvim*), even though it should certainly carry less weight than a verse from the Torah itself. The following is the wording there: "R. Ilai further stated in the name of R. Eleazar son of R. Shimon: Just as one is commanded to say that which will be obeyed, so is one commanded not to say that which will not be obeyed. R. Abba stated: It is an obligation; for it is said in Scripture, 'Reprove not a scorner, lest he hate you; reprove a wise man and he will love you' (Proverbs 9:8)."

Indeed, the Rabbis of Old instituted many regulations to ensure that one might not embarrass one's neighbour. Thus, for example, we learn in *B. Moed Katan* 27b that:

> In the beginning they used to place incense under the bed of a corpse that had died of a stomach ailment. And those who suffered from stomach ailments were embarrassed, (i.e., that after their death, everyone would know that they had died of such a disease, since under the funerary bed there would be aromatic incense). The rabbis made an amendment that there be placed incense beneath all corpses, out of respect for those living with stomach ailments.

The above demonstrates clearly rabbinic sensitivity to shame and embarrassment.

In parenthesis it should, however, be noted that in later sources, the use of aromatic incense near the dead body was given a totally different interpretation, (or perhaps another symbolic level of interpretation, especially as to the specific choice of which kinds of fragrance to use.) Thus in *Perek Mishnat ha-Meit*[22] we read:

---

22. See Meir Benayahu, *Sefer Zikaron le-ha-Rav Nissim Zecher Tzaddik le-vra-*

And one places in a pan at its head pure frankin- cense and at its feet aromatic branches, for the Angels of Injury sit at its feet and the fragrance of these aromatic branches frighten them off. And the Angels of Mercy surround its head, and with the fragrance of the frankincense they rise up to the heavens and tell of its merits before the Holy One blessed be He.

Though this kabbalistic text is so very different from our Talmudic sources, ultimately, it too expresses the basic desire to guarantee respect for the dead, which in them serves to alleviate elements of the fear and shame of the living at the possibility of their being harmed by the Angels of Injury.

In *Moed Katan* ibid. we also read:

In the beginning they would purify by immersion [in the *mikveh*] vessels touched by menstruant women [who by touching them transmitted to them a degree of impurity] even after their death. The rabbis made an amendment, namely that they would immerse vessels of all women [who had died], out of respect to the menstruant ones.[23]

This kind of degree of sensitivity expresses itself in what might have appeared to be a paradoxical ruling found in the Rambam, *Hilchot Avadim* 1:7. There we are told that one may not employ a Jewish slave in demeaning activities, and the Rambam gives a number of examples to illustrate what he means. On the other hand, one may engage a regular employee for just such degrading types of labour. At first blush it would seem strange that the rights of the slave are more equitable than those of a hired labourer. However, the Rambam ends that section as follows:

When do we say [that one may not employ them for such unpleasant tasks]? When we are speaking of a Jewish slave, *because his spirit is low* (i.e., object) is *that he had to sell himself* [because of his penury] But as to an ordinary Jew, who was not sold [into slavery], one may make use

chah, ha-Rishon le-Tziyyon ha-Rav ha-Rashi le-Yisrael, vol. 6, *Maamadot u-Mishma-rot*, Jerusalem, 1985, p. 333, and cf. p. 340.

23. Cf. *Tosefta Niddah* 9:16, ed. Zuckermandel, p. 651, and also previous section on "Human Dignity" and upcoming section on "Sensitivity to the 'Have-Nots'".

of him as a slave [i.e., in lowly taks], for he does his work of his own free will and volition.

The rabbis (interpreting the biblical verse in Leviticus 25:40) were keenly aware of the traumatic emotional state of mind of a person who felt forced to sell himself into servitude because of his impossible economic position. Hence, his owner is cautioned against any demands that might lead to an additional loss of self-respect. Not so the regular hired laborer, who does not have this "emotional baggage," and therefore feels little constraint against any kind of employment.[24] Incidentally we might take notice of the fact that those who used to be called "rubbish collectors" or "garbage collectors" are now termed "sanitary officers"!

Now returning to the issue of shame, though the prohibition of embarrassing someone is itself not mentioned explicitly in the Torah, the rabbis derived it from biblical verses, such as the teaching of R. Yohanan in the name of Rabbi Shimon bar Yohai in *Sotah* 10b: "Better for a man to cast himself into a fiery furnace rather than shame his fellow in public. From where do we know this? From Tamar, as it says: 'She was taken out and she sent to her father-in-law, saying: By the man whose these are, am I with child' (Genesis 38:25)." This can be compared to *Baba Metzia* 59a where Rashi explained: "Even though she was being taken out to be burned, she did not say to them that she had been impregnated by Yehudah." (See notes 121 and 239.) If so, this transgression is derived incidentally from the story of Tamar.

So too we read in *Tanhuma Va-Yigash* 5: R. Shmuel bar Nahman said: Josef put himself in great danger, for had his brothers killed him no one would have recognized him [i.e., would have noticed his death]. And why did he say, "Remove everyone from me" (*Genesis* 45:1)? For Josef said unto himself, "Better that I be killed and I will not shame my brothers before the Egyptians."

Similarly, in *B. Baba Metzia* 58b-59a, we hear from Raba bar Bar Hana in the name of R. Yohanan that "Better that a man have relations with a doubtfully married woman (*safek eshet ish*) than that he shame his fellow in public." And they derived this (anachronistically) from a

---

24. All this is derived from a simple word in Leviticus ibid. עמך "with thee," the full verse being, "But as a hired servant, and as a sojourner, he shall be *with thee* . . ." See M.M. Kasher, *Torah Shelemah*, vol. 34, Jerusalem, 1981, pp. 98–100 for sources.

homily of Rava who stated that people tried to embarrass King David by asking him a question, namely: what is the punishment for one who has had relations with a married woman? His reply was: that he is executed by strangulation, but he has a part in the World to Come, whereas one who shames his fellow in public has no part in the World to Come. Indeed the rabbis stated in this regard: "One who publicly embarrasses another person has no portion in the world to come, even if he has observed the Torah and performed good acts, because man was created in the image of God" (see Avot 3:15).[25]

And in the Maharil, R. Yaakov Moellin (1355-1427), *Hilchot Milah* 19 (ed. S.Y. Spitzer, Jerusalem, 1989, p. 485), we are told of:

> An unmarried woman gave birth to a son [some versions say in harlotry], and gave him to a certain person claiming that he was the boy's father. And he denied it. And they wished to name the son in the name of that person, that is to say [to call him] the son of Y. And Mahari Segal warned them not to do so as it would cause him shame, since he denies paternity. And the person carrying out the circumcision blessed the benediction [to sanctify him in the covenant of our forefather Abraham]. And when the circumciser reached the point in the benediction "who has sancti-fied" . . . instead of continuing "Praise ye the Lord, for He is good," he said, "Praise the Lord for His mercy endureth forever," (Psalm 106:1). And he skipped over the words "for He is good," saying that he could not mention goodness, since the child was born out of harlotry. [Some versions have: One does not mention goodness in connection with evil people.] And Mahari Segal rebuked him, ordering him to repeat the

---

25. See on this subject, Daniel Z. Feldman, *The Right and the Good: Halakhah and Human Relations*, 2nd edition, New York, 2005, pp. 1–28, a chapter very meaningfully entitled "Emotional Homicide: Embarrassing Others." As to whether these statements are to be taken literally, see the discussion in my father's *Maamarot*, Jerusalem, 1978, pp. 197–205; and Yitzhak Yosef, *Maarechet ha-Shulhan*, vol. 2, Jerusalem, 2010, pp. 564–569, who shows this is a controversy among the *Rishonim*, idem, *Ein Yitzhak*, vol. 1, Jerusalem, 2009, p. 151–155, and see further S.Z. Auerbach, *Minhat Shlomoh*, vol. 1, Jerusalem, 1986, *Orah Hayyim* sect. 7, p. 55; and, most recently, Eliyahu Berachah, *Toldot Noah*, Jerusalem, 2012, pp. 221–223, citing, inter alia, R. Ovadiah Yosef, *Yabia Omer*, vol. 6, *miluim* to *Yoreh Deah*, no. 13, etc.

See also Aviad Hacohen, *Parshiyot u-Mishpatim: Mishpat Ivri be-Parshat ha-Shavua*, Tel Aviv, 2011, pp. 105–111.

verse in full, since the child's status was equal to that of any other child born in wedlock.

The Maharil here sought to avoid showing both the suspect father and the newborn babe embarrassment. (However, see editor's note 2, ad loc., that R. Akiva Eiger, in his notes to *Yoreh Deah* 265:4, cites Ri Castro, said that any child whose birth is somehow suspect of being the result of a sinful relationship, one omits certain verses from the circumcision ceremony and one takes care not to shower praises over the parents.)

A very interesting example of rabbinic sensitivity not to cause shame and embarrassment may be found in a responsum of the great 19 cent. Galician authority, R. Shlomo Kluger. The background to his discussion is a statement in *B. Baba Batra* 119b where we read in the name of Rav Hida that a woman of forty can no longer give birth. The question that was put before the Rabbi concerned a man who only had one daughter, and his wife had died (and therefore he had as yet not fulfilled the obligation of *periah u-reviah*) and he was now engaged to a "virgin" who was forty years old. Some trouble-makers told him to cancel the engagement since he would have no children from his bride (and therefore would again be unable to fulfil his obligation). The response of R. Kluger was as follows:

> He should certainly take her in marriage, just as the daughters of Tzelofhad got married even though they were forty. See the *Ein Yaakov* in the name of the *Ritba* that the husbands relied upon (i.e., were even confident of) a miracle because of their virtue . . . And even though the Sages said that one should not rely upon miracles, not all miracles are equal . . . , for if we do not see great miracles, we do see minor ones. And hence, it is clear that when a forty-year-old woman gives birth, this is a minor miracle, and it is not infrequent, and for this reason they [the husbands of the daughters of Tzelofhad] relied upon such a miracle. So too can our bridegroom rely upon one. And especially since he is already engaged, and has sent presents, and the *shame would be great* (if he cancelled the wedding). And the virtuous act of not shaming (his bride) . . . in itself merits him to have a family with her . . . [*Ha-Elef Lecha Shlomo*, Bilgurai 1932, no. 9, p. 4].

See the continuation of his discussion where he limits the Talmudic statement in a certain fashion to strengthen his argument. However, what emerges very clearly from this responsum is that R. Shlomo Kluger was willing to make a ruling, despite an explicit statement in the Talmud that prima facie negated such a ruling, emphasizing the paramount importance of not causing shame, even to the extent of virtually promising a "minor miracle" as a reward from desisting from causing such shame. (See also most recently Eliezer Zeev Raz, *Mi-Tzion Orah*, 2007, p. 330, to *Even ha-Ezer* 1.)

Furthermore, the need for extreme sensitivity not to mortify a person, when he is mistaken, and even if he is sinful, is vividly expressed in a tale told of the father of the Baal Shem Tov (1700–1760), as recorded in Martin Buber's *Tales of the Hasidim: The Early Masters*, New York, 1947, 35–36:

> Rabbi Eliezer, the Baal Shem's father, lived in a village. He was so hospitable that he placed guards at the outskirts of the village and had them stop poor wayfarers and bring them to his house for food and shelter. Those in Heaven rejoiced at his doing, and once they decided to try him. Satan offered to do this, but the prophet Elijah begged to be sent in his stead. In the shape of a poor wayfarer, with knapsack and staff, he came to Rabbi Eliezer's house on a Sabbath afternoon, and said the greeting. Rabbi Eliezer ignored the desecration of the Sabbath, for he did not want to mortify the man. He invited him to the meal and kept him in his house. Nor did he utter a word of reproof the next morning, when his guest took leave of him. Then the prophet revealed himself and promised him a son who would make the eyes of the people of Israel see the light.[26]

An interesting example of this sensitivity may be found in *Shulhan Aruch, Yoreh Deah* 335:1 where, after the Mehaber (R. Yosef Karo) states that it is a mitzvah to visit the sick, the Rema adds (ibid. 2):

> There are those who say that one who hates his fellow may visit him when he is sick (Maharil sect. 197), but this does not seem right to me. Rather he should not visit him and not comfort him if he is in mourning

---

26. See my *On the Relationshp of Mitzvot between Man and His Neighbor and Man and His Maker*, Jerusalem and New York, 2014, pp. 104–106, and indeed that whole chapter entitled "Human Dignity and Avoiding Embarrassing Others," ibid., pp. 102–114.

if he hates him, lest [the sick person or the mourner] suspect that he is happy at his hour of distress, and this would only cause him anguish. So it would appear to me. (He bases himself on *B. Sanhedrin* 19a. And see in greater detail in his *Darchei Moshe* to *Yoreh Deah* ibid.)

The great importance of visiting the sick and comforting the mourner is offset by the counterproductive effects of the visit by the hateful neighbour, which would not bring relief or condolence, but added suffering.[27] The Maharil, R. Yaakov Moelin (1355–1427), had been well aware of the Rema's reasoning, (see his responsum ibid., ed. Y. Satz, Jerusalem 1980, pp. 313–314), but had rejected it, ending his response

And all Israel (i.e., any Jew) is not suspect that he will rejoice at the distress of the sick fellow, even if he hates him, [and] he is not gleeful at his death, or his critical sickness . . .

(See editor's note 18.) This demonstrates his confidence is the basic goodness of heart in every Jew, and determined his ruling, backed, of course, by Talmudic presedents. The Rema, on the other hand, was of the opinion that even if there was a slight chance of such a visit resulting in greater distress, it should be forbidden. We have here an interesting example of a clash of basic values: confidence in the moral qualities of the Jew versus the possibility of causing further distress to one already in a state of distress. See further the discussion of R. Yaakov Hayyim Sofer, in his article in *Mekabtziel* 17, 1992, "*Hiddushei Torah*," no. 18, pp. 88–89, his *Zechut Yitzhak*, Jerusalem, 1992, sect. 58, pp. 222–223 (referring us to R. Yehuda Ayash's *Shevet Yehudah*, Livorno, 1783, *Yoreh Deah* 335, 356b) adding his own additional comments, in which he explains the Talmudic sources describing a sick call on the part of Sages who certainly were at loggerheads with the person they were visiting. He is referring to *B. Sanhedrin 68a*, where R. Akiva and the Sages visit the dying R. Eliezer who had been excommunicated by them. He reinstates R. Yehuda Ayash's suggestion, which he himself

---

27. On hating a fellow Jew in Jewish Law, see Norman Lamm, "Loving and Hating Jews as Halakhic Categories" apud *Jewish Tradition and the Non-traditional Jew*, ed. J.J. Schacter, Northvale, New Jersey and London, 1992, pp. 139–176; and R. Ovadiah Yosef, *Yabia Omer*, vol. 5, sect. 64.

had rejected, that there is a difference between Sages, who can control their emotions and rise above their differences and ordinary people. The former may visit those whom they oppose, the latter may not.[28] However, this argument is also not persuasive, since the Sages that banned R. Eliezer did not hate him, but merely felt that their act was necessary in order to squelch a conflict that could have led to a splintering of rabbinic authority.[29]

An additional ruling relating to the mitzvah of visiting the sick is to be found in a *beraita* in *B. Nedarim* 41a. There we read that one does not visit those who suffer from a stomach ailment. Rashi ad loc. explains that this is because they may need to relieve themselves during such a visit and this would be a source of embarrassment for them. Rashi writes "*u-metzaarei leih*," (and this would discomfort him), while the Talmud's formulation is "*mi-shum kisufa*," (because of shame). And cf. *B. Nedarim* 41b:

> Said R. Yohanan: "One does not visit someone who is sick with *bordam* (dysentery)." Why? Said R. Eleazar: "Because he is like a growing spring."

Rashi explains that he has diarrhea, with a constant flow, and it [the disease, the virus] jumps from one to the other, i.e,. it is contagious. However, it may be that R. Yohanan regarded this malady as a source of embarrassment, and it was also for this reason that he counseled not even mentioning by name, i.e., identifying him as being sick in this manner.[30]

This ruling is brought in the *Shulhan Aruch, Yoreh Deah* 41:8. (And cf. above in this section on the treatment of those who died of stom-

---

28. Further discussion may be found in R. David Meir [ha-Levi], *Siah ha-Sadeh: Dinei Bikkur Holim*, Mexico 2013, pp. 48–50, especially note 24 ibid.; according to the Rema.

29. See further R. Ovadiah Yosef, *Hazon Ovadiah*, vol.1, Jerusalem, 2010, pp. 10–11.

30. On *burdam* or *burdas*, see *Aruch Completum* ed. Kohut, vol.2, 2nd ed., New York, 1955, p. 187a, s.v. ברדם ; S. Krauss, *Griechische und Lateinische Lehnwörter im Talmud, Midrash und Targum*, vol. 2, Berlin, 1899, p. 144b, s.v. בורדס, with Löw's comments; and J. Preuss, *Biblisch-talmudische Medizin*, 2nd edition, Basel, 1923, pp. 213–214. The etymology remains unclear. And as to whether one may visit a contagious patient, or whether one is permitted to avoid visiting him – an interesting ethical question – see R. Ovadia Yosef, *Hazon Ovadiah*, vol. 1, Jerusalem, 1970, pp. 14–15.

ach diseases.) The notion of *Kisufa* (shame) is found frequently in the Talmud, e.g., *B. Ta'anit* 9b, *B. Ketubot* 108b, *B. Baba Metzia* 22a, *B. Horayot* 13b, etc, and it is evident that every effort was to be made to avoid causing it.

Returning to the issue of people's sensitivity to feelings, we may note that numerous rules were enacted by the rabbis in order to avoid causing embarrassment to others. Thus, the *Amidah* (*Shemonah Esrei*) is said silently, so that no one might hear one's neighbor's secret confession of his sins when begging for forgiveness (see *B. Sotah* 32b and *Shulhan Aruch, Orah Hayyim* 101:2). One should also bear in mind the view of the *Pnei Yehoshua* to *B. Baba Kama* 92a, that one may not publically reveal sins between man and his maker.[31]

For much the same reason, according to the Tosafot in *Moed Katan* 27b, nowadays one has a reader, a *baal kore*, to read the Torah in the synagogue, as opposed to Talmudic times when each one called up would read his own portion, so as not to embarrass one who does not know how to read from the Torah.

The degree to which one must take great care not to embarrass people, for instance by revealing their ignorance, is well demonstrated in the remarkable ruling found in R. Yaakov Hayyim Sofer's *Kaf ha-Hayyim*, to *Orah Hayyim* 135, note 16, 119b–120a. There he discusses the question whether a person who is so ignorant in things Jewish that he can not read Hebrew, even when another person prompts him, can be called up to the Torah. He rules that one cannot call him up, unless:

> If he is a bridegroom or [the father] of a child to be circumcised, and he will be ashamed if he is not called up, then, it would appear, one may rely on those who hold a lenient position, namely that he may be called up and make the blessing [presumably being helped by someone else, such as the cantor], but he cannot be counted as one of the seven *aliyot*, (i.e., he must be called up as an extra *aliyah*). And if it is possible, the cantor should make the blessing for him, and he shall [stand] as a wooden block before the public, who will see that he has been called up [and may not

---

31. See also Rambam, *Hilchot Teshuvah* 2:5, the note of the Raavad ad loc., and the *Kesef Mishnah*, and the *Lehem Mishnah* ibid., and what R. Yaakov Hayyim Sofer wrote in his *Shuvi ha-Shulamit*, vol. 5, Jerusalem, 2008, p. 38.

even notice that it is not he who has made the blessing].And this is the better option, and the cantor will be counted as one of *olim* . . .[32]

And at weddings, the *birkat erusin* is usually said, not by the groom, but by someone else, in order to not embarrass a groom who does not know to recite the blessing (R. Shmuel Vladislaver, *Beit Shmuel*, Dhyrenfürt, 1689, to *Even ha-Ezer* 101:2).

Similarly, we read in R. Naftali Katz's *Shaar ha-Hachanah*, Lvov 1794, 7b, that the *Taz*, R. David ha-Levi Segal, was always accustomed to recite the *Kiddush* on Shabbat from a *siddur*. He explained that in addition to the fact that there is holiness in the [printed] letters, he sometimes entertained guests who were ignorant, and sat with such persons in another's home, and those unlearned persons would be ashamed at not knowing the *Kiddush* by heart, and would feel awkward to have to read it from a *siddur*. For that reason he would present himself as someone who had to recite it from a *siddur*. Indeed, much the same is told of the Tchebiner Rav, who made *Kiddush* and the grace after meals and read all the *tefillah* from a *siddur*, for the same reason.[33] Similarly, R. Hayyim Palache, in his *Kaf ha-Hayyim* (sect. 35:4) insists that one bless the new moon (*kiddush levanah*) from a *siddur*, in order not to embarrass those who do not know the blessing by heart.[34]

In my book *On the Relationship of Mitzvot between Man and His Neighbor and Man and His Maker*, Jerusalem and New York, 2014, in a chapter (18) dealing with this subject, entitled "Human Dignity and Avoiding Embarrassing Others," pp. 104–106, I cite two remarkable stories illustrating how this principle functioned in practice. The first relates to Rabbi Moshe Kleers, the rabbi of Tiberias around the year 1934. It is related in A. Tobolsky's *Hizaharu bi-Chevod Haverchem*, Bnei Brak, 1981, 326–327 (citing the pamphlet *Mi-Pi Dodi: Zichronot mi-Pi R"M Kleers Shnat 1934, Meorot* 12):

---

32. See further on this subject Akiva Meller, *Ha-Keriyah ba-Torah ve-Hilchotehah*, Jerusalem, 2009, p. 278, sect. 8 and note 24 ibid.; and cf. ibid., pp. 213–215.

33. *Sar ha-Torah*, p. 312, cited in *Malchut David* (on the history of the *Taz*). Jerusalem, 2013 p. 80, note 287.

34. See Z.W. Zicherman, *Otzar Pelaot ha-Torah*, vol. 2 (*Exodus*), Brooklyn, 2014, pp. 200–201.

On one of the Sabbaths, Rabbi Kleers, the rabbi of Tiberias, was informed that it appeared that the *eruv* was faulty [and, as a consequence, people could not carry things within the town], and had not been correctly organized before the Sabbath. He looked into the matter and ascertained that it had been set up by the local Sephardi rabbi under his directions. He turned to those who questioned its *kashrut*, and ruled that it was in order, but that he had not the time to explain his reasoning.

He was on the very best of terms with this Sephardi rabbi, and they both ho2ad the deepest respect for one another. On the following Sunday he came to the rabbi and said to him: "I have to clarify a difficult halachic issue, and I require your help." The Sephardi rabbi smiled and said: "Surely you do not need my help. Are you teasing me?" He replied: "I am not feeling well; I am rather weak and find it difficult to sort this issue out by myself." "Please come in," said the rabbi, "and we will study the matter together." "No, I would prefer if we could both go together to the synagogue," which was a little further away.

They both went to the local *beit midrash* which was empty, and R. Moshe pulled out a volume of the Talmud, the Tractate *Eruvin*, and they both sat at length analyzing an issue in depth, with the various commentators until finally the Sephardi rabbi understood what this was all about. Deeply disturbed, he cried out: "I erred last Friday in the preparation of the *eruv*." Rabbi Kleers calmed him down, explaining that it was for this reason that he had come to him. "And how did you act, last Shabbat?" asked the Sephardi rabbi. "I ruled that the *eruv* was *kasher*, in order," he replied. The rabbi was astounded: "How come?" he asked. Rabbi Kleers smiled: "The laws of *eruvin* are merely of rabbinic authority, while the dignity of the Torah [i.e., the Rabbi] and the individual is of biblical authority (*mi-de-Oraita*) . . ." he replied.

And yet another very moving story in this vein is recorded by the great Maspid, Reb Shalom Schwadron, in R. Paysach J. Krohn's *The Maggid Speaks: Favorite Stories and Parables of Rabbi Shalom Schwadron Shlita, Maggid of Jerusalem*, Brooklyn, N.Y., 1987, pp. 64–65:

> In a small town far away from Kovno, a local *rav* had erred in a ruling he had made on a religious question posed to him. Though not everyone realized his mistake, two devious and mischievous individuals knew that their *rav* had blundered badly. He had forgotten that the very same

situation on which he had ruled was discussed in the Shach, one of the primary commentaries of the *Shulhan Aruch* (Code of Jewish Law).

Seeking to humiliate their *rav*, the two miscreants sent a letter to R. Yitzchak Elchanan, Spektor (1817–1896], in which they posed the same question. They knew that R. Yitzchak Elchonon's answer would be in accordance with the Shach's ruling as opposed to their *rav*'s opinion. Once armed with R. Yitzchak Elchonon's letter of reply they would show it around to the community at large and this would shame and disgrace the *rav*.

When R. Yitzchak Elchonon received the letter, his first reaction was one of surprise. For although he had received queries from people in this particular town before, he remembered that he had never received any from either of these men. Why would they be writing now, he wondered, and why would they be sending a question with which any rav, including their local *rav*, would surely be familiar?

Therefore, he investigated and learned that these men were exceptionally argumentative and had a history of causing trouble in the community.

R. Yitzchak Elchonon suspected at once that the two men were contemplating a plot to embarrass their *rav*, and he thought to foil their plot. First he sent a letter to the two men with the wrong answer to the question, ruling exactly as their *rav* had ruled. Then, the very next day, he sent them a telegram which would arrive before the letter, saying that he had erred in his written ruling, and that they should disregard the letter with the wrong ruling that would soon be coming.

Thus the mischievous twosome would not be able to use either the letter or the telegram to defame their *rav*, for the letter agreed with the *rav* and the telegram clearly indicated that even the great and sainted R. Yitzchak Elchonon had erred in this matter – just as their *rav* had.

Reb Shalom heard this story from R. Isser Zalman Melzer (1870–1953) who, when he told it, his eyes filled with tears, because he was so deeply moved by the length to which Reb Yitzachk Elchonon would go to save another Jew from embarrassment.[35]

---

35. See continuation of that chapter for additional material on this subject. And on the required relationship between the local rabbi, the *mara de-atra*, and other scholars, *talmidei hachamim*, in his neighborhood, see B. *Horayot* 14a, and the article by R. Matanya ben-Shahar, "*Ha-Rav ve-Talmidei Hachamim be-Kehilato*" in *Ha Rav ve-ha-Ketubah: Assufat Maamarim*, ed. R. Benaya Broner, Jerusalem, n.d.

Similarly, though in a slightly different halachic context, part of the confession on separation of tithes – *Vidui Maaser* – (the first two verses of Deuteronomy 26:12–16) is said silently so as not to embarrass those who could not state that they had separated their tithes.

Similarly, in *B. Yoma* 21a we are told that in the Temple during the foot-festivals, one of the ten miracles that took place was that even though the temple area was full of closely-packed pilgrims, when they bowed down and prostrated themselves, they felt there was plenty of room. Rashi ad loc. explains that "they had a space of four cubits surrounding them, in order that their neighbours should not hear their confessions, lest they be ashamed." And R. Moshe Premischle, in his *Mateh Moshe* sect. 204, ed. H.H. Knoblowicz, London, 1958, pp. 96–97, following Rashi's explanation, adds that this is the reason we hide our faces during the *Tahanun* prayer, "and we do so . . . as though each one neither sees nor knows for what his fellow is praying."

Along this same line of thought, Sar Shalom of Belz sought to explain the apparent inconsistencies in the verses in Exodus chapter 29. There in the passage on sacrifices it mentions that Aaron and his sons offered these distinct sacrifices: a young bull as a sin-offering, two rams, one as a burnt offering and the other as one of consecration. Now in verse 10 it says, "and Aaron and his sons shall put – *ve-samach* (in the singular) – his hands upon the head of the bullock." In verse 15, it says, "and Aaron and his sons shall put – *ve-samchu* (in the plural) –their hands on the head of the ram." And in verse 19, it says, "And Aaron and his sons shall put – *ve-samach* (again in the singular) – their hands on the hand of the ram." His explanation for this difference of *ve-samach, ve-samchu, ve-samach,* is due to the fact that the first and last offering were accompanied by confessions (*viduim*), hence Aaron and his sons had to be separated so as not to hear one another, while the burnt offering was not accompanied by a confession, so that they could all stand together.[36]

And interestingly enough R. Simon ben Tzemah Duran (Algiers, 1361–1444) in a responsum (*Tashbetz,* vol. 2, no. 39, ed. Y. Katan,

---

pp. 15–27. And see the index volume to R. Ovadiah Yosef's *Yabia Omer* (vol.11), Jerusalem, 2009, pp. 336–337, s.v. *mara de-atra*.

36. See David Baer Meir, *Dvash ha-Sadeh*, Bilgurai, 1909, sect. 33, quoted by Tzvi Adler, *Kabel Rinati*, Bnei Brak, 2011, pp. 51–52.

Jerusalem, 2002, pp. 41–42), when asked concerning the custom that a bridegroom reads, on the Shabbat before his wedding, the chapter in Genesis 24, *"Ve-Avraham Zaken"* (And Abraham was old . . .), gives quite an illuminating answer, he writes:

> . . . the majority of bridegrooms are ignorant and do not know how to read, and [so] they have been trained to read [only] this [one] chapter, even the ignorant among them.

In other words, again in order not to betray their ignorance in public, they had been taught this one chapter which they would be able to recite in the synagogue at the eve of their wedding without any embarrassment. This motif, as a decisive halachic principle, is reflected in a great variety of halachic discussions. Thus, in *Sefer Hasidim* we have a number of sections dealing with student-teacher relationships, in which there is a stress on the student not asking questions that the teacher will not be able to answer, thus shaming him.[37] The rabbis went even further, instituting special regulations not to embarrass the poor. Thus, the Talmud in *B. Moed Katan* 27a–27b tells us that at first there used to be very opulent funeral arrangements, but the poor people were embarrassed, so they issued a series of regulations making all such arrangements far more modest. As an example, the early practice was to bare the faces of the rich corpses, whereas those of the poor, black with hunger, were left covered. In order to avoid shaming the poor, the rabbis decreed that the faces of all corpses remain covered.[38]

In the medieval period yet another somewhat similar regulation was instituted, namely that all bridegrooms take upon themselves the monetary obligation in their *ketubah* (marriage document) to the amount of "two hundred pure silver pieces." The question that immediately raises itself is how they could institute a *single* sum for all bridegrooms. Surely, each one obligates himself to an additional sum (*tosefet ketubah*) according to his will and means. And not all the brides bring along an identical dowry (*nedunia*).

It appears that about one-thousand years ago two things happened:

---

37. See ibid. vol. 2, index 64c, s.v. Rav ve-Talmid.
38. But see *Massechet Semachot* 8:7, and D. Zlotnik's note in *The Tractate "Mourning,"* New Haven and London, 1966, p. 137.

The value of "two hundred *zuzim*," which the Sages fixed as the main obligation in the *ketubah* (*ikkar ketubah*), went down in value to such an extent that it was no longer a significant amount, and would no longer cause the husband to hesitate and give additional thought before deciding to divorce his wife. Consequently, the leading authorities of that time fixed a higher standard. After coming to that decision, they further ruled that *all grooms* obligate themselves to the same sum, both in the *tosefet ketubah* and also in the *nedunia*, so that those who were poor would not be embarrassed, as all *ketubot* were identical.[39]

In a slightly different context we find in *Sefer Hasidim*, ed. Gutman, sect. 572, p. 521, that:

> If there is a good Jew and he has a wicked father, and he is ashamed when his father is mentioned to him, do not mention him and do not cause him distress . . .

And in sect. 791, p. 657 we read:

> He whose father is an apostate we do not call him up to the Torah in the name of his father . . .

So too wrote R. Yisrael Isserlein in his *Terumat ha-Deshen* sect. 21 (who also wrote that he heard in the name of one of the great scholars that they should call the son by his own name alone).

On the basis of this, the Rema in *Orah Hayyim* 139:3 rules that:

> He whose father is an apostate, one calls [the son up to the Torah] in the name of his grandfather, and not in his father's name, so as not to shame him in public.

Cf. Rema in *Even ha-Ezer* 129:10, who writes that in a *get* one writes his father's name, even though in the synagogue service one calls him by his grandfather's name. However, the *Pithei Teshuvhah*, ibid. no.

---

39. See Tur, *Even ha-Ezer* 66; *Teshuvot Maimoniyot, Hilchot Ishut* 6, responsa of the Maharik [Mahari Colon] 81, etc. And see *Meorot ha-Daf ha-Yomi* to B. Ketubot 53–59, Heshvan 2008, no. 438. And see also below section entitled "Sensitivity to the 'Have-Nots'".

29 cites the *Get Pashut* by R. Moshe ibn Haviv, Stilkov 1834, sub sect. 55, that one may write the grandfather's name in a *get* under such circumstances.[40]

And indeed the rabbis pointed out that the Torah, on occasions, omitted certain information out of respect for someone and not to embarrass him or sully his reputation.[41]

It should be noted that already Rabbenu Gershom Meor ha-Gola had ruled that a priest who had apostatized and then repented may participate in the communal priestly blessing (*birkat-Kohanim*), and be honored as a priest to be called up first to the Torah reading. This is despite the fact that many considered it shocking that a former apostate should bless the community, citing biblical verses to demonstrate its odiousness. Rabbenu Gershom stated that there is no proof from the Bible or the *Mishnah* to disqualify him; on the contrary there is proof from those sources not to disqualify him, and he further argued that by denying a *Kohen* his rights one would be publically humiliating him for past sins, conduct that both the Bible and the Talmud strictly enjoin (*ona'at devarim*).[42]

A very instructive example of the degree to which one must go to avoid embarrassing a person is to be found in the ruling of R. Shlomo Zalman Auerbach of blessed memory. He stated that

> If one has a guest who is likely to be embarrassed if he be left alone, the host should stay with the guest, even if by doing so he will miss praying with the congregation, because in such a situation the hosting of a guest takes precedence over praying with the congregation.[43]

---

40. See further *Maharam Padua* (R. Meir of Padua, Cracow, 1882) sect. 87, fol. 117b who also discuses this issue, and *Sefer Hasidim*, sect. 191, p. 222.

41. See Ramban to Genesis 35:8, and *Torah Shelemah* of R.M.M. Kasher, Genesis, vol. 5, Jerusalem, 1935, p. 1347, note 35.

42. See on this Haym Soloveitchik, *Collected Essays*, vol. 2, Oxford Postcard, Oregon, 2014, pp. 88–89, with the relevant references.

43. See *Halichot Shlomo al Hilchot Tefillah*, Jerusalem, 2000, p. 66, note 28, subnote 50. This ruling is further quoted in Y.Y. Fuks, *Ha-Tefillah ke-Hilchatah*, Jerusalem, 1989, p. 141, note 50, and M.M. Shklarsh, *Hayyei Moshe* to *Yoreh Deah*, Bnei Brak, 2001, p. 327, no. 20. And this despite the importance of praying with a congregation, see e.g., *Ha-Tefillah ke-Hilchatah*, pp. 21–30, 105–106, etc. On the importance of hosting guests, see my *On the Relationship of Mitzvot between Man and His Neighbor and Man and His Maker*, Jerusalem and New York, 2014, index 1–220 s.v. Hospitality.

An edifying example of extreme sensitivity not to embarrass a person in public is related by R. Yosef Scheinberger, in his biography of R. Yehoshua Yehuda Leib Diskin, Jerusalem, 1954, pp. 149–150:

> It was the practice to gather together after Shabbat to hear the weekly lesson [from Rabbi Diskin], and everyone would receive a glass of tea, including the Rabbi.
>
> However, once it happened that the person preparing his glass of tea by mistake substituted salt instead of sugar, and handed over the drink to the Rabbi. The Rabbi required a goodly portion of sugar due to his ill-helath and weakness, but, instead, got a plentiful dose of salt in his tea. He took the hot glass in his hands and slowly drank the tea down without any indication of displeasure or discomfort, so that the disciples sitting around the table noted no change of expression. However, his wife, the Rabbanit, when she tasted her tea noticed that the server has mixed up the sugar for salt, and hurriedly turned to her husband with a worried cry, "Hey, there is salt in your glass of tea!" The disciples, who also tasted the remnants of the salt in their glasses, were astounded at the self-control of the Rabbi, and that he was able to drink down these salty waters with a murmur. After they began to disperse, the Rabbanit asked her husband how he had not demurred, bearing in mind that this could be harmful to his health, and [the Torah demands that] "Take ye good heed unto yourselves" (Deuteronomy 4:15). To which he responded in astonishment, "What? To embarrass someone publicly!"

Perhaps we may term such behavior as "extreme menschlechkeit."

Returning to the area of practical halachah, we may point to the ruling of R. Joseph Messas that there are no prohibitions against offering a guest something to eat, even though he will not make the requisite blessings over the food. He writes that the *Shulhan Aruch, Orah Hayyim* 163:2 (based on B. *Hulin* 107b) prohibition against such action is not to be regarded as a real prohibition, but a stringency and more of a warning, and it is preferable to take a lenient position and treat guests graciously and with warmth.[44]

---

44. See his *Otzar Michtavim*, vol. 3, 1815:3, cited in Zechariah Zarmati, *Hod Yosef Hai*, Jerusalem, 2008, p. 102, no. 81. See also the detailed analysis of Avraham Wasserman, *Reiacha Ka-Mocha: Birur Halachot be-Sugyot she-bein Datiim ve-Hiloniim*, Petah-Tikvah [n.d. but c. 2007], pp. 136–138. The permissive position is based on the

In a recent article by R. Barry Selman in *Milin Havivin* 3, 2007, p. 88, on the subject of *Takkanat ha-Shavim* (see below near note 105), he writes as follows:

> Rabbi Sherlow further addressed the issue of women who were uncomfortable with the mikvah attendant doing a full body check before immersion (responsa *Reshut-Ha-Yahid*, pp. 209–210). The question stated that women refrained from immersion in the mikvah due to what they perceived as a breach of privacy on the part of the mikvah attendant. The questioner (rightly) states that since immersion is only disqualified by the presence of a foreign substance that covers most of a woman's body, or by a small amount of foreign substance about which the woman cares, there is no real reason for the mikvah attendant to do a full body check for such substances.
>
> Rabbi Sherlow quotes Rabbi Yaakov Ariel, Chief Rabbi of Ramat Gan, who allows the attendant to only view the woman while immersing in the mikvah, to make sure that all of her hair has gone below the surface, and states that he was willing, for the sake of making it more comfortable for women to use the mikvah, to do away with the full body check that is prevalent in most mikvahs. In this case, the attendant would only enter the mikvah chamber once the woman has already descended into the water. Once again we see a *posek* who is willing to recognize that issuing lenient rulings can lead to further observance.
>
> Here too it was the issue of embarrassment that motivated the leniency of *psak*, in addition to the principle of *Takkanat ha-Shavim*.

(And see below section entitled "Encouraging Repentence.")

Another interesting example of rabbinic sensitivity is to be found in a discussion of the personal relationship between a husband and his menstruant wife. In *B. Eruvin* 63b we read:

> R. Brona said in the name of Rav: Anyone who sleeps in a compartment (*Kila*) in which a husband and wife are, concerning him does the verse say, "The women of my people have ye cast out from their pleasant

---

view of R. Yonah to *B. Berachot 34b*, that feeding the guest is an act of charity, and this view is cited in the *Shulhan Aruch* ibid. as another opinion.

homes . . ." (Micah 2:9). And Rav Yosef said, "Even [when we speak of] his menstruant wife . . ."

To the above, Tosafot Rosh in *B. Yevamot* 62b writes:

> Even a woman during her period of menstruation should be visited [by her husband] and spoken to lovingly for that whole period, even though she is prohibited [to him] from sexual relations. Nonetheless, he is to her a source of happiness and pleasure, since he wishes to depart on his way. And so we say in *Eruvin* (ibid.):
>> Anyone who sleeps in a compartment in which a husband and wife sleep, concerning him does the verse says, "The women of my people have ye cast out from their pleasant houses . . ." And Rav Yosef says: "Even [when we speak of] his menstruant wife . . ."

This basic notion expresses itself in another area of halachah. For the rabbis were troubled by the fact that so many people in so many different communities do not sleep in their *Sukkot* at night. A little further below in our discussion of the *mitz'taer* in the *sukkah* (in the chapter entitled "Leniency to Prevent Distress and Suffering,"ad init.) we offer the Rema's explanation. But R. David b. Shmuel ha-Levi (1586–1667, Poland), in his *Turei Zahav* (usually called *Taz*) to *Orah Hayyim* 639:9, gives quite an alternative explanation too that of the Rema. He writes that the reason is that a husband is obligated to please his wife during the festival periods, and since women are not obligated to dwell in the *sukkah* – because dwelling in a *sukkah* is a time-related mitzvah – if he does not wish to separate himself from his wife, this is considered a mitzvah, *and this is the case even when she is a menstruant (niddah)*, for it is pleasing for her to be in the same room as her husband (cf. *B. Eruvin* 63b). And this constitutes the mitzvah, because of the principle of *teshvu ke-ein taduru* , one's dwelling in the *sukkah* should be of the same nature as when one normally dwells in one's home (*B. Sukkah* 28b, and cf. 26a, and cf. *Tosafot* 28b, s.v. *teshvu*).[45]

---

45. This reasoning appears in a variety of *Rishonim* and *Aharonim*, as arrayed by R. Ovadiah Yosef in his *Hazon Ovadiah: Sukkot*, Jerusalem: 2005, pp. 195–196. And see further in my *On the Relationship of Mitzvot between Man and his Neighbor and Man and His Maker*, Jerusalem and New York, 2014, pp. 26–27.

So even when a couple have to keep apart, they still want to be together in some measure and require privacy for intimate conversation, which would be spoiled by the presence of a third person – an outsider, and would be the cause of their embarrassment and thus reduce their ability to take pleasure in their emotional, non-sexual intimacy. And even if they do not speak to one another, (See *Rema Yoreh Deah* 195:1), the feeling of "togetherness" is most rewarding, and would be sullied by the presence of a third person.

A further example of the fine sensitivity towards people: feeling, that the Rabbi requires, is beautifully illustrated in what Marc C. Angel relates in his *Loving Truth & Peace: The Grand Religious Worldview of Rabbi Benzion Uziel*, Northwale, N.J. and Jerusalem, 1999, pp. 115–116:

> A question arose in a synagogue where the custom was for each man who was called to the Torah to read his own section. One man read his section but made a number of errors in the musical notations. The man who was called next, instead of beginning with his own portion, went back to the portion of the previous man and began to read it again. He felt that the former reader had made errors and that the reading was therefore not valid. Yet, by rereading the previous section, he was causing embarrassment to the man who had read that section. Rabbi Uziel ruled that the second man was guilty of causing public humiliation to the previous reader. Mistakes in the musical notations do not in themselves invalidate the Torah reading (*Mishpetei Uziel, Hoshen Mishpat*, Jerusalem 5700, *Miluim*, p. 226). Rabbi Uziel was distressed that self-righteousness was cloaking itself in religiosity in order to shame another person.

Angel adds that:

> Throughout his response, Rabbi Uziel demonstrated his commitment to proper legal argumentation along with an overarching sense of moral righteousness. He was deeply sensitive to the situations of those who would be affected by his rulings. He was motivated by his belief that halachic decisions should reflect the principle that *the ways of the Torah are ways of pleasantness*. (My emphasis – D.S.)[46]

---

46. Cf. my *Netivot Pesikah*, Jerusalem, 2008, pp. 195–197. Cf. above section

An interesting example of such halachic thinking and argumentation may be found in R. Israel Isserlein's *Terumat ha-Deshen*, vol. 1, Warsaw, 1882, sect. 285, p. 102. The question concerns a *Kohen* who slept naked and suddenly someone died in his house, whether to tell him immediately so that he jump out of bed and immediately exit the house naked, so as not to linger in an area of impurity, or to delay his exit out of concern for his dignity and not to embarrass him by forcing him to stand naked outside in the open. His reply is that *kevod ha-briyot*, while it cannot supercede a biblical prohibiton – such as the *Kohen*'s staying in an area of impurity – it is still significant. Therefore, those that have to inform him of the decease should preferably tell him to get up and leave the house without telling him of the death, thus giving him the opportunity to get dressed while he is unaware of the reason. He proves this from earlier sources dealing with the laws of *kilaim*, namely that as long as he is unaware, i.e., a *shogeg*, the principle of the dignity of the individual prevails, so allowing him to avoid shame by getting dressed, even at the expense of delaying his exit from a place of impurity, is permitted. (See above chapter entitled "Human Dignity," ad init.)

And as to shaking hands with a woman, or rather refusing to do so when her hand is outstretched for a handshake, which could surely embarrass her, see the discussion in Malka Puterkovsky's *Mehalechet be-Darkah*, Tel-Aviv, 2014, pp. 451–451 and 561, note 26, who brings the relevant sources, concluding that one should be more stringent in *kevod ha-briyot*, thus permitting such a handshake.

Thus, this ethical value, to do all that is possible to avoid shaming or embarrassing the other, which was only insinuated in the biblical text and was derived from an aggadic story, steered the course of the rabbis in establishing the guidelines for a variety of instructions, including the commandment to rebuke one's neighbor that is stated explicitly in the Torah. This is yet another example of a fundamental ethical principle that serves as a foundation for halachic decision-making.[47]

---

entitled "Its Ways Are the Ways of Pleasantness."

47. See what my father wrote in his *Maamarot*, Jerusalem, 1978, pp. 197–201, on whether this is really halachah or [only] *aggadah*. And see below pp. 128–131. See further sections entitled "Compassion and Casting a Blind Eye" and "Sensitivity to the 'Have-Nots'".

Leniency to Prevent Distress and Suffering

Perhaps it is self-understood that for the same reason, physical discomfort and distress are justifications for seeking leniencies, such as permitting shaving during the three weeks of mourning for those who are accustomed to shaving daily and for whom facial hair would seem like thorns, permitting swimming during this period in hot climates in order to wash away perspiration, cancelling the requirement of emersion during the winter in very cold climates for men who have an emission, and not sleeping in the *sukkah* during the cold winter months.[48]

A related case is cited in R. Yair Hayyim Bachrach's *Havvat Yair*, Jerusalem, 1973, no. 191, p. 98b concerning a *Kohen* who was standing in his courtyard during the winter on a very cold and windy day. When he was informed that there was a dead person in his house, he wished to run quickly through his house to that of his neighbor, rather than to be kept out in the windy wintery cold. R. Bachrach tends to permit this basing himself on a number of premises, and taking into account the distress and pain involved (*tza'ara*), and citing a number of tangentally related rulings. Likewise, if he had to relieve himself under similar circumstances, R. Bachrach would permit it.[49]

And, of course, we recall the halachic ruling that the "*mitz'taer*" who feels uncomfortable [because of the cold, etc.] is exempt from sitting in the *sukkah* (B. Sukkah 26a). Likewise if it rains into the *sukkah* (B. Sukkah 29a, Mordechai ad loc. Shulhan Aruch, Orah Hayyim 639:5–7, and see Shaar ha-Tziyyun ibid. 67). Here again, physical distress or discomfort is sufficient reason to be exempt from fulfilling the biblical commandment of dwelling in the *sukkah*, and furthermore sitting in

---

48. See *Minhagei Yisrael*, vol. 1, pp. 110, 112–117; vol. 3, p. 48–49, note 25; ibid., pp. 102–106, etc.; and see R.M. Mazuz-Neeman Sat's discussion in *Ve-Al Titosh et Torah Imecha*, by Y.B.A. ha-Levi, Jerusalem, 2014, pp. 8–10; Maharatz Chajes, *Darkei Horaah*, chapter 4, apud *Kol Sifrei Maharatz Chajes*, vol. 1, Jerusalem, 1958, p. 230, referring to *Rema, Shulhan Aruch, Orah Hayyim* 639.

49. However, see the end of the responsum where he writes that his permission is not because we learn a *kal va-homer* from *tzaar baalei hayyim*, from the leniencies in the case of an animal's pain and distress. See further the discussion in R. Ovadiah Yosef's *Yabia Omer*, vol. 9, Jerusalem, 2012, *Orah Hayyim* 30:8, p. 49, who brings sources from the *Rishonim* that permit a woman who has an excess of milk in her breasts which causes her much pain to express that milk on Shabbat but wasting, i.e., not saving it, on which latter see Y.Y. Neuwirth, *Shemirat Shabbat ke-Hilchatah*, 2nd edition, Jerusalem, 1988, 36:20, pp. 493–494, with references.

it while it is raining is not considered fulfilling the commandment but acting as a boor (*Shulhan Aruch* ibid., 7; responsa *Shvut Yaakov*, by R. Yaakov Reischer, vol. 3, Metz 1789, no. 45; and see further ibid., 640:4, and *Shaar ha-Tziyyun* ibid., 20, for further aspects of *mitz'taer*).

Indeed, there is a well-known question that troubled the rabbis throughout the generations, namely, why is it that so many people in so many different communities do not sleep in their *sukkot* at night. Surely one is obligated to spend all of one's time in the *sukkah* during the seven days of the festival, in so far as is possible, and even a short nap is mandated in the *sukkah* (lest it becomes a long sleep), according to the *Shulhan Aruch, Orah Hayyim* 639:2 (based on *B. Sukkah* 26a and *Y. Sukkah* 2:5 ad fin.).

The socio-historical explanation, offered by the Rema, R. Moshe Isserles, in *Orah Hayyim* 639:2, is that in northern European communities *Sukkot* falls during a wintry period, which can be both very cold and rainy, and therefore sleeping in a *sukkah* would be most uncomfortable and even stressful, and, as is well-known, a *mitz'taer* – he that feels uncomfortable (cold, etc.) – is exempt from sitting in the *sukkah* (*B. Sukkah* 26a, in the name of Rava, *Shulhan Aruch, Orah Hayyim* 640:4).[50]

---

50. See my *Minhagei Yisrael*, vol. 3, Jerusalem: 1944, 75–77), and my *On the Relationship of Mitzvot between Man and his Neighbor and Man and His Maker*, Jerusalem and New York, 2014, pp. 25–27, where I give additional explanations. On the notion of acting as a boor, see ibid., pp. 69–78.

Here it is worth noting what R. Yosef Shaul Natansohn, wrote in his *Shoel u-Meshiv Kama*, vol. 2, Lvov, 1869, sect. 22, on the question whether one can allocate a section of the (man's) synagogue for the women in the winter, even though the sanctity of the women's section is considered less that that of the men's section. And he writes as follows:

And we see that it is impossible for the women to pray in their women's synagogue in the winter because of the cold, and [therefore] they do not come to pray at all, and women's prayer in the women's synagogue is almost forgotten, for they are delicate and find it impossible to pray in the [freezing] cold. And therefore it is only right and proper to allocate them an area in the [men's] synagogue, so that they too may share [the warmth of] the stove in the [men's] synagogue, and in this way they will be able to pray as they should, and this is not to be regarded as reducing the sanctity of the [men's] synagogue, since [their section] also has a degree of sanctity . . .

See R. Ovadiah Yosef, *Yabia Omer* vol. 10, Jerusalem, 2004, *Orah Hayyim*, sect. 15, pp. 20–21. See also *Minhagei ha-Kehilot*, by R. Bunem Yoel Taussig of Mattersdorf, ed. Yehiel Goldhaber, vol. 1, Jerusalem, 2005, p. 27, no.17:

In the [men's] synagogue there was no stove to heat it up, and therefore they prayed in the women's section during the winter (where there was a stove).

Another example, also related to *Sukkot*, may be found in Hafetz Hayyim's ruling in his *Shaar ha-Tziyyun* to *Shulhan Aruch, Orah Hayyim* 639, subsection 67. The issue under discussion is whether one waits until midnight to eat one's meal in the *sukkah* when it is raining, hoping that it might stop raining (see *Shulhan Aruch* 639:5). The *Mishnah Berurah* (ibid.) writes in the name of some latter-day authorities

---

The continuation (p. 28) describes how they would dress in heavy clothing because of the cold. The editor adds additional description of the extreme cold, so much so that at times R. Yosef of Pozna (the son-in-law of the *Noda bi-Yehudah*) would find himself in the winter with his beard frozen into a solid block of ice.

I cannot restrain myself from adding that despite these extreme climatic conditions in the northern regions of Europe, which prevented people from coming regularly to pray in the synagogue during the winter months, the local rabbinic authorities did not allow placing stoves in the men's synagogues, because this could constitute an innovation contrary to their tradition. They offered additional reasons which are most unconvincing. See editor's citations ibid., pp. 29–30. (We may add that since most these synagogues were wooden, there may have been a better reason for not introducing stoves.)

This implacability expresses itself in other places in this work, such as the unwillingness to change "*shtenders* (lecterns) into tables and benches, nor to introduce clocks into the synagogue nor indeed make any other such changes all of which were not permitted" (see ibid., pp. 21–26, etc.).

For yet another example of the influence of cold on the halachah, see what I wrote in my *Minhagei Yisrael*, vol. 3, Jerusalem, 1994, pp. 102–106, on oblutions for seminal flow (*tevilat baalei keri*).

For the effect of *hot* weather during the summer months on the halachah, see, for example, R. Ovadiah Yosef, *Yabia Omer*, vol. 5, 2nd edition, Jerusalem, 1986, *Orah Hayyim*, no. 41, p. 143, who cites sources permitting one to wash oneself in warm water from the first of Av until the week of *Tisha b'Av*, and in cold water during the week of *Tisha b'Av*, because "due to the heat during the month of Av one is covered in sweat and one becomes super-sensitive (*istenis*) which makes it permissible" (*B. Berachot* 16b, and Tosafot ibid.). This is cited in *Mahari Brona*, responsum 12, and this in contradistinction to a variety of earlier sources, but following the Rambam and the Ramban, and such was the practice in Soloniki.

On the basis of the "*sukkah heter*," the author of *Yosef Ometz* (sect. 40) cited *Maharikash* (R. Yaakov Castro, 1525–1610), in his *Ohalei Yaakov*, sect. 98, that there is discomfort one may shave (one's beard) during the *Omer* period, and so too ruled R. David ben Zimra, the *Radbaz* (1480–1574), in his responsum (part 2, no. 687) that "this is no more weighty a custom than the positive (biblical) commandment of *sukkah*, where we rule that a *mitz'taer* is not obligated [to sit therein]. . . ." (See my *Minhagei Yisrael*, vol. 1, Jerusalem, 1989, p. 115, for additional sources.)

One could greatly multiply examples of the use of the principle of *mitz'taer* leading to halachic leniencies, but this note is already overleaded, and therefore let these sources suffice.

that, at least on the first day, one should wait until midnight. But in the *Shaar ha-Tziyyun* (66) he adds:

> If by waiting he is distressed by his hunger or (lack of) sleep (and especially when he invites poor guests, and in all probability they have not eaten the whole day long and are ravenously hungry and distressed), he should not wait . . . , and especially for poor people it is sinful to delay their meal . . . , etc.

And on yet another aspect of *mitz'taer,* see *Shut Maharshal* (R. Shlomo Luria), sect. 33a.[51]

The principle of *mitz'taer* has a number of applications in other areas of halachah. Thus, for example, although one is not permitted to fast on Shabbat (*Shulhan Aruch, Orah Hayyim* 288:1) if one finds eating distressing – for health reasons – so that fasting is pleasant for him, he is permitted to do so on Shabbat (ibid. 2). Similarly, if crying helps to alleviate one's distress, one may cry on Shabbat (ibid.). And there are other such cases, which go beyond the scope of this study. So too in *Shulhan Aruch, Orah Hayyim* 38:1, we read that a person who is in distress because of some form of sickness is not obligated to wear *tefilin* (see supercommentaries ad loc.). Furthermore, a *mitz'taer* does not have to wear his *tefillin* (*Rambam, Hilchot Tefillin* 4:13).[52]

Indeed, it is for precisely this reason, i.e., compassion for the suffering, that the rabbis permitted one to pray for the death of one terminally sick, who suffers with unbearable pains. (See *Raviah* to *Nedarim* 40a, going back to B. *Ketubot-*107a; and see *Tiferet Yisrael* to M. *Yoma* 8:7, *Boaz* note 3.)

Yet another example of the application of the concept *mitz'taer* may be found in the ruling of R. Joseph Messas, in his *Otzar ha-Michtavim,* vol. 2, no. 1061 (cited in Zechariah Zarmati's *Hod Yosef Hai,* Jerusalem, 2008, p. 258, no. 229), namely that though according to the halachah a mourner may not sit on a regular chair, but be seated on the bare ground (*Shulhan Aruch, Yoreh Deah* 387:1); nonetheless, since such a form of sitting is difficult for many, the rabbis ruled leniently for

---

51. But see also Yitzhak Yosef, *Ein Yitzhak,* vol. 1, Jerusalem, 2009, pp. 495–499, on the limitations of this principle.

52. See on this M.M. Kasher, *Divrei Menachem,* vol. 1, Jerusalem, 1977, pp. 79–80.

the aged and infirm, and even for those who are accustomed to sit only on chairs, to be seated on cushions, and even on a chair – usually a low one, or a bench, because otherwise he would be a *mitz'taer*. Indeed, to sit for an extended period on the bare floor would be for most people not merely discomfort but, after a while, even painful.[53]

Into this generic concept of *mitz'taer* we should also include the principle of *bi-mekom tza'ar lo gazru rabbanan*, found in B. *Ketubot* 60a, where even an act that is prohibited by biblical law may be performed in order to relieve pain, if performed abnormally, in which case the prohibition is reduced to a level of *mi-de-rabbanan*, of rabbinic status. This principle is again to be found in the Rema's gloss in *Shulḥan Aruch, Orah Hayyim* 317:1, where he permits untieing knots, when their unraveling is only prohibited by rabbinic law, in a case where there is pain and discomfort, *bi-mekom tza'ara*, because of the above cited statement in B. *Ketubot*. R. Aharon Lichtenstein, (in his essay '"*Mah Enosh*': Reflections on the Relation between Judaism and Humanism" *The Torah u-Madda Journal* 14, 2006–07, p. 41), comments that since

> in this case his explanatory assersion, *de-bi-mekom zaar lo gazru*, nowhere appears in the *gemara*, one can only presume that Rema expounded and extrapolated from Ketubot into a general principle . . .[54]

In parenthesis, as a sort of different aspect (almost interpretation) of his principle, we may note that the *poskim* ruled that a rabbi who is in a state of distress should not give *piskei halachah*. So we read in the Bah, *Yoreh Deah* 242, cited further by the Shach (ibid., sub sect.21), that:

> One who is in distress and his mind is not at ease should not give rulings, as it is written "while in distress do not rule" (*Ben Sirah* 7:3; B. *Eruvin* 65a; see Rashi and Tosafot ad loc., referring to Y. *Berachot* 5:1).

(See L. Ginzberg, *Peirushim ve-Hidushim ba-Yerushalmi, Berachot* vol.

---

53. Cf. Shach, *Yoreh Deah* 387:1, and the extended discussion of R. Ovadia Yosef, in *Yabia Omer*, vol. 9, *Yoreh Deah* 40:2, p. 341.

54. See his continued discussion, referring to the Rema in *Yoreh Deah* 240:25 based on a Responsum of the Maharik (R. Yosef Colon) no. 167; *Tosfot Ketubot* ibid. s.v. *Goneah Yonek*, and his note 191 on p. 60 on the nature of *mitz'taer*. See also *Tosfot Yevamot* 114a s.v. *Shabbat*.

4, ed. D. Halivni, New York, 1261, pp. 3–5; Y. Tamar, *Alei Tamar*, vol.
1, Givataim, 1999, p. 177.) And indeed, such was the practice of great
decisors, such as the *Noda bi-Yehudah*, who writes at the end of one
of his responsa (*Tinyana, Even ha-Ezer* sect. 15):

> But because my head and heart are not with me, because the Rebbetzen
> is mortally sick for more than three weeks, therefore you cannot now
> rely upon me, and [you should] clarify the issue [with others], and if they
> find it so, you can rule permissively . . .[55]

I believe we may discern yet another example of rabbinic sensitivity
and deep psychological insight, in a responsum of the Radbaz, R. David
ben Zimra [*Shut ha-Radbaz* vol. 8, ed. Y. Tzvi Sofer, Bnei Brak [n.d.]
no. 135, pp. 82–83). Paradoxically it deals with women, who during
the period of mourning, out of deep distress, strike their faces drawing
blood. He is asked whether they should be chastised and prevented
from such actions, since this would appear to be forbidden by biblical
law. In his response he argues that scratching and slashing oneself thus
drawing blood on a part of mourning activity is biblically prohibited,
expounding the relevant sources, and should therefore certainly be discouraged. However, he does find, in the continuation of the responsum,
a way of viewing this with leniency. For the Talmud (*B. Sanhedrin* 68a)
reports how R. Akiva would beat himself over the death of R. Eliezer,
even until the blood poured out of his wounds. And surely R. Akiva
could not have transgressed the law of "do not cut yourself . . . for the
dead" in *Deuteronomy* 14:1! He then cites the Ritba and the Tosafot (to
B. Yevamot 13b) who argue that *cutting* is prohibited, but not *beating*.
Having said that, he adds that one should not rule thus, since people
might take it that "cutting" is also permitted, and that probably there
is some measure of prohibition involved; nonetheless, if one feels that
one cannot dissuade them from doing so, better they do it unwittingly
(*be-shogeg*) than knowingly (*be-mezid*). Here one may feel a measure
of sympathy and understanding as to the need to express one's grief
even in such extreme a manner. It may however be that I am reading too

much into this responsum, and that the Radbaz merely wishes partially to justify a somewhat problematic practice.

We might mention in passing the view expressed in *Tosafot Yeshanim* to *B. Eruvin* 40b, that the reason that (according to some opinions) one (i.e., the father) does not make the *shehehiyanu* blessing at *brit milah*, is because of the pain the newly-born experiences during the circumcision ceremony. In this way they express sympathy for the child's suffering, even though it is *le-shem mitzvah*. To this it may be added that it has been suggested that the reason the Rambam (*Hilchot Milah* 2:8), after listing the materials that may be used as the circumcision "knife," writes that the best way to do it is with metal knife, because a metal knife is sharp and cuts cleanly, minimizing the pain for the child.[56]

The extreme degree of sensitivity towards the feelings of the other expresses itself in the care one has to take not to cause any manner of distress towards the other, which would make him or her a *mitz'taer* (or a *mitz'taeret),* and in order to avoid this the halachah should, on occasions seek lenient solutions.[57]

Indeed, R. Moshe Feinstein was deeply sensitive to the problems of emotional and psychological distress, and this was a major element in his very bold and problematic ruling on artificial insemination from a gentile donor. Thus when asked about a couple "who are suffering greatly because of their yearning for a child," and the only way in which they could have a child was through artificial insemination, he responded:

> [The procedure] should be permitted with use of sperm from a gentile, for since the offspring will be a Jew because its mother is Jewish, there are no concerns of any sort. The offspring's paternity would not be attributed to the gentile father even had it been conceived though intercourse, and that is so a *fortiori* when it is conceived not through intercourse but in a bath . . . and the fact that the sperm is from a gentile also addresses the concerns of those who maintain that [a child born of] other semen [than that of the woman's husband] is a *mumzer* even [if conceived] without

---

56. See *Sefer ha-Brit*, 264:2, cited in *Meorot ha-Daf ha-Yomi* 811, to *Yevamot* 64–70, 2015, p. 2.

57. See also Zeev Fund, "*Be-Inyan Shvut b-Mekom Tzaar,*" *Hitzei Giborim* 6, 2014, pp. 152–157, but especially on heating the house on Shabbat by a gentile in cold weather.

intercourse. . . . And so, *in exigent circumstances when they are suffering greatly because of their yearning for a child,* it is permitted to cast into the woman's innards semen coming specifically from a gentile. . . . As for the statement in *Otsar Ha-Poseqim,* quoting *Sefer Menahem Meishiv,* that it would be terrible for a daughter of Israel to abandon herself to the artificial prostitution invented by the doctors – those are empty words, for this has nothing whatsoever in common with prostitution and the only prohibition is the possibility that the offspring might unknowingly come to marry his half sister on his father's side. Without the husband's consent, it would be forbidden on the grounds of her subservience to her husband . . . but with the husband's consent, *and where they are suffering greatly,* it should be permitted, but only with semen from a gentile. (*Igrot Moshe, Even ha-Ezer* 1:71.) (My emphasis – D.S.)

This ruling elicited vehement opposition from his contemporaries and criticism often formulated in vitriolic style. Thus R. Yaakov Breisch expresses grave surprise, writing:

> Is it possible that a renowned decisor would permit something so revolting and disgusting? It is something that even the Catholics and their leaders have forcefully attacked, forbidding such vile actions, which resemble the ways of Egypt and Canaan with their abominations. Should we, the precious and chosen people, permit something as revolting and disgusting as this? Is it not the greatest desecration of God's name? (*Helkat Ya'akov, Even ha-Ezer* 14:1.)

But despite this frontal attack on his ruling by very prominent rabbis, such as R. Moshe Charlap, R. Moshe Efraim Bloch, and others, R. Feinstein did not recant, though he did modify his position.[58]

Thus, in *Igrot Moshe, Even ha-Ezer,* vol. 4 no. 32, he wrote:

> Everything I wrote in my responsum is true and clear as a matter of law, and there is no reason to regret my words and no concern related to injection of gentile seed. As a practical matter, however, I did not teach that this should be done, for it is ineffective in fulfilling the husband's obligation to procreate, and the woman has no such obligation; and it may

---

58. See below section titled "On an Independent Stance."

result in great jealousy on the part of her husband, so it is ill-advised. . . . Certainly one should not advise doing this, for the reasons I have set out, but if one did so, the offspring is fit even for the priesthood. . . . As for what his Torah Excellency [an honorific applied to the correspondent] wrote regarding the main concern being that of [the offspring] marrying his [half] sister, that does not apply with respect to [seed from] gentiles, as I wrote in my responsum.[59]

Perhaps into this category we can also include the ruling of R. Jack Simchah Cohen, a prominent American Orthodox rabbi, on the issue of converting children born to Jewish fathers and gentile mothers. In this specific case, a Jewish family who had adopted a gentile girl and after a few years came to the rabbis to formally convert her, and they were informed that a *beit din* could not properly convert their adopted daughter (aged five) because the parents did not observe the laws of Shabbat. "Imagine the trauma attendant upon such an episode," declared Cohen, as part of his legitimation to ruling a permitted conversion, against the prevailing rulings of such Torah giants as R. Moshe Feinstein and R. Yehiel Weinberg. "While Feinstein, or even Weinberg, might not have denied the emotional difficulty for a family that was denied conversion, it is clear that any such trauma was not a legally relevant factor for them. For Cohen, however, it was."[60]

And from a totally different angle we may refer to the fact that the Maharsham, R. Shmuel Mordechai mi-Brezen [Berezyna], in his responsa, *Shut Maharsham*, Jerusalem, 1974, vol. 2, no. 210, records that he gave distinct directions to his family that if someone came with a question, even if he is in the middle of a meal or even asleep, they should not delay the questioner, but bring the issue before him, even when it meant waking him up. He explained that a person is prohibited

---

59. See also *Igrot Moshe, Even ha-Ezer* vol. 3, no.14. And for a fine and detailed analysis of this whole issue, see Ronit Irshai, *Fertility and Jewish Law: Feminist Perspectives on Orthodox Responsa Literature*, Waltham Mass. 2012, pp. 237–241 and the whole of chapter 6, pp. 225–268.

60. See David Ellenson and Daniel Gordis, *Pledges of Jewish Allegiance: Conversion, Law and Policymaking in Nineteenth and Twentieth-Century Orthodox Responsa*, Stanford, California, 2012, pp. 112–113; Jack Simcha Cohen, "The Conversion of Children Born to Gentile Mothers and Jewish Fathers", in *Inter-marriage and Conversion: A Halakhic Solution*, Hoboken, N.J., 1987, p. 7. Of course, this was only one single element in his halachic argument.

from causing any sort of distress, even of the slightest nature to anyone of Israel, for the verse in Exodus 22:21, "Ye shall not afflict any widow, or fatherless child" applies to every person. He was basing himself on *Massechet Semachot* 8:8 (ed. M. Higger, New York, 1931, pp. 153–154; transl. Dov Zlotnik, "The Tractate Mourning," New Haven and London, 1966, pp. 59–60):

> When Rabban Simeon and Rabbi Ishmael were seized and sentenced to be executed, Rabbi Ishmael wept.
>
> "Son of the noble," said Rabban Simeon to him, "you are but two steps away from the bosom of the righteous, and you weep?"
>
> "It is because we are about to be killed that I weep," he replied. "I weep because we are being executed like murderers and like Sabbath breakers."
>
> Rabban Simeon then said to him: "Perhaps while you were dining or while you were sleeping, a woman came to ask for a ruling about her menses, her defilement, or her cleanness, and the servant told her, 'He is sleeping.' Whereas the Torah states: *If thou afflict them in any wise* (Exodus 22:22). And what is written after this? *My wrath shall wax hot, and I will kill you with the sword*" (ibid. 22:23).

However, this does indeed entail a degree of ultra-sensitivity, which, perhaps, we cannot expect of ordinary folk.[61]

Of a somewhat related issue is the discussion found in the *Shulhan Aruch, Orah Hayyim* 511:1, where the Rema brings a difference of opinion as to the permissibility of heating a house on *Yom Tov* during a period when it is not "very cold," but when, nevertheless, those who are ultra-sensitive to cold (*ha-mefunakim*, nowadays translated as "pampered") feel it necessary to heat the house. (Cf. above note 58.)

We should explain, by laying out the general background to this discussion, that on *Yom Tov* food-cooking activities (*melechet ochel nefesh*) are permitted. And since one may light a fire (from an existing

---

61. See Moshe Mendel Sklarsh, *Hayyei Moshe* to *Yoreh Deah*, Bnei Brak, 2001, pp. 250–251, for a further discussion as to whether the category of "the widow and the fatherless child" should indeed be broadened to include every person, and that according to the *Minhat Hinuch, Mitzvah* 65, this indeed is a difference of opinion among the *Rishonim*. Cf. above pp. 59–61 note 17, where clearly *kevod ha-briyot* is a related concept.

fire) in order to cook, such fire-lighting is permitted also for other, non-food related activities. The question then is: must these other activities, such as heating a house in cold weather, be only when the requirement is for the majority of people (*shaveh le-chol nefesh*), or also when the requirement is merely for a small minority. Some argue that when the act of heating the house is unnecessary for the general public, and only the *"mefunakim"* require it, it should be forbidden. While others respond that since the generic act of heating is basically permitted to the general public (*shaveh le-chol nefesh*), it should be permitted for the *"mefunakim"* as well. The Rema summarises: And the custom is to be lenient, i.e., to permit it, again demonstrating a sensitivity to the "sensitive."[62]

Beyond the Letter of the Law

The rabbis established a principle that we obligate people to follow behavioral guidelines that are apparently beyond the letter of the law (*lifnim mi-shurat ha-din*).[63] Based on the verse "And you shall do that

---

62. For further elaboration of this issue, see R. Yechiel Michel Epstein (1829–1908), *Aruch ha-Shulhan* (1903–1907), *Orah Hayyim* 511:3–4 (vol. 3, p. 48), on the Rambam's position on this issue, namely that he does not mention the principle of *davar ha-shaveh le-chol nefesh*; cf. ibid. 495:19, and see also *Meorot ha-Daf Yomi*, to *Beitzah* 22b, no. 777, Nissan 2014, p. 4, citing, inter alia, R. Shlomo Zalman Auerbach's explanation in his *Minhat Shlomo* ad loc. See further what I wrote in *Minhagei Yisrael*, vol. 4, Jerusalem, 1995, pp. 322–329, on "Coldness as an influence on the formation of *halachah* and *minhag*."

63. See Rabbi Moshe Isserles (Rema), *Hoshen Mishpat* 11:2; see also, Elon, *supra* note 5, pp. 176–180.

See below pp. 101–103 note 66 where we discuss the degree to which the judge is *obligated* to go beyond the letter of the law. At this stage we should clearly point out that this is the subject of considerable controversy among the *poskim*. Thus in Talmudic times there seems to have been a clear distinction between the *law* and the *advice* to go beyond it, as opposed to an *obligation*.

Thus, for instance, in B. *Ketubot* 50a we read that R. Eleazar gave an order to feed daughters from the "moveables" (*metaltelin*) that were part of their dead father's estate, even though the conditions of the *ketubah* only obligate that they receive their sustenance from "immovable" (*karkaot*) of the estate. R. Shimon ben Eliakum then argued: "Rabbi, I know that you acted not according to the Law, but out of the spirit of mercy, but [I fear] lest your disciples will see [your practice] and adopt it as law for future generations." R. Shlomo Luria, the Maharshal, explains that R. Eleazar did not want to force his views on the heirs, but only to persuade them with words. But

which is right and good" (*Deuteronomy* 6:18)[64] examples, such as *Dina*

R. Shimon ben Eliakum objected even to this, lest future generations see this as an enforceable ruling.

In later periods, however, this distinction was blurred among certain authorities, who saw the element of *obligation* to be paramount. Thus, the Raviah (cited in *Haga-hot Maimoniyot* to *Hilchot Gezeilah* 1:7) obligates returning a lost object to its former owner even after *yiush* – i.e., even when the owner had given up hope of getting it back, if the finder is rich. While the Rosh (to *Baba Metzia*, chapter 2) disagrees, ruling that we do not force him to do so, and so too the Rema (*Hoshen Mishpat* 12:2). The Bah, on the other hand, disagrees with the Rema, stating explicitly that "it is the practice in all the courts of Israel to force the rich man to act in a proper and correct fashion, even though this is not the [real] law." And so too ruled the *Tzemach Tzedek* (Responsum no. 89), the *Hatam Sofer* (*Yoreh Deah* no 239, and cf. Rema to *Hoshen Mishpat* 250:7). See on this Shimon Federbush, *Ha-Musar ve-ha-Mishpat be-Yisrael*, Jerusalem 1979, pp. 74–86, especially pp. 85–86, for his clear and extensive discussion of this subject. (Cf. *B. Berachot* 5b for a partially related example.)

64. See Nahmanides at the beginning of *Parshat Kedoshim* (Leviticus 19). On verse 2 he writes:

What does the command to be holy mean? The Torah prohibits certain types of sexual relationships and certain types of foods while it permits relations with one's wife and eating of meat and drinking wine. This might lead lustful people to be preoccupied with their wife or to have many wives. It might lead them to constantly drink wine and eat meat. They might think that they can speak in a disgusting way – since none of these things are specifically prohibited in the Torah. Thus, a person apparently can be totally disgusting while precisely keeping all the commandments of the Torah. Therefore this verse comes to teach that after specifying those things which are absolutely prohibited, there is a general rule to be moderate in that which is permitted. Thus one should not have unlimited sexual relations and should minimize the amount of wine he drinks. He should stay away from impurity, even though these things are not specifically prohibited in the Torah. . . . Similarly he should guard his mouth from gluttony and disgusting speech. . . . He should sanctify himself and act in a holy manner. . . . This is the purpose of having a general principle after specific examples of that which is prohibited and permitted. . . . Even these additional commandments are rabbinic in origin – they are based on this Torah principle to be clean, pure, and distinct from the average man who is focused on pleasure to a disgusting degree. This is the manner of the torah to specify examples and then to give the general principle to enable generalization to new situations. We find this also concerning the laws of business and proper relations between men concerning theft, and fraud etc., then the Torah says "Be uprights and good in G-d's eyes" (Deuteronomy 6:18). This tells you how to evaluate the appropriateness of all activates – not just those specified in the Torah.

And on Deuteronomy 16:18, he writes:

"You should do that which is upright and good in the eyes of G-d." This principle is very important since it is impossible to mention in the Torah every detail of how a person should conduct himself with his neighbors and friends and all aspects of business, society and politics. However, after mentioning many – such as not gossiping and not taking revenge, not to allow harm to occur to others, not to curse the deaf, to respect the elderly and others – it now tells you that there is a general principle to guide

de-Bar Metzra (*Baba Metzia* 108a – the first right of refusal to the adjacent landowner regarding property for sale) and *Shuma Hadra le-Olam* (*Baba Metzia* 35b) have been formulated. The latter example ensures that one whose land was appropriated by a creditor as payment for a debt can always redeem the land from the creditor because of the verse "And you shall do that which is right and good."[65] Even more radical are the rulings of Rav in the famous story recorded in *Baba Metzia* 83a in which he ordered Raba bar Bar Hana to return the garments that he had taken from workers who had broken his wine barrels. When Rabah asked him if this was indeed the law, Rav responded: "Yes, 'That you may walk in the way of good men' (Proverbs 2:20)." Rabah gave them back their garments. Nevertheless, the workers said to him: "We

---

your actions. That principle is to be good and upright in all matters. Consequently, one should compromise rather than on insisting on all monetary rights and that one should go beyond the letter of the law. . . . Thus this even includes speaking pleasantly with others – all that can be considered perfect and upright.

(Translation Daniel Eidensohn, *A Jewish Sourcebook: Daas Torah*, Jerusalem, 2005, pp. 170–171.)

See *Maggid Mishnah* on Maimonides, *Mishneh Torah, Hilchot Shechenim* 14:4.

We may note that, according to some authorities, there is a sort of incentive to act beyond the letter of the law. For although there is a general principle that there is no reward for carrying out mitzvot in this world (*Schar mitzvot be-hai alma leka* – B. *Kiddushin* 39b, and B. *Hulin* ad fin.), R. Yehonatan mi-Lunel states that for acting beyond the letter of the law one *does* receive a reward in this world (*Shitah Mekubetzet* to *Baba Kama* 109b). R. Yaakov Hayyim Sofer, in his booklet *Lecha Naeh le-Hodot*, Jerusalem, 2010, pp. 86, no. 30, brought additional references, such as Y. Pachnovsky, *Pardes Yosef*, Lodz, 1931, Bereishit 27:44, and several others.

65. This principle of *Shuma Hadra le-Olam* rules that property that was claimed by a creditor in lieu of the payment of the debt can always be reclaimed by the debtor, by the authority of the court, if he can repay the debt. The rabbis granted authority to the debtor to reaquire his property from the creditor, even though he had acquired it rightfully and legally with the court's authority. The Talmud (*Baba Metzia* 16b) states that "according to the law (*mi-dina*) the land need not return [to its former owner], but because [the Bible states] 'Thou shalt do that which is right good . . .' (Deuteronomy 6:18), the rabbis ruled that [the property] should be returned." On the relationship between *Dina de-Bar Metzra* and *Kofin al Middat Sedom*, see most recently Yitzhak Rones, "*Nizkei Shecheinim: Internet Alhuti*" *Le-Shichno Tidreshenu: Kovetz Maamarim be-Hilchot Shecheinim*, Ha-Machon ha-Gavoah le-Torah: Universitat Bar-Ilan, 2013, pp. 124–130. See A. Lichtenstein, " *Middot Sedom*," *Alei Etzion* 16, 2009, pp. 31–70. On these concepts, see A. Kirschenbaum, *Equity in Jewish Law: Halakhic Perspectives in Law-Formalism and Flexibility in Jewish Civil Law*, Hoboken, N.J. and New York, 1991, pp. 255–268; M. Higger, *Nezir Ehav*, vol. 3, pp. 153–154. And see *Magid Mishnah* to *Hilchot Shekhenim* 14:5 and Shlomo Brin, "*Be-Inyan Shuma Hadar ve-Lifnim mi-Shurat ha-Din*" *Alon Shvut* 100, Kislev 1983, pp. 95–109.

have labored all day and we are hungry, but we have nothing." Rav said to Rabah: "Give them their wages." When Rabah asked him if this was indeed the law, Rav responded: "Yes, 'And keep the paths of the righteous.' (ibid.)" Thus, Rav obligated Rabah to go beyond the letter of the law.[66] We understand from this story that Rabah was correct

---

66. However, in B. Baba Kama 11a, when Rav in a different case was asked if this was the law, he remains silent. The Tosafot to B. Baba Batra 62a explains that he recanted. However, there are other cases where the lack of a response is not equal to an acceptance of the criticism. See Shilem Warhaftig, Talmidei Hachamim ve-Halichotehem, Jerusalem, 1988, p. 58. See further Shmuel Shilo's article, "On the Aspects of Law and Morals in Jewish Law: Lifnim Mi-Shurat ha-Din" Israel Law Review 13(3) (1978), pp. 359–390; J.D. Bleich, The Philosophical Quest Philosophy, Ethics, Law and Halakhah, Jerusalem, 2013, pp. 125–133; Isaac ha-Levi Herzog, The Main Institutions of Jewish Law, London, 1936, vol. 1, pp. 383–385; Eliezer Bashan, "Li-fnim mi-Shurat ha-Din be-Sifrut ha-Halachah," Deot 39, 1970, pp. 236–243; Saul Berman, "Lifnim Mi-Shurat ha-Din," Journal of Jewish Studies 26, 1975, pp. 86–124; idem, "Lifnim Mi-Shurat ha-Din 2," Journal of Jewish Studies 26, 1975, pp. 86–104, and ibid. 28 (1977), pp. 181–193; A. Kirschenbaum, Equity in Jewish Law: Vol. 18: Beyond Equity – Halachic Aspirationism in Jewish Civil Law, Hoboken, N.J. and New York, 1991, pp. 109–136 (and pp. 212–222, the critique of Berman's approach); and Lichtenstein, "Mussar ve-Halakhah be-Messoret ha-Yehudit" and also his "The Human/and Social Factor in Halakha," Tradition 36:1, 2002, pp. 1–25. cf. near supra note 6. See also the Rema, Hoshen Mishpat 12:2: "The court cannot force someone to go beyond the letter of the law, even if it seems to them to be appropriate (Beit Yosef there in the name of Ri in the name of the Rosh), and there are those who differ (Mordechai, Chapter 2 of Baba Metzia) . . ." Hoshen Mishpat 259, Shach ibid.; Urim ve-Tumim (by R. Yonatan Eibeschutz) to Hoshen Misphat 12, etc. To which we may add: Semak, Ketzot ha-Hoshen 12; Pithei Teshuvah to Hoshen Mishpat 251:5; Aruch ha-Shulhan, Hoshen Mishpat 259:7. See Higger, Nezir Ehav (below, note 70), pp. 150–162. See also Emanuel Quint's summarizing article entitled "Lifnim Mishurat HaDin" in The Annual Volume of Torah Studies of the Council of Young Israel Rabbis in Israel, vol. 2, Jerusalem, 5748 (1988), pp. 97–122.

Of tangential interest is the statement in Seder Eliyahu Rabbah, chapter 15 (16), ed. M. Ish Shalom, Vienna, 1901, p. 80, translation W.G. Braude and I Kapstein, Philadelphia 1981, p. 215, which would appear to give a different message. There we read:

From here they said, a worker who accepts a task from a householder is under obligation to perform it as the householder wishes him to; and if he does not please the householder, of him is it said, "Cursed be that doeth the work of the Lord with a slack hand" (Jeremiah 4:10).

However, this statement should be seen in its fuller context. For it is preceded by an imprecation over those who rise early to sit late over wine, referring to the verse in Habakuk 2:5, "Yea also, because he transgresseth by wine, he is a proud (perhaps arrogant) man . . ." But this is an aside.

Further on the rights of a laborer and the various types (status) of laborers, see Israel H. Weisfeld, Labor Legislation in the Bible and Talmud, New York, 1974; Menachem Assaf, Ha-Avodah ba-Mekorot, Jerusalem, 1985; Hayyim Zack, Avodat

Hayyim ve-Avodat Avodah, Givataim, 1947; Meir Ayali, *Poalim ve-Omanim: Melach-tam u-Maamadam be-Sifrut Hazal*, Givataim, 1987; Shilem Warhaftig, *Dinei Avodah be-Mishpat ha-Ivri*, Jerusalem, 1982; Moshe Aberbach, *Labor, Crafts and Commerce in Ancient Israel*, Jerusalem, 1984; David J. Schnall, *By the Sweat of Your Brow: Reflections on Work and the Workplace in Classic Jewish Thought*, Hoboken, N.J., 2001. And most recently, Henech Yitzhak Rosenblat, *Hilchot Oved u Maavid*, Jerusalem (c. 2013). This is merely a sampling of the literature on the subject.

Returning to the main issue, we note that though the Rema in general prefers the first opinion that he cites (*Hochmat Shlomo*, ibid.), it seems from the responsa of the Rema 32 that he suggested enforcing going beyond the letter of the law (Kirschenbaum, *Equity in Jewish Law. Vol. 18: Beyond Equity*, p. 125, note 82), and this is the language of the Rema (A. Ziv edition, Jerusalem, 1971, p. 188):

Nevertheless, I say that if in opening the windows of the synagogue to his house or courtyard the damage to the aforementioned Reuven is not very large, he should not stand on the letter of the law, but should rather go beyond the letter of the law in order to give honor to his God and to glorify the house of our Lord. And one who does not have concern for the honor of his Maker (according to *Mishnah Hagigah* 2:1: "One who does not have concern for the honor of his maker, it would be better had he not come into the world."), etc. And we compel one to go beyond the letter of the law as stated by the Mordechai in Chapter *Elu Metziyot* (257), although there are authorities that differ.

See also the words of the editor there, note 4, who referred to Tosafot *Baba Metzia* 24b "*Lifnim*," *Baba Kama* 100a "*Lifnim*," and *Bayit Hadash, Hoshen Mishpat* 12:4 and 304:1, who wrote there: "We have discussed this law at length as it appears that Rav forced Raba bar Bar Hana to act beyond the letter of the law." See further Yisrael Roth, "*Lifnim mi-Shurat ha-Din: Mashmaauto*," *Shematim* 28/104–105, 1991, pp. 89–93.

Apparently the Rema saw it as a moral imperative here to go "beyond the letter of the law." His ethical position expresses itself in his ruling in *Shulhan Aruch, Orah Hayyim* 343 ad fin., in which he states concerning a child who sins in his childhood days, and then grew up to adulthood:

Even though he is not required to do repentence when he grows up, nonetheless, it is good (or perhaps right) that he take upon himself some form of penitence and atonement, even though he sinned before he became culpable.

And the *Mishnah Berurah* ad loc., note 8 adds (on the basis of the Taz and the *Hayyei Adam*, and perhaps the Gra), that:

All this is in accordance with the [letter of] the law. But beyond the letter of the law, either in a case where he did bodily harm [to someone] or monetary damage, he has to pay up [when he comes of age].

The *Mishnah Berurah*'s formulations does not sound as though this obligation is optional. And indeed, the Taz refers us to *Sefer Hasidim* no. 692, ed. Gutman, vol. 2, pp. 603–605, where we read:

Someone came before a wise man and said to him, "I remember that when I was small I used to rob people, and I sinned in other ways." He added, "Perhaps I am not required to repent [and] to pay back the thefts, for when I sinned I was not yet thirteen years and one day old. And since I was young, why should I [be obligated to] repent and pay back my thefts?" He replied, "Every sin that you remember, and all that you

according to the simple letter of the law, but that the ethical value of following the ways of good men and the paths of the righteous overrode the letter of the law, and he was therefore obligated to pay more than the law required, that is *Lifnim m-Shurat ha-Din.*

A similar case is reported in *Y. Baba Metziah* 6:8, 11a. There we read that:

---

robbed, you must return. For Josiah repented all the sins he committed and paid back all the cases when he judged incorrectly, and where he caused monetary loss in his youth (*B. Shabbat* 56b). . . . However, if he said, "I was very young when I used to steal," since he no longer remembers [what he did], he need not pay up.

(Cf. responsa of *Radbaz* 301, 314; *Shulhan Aruch, Hoshen Mishpat* 349:3, ibid. 96:3; the story of Rafram bar Papa and Rav Ashi in *B. Ketubot* 86a, according to Rashi's interpretation, and the extensive discussion in Gutman's note to *Sefer Hasidim* ibid.)

See further the very important extended discussion of the *Shlah* (*Shnei Luhot ha-Brit*), by Yishayahu Horowitz (c. 1570–1626, Poland), ed. Meir Katz, vol. 1, Haifa, 202, pp. 200–202 (nos. 199–203), who begins the discourse with the question: If God required that we go beyond the letter of the Law, why is this not stated explicitly in the Torah? He then moves on to explaining the view of the Ramban to *Kedoshim* (Leviticus 19:2), and moves on the *sugya* in *B. Baba Kama* 99b on R. Hiyya and the denarius, then to *B. Baba Metzia* 30b and on to a more spiritual discussion. The upshot of the whole discussion is that different halachic areas require differing treatments, also depending on the individual characteristics of the various cases and those involved in them, and, hence, this principle was not formulated as an absolute ruling, but latitude was given to the judge for a discretionary decision on the issue. See also Moshe Mendel Shklarsh, *Hayyei Moshe*, Bnei Brak, 2001, p. 279.

We should also take account of the principle of *Shuda de-Dayyanei*, which we cannot discuss in this context. But see Benzion Meir Hai Uziel, *Ha-Shofet ve-ha-Mishpat*, Jerusalem, 2006, pp. 68–84, for a full analysis.

For *Shuda de-Dayyanei*, "the discretion of the judges," which gives authority to judges to make increments that bring judicial procedure more in line with individual cases whose justice and fairness are better served by those refined modifications, see Aaron Kirchenbaum, *Equity in Jewish Law. Vol. 15: Halakhic Perspectives in Law – Formulation and Flexibility in Jewish Civil Law*. Hoboken, N.J. and New York, 1991, pp. 82–86. In note 112, on p. 83 he gives the following references:

On *shuda de-dayyanei*, see the classical commentaries to *B. Ketubot* 85b, 94a–b and the literature cited in R. Isaac Lampronti, *Pahad Yizhak s.v. "shuda de-dayyanei."* It is interesting to note that Rav Nahshon Gaon is cited as having applied the term *shuda de-dayyanei* to nonmonetary matters, namely, to a problem in the sphere of ritual and prayer that has not been resolved. The *Gaon*'s statement is found in R. Isaac b. Abba Mari, 12th century, *Sefer Ha'ittur, "Ma'amar Teshii al Hamezranim"* (Warsaw ed.; rep., Jerusalem, 1970), vol. 1, 66; R. Mordecai b. Hillel Ashkenazy, *Sefer Mordekhai-Ke-tubot*, "Glosses," ch. 10, para. 303. (*Cf.* R. Jacob Kanevsky, *Kehillot Ya'akov-Berakhot*, sect. 1, citing R. Hayyim Kanevsky, as the source of this bibliographical note.)

On the Rambam and *shuda de-dayyanei*, see Yaakov Blidstein, *"Ha-Emet shel ha-Dayan ke-chli Pesikah," Dinei Yisrael* 24, 2007, pp. 120–122.

A certain trade in pots and pans handed his wares to a porter to transport them for him. When the porter broke the pots in his care, presumably through negligence, his employer confiscated his coat as part-compensation. The porter complained before R. Yose bar Hanina (3rd century C.E.), described elsewhere as "a judge able to penetrate to the innermost intention (or deeper meaning) of the Law" (*B. Baba Kama* 39a). R. Yose ran true to form and told the porter to go to his employer and demand not only the return of his coat but also payment of his wages, again on the basis of Proverbs 2:20. Although the trader was not personally present in court, he yielded on both counts.

This story differs from the previous one, since in this case the judge himself spontaneously advised the plaintiff to demand his wages, whereas in the previous account Rav merely responded to the porters' request.

Rav's position on this issue also is reflected in yet another *sugya* in the Talmud. In *M. Baba Metzia* 2:11 we read (in Herbert Danby's translation, Oxford, 1933):

[If a man went to seek] his own lost property and that of his father, his own has first place.

Upon which the Talmud explains (*B. Baba Metzia* 33a):

How do we know this? Rav Yehudah said in the name of Rav, "The Scriptures say, 'Save when there shall be no poor among *you*' (Deuteronomy 15:4) – Yours has precedence over that of any other person."

Nonetheless, the *sugya* continues:

And Rav Yehudah said in the name of Rav, "Anyone who [actually carries this out for himself, in the end will come to this" (i.e., penury).

And Rashi comments on this:

Even though the Scriptures did not obligate him to this (i.e., to give precedence to his father's loss), a person should take upon himself to act beyond the letter of the Law, and not to adopt a formal pedantry, [saying] "Mine comes first," unless there be a proven loss. But if he always acts in this way, he divests himself of the burden of beneficence and charity, and in the end he will require the help of others.

We see, then, that even though Rav admits that the strict letter of the Law gives him precedence, nonetheless, he counsels that from an ethical point of view one should rule beyond the letter of the Law.

Indeed, Rav attributes this characteristic to God himself, as we learn from *B. Berachot* 7a:

> What prayer does the Holy One blessed be He pray? Said Rav Zutra bar Tuviah in the name of Rav: "May it be My will that My [feelings of] mercy overcome My anger, and My mercies prevail out my [other] dispositions, and I deal with them [i.e., Israel] beyond the letter of the Law."[67]

Interestingly enough, Rava seems to have followed his master's prima facie position, as opposed to that of Rav. For in *B. Baba Metzia* 109ab we are told how Ravina (4th century C.E.) employed a gardener to tend his plot. Unfortunately, the gardener was incompetent and ruined the garden. Ravina instantly fired him. The gardener then complained to Rava, the leading authority of his time, claiming that he had been treated unfairly. But Rava responded by saying that Ravina had been within his rights. The gardener argued that he had not been warned, to which Rava retorted that no warning was required, since when people are employed there is an explicit understanding that if they fail to give satisfactory service, they are liable to be dismissed without warning. This passage, however, does not tell us whether Ravina paid the gardener, or indeed whether the gardener requested payment. Had he done so, perhaps Rava would have awarded some payment in accordance with Rav's directive. In the first story, on the other hand, one is pretty certain that those porters would never be employed by Rabah again; presumbably they were day-workers, hence the question of their dismissal never arose.

This principle of acting (and ruling) beyond what the law formally requires is very basic in Jewish legal thought, and requires that law

---

67. Compare the *beraita* attributing this position to the arcangel Akatriel, in *B. Berachot* ibid. And see Shimon Federbush, *Ha-Musar ve-ha-Mishpat be-Yisrael,* Jerusalem, 1979, pp. 67–68, 72.

(*din*) be tempered with *hesed* (charity and benevolence). See, for example, the well-known story of R. Haninah ben Dosa and his wife in
B. *Ta'anit* 25a.[68]

The story appears at the end of a series – a *catena* – of tales describing
the piety and poverty of R. Haninah ben Dosa and his wife. They
both lived in penury, and were miracle workers, but for others rather
than themselves. One of the stories tells how he had goats, which the
neighbors claimed were doing them damage. He replied that if this was
the case, then bears would devour them by night. But, if the claim was
untrue, they would carry the bears on their horns by nightfall. And so it
was that by nightfall the bears appeared borne on the horns of the goats.
There then follows another tale about how he helped a neighbor who
had planned building his house, but mistakenly had ordered roof beams
that were too short. R. Haninah ben Dosa miraculously lengthened the
beams so that they protruded a cubit on either side, and Pelimo asserts
that he saw this building.

The Talmud then asks: How come R. Haninah ben Dosa had goats?
Surely he was extremely poor, and, furthermore, one was not permitted
to have goats in Palestine (*B. Baba Kama* 79b). The reply, in the name
of Rav Pinhas, is as follows:

> It once happened that someone passed by the entrance to R. Haninah's
> house, and left there some chickens [two, according to a manuscript that
> Malter found]. His wife found them, and brought them in. R. Haninah
> told her not to eat the eggs, and they hatched, and soon there were
> many chickens, which troubled the couple. So they sold them and with
> the proceeds bought goats. Some time later the original owner of the
> chickens was passing by with a friend, and remarked to him that it was
> here that he had left his chickens. R. Haninah heard him, called him in
> and asked him if those chickens had any sign to identify them as his.
> He replied, yes, and gave the signs, and R. Haninah gave him the goats.
> And these are the goats, says the Talmud, which bore the bears on their

---

68. In point of fact it is not found in most manuscripts, nor in early testimonies, such as *Ein Yaakov, Menorat ha-Maor,* etc., and was declared both by scholars
(*Dikdukei Soferim* ad loc. and Malter's edition of *Ta'anit, The Treatise Ta'anit of the
Babylonian, Talmud,* New York, 1930, p. 112, note to line 10), as well as classical
commentaries (Maharsha) to be a late addition.

horns. [This latter statement is in Aramaic, whereas the story, unlike the other ones in the series, is in Hebrew.]

We have already noted that R. Haninah ben Dosa was extremely poor. Indeed, the Talmud, *Ta'anit* 24b, relates in the name of Rav Yehudah in the name of Rav (Babylonian *amora*, mid-3rd century C.E.) that each day a voice (*bat kol*) came forth from heaven declaring: "The whole world is nourished by the merit of Haninah my son, and for Haninah my son it suffices that he has a *kav* of carobs from Sabbath eve to Sabbath eve." Yet despite his poverty he took upon himself to look after what he found, until its owner was identified.

Now according to *B. Baba Metzia* 28b, and thence to Rambam, *Hilchot Gezeilah ve-Aveidah* 13:15, and *Shulhan Aruch, Hoshen Mishpat* 267:26, chickens found should be publicly announced for several months (perhaps twelve), the eggs sold, and the proceeds used to cover the expenses involved in feeding them, etc. If, in the end, the income is greater than the outlay, the profit is shared equally by the finder and owner. Sales are carried out in the presence of a *beit din*. However, none of these procedures were carried out by R. Haninah. He did not sell the eggs to cover his expenses, but fed the chickens at his own expense, despite his extreme penury. Only when the number of chickens became too troublesome did he sell them – it is not mentioned whether this was before a *beit din*, or not – and bought goats with the proceeds. He then continued to feed and look after the goats, which obviously required more food and were worth much more than (two) chickens, until the owner was identified. He then gave him the goats, not requesting any payment for his work and monetary outlay, and not requesting an equal share in the increased value of the find. All in all, the message of the tale is that he went far beyond the letter of the law in the mitzvah of returning a lost object (השבת אבידה). This, of course, is an extreme example of לפנים משורת הדין, in the case of a mitzvah between a person and his neighbor.[69]

---

69. See my discussion in my *On the Relationship of Mitzvot between Man and his Neighbor and Man and His Maker*, Jerusalem and New York, 2014, pp. 20–21. Here we may add a reference to *B. Baba Metzia* 24b, where we read that Shmuel's father found some asses in the wilderness and returned them to their owner after twelve months, and the Talmud adds that this was "beyond the letter of the law." See the continuing discussion there.

Incidentally, this tale does not answer the Talmud's question on how R. Haninah had goats, when they were not permitted in Eretz Yisrael. The later commentaries make various suggestions in this regard, but they are all somewhat forced. Indeed, this is one of the arguments that the Maharsha brings to prove that this is a late addition.

This tale was very popular, and appeared in numerous folkloristic collections, such as *Sefer ha-Maasiyyot*, and is frequently related in kindergartens. A similar tale is told of the very pious R. Pinhas ben Yair in *Y. Demai* 1:3. There we read how:

> Two poor people deposited two *seahs* (bushels) of barley with R. Pinhas ben Yair. He sowed them and afterwards reaped them. Later on they came back to reclaim their barley. He said to them, "Bring camels and donkeys to transport your barley."

Indeed, there are many similarities between these two personalities.

This story falls into much the same category as that which we read in *B. Baba Metzia* 24b:

> Rav Yehudah was walking along with Shmuel in the grain market. He asked him, "What should one do if one finds here a purse?" He replied, "It belongs to him." "And if a Jew comes along and [claims it as his] giving a sign [identifying it] – what then?" "He must return it." "Surely these two rulings contradict one another (*tartei*)!" "Beyond the letter of the Law," he replied. Just as Shmuel's father found some donkeys in the desert and reclaimed them to their owners after twelve months (even though by then he did not need to return them according to the strict Letter of the Law; but he did so *li-fnim mi-shurat ha-din*).[70]

Incidentally, we can learn of the halachic character of Shmuel's father from the following incident found in *B. Ketubot* 23a. There we learn of Jewish women who had been taken captive and came to Nehardea with their captors. Shmuel struggled with the question of their marriageabil-

---

70. See Higger, ibid., *supra* p. 101, as to whether returning a lost object after the owners' have given up hope of its return – *yiush* – is obligatory or just good advice, and whether the courts can force the return or not. See Rambam, *Hilchot Gezeilah* 11:7, *Shulhan Aruch, Hoshen Mishpat* 259:5, 7; Mordechai to *Baba Metzia* ibid.; *Hagahot Maimoniyot* to Rambam ibid., etc.

ity, concerned that they might have been defiled by their captors before coming before him. Shmuel's father rebuked him for his concern, saying, "were they your daughters would you demean them in this way?"

R. Benjamin Lau, in his article "the Challenge of Halakhic Innovation," *Meorot* 8, 2010, p. 54 (first published in Hebrew, in *Akdamot* 23, 2009), writes:

> Those words should resonate inside the head of every decisor as he considers every question that comes before him: "If she were your daughter . . ." Everyone knows that a parent will make every effort to help his child, overturning the world if need be.

He then continues as follows:

> The *Gemara* (*Shabbat* 55a) tells of a woman who came to Samuel in distress. He disregarded her, and his student, Rabbi Judah, questioned his doing so. Samuel replied that the responsibility was not his but that of the Exilarch. That would appear to end the story, but another passage (*Bava Batra* 10b) cites a tradition about the son of Rabbi Joshua ben Levi (the first generation of *Amora'im*), who fell ill, died, and returned to life. His father asked him what he had seen while dead, and the son replied "I saw a world turned upside down, the exalted below and the lowly elevated." Tosafot ad loc. says that the *Ge'onim* had an oral tradition, passed from rabbi to rabbi, "that in the upside-down world he had seen Samuel seated [as a student] before Rabbi Judah his student, who had protested Samuel's conduct." One need not agree with a plea, but one may not close his ears to it.

Perhaps Shmuel was less hesitant in matters of ownership, or perhaps he subsequently learned something from his father's reprimand.

Perhaps we may support such a contention from the fact that in *B. Gittin* 37b that same Shmuel is called *Avi ha-Yetomim*, the "father of orphans." And in *B. Baba Metzia* 70a he permitted orphans to loan out money receiving interest on the loan, despite the fact that usury is considered a very serious sin of biblical status (see Leviticus 25:36, Deuteronomy 23:20, etc.). Likewise, in *Gittin* ibid. he did not require a *prozbol* from orphans (i.e., enabling them to claim back their loans from debtors even after the Sabbatical year.) He also empowered women in distress, ruling that "One who says, 'I will not feed nor support [my wife],' one forces him to feed [her]" (*B. Ketubot* 77a), and in a similar vein, a daughter supported by her brothers is entitled to her own earnings (*maaseh yadehah shelah*, ibid. 43b). He also kept a sharp eye on business activities, and was willing to act vigorously to maintain norms of economic rectitude. He took pains to make sure prices did not unfairly soar (*B. Baba Batra* 90b). After the Passover, when there was a great demand for new earthenware utensils and the price of such pots became impossibly high, he forced the prices down by declaring he would permit the use of the old pots (which had been used for *hametz* before the Passover and normally would no longer be used after the Passover, *B. Pesahim* 30a). In this he was, indeed, following in the directions already pioneered by Rabban Shimon ben Gamliel in *M. Keritot* 1:7. (See below section entitled "Sensitivity to the 'Have-Nots'".) In a like manner, when the price of *hadasim* (myrtle branches, used as part of the four species on *Sukkot*) was raised unreasonably by the vendors, he permitted using them with broken tops (*ketumim, B. Sukkah* 34b; and see above note 10, on how the Rabbi of Sombar brought down the price of *schach*). He also established what he believed to be the maximum profit permitted – one sixth – which became the halachic norm (*B. Baba Batra* 90a). We see, then, a whole range of areas of legislation which reveal his sensitivity to the needs of the poor.

Returning to the subject of *lifnim mi-shurat ha-din*, we may also learn this message from the tale told of R. Hiyya, an expert money-changer, who declared a certain coin valid. Later, when that certain coin was proven to be invalid, he reimbursed the owner of the coin, or actually exchanged it for a full-value coin, even though strictly according to the law he did not have to, being an expert. Nonetheless, he did so *li-fnim mi-shurat ha-din* (*B. Baba Kama* 99b).

A variant version of this tale is to be found in *Deuteronomy Rabba* 3:3. It reads as follows:

> It happened that R. Pinhas ben Yair was living in a city in the South when people came to do business there and they had in their possession two bushels of barley which they deposited with him. But they forgot about them and went away. R. Pinhas ben Yair planted them every year, harvested their yield. Seven years later those same businessmen came

back to claim, forthwith their two bushels. R. Pinhas ben Yair recognized them, and said to them, "Come and take your treasures," (i.e., the huge crop) . . .

And futher on in that section we are told that:

> R. Shimon ben Shetach borrowed an ass from an Ishmaelite. His disciples found a precious stone tied around the ass's neck. They said to him, "Rabbi, 'The blessing of the Lord, it maketh rich' (Proverbs 10:22)." He replied to them, "I took an ass from him; a precious stone I did not take," and he went and returned it to the Ishmaelite. And that Ishmaelite then said of him, "Blessed be God of Shimon ben Shetach."

Cf. Y. *Baba Metzia* 2:5 for a further version of this tale. There we are introduced to Aba Oshaiah of Turia and also R. Shmuel ben Sosartai who was a laundry-man and who found some jewelry on the banks of the river where he did his washing. He did not want to return them to the princess who had lost them, (cf. Y. *Baba Kama* 10:11), but Aba Oshaiah of Turia insisted on returning them. (See further on these passages, Y. Tamar, A*lei Tamar, Nezikin*, Givataim, 1982, pp. 27–28, and also ibid., p. 23.)

Perhaps the most remarkable example of acting in accordance with this principle is to be found in B. *Baba Metzia* 30b:

> R. Yishmael ben Yossi was walking along a road when he met up with someone who was carrying a bundle of sticks. He paused to rest, and asked R. Yishmael to help him [carry the load]. He asked him, "How much are they worth?" "Half a *zuz*," [i.e., he bought the sticks from him] and declared them ownerless (*hefker* – i.e., so that he would not have to carry them). The fellow immediately took possession of the bundle. R. Yishmael again gave him half a *zuz* and declared [the bundle] ownerless, and the fellow again took possession of it. R. Yishmael saw that he would repeat this process, so he said to him, "I declare it ownerless to the whole world excepting you."

The Talmud then asks:

> But surely R. Yishmael ben Yossi was an old man and it was not in accor-

dance with his dignity [to carry such a burden, i.e., he was halachically exempt from doing so (*zaken ve-aino le-fi chevodo*)].

The answer given is:

R. Yishmael ben Yossi [acted] beyond the letter of the law (*lifnim mi-shurat ha-din*) as Rav Yosef taught, (relating to the verse in Exodus 18:20): "which they should do" – that is *lifnim mi-shurat ha-din*.[71]

Similarly, the rabbis established that one can be obligated not to behave in a manner that is termed "*Middat S'dom*" (*Ketubot* 103a – a behavior that is not technically illegal but is characteristic of the people of S'dom).[72] For example, if brothers are dividing an inherited field in which each has a portion, and one says "Give me my portion on the side that it adjacent to another field that belongs to me so that it create one big field," we obligate the brothers to do so because not doing so would constitute *Middat S'dom*. Thus, we obligate the brothers to go beyond what would be required by the simple law and to behave according to a higher ethical standard.

Adaptability of Halachah to Changing Circumstances

It is clear that what may appear to be laws carved in stone can actually be modified with the changes that take place in society. As societal norms and practices evolve and undergo alteration, so too, the law has to adjust itself to the new cirumstances. An obvious example of this is in the variety of rules relating to feminine modesty (*tzniut*).

---

71. See my *Netivot Pesikah*, Jerusalem, 2008, p. 185, note 270; and on this principle in general see bibliographic references in Nahum Rakover, *Otzar ha-Mishpat: Mafteah Bibliografi la-Mishpat ha-Ivri* (*A Bibliography of Jewish Law*), vol. 1, Jerusalem, 1975, p. 35, nos. 893–899.

72. On this principle, see the article of Shmuel Shilo, "'*Kofin al Midat S'dom*': Jewish Law's Concept of Abuse of Rights," *Israel Law Review* 15(1) (1980), pp. 49–78. We should also note the Ramban's famous passage in his commentary to Leviticus 19:2 (cited above p. 99 note 64), on the issue of *naval bi-reshut ha-Torah*, how a person could be disgraceful and obscene without actually transgressing any explicit commandments. The biblical directive (ibid.) to be "Ye shall be holy: for I the Lord your God are holy" comes, as it were, to close this legal loophole, and prohibit any such behaviour. And see Rones, *supra* p. 100 note 65.

Thus, at times our classical halachic sources give us a ruling that seems totally impractical in contemporary terms, and it is instructive to see how the rabbis deal with such a situation. A case in point is that of a man walking behind a woman. In the Babylonian Talmud *Berachot* 61a, we read in a *beraita*:

> A man should not walk on a pathway behind a woman, even his wife. And if he meets up [with a woman] on a bridge, he should push her to the side. And whoever walks behind a woman by the riverside has no place in the World to Come.

This ruling is cited by the Rambam in *Hilchot Issurei Biah* 21:22 in the following formulation:

> He who comes upon a woman in the marketplace is forbidden to walk behind her, but pushes her to the side or behind him. And whoever walks behind a woman in the marketplace is of the simplest, of the ignorant (*mikalei amei ha-aretz*).

Perhaps this formulation is a little less strident than that of the Talmud in that it does not explicitly deny the transgressor a place in the World to Come. However, in present-day terms, it is still rather severe, to say the least. And Rambam's formulation is quoted verbatim by R. Yosef Karo in his *Shulhan Aruch, Even ha'ezer* 21:1.

Now this might have been deemed acceptable behavior in the time of the *baraita* (2nd century C.E.), when women generally kept to themselves within their homes, the marketplace was populated mostly by men, and it would not be considered proper for a man to come down to the riverside while the womenfolk were doing their washing. However, in our days, with our crowded sidewalks and bustling throngs, and our totally different attitude to women and modesty, such rulings are wholly unacceptable.

Practically speaking, how would men deal with such a situation, for example, when standing in a line waiting for a bus or at the checkout counter at the supermarket? Would they push the woman in front of them aside, or shove themselves forward to get in front of her? Obviously not.

This problem was already recognized in the medieval period. Thus, the author of the *Leket Yosher*, R. Jacob ben Moshe (ed. Freimann,

Berlin, 1903, *Yoreh De'ah* 37), cited his master, R. Israel Isserlein (1390–1460, author of the famous *Terumat ha-Deshen* and of the school of R. Meir of Rothenberg), saying:

> It is permitted to walk behind a friend's wife or his mother. For nowadays, we are not all that prohibited from walking behind a woman.

So, in Weiner-Neustadt, where R. Isserlein lived much of his life, apparently the men did not adhere strictly to the Talmudic-Maimonidean ruling.

How did this great authority partially reject, or at least greatly modify, the Talmudic ruling? R. Yehuda Henkin, in an important article in *Tradition* (34/3), 2000, entitled *"Ikka d'Amrei* Others Say: The Significance of Habituation in Halakha", discusses this issue as follows:

> What is the meaning of "nowadays we are not all that prohibited . . ."? It means that although the Talmud forbade men from walking behind women, lest it cause *hirhur* (sexual arousal), nowadays women go everywhere and we are used to walking in the back of them, so no *hirhur* results.

R. Henkin then refers to a responsum of the great contemporary authority, R. Eliezer Waldenberg (in his *Tzitz Eliezer*, vol. 9, no. 50:3, p. 195), who writes:

> We may further say that the intention of the *Terumat Hadeshen* was as follows. For our days are different from those of olden times. For in olden times a woman was not wont to walk about the streets, but would sit in the confines of her home, in accordance with the words of the Rambam (*Hilchot Ishut,* 13:11), namely that it is only seemly for a woman to dwell in the corner of her house, as it is written, "the King's daughter is all glorious within" (Psalms 45:14). And so ruled the Rema in *Even ha'Ezer* 73:1, that a woman should not accustom herself to going out [of her house] much. . . . And then on meeting her, walking after her in the street will most likely lead to *hirhur*. But this is not the case nowadays; the situation is different. For women do not confine themselves to their home as they did in olden times, and it is most usual to see them in the streets. . . . So nowadays, there is little likelihood of *hirhur* when

walking behind her. . . . And it is for this reason the *Terumat Hadeshen* was lenient, at any rate in the case of a friend's wife or his mother.

If this was true in 15th century Austria, how much more so in the 21st century, when walking along Broadway, Dizengoff, or Rechov Yafo! Rabbi Henkin put forward a theory of habituation, bringing several examples to exemplify his argument. Briefly stated, he reasons that:

> When men are accustomed to seeing women constantly, as in present-day society, many halachic stringencies designed to curb male *hirhur* (erotic thoughts) do not apply, for when men are habituated to women, *hirhur* concerns are no longer an issue.

Interestingly enough, R. Joseph Messas of Meknes, Morocco, wrote a responsum in 1954 (*Otzar Michtavim*, vol. 3, p. 211, no. 1884) dealing with the question of women's head covering, and most remarkably he writes as follows:

> The covering of a woman's hair is only a custom because in antiquity it was thought to be modest, and not to do so was regarded as immodest and licentious. But nowadays that the consensus is that there is no immodesty in uncovered hair . . . the prohibition is no longer effective. . . . And just as for unmarried women it was permitted, for there is no erotic thought (*hirhur*) in what one is accustomed to see, so too for married women nowadays. And each man can judge for himself that he sees thousands of women every day with uncovered hair and he pays no attention to them and has no licentious thoughts because of this uncovered hair.

(However, see the critical article of Michael Avraham and Rinat Ankri, *Hiddusho shel ha-Rav Yosef Messas le-Gabei Hisui Saar Rosh ha-Ishah,*" in *Derishah* 1, 2016, pp. 54–84.)

We see then that this concept of habituation, which both R. Henkin and R. Messas put forward, may serve as a key to solving untenable halachic situations presented by contemporary society. We must, however, bear in mind R. Henkin's own important caveat: "certainly the principle of habituation has the potential of being abused and misused by the irresponsible" (ibid., p. 49). Nevertheless, careful and judicious application of this principle may ease some of our potentially discomforting situations that face contemporary society.

R. Henkin further expanded on this theme in his *Understanding Tzniut: Modern Controversies in the Jewish Community*, Jerusalem and New York, 2008, in a chapter entitled "The Significant Role of Habituation in Halachah" (pp. 73–84). R. Emanuel Feldman had vigorously contested Henkin's thesis in *Tradition* ibid. p. 49–57, in a response entitled "Habituation of Halakhic Void with Risky Implications," and R. Henkin replied in his *Understanding Tzniut* very convincingly, to my mind, in a chapter entitled "On the (Alleged) Hazards of Habituation" (pp. 85–91; and see what I wrote in *JOFA Journal* 6/4, 5767).

Incidentally, since we mentioned 15th century Austria, we may call attention to Shlomo Eidelberg, *Jewish Life in Austria in the 15th Century*, Philadelphia, 1962, p. 84 where he writes as follows:

> Despite their opposition [to gambling and card-playing] the rabbis were forced to tolerate gaming, and turned their efforts to restraining it in various ways. This is evidenced by their admonition against playing cards in the period between Rosh Hashana and Yom Kippur, (*Leket Yosher* 11, p. 118).

Here too, we see how these authorities came to grip with the new reality presented by their times.

Much the same argument can be used with regard the principle of *Kol be-ishah ervah*, (*B. Berachot* 21a), namely that one may not listen to a woman singing. This prohibition comes together with the prohibitions against seeing a woman's hair or her calf. The Raviah (vol.1, *Berachot* 76, ed. A. Aptovitzer, 2nd edition, Jerusalem, 1964, p. 52) writes that "all these prohibitions concerning *ervah* are limited to those parts of the body that are not usually open to display. But, [for example], an unmarried girl who regularly goes with uncovered hair – concerning her we do not suspect [that it be inciteful of] erotic thoughts (*hirhur*), and so too concerning her voice." This view was accepted by the *Beit Yosef* (*Orah Hayyim* 75), quoting *Hagahot Maimoniyot*. So too ruled the Rema (ibid., 75:3), further expounded by the *Mishnah Berurah* (ibid., note 18), that "since one is accustomed to this, (i.e., hearing female voices), this will not lead to *hirhur*, even from a married woman ..." So this principle of habituation, i.e., being accustomed to something, has been readily applied to these various Talmudic prohibitions, leading to an acceptable way of circumventing them.[73]

Similarly such an argument can be applied – and indeed has been applied – to the question as to whether one may walk between two women (*B. Horayot* 13b, *B. Pesahim* 111a). The stringent position is set out by R. Yosef Hayyim Masud Abuhatzeira, in his Kuntres *Be-Hukotav Teleichu*, Afulah, 2012, and indeed the Hazon Ish took just such a position. (See Y.Y. Lerner, *Shmirat ha-Guf ve-ha-Nefesh*, vol. 1, Jerusalem, 1988, no. 111: 1–2, p. 328–331, especially note 3). However, R. Yosef Hayyim of Bagdhad, in his *Ben Yeho'yada* (to *Pesahim* III, Jerusalem 1898–1904) wrote that these prohibitions "were only stated in times of antiquity when evil harmful spirits were commonly to be found, . . . but nowadays . . . their powers have been weakened . . ." This is a sort of kabbalistic solution, whereas the argument from habituation is a more rational one.[74]

Similarly, we may call attention to the view of the *Levush* (*Orah Hayyim, Minhagim* 3b), that even though in *Sefer Hassidim* we are told that anywhere that men and women are seated together and see one another, one may not make the blessing (at *Sheva Berachot*) "that joyfulness be in his abode" (*she-ha-simchah bi-Meono*), because there is no joy before God when there are erotic thoughts. Nonetheless, nowadays we do not take care in this matter, because nowadays women are frequently accustomed to be among men, and [therefore] they do not incite erotic-thoughts. This view of the Levush is frequently cited among the *Aharonim*. For example, the Hida in his responsa *Yosef Ometz*, no. 47, and a host of other sources cited by R. Ovadiah Yosef in his *Yabia Omer*, vol. 6, 2nd edition, Jerusalem, 1986, *Orah Hayyim* no.13:5, pp. 43–44, summarizes, concerning other related issues, that:

> Since the reason is because erotic thoughts, wherever the case may be, is no longer applicable, because the women walk abroad so much, the prohibition is annulled, and it ceases to be a matter of concern.

---

73. See Henkin, ibid., pp. 11–28, 51–66 for detailed analysis of these issues. There is considerable literature on this subject. And for a completely opposite approach, see R. Pesach Eliyahu Falk, *Modesty: An Adornment for Life*, Gateshead, England, 1998; and see Henkin's responses in his *Shut Bnei Banim*, vol. 3, Jerusalem, 1998, pp. 86–96.

74. See further Lerner ibid., pp. 332–334, for additional "traditional" solutions to the dilemma.

And even though conversing with a woman was not considered an act of modesty (see *M. Avot* 1:5, *B. Eruvin* 53b), the author of *Derech Pikudecha*, Lvov, 1851, R. Tzvi Elimelech Shapiro, wrote (*Lo Taaseh* 35), that

> Since we are used to having women among us, there are no erotic thoughts; ... only during those days when women were not outside ... seeing and conversing with a woman might lead to erotic thoughts, but nowadays that women are involved in business ... people are no longer aroused at seeing them or conversing with them, and such activities do not lead to erotic thoughts.[75]

And for yet another example of such a change in halachic perspective due apparently to sociological development, we can call attention to the fact that R. Yohanan, in Talmudic times (mid 3rd century C.E.) greatly discouraged the marriage of the daughter of a *Kohen* to a *Yisrael*, and that of a *talmid hacham* to an ingroramus – *am ha-aretz* (*B. Pesahim* 49b). Indeed, the Tur, *Even ha-Ezer* 2, adds the frightening statement that "such a marriage will not work out, and either he or she will die quickly, or some form of misfortune will beset them." In the *Shulhan Aruch, Even ha-Ezer* 2:8, the ruling is that an ignoramus should not marry the daughter of a *Kohen*. (This ruling is also cited by the *Magen Avraham* to *Orah Hayyim* 415:1, where however, it is said that such a marriage is not a mitzvah, rather than *lo tisa kohenet* – he *shall not* marry the daughter of a *Kohen*.) Thus what was once a cautionary discouragement became an absolute prohibition. (See, for example, R. Yehoshua Arditi, *Hina ve-Hisda*, vol. 2, Izmir, 1864–1877, to *Ketubot*, 238a.)

However, R. Yair Bachrach, in his *Havat Yair* no.70, (in a long discussion on the concept of *seudat mitzvah*) states clearly that "In our day we do not apply the law of the *am ha-aretz* ... as mentioned in *B. Pesahim* 49b." His position was brought in the *Pithei Teshuvah* to *Even ha-Ezer* ibid. note 9, and so too in the *Mishnah Berurah* to *Orah Hayyim* 415:2, (and see his *Shaar ha-Tziyyun* no.6). So too R. Shlomo Kluger, in his *Tuv Taam ve-Daat Tlitaa*, vol. 1, Zitomir, 1884, no. 263, ad fin., follows the *Havat Yair*, while R. Yekutiel Yehuda Teitelbaum, in

---

75. See also above p. 40, on issues of *yihud*.

his *Avnei Tzedek* to *Even ha-Ezer* 5, (Lvov, 1885–1886) states explicitly that "in our lands there are no *amei ha-aretz* and no certain *Kohanim*," and consequently this prohibition is not relevant.[76] Indeed, already the Rivash, R. Yitzhak ben Sheshet (1326–1407), in his response, no. 15 (ed. D. Metzger, vol. 1, Jerusalem, 1993, p. 20, col. 2) wrote that the courts do not object to such marriages.[77] So here again, societal changes, and perhaps the spread of elementary education, have brought about a different understanding of the status of the *am ha-aretz* with the attendant halachic implications, such as in relation to the laws of evidence, etc.[78]

This general concept of change in halachah because of changes in time is also clearly formulated in *Shulhan Aruch, Yoreh Deah*, 148:12:

> There are those who say that all these things (cited above) only applied in their days (i.e., those of the Talmud), but nowadays they are not idolators and hence one may do business with them on their holy days and give them loans etc.

However, here we touch upon a very complex issue which we cannot deal with in this context.[79]

Finally, we should recall the famous sugya in *B. Berachot* 28a, where we read how Yehudah the Ammonite convert came to the *beit midrash* of Rabban Gamliel and asked whether he could marry a Jewish woman. Rabban Gamliel replied that he may not, basing himself on the biblical verse in Deuteronomy 23:4, which states explicitly that "An Ammonite or Moabite shall not enter into the congregation of the Lord; even unto

---

76. See further Yosef Yitzhak Lerner, *Shemirat ha-Guf ve-ha-Nefesh*, vol. 2, Jerusalem, 1988, sect. 164, pp. 478–480.

77. See further R. Ovadiah Yosef, *Meor Yisrael*, vol. 3, Jerusalem, 2005, to Eruvim, chapter 6, p. 172, and in his *Yabia Omer*, vol.3, 2nd edition, Jerusalem, 1986, *Yoreh Deah* 7:3, pp. 133–134, following the view of the *Havat Yair*, and R. Shlomo Kluger, etc.

78. On the nature of the *am ha-aretz* in the Talmud, see A. Büchler's classic study, *Der galidäische Am ha'ares der zeveiteh Jahrhuderth*, Vienna 1906; and also N.S. Greenspan, *Mishpat Am ha-Aretz be-Sifrut ha-Halachah shel Kol ha-Tekufot*, Jerusalem, 1946. See also below Appendix 1.

79. Additional examples may be found in Neria Gotel's, *Hishtanut ha-Tevaim ba-Halachah*, Jerusalem, 1995, pp. 106–117, 121–122 (e.g., R. Shlomo Luria, *Yam shel Shlomo, Baba Kama* chapter 5, sect.7, R. Moshe Feinstein, *Igrot Moshe, Yoreh Deah*, vol. 3, no. 47:2), 229, etc.

the tenth generation shall they not enter into the congregation of the Lord for ever." R. Yehushua, on the other hand, permitted it, disagreeing with Rabban Gamliel, and arguing that Ammon and Moab no longer dwell in their former habitation because Sennacherib scattered them among the nations (see Isaiah 10:13), so that we can no longer be certain that he was indeed an Ammonite. The halachah is in accordance with the opinion of R. Yehushua, (see *Shulhan Aruch, Even ha-Ezer* 4:3). We see, then, that historical events, such as the dispersal and redistribution of populations as an outcome of war etc., can bring about a change in practical halachic decision-making, even if it might be contrary to biblical law.

One could greatly expand on this theme, but let the above random examples suffice to highlight how changes in norms of behaviour necessitate reevaluation of time-venerated rules, which may at times clash with contemporary ethical standards, and cause meaningless stress and discomfort, and even distance people from respecting the halachah.

The common denominator in all of these examples is that changing circumstances bring about changes in the law. Furthermore the simple law is not necessarily the determining factor, but on occasions it is rather a standard that goes beyond it, a fundamental ethical value of kindness and pleasantness that overrides the legal requirement. In the words of the *Maggid Mishnah* on Maimonides, *Mishneh Torah, Hilkhot Shecheinim* 14:5

> Behold the Torah stated: "And you shall do that which is right and good" (Deuteronomy 6:18), meaning that you should conduct yourself in a good and just manner toward other people. And it would not have been appropriate to give details in this regard because the commandments of the Torah are for all times and circumstances which necessitate doing so, and a person's traits and behavior change in accordance with the time.[80]

This teaches that specific halachot may change in their relation to time and place, but must always be in accordance with these fundamental values, such as "And you shall do that which is right and good." As such, the *posek* should not see himself bound and forced to rule in accordance with a firm, set order of absolute laws, for he would then

---

80. Cf. what was quoted above p. 20.

be considered among those who destroy the world. The reference is to those who decide points of law from their teachings (*Sotah* 22a).[81]

---

81. See the important article of Pinhas Shifman, "*Ish ha-Halachah Nidon le-Herut*" in Zev Safrai and Avi Sagi (eds.), *Bein Samchut le-Autonomiah be-Masorat Yisrael*, Tel Aviv, 1997, pp. 243–251.

See, e.g., responsa of Rema, no. 19, ed. A. Ziv, Jerusalem, 1971, p. 128.

There are, of course, all too many examples of how the halachah changes according to circumstances. Thus, for example, the *Mishnah* in *Terumot* 8:4 rules that:

Three liquids become forbidden through being uncovered: water, wine and milk. . . . How long must they have remained [uncovered] to become forbidden? Such time as it could take a serpent to come forth from a place near by and drink.

The Rambam in *Hilchot Rotzeah* 11:11 expands this ruling, stating that:

All liquids that were uncovered, whether by day or night, are forbidden, even if a person slept next to them, because the creeping creatures fear not sleeping person.

This ruling is followed by the *Tur Yoreh Deah* 116, who explains that the rabbis forbade things which they regarded as dangerous, such as uncovered liquids, for they feared that a snake put its poison in them. But, adds the Tur, "nowadays it is the custom to be lenient in this matter, even if it is certain that the liquids remained uncovered, because such poisonous creatures are not to be found now." He continues to explain why the rabbis' ruling can be annulled, arguing that the original enactment was instituted because of the fear of snake-poison, and since now there are no longer such snakes around, the enactment no longer applies. This is how the *Shulhan Aruch* rules, (ibid. 116:1).

However, the *Pri Hadash* (ad loc.) comments that in the Magreb there are many places where snakes and scorpions are to be found, and in these places people are careful not to drink uncovered water. And in Jerusalem and its surroundings, even though snakes are not common, but there are some, people should take heed of this prohibition. And so too, R. Yosef Hayyim of Bagdhad (1833–1909), in his famous *Ben Ish Hai* (*Pinhas* sect.9) despite the lenient ruling of the *Shulhan Aruch*, nonetheless, cautions his community to take heed of this ruling; and so too does the Hungarian, Shlomo Ganzfried (1804–1886), in his highly popular *Kitzur Shulhan Aruch* 33:5.

And for further references to the rabbis of North Africa, who follow the original Talmudic ruling, see Moshe Suissa, *Ateret Avot*, vol. 3, Israel (no date, but c. 2013), p. 295, note 20; but R. Joseph Messas, in his *Otzar ha-Michtavim* no. 1884, vol. 3, Jerusalem, p. 211, clearly states that nowadays this decree no longer applies.

We see, then, that despite the fact that the rabbis instituted a prohibitional regulation (*gezerah*), when (and where) the reason for its enactment was no longer applicable, the prohibition was ignored or rejected with the consent of the rabbis. Indeed, there are many other such examples of halachic regulations enacted because of the fear of some sort of danger – *mi-shum sakanah* (or *mi-shum hashasha*) – that subsequently became regarded as irrelevant and fell into desuetude, again with the approbation of the rabbis. Or in the words of Schepansky ((*Ha-Takkanot be-Yisrael*, vol. 1, Jerusalem 1991, p. 865):

That which [the rabbis] forbade *mi-shum hashasha*, out of fear or apprehension (of some kind), even if they enacted it *be-minyan*, i.e., through the agency of a court of law (*beit din*), if that fear is now allayed, one does not require a court of law to permit it.

He then gives the example we have cited above, adding that nowadays we do not

This idea is expressed explicitly in the famous statement (*Baba Met-zia* 30b) that "Jerusalem was only destroyed because they ruled there

---

observe strictly the practice of *mayyim aharonim* (rinsing the hands at the end of the meal) required by the Talmud (*B. Hulin* 106a), because we no longer use *melech sedomit,* a kind of salt which, if left on one's hands and reaches one's eye, might blind them (*Tosafot Berachot* 53b). See below Appendix 3.

And see the additional example cited by Schepansky, ibid., p. 87, note 22, and *Entziklopedia Talmudit* vol. 26, Jerusalem, 2004, 669, on looking in a mirror.

We may bring yet another example. For in *B. Nidah* 17a we read:

Said R. Shimon bar Yohai: Five things there are which if one does them one en-dangers one's life (*mithayev be-nafsho*): he who eats peeled garlic, peeled onion, a peeled egg that passed a night, and who drinks water that was uncovered over night, and he who sleeps in a graveyard and pares his nails throws away the pairings into the public domain. . . .

However, *Hagahot Mordechai* to *Shabbat* chapter 8 shows that the reason we are not careful with peeled eggs is because we do not concern ourselves (*lo haishinan*) with evil spirits. (See R. Ovadiah Yosef, *Yabia Omer,* vol. 10, Jerusalem, 2004, *Orah Hayyim,* sect 9, p. 217, for numerous additional references; Neriah Moshe Gotel, *Hishtanut ha-Tevaim ba-Halachah,* Jerusalem, 1995; Yosef Yitzhak Lerner, *Shemirat ha-Goof ve-ha-Nefesh,* 2 vols., Jerusalem, 1988, etc.) R. Ovadiah (ibid.) even cites an opinion (of the *Terumat ha-Deshen,* no. 311) that perhaps the law of the *Katlanit* no longer applies, with the reasoning behind such a suggestion. (See below p. 155 note 107). This is a vast field which deserves a full-scale treatment of its own, and which we must leave to a different framework. See above section entitled "Dynamism in Halachah."

And returning to the peeled egg issue, I found an interesting comment in a note (48), in R. Shimon Gutman's *Minhagei ben Shalosh* (c. 2003), p. 47. After discussing this issue, he cites R. Meir Shapiro, in his approbation to *Shulhan Hai* (by R. Hayyim Yaakov Edelsberg, Lublin, 1933), who notes that the Rokeah by R. Eleazar of Ger-maiza [Worms] (*Hilchot-Shevuot* no. 296, ed. B.S. Shneursohn, Jerusalem, 1967) wrote that it was the custom on Shavuot to sit down with small children to learn (Torah). Afterwards, they would bring them a (hard-boiled) peeled egg with the egg-shell, and on it was written "And he said unto me: Son of Man [cause thy belly to eat; and fill thy bowels with this roll that I give thee, then did I eat it; and it was in my mouth honey for sweetness]" (Ezekiel 3:3). The rabbi would read each word and the child after him. However, since on Shavuot they had not written on the egg-shell, obviously he did so before the festival, and therefore the egg had been peeled overnight, and nonetheless they were not put off by the "peeled egg" dangers. Or perhaps, he added, the holy words protected him.

The verse in Ezekiel of course is relating to the practice of feeding the child with a cake baked with honey on which is written the verse in Isaiah 50:4–5: "The Lord God hath given me the tongue of the learned, that I should know how to speak a word in season to him that is weary: he wakeneth me morning by morning, he wakeneth mine ear to hear as the learned. The Lord God hath opened mine ear, and I was not rebellious, neither turned away back." (See Rokeah ibid.) Of course, they may have written the verse before Shavuot and only peeled it on Shavuot. Nonetheless, this is an interesting comment.

according to the laws of the Torah." This statement, which at first blush seems strange and irrational, was explained as follows in the Drishah on the Tur, *Hoshen Mishpat* 1:

> It appears to me that we should interpret this statement as meaning that their intent was that a legal ruling should be the absolute truth, meaning in accordance with the time and place in a manner that it be an absolute truth, precluding that one should always rule according to the literal letter of the law of the Torah. For there are times when the *dayan* (judge) must rule beyond the letter of the law in accordance with the time and the circumstances, and when he does not do so, it is not the absolute truth even though it is "true." On this point, the rabbis stated: "Jerusalem was only destroyed because they ruled there according to the laws of the Torah, and did not go beyond the letter of the law."[82]

Conflict Between Legal Formalism and Morality

The values under discussion come to expression most prominently in cases where there is conflict between what appears to be the correct formalistic ruling and what appears to be required by the standards of

---

82. It is interesting to note that Rabbi Hayyim Sofer used this saying to justify a stringency, stating that even if there are formalistic halachic means to refrain from imposing the status of one who publicly profanes the Sabbath on certain individuals, even if we know that they in fact profane the Sabbath, we should not stick to the formalistic halachic ruling, but should label them as transgressors from whom we should distance from the community and forbid their wine. See responsa R. Hayyim Sofer, *Mahaneh Hayyim* 2, Jerusalem, 1969, *Yoreh Deah* 1, who wrote: "Because they based their words on the Torah law in the generation of the destruction – asking if this person who profanes the Sabbath makes wine prohibited, if his ritual slaughtering is kosher, or if he can be counted as part of a quorum for prayer according to the law of the Torah – for that reason Jerusalem was destroyed." See the discussion in Avi Sagi and Tzvi Zohar, *Ma'agalei Zehut ha-Yehudit be-Sifrut ha-Hilchatit*, Tel Aviv, 2000, p. 194. On the other hand, see the rulings of Rabbi Joseph Messas, cited by Tzvi Zohar in *Peamim* 82, 2000, pp. 150–162, for his extreme leniency in such matters.

See also Rav Amital's position on non-observant Jews as articulated in his brief essay in *Alon Shvut* 13, Hannukah 1988, pp. 1–17. This too is a very broad subject to which we cannot do credit within the scope of this study. (See below note 170.)

We should further add to this discussion the category of *mi-pnei darchei shalom*. This is too broad a subject to be dealt with here. But see Shimon Federbush, *Ha-Musar ve-ha-Mishpat be-Yisrael*, Jerusalem 1979, pp. 129–130. Indeed, his whole book deals with the tension and conflict between legal formalism and morality.

human justice and religious morality. The classical example is that for the sake of *agunot* (women whose husbands are missing and cannot remarry) the rabbis were lenient. In order to relieve the *agunot* of their distress, the rabbis found leniencies. In this regard, Maimonides wrote (*Mishneh Torah, Hilchot Gerushin* 13:29):

> Do not wonder at the fact that our Sages discharged the prohibition [against a married woman], which is considered a very severe matter, on the basis of the testimony of a woman, a servant or a maidservant, statements made by a gentile in the course of conversation, a written statement or [testimony] that was not investigated by the ordinary process of interrogation, as we have explained. [These leniencies were instituted] because the Torah requires only testimony of two witnesses, and all the other details of the laws of witnesses with regard to matters that cannot be verified definitively except via witnesses and their testimony [. . .] but something that can be clarified without a witness . . . and a witness will not lie about it . . . for this reason our Sages were lenient in this matter – so that the daughters of Israel will not be forced to remain unmarried.

Although Maimonides found a halachic justification for this approach that "a witness will not lie about something that can be verified" (ibid.), it seems that his primary motivation was "so that the daughters of Israel will not be forced to remain unmarried."[83] We find that in other circum-

---

83. Despite the fact that we derive the standard case of *arayot* specifically from the cases of monetary affairs (*Shitah Mekubetzet* to *B. Baba Metzia* 60b), in the case of monetary matters witnesses are not required unless a financial claim is challenged and brought to court, whereas acts of marriage and divorce are ineffectual, if witnesses are not present. (See Daniel Mann, *A Glimpse at Greatness: A Study in the Works of Giants of Lomdus [Halachic Analysis]*, Jerusalem, pp. 102–103, in his discussion of the *Ketzot ha-Hoshen.*)

See Maharsha (R. Shmuel Eliezer ha-Levi Eidles) to *B. Yevamot* 121a:
And it says, "Great peace have they which love Thy Law" (Psalms 119:165) – that this is not an abrogation of the value of peace, that a woman be not left abandoned, and it says, "Her ways are the ways of pleasantness . . . (Proverbs 3:17), and it [Psalm 29] ends, "The Lord will give strength unto His people . . ." – meaning that this is not an abrogation of something biblical. For the Holy One blessed be He gave strength and power to His people, who are learned scholars, to act leniently in this matter, for "God will bless his people with peace" (ibid.), as it is said, "and all her paths are of peace" (Proverbs 3:17), and there can be no peace [for her] if she is abandoned.
This is somewhat contrary to the view of R. Yosef Dov Soloveitchik, as expressed in his *Divrei Hagut ve-Haarachah*, Jerusalem, 1982, pp. 77–78, who says that the

stances, the rabbis were afraid to take such a radical step – essentially changing all of the rules of testimony – as we see in *Gittin* 67a: "We are afraid lest she might bribe the witnesses" and *Yevamot* 111a: "That a woman not gaze at one and thus ruin her husband."[84]

Furthermore, despite the general principle that in halachah we follow the majority opinion, in order to find solutions for the *agunah* problem the rabbis were willing to base themselves as minority opinions. (See also Appendix 2.) Thus we find the great 16th century rabbi Avraham

---

rabbi rules in accordance with halachic principles divorced from his personal feelings of sympathy and compassion. See Avi Sagi, apud *Rabbanut: Ha-Etgar*, eds. Y. Stern, S. Friedman, vol. 2, Jerusalem, 2011, p. 710 and idem, *Yahadut, Bein Dat le-Musar*, Tel-Aviv, 1988, pp. 235–241. His studies raise a number of important issues which are beyond the scope of this study.

84. There is vast literature on the *agunah* problem. I shall only refer to Aviad ha-Cohen's *The Tears of the Oppressed: An Examination of the Agunah Problem's Background and Halakhic Sources*, Jersey City, N.J., 2004, which is a fine introduction to the issue. Note also my "Revisiting the Agunah Problem," in *JOFA Journal* VI/1, 2006, p. 20; and my "A Plea for the Chained Daughters of Israel: Comments on Aviad Cohen's '*Tears for the Oppressed*,'" *The Edah Journal* 5:1, 5765, pp. 1–4.

As to the issue of conflicts of values in law, to which we alluded to above, see R. Dworkin, "The Liberal Values Conflict" *The Legacy of Isaiah Berlin*, eds. M. Lilla, R. Dworkin, and R. Silvers, New York, 2001, pp. 73–90; and most recently R. Shmuel Lewis, *Ve-Lifnei Kavod Anavah* ('*And Before Honor-Humanity*'), Jerusalem, 2013, pp. 214–216.

Note that already almost two-hundred and fifty years ago the Mahari Yavetz, in his responsa *Sheilat Yavetz*, part 1, Altona 1738, sect. 32, noted that up to his time the number of responsa dealing with the *agunah* problem ran into tens of thousands.

We may bring yet another example of leniency with regard to the *agunah* problem. It is well known that the Sages forbid judges sititing in judgement on Shabbat, lest they be tempted to write out their judgements, (*B. Beitzah* 36b, Rashi ad loc. 37a). This prohibition was extended to forbid any sort of punishment and/or imprisonment carried out on Shabbat, despite the fact that no writing was required for such custom, on the part of the Rema (*Orah Hayyim* 339:4), basing himself on the *Shibolei ha-Leket*. The reason given is that there is a Torah prohibition not to exact punishment on Shabbat mentioned in *Y. Sanhedrin* 4:6, and followed by the Rambam (*Hilchot Shabbat* 23:14). However, is imprisonment a punishment or merely a means of holding on to the culprit until he can be justly punished? The *Magen Avraham* (ibid., sect. 3) rules that though encarceration is not considered a biblical punishment, and hence from the point of view of biblical law might be permitted on Shabbat, it is forbidden by rabbinic law. However, in the case of a husband who intends to desert his wife without giving her a *get*, the law permits him to be imprisoned on Shabbat, since this imprisonment is not intended as a punishment, but merely to prevent him from making his wife an *agunah*, (*Shaarei Teshuvah* ibid. sect. 3; and see *Meorot ha-Daf ha-Yomi* to *Beitzah* 35 – *Rosh ha-Shanah* 2, no. 780, Iyyar 5774, for further details).

ha-Levi, who lived in Egypt, in his response *Ginat Veradim, Even ha-Ezer*, part 3, sect. 20 (Jerusalem, 1951):

> If we were to examine the opinions of the sages of ancient times – in order to fulfill what they obligate us to do and as we do in all other areas of law – and follow the majority rule so that there would never be any challenges to our decisions, then there would never be freedom for the *agunah* from any rabbinic teacher. And it is our fault that there are terrible situations which result in the daughters of our father Abraham remaining grass widows with living husbands. And there is none to be gracious or kind to them, and they are left starving and thirsty and destitute. And we should also be concerned lest they follow paths of immorality: great poverty can lead one to such a path. Moreover, these women are young and virile (and will not be able to wait with restraint). Yet, if we want to follow the lenient decisions, the seriousness of the issue holds us back. Therefore, we have no alternative but to follow the path that was firmly established by our earliest rabbis – to follow the path of straight thinking even if it is against the consensus of the *gedolim* from whose waters we drink, as it is written in the Talmud, "It is sufficient to rely on (the minority opinion) of Rabbi X, even though it is not the accepted halachah." And it has already been stated at the end of Y. *Yevamot* 122a, "We allow a woman to marry on the authority of an echo," *i.e.*, that they were lenient with her because of her *iggun* (enchainment).

In a similar vain, we find friendly voices on the issue of the *mumzer* (an illegitimate child), who is stigmatized through no fault of his own. Indeed, the tragic and even unfair stigmatization of the *mumzer* was already recognized and openly admitted by the Sages of old. Thus, in *Leviticus Rabba* 32:8, ed. Margaliot, pp. 754–755, we read on the verse in Ecclesiastes 4:1 as follows:

> Hanina the tailor interpreted this verse as referring to *mumzerim*. "So I returned, and considered all the oppressed . . ." – these are the *mumzerim*. "And behold the tears of these oppressed" (ibid.) – the mothers of these committed a sin, and these wretched people are sent away. Their fathers had forbidden relations, but what did [the *mumzer* do], why should this matter to him? "But they have no comforter, and on the side of their oppressors there was power" (ibid.), – this refers to the Great Sanhedrin of Israel which comes upon them with the power of the Torah, and sends

them away. And [it does so] by force of the verse in Deuteronomy 23:3, "A *mumzer* shall not enter into the congregation of the Lord," "and they have no comforter" (Ecclesiastes ibid.). Said the Holy One blessed be He, "I have to comfort them. For in this world they have dross, but in the world to come . . . [they will be regarded as pure] . . ."[85]

So in this instance as well, the rabbis found unique ways to allow permissive circumstances. Let us see the degree to which the rabbis were prepared to push the limits in this effort. They established that "a woman whose husband had gone to a country beyond the sea and remained there for a full year of twelve months, if she gave birth within twelve months, the child is legitimate for we attribute it to the possibility that the baby remained in the mother's womb for twelve months" (*Yevamot*, 80b). After twelve months, the child would be considered illegitimate by most sources.[86]

A remarkable example of the practical application of this principle

---

85. This too is the view of R. Yose in *Leviticus Rabba* 32:7 ad fin.; see editor's notes ad loc.

86. See George M. Gould and Walter L. Pyle, *Anomalies and Curiosities of Medicine*, Philadelphia, 1896, pp. 68–72, on cases on protracted gestation.

Perhaps this is how we are to understand the story told of R. Hayyim Brisk, in Shimon Yosef Meler's *Uvdot ve-Hanhagot le-Beit Brisk*, vol. 1, Jerusalem, 1999, p. 62. He relates the following tale:

Once a woman came to R. Hayyim *zt"l*, and poured out before him her distress. She was pregnant, and she had nothing . . . she was desperately poor. . . . R. Hayyim turned to his wife the Rabbanit and asked, "Where is the women's committee? . . . Why does it not deal with this poor woman?"

R. Hayyim saw that the Rabbanit was in a state of consternation, and she was whispering to the daughters of the house. . . . R. Hayyim felt that there was something . . . and began to enquire closely [what was troubling them]. His wife told him, "The lady's husband left his house and has not returned for the last eleven months." "If so," said R. Hayyim, "this poor wretched woman has no one to care and take pity over her. How much more so that we are obligated to help her. . . . Let us prepare a room for her in our house for the next two weeks, and all her needs will be upon us. After that we shall give her a fixed sum every month for two years to enable her to look after the baby. And so it was; they looked after the woman in the house of R. Hayyim for the next two weeks . . . within which time she gave birth to a son, and R. Hayyim arranged his *brit* (circumcision) in his own house, and for two years the woman received a monthly sum to support her.

This story was brought to illustrate R. Hayyim's incredible concern for the welfare of all, and his remarkable degrees of charity. But perhaps we may assume that he also dealt with the halachic problem as to the status of the child, again in the spirit of charity and compassion, but on the basis of the above-mentioned halachic view.

is cited by Marc C. Angel, in his *Loving Truth and Peace: The Grand Religious Worldview of Rabbi Benzion Uziel*, Northvale, N.J., Jerusalem, 1999, pp. 111–112, which I quote fully:

> Rabbi Uziel's concern to mitigate the possibility of a child being declared a *mumzer* is demonstrated in a remarkable case. A married woman left her husband without having received a Jewish divorce, a *get*. In the eyes of Jewish law, therefore, she was still considered to be legally married to him. She then went to live with another man and had a baby ten months after having left her husband. The question arose: What is the status of the baby? The answer, of course, depends on who the father is. If the father is her husband, then the child is legitimate. If, however, the new partner is the father, then the child is a *mumzer*.
>
> A simple analysis of the case would lead one to conclude that the child, indeed, is illegitimate. After all, the woman herself admitted that the child had been born ten months after she had left her husband. And during those ten months, she had been living with her new partner, who presumably fathered the child.
>
> Yet, Rabbi Uziel found a way to declare the child to be legitimate. He drew on a halachic notion that pregnancies sometimes last longer than nine months – as long as twelve months (see the Rema on *Even ha-Ezer* 4:13). Thus, it can be argued that the child was actually fathered by the woman's husband before she had left him. Even though the woman had demonstrated immoral behavior by living with another man while still legally married to her husband, and even though she and her partner considers the child to be theirs, the halachah considers the child to belong to her husband – and the child is, consequently, not a *mumzer* (*Mishpetei Uziel, Even ha-Ezer*, Jerusalem, 5724, no. 12). Rabbi Uziel's halachic ingenuity freed this child from a lifelong stigma.[87]

And the author of *Halachot Gedolot* uniquely indicated that even if the child would be born after twelve months it would be considered legitimate, as we may assume that the father returned to his house secretly, unless he admits that he was not there with his wife. Furthermore, "if a woman gained a reputation as an adulteress and everyone is gossiping about her, we are not concerned that her children are illegitimate since

---

87. Cf. Shaarei Uziel, vol. 2, *Mishpetei Yatom ve-Almanah*, Jerusalem, 1991, p. 217.

the majority of the acts of cohabitation are ascribed to the husband" (*Sotah* 27a). Similarly, "even if she claims that her fetus is not from her husband, she is not to be believed to stigmatize him" (*Yevamot* 47a). So too, for an illegitimate child to be excluded from the community, it must be certain that it is illegitimate, for "a questionably illegitimate child may come [into the community]" (*Kiddushin* 77a).[88] The rab-

---

88. Once again we will call attention to Rav Uziel's saying, as cited by Angel, ibid., pp. 109–111:

A complex halachic problem arose when a married woman had intimate relations with a man other than her husband and then became pregnant and gave birth. Who was the baby's father? If it was the woman's husband, then the child was halachically legitimate. But it if was the other man, then the child was the result of an adulterous affair and was deemed a *mumzer*, an illegitimate child. This is a terrible stigma for the child, and Jewish law forbids a *mumzer* to marry a legitimate Jewish person.

One of the principles in determining such cases is that we assume – unless there is clear evidence against the assumption – *that the majority of the woman's intimate relationships were with her husband*. [B. Sotah 27a, Tashbetz sect.19; see also *Shaarei Uziel* vol.2, *Mishpetei Yatom ve-Almanah*, Jerusalem, 1991, pp. 191, 196–197, 213.] Thus, it is far easier to declare a child born of this woman to be legitimate, the child of her legal husband. Rabbi Yitzhak Herzog suggested that newly developed blood tests could provide evidence as to the identity of the real father. Rabbi Uziel was unhappy with this suggestion, feeling that the determination of fatherhood should be made only on the basis of halachic arguments, not on new scientific methods. In articulating his position to Rabbi Herzog's opinion, Rabbi Uziel was concerned that the blood tests might result in declaring more children to be *mumzerim*. Rabbi Herzog responded: So be it. Since we have scientific tests to determine paternity, we should use them. On the face of it, Rabbi Herzog's position seems more reasonable and progressive. Yet Rabbi Uziel's argument was based on a compelling sympathy for children born in dubious situations; he did not want them to be declared *mumzerim* if there were halachic arguments to free them from that designation. To allow the blood tests, even if they would provide greater possibility of objective truth, would increase the possibility of children being declared illegitimate. Rabbi Uziel preferred to stick to the Talmudic principles, since they would be more helpful to lenient rulings in these cases. Rabbi Uziel's opposition was so strong that Rabbi Herzog backed down a bit, concluding that in his opinion blood tests should be used not to determine paternity but to provide additional information to the posek who must judge each case (R. Herzog, *Pesakim u-Khtavim*, vol. 6, Jerusalem, 1989, p.76f). (My emphasis – D.S.)

See the very detailed discussions of the notion of a *safek mumzer* being certainly permitted to marry, in my grandfather, R. David Sperber's *Afracasta de-Anya*, vol. 3, Brooklyn, 2002, sect. 265, pp. 319–326, and index, ibid., pp. 405–406. We should clarify that a questionable bastard on the Torah level is not considered a bastard, but the rabbis required that there be two degrees of doubt to permit the child to become part of the community. See in R. Ovadiah Yosef's responsa *Yabia Omer* 5, *Even ha-Ezer* 2, Section 9, p. 274; 7, *Even ha-Ezer* Section 8:11, p. 331; 10, *Yoreh Deah*, 6:2–3; ibid, *Even ha-Ezer* 6, p. 392, for a clarification of the matter. In addition, the rabbis established (*Kiddushin* 71a) that "a family that has been mixed up remains mixed up." In other words, if a family has bastards absorbed in it, "they should not be separated and distanced from the community in order to clarify the doubt as to who was assimilated and who not, but they should remain in a state of uncertain legitimacy forever." Based on this principle, R. Yohanan swore by the Temple (*Kiddushin*, ibid.): "It is within our power [to identify the families of impure birth in the Land of Israel – Rashi], but what can I do, seeing that the greatest men of the generation are mixed up in them." In light of Rabbi Yitzhak's dictum, the Ran established at the beginning of chapter *Assarah Yuhasin* that anyone who knows about the existence of a bastard is forbidden to publicize it and question the assumed legitimacy of the family. There is support for this approach from an ancient *Mishnah* (*Eduyot* 1:7): "Elijah will not come to declare things pure or impure, to distance and draw near."

There is a similarity we learn from B. *Yevamot* 45a where Rav Yehudah advises a convert, who is tainted with a certain stigma but not one forbidding him to marry a Jewish woman, to go to a place where no one is acquainted with him, and not to reveal his taintedness, so that he may be able to find himself a wife. From this testimony certain *Aharonim* learn that one may hide or suppress information concerning that which is not a defect that forbids marriage, but merely a stigma, in a case where it is most likely that de facto the other side will accept the stigma, and not demand the cancellation of the marriage, should that stigma be revealed.

This is not dissimilar from the discussion we find in *Sifrei Numbers* sect. 113, ed. Horowitz, Leipzig 1917 (2nd edition, Jerusalem, 1966), p. 122:

R. Yehuda ben Beteirah says: Anyone who says Tzelophad was he that gathered the faggots will be judged by [God]. For He who spoke and the world was created, hid his name and you [R. Akiva] wish to reveal it. . . .

(See below section entitled "Compassion and Casting a Blind Eye.")

In the preceding section we read that R. Akiva sought to identify the faggot gatherer with Tzelofhad by means of a *gezerah shavah* (an analogy based on verbal congenity between two different texts).R. Yehuda ben Beteirah criticizes him for revealing what the Torah did not identify. He suggests an alternative identification which leaves him in anonymity. (See Y. Copperman's analysis of this text in his *Kedushat Peshuto Shel Mikra*, vol. 2, Jerusalem, 2009, pp. 333–335.)

See further the Reshash's comment to B. *Baba Batra* 58a, on the story of R. Benaah who did not want to actively reveal which sons were *mumzerim*. (And cf. above section on "Care Not to Shame or Embarrass.")

See also the Rema on *Even ha-Ezer* 2:5; the Hazon Ish on *Even ha-Ezer* 1:18, p. 8, where he implies that if there is testimony of one person (as opposed to two witnesses) who knows that there is a bastard in a particular family, that person may marry into that family – i.e., that a family in which a bastard has been assimilated is absolutely permitted. See also Berkowitz, *Ha-Halakhah Kohah ve-Tafkidah*, Jerusalem, 2001, pp. 116–117. See also Rabbi Moshe Feinstein, *Igrot Moshe, Even ha-Ezer* 2, 9:3, who wrote that the prohibition is to knowingly marry a bastard, but there is no prohibition at all if he did not know, and it is even not as if he violated a prohibition accidentally. See also in the responsa of Rabbi Yitzhak Isaac Halevi Herzog, *Heichal Yitzhak, Even ha-Ezer* 1, Jerusalem, 1960, 10:2, pp. 62–63. It is also appropriate to add here what was written about the legitimization of a questionable bastard by Rabbi Ovadiah Yosef, "*Histamchut Al Bedikat Rikmot*" in Rabbi Yosef Halevi Movshovitz (ed.), *Sefer Zikaron la-Gaon Rabbi Shilo Rafael*, Jerusalem, 1998, p. 496:

bis developed a different language through which they revealed for themselves leniencies and even permits in those situations where the formalistic law might tend toward stringency in other circumstances. For in such cases, kindness and justice cry out for a solution that is both logical and humane.

A very remarkable example of creative halachic thinking overcoming the apparent constraints of formalism may be found in a long passage in R. Moshe Isserles' *Darchei Moshe* to *Even ha-Ezer* 7:13, citing the *Terumat ha-Deshen*, by R. Yisrael Isserlein (1390–1450), no. 241. The issue under discussion concerns women who were taken captives by gentiles and suffered dire threats. They did not attempt to escape from their captors, and presumably were raped, but afterwards were saved. Can they return to their husbands, and especially to a husband who is a *Kohen*? The simple ruling ought to be that they cannot, even to their non-*Kohen* husbands. However, the *Darchei Moshe* informs us:

It is well known that the Rivash [R. Yitzhak ben Sheshet Perfet, 1326–1408] wrote in responsum 447 that we should never ascribe promiscuity to a woman when it is possible that the children were from her husband, even if it is an unlikely possibility, because we have established that a promiscuous woman uses an absorbent in order to prevent conception (*Yevamot* 35a). And so wrote the *Beit Meir* 156:4, and I have written in several places that we can rely on the remarkable interpretation of *Panim Yafot* (*Parshat Aharei Mot*) that the concept that a majority of intercourse is with the husband means that a majority of conceptions are by the husband. Thus, even if the husband was only with her one time, the law is so. And so wrote *Netivot le-Shabbat* 4:9. The members of the Great Rabbinical Court of Rabbi Zolti and Rabbi Goldschmidt agreed with me that one can rely on this reasoning to be lenient. So too in our case we can rely on this to attribute the child to the husband even if she is very promiscuous, . . . And the *Ahronim* wrote that one can add the doubt that perhaps she was impregnated by a non-Jew, and they dismissed the objection of the Bah in 4:46. [See responsa *Beit Shlomo*, *Even ha-Ezer* 6; responsa of the *Hatam Sofer, Even ha-Ezer* 13; and the responsa of Rabbi Akiva Eger 106; responsa *Bnai Yaacov* 10; Responsa *Nediv Lev, Even ha-Ezer* 3; responsa *Mateh Lehem* 23; responsa *Tzeil ha-Kesef, Even ha-Ezer* 4; the book *Einei Kol Hai* 115c; responsa *Pnei Yitzhak Abulafia, Even ha-Ezer* 7; etc.] And all of these conditions enable the master to add this doubt in order to make it a second degree doubt [*sfek sfeika*] in order to be lenient. More power to the master who utilized his power of leniency – he has ruled well and taught well, and my hands are joined with him.

On the question as to whether a double-doubt, a *sfek sfeika*, may be used to permit a *mumzer* to marry freely, see the detailed examination of R. Nissim Rebibo, in his article "*Be-Inyan Heter Mumzer be-Sfek Sfeika*" in *Shevillim* 22, January, 2005, pp. 81–99. See also R. Ovadiah Yosef, *Yabia Omer*, vol. 8, 2nd edition, Jerusalem, 1995, *Even ha-Ezer* 9:1, pp. 401–402.

During the Austrian evil decrees (*gezerot*) [1360–1361], great authorities permitted (all of) them [to return] to their husbands, and even to those who were *Kohanim*. And possibly these women had some sort of excuse to justify themselves (*amatlaot le-divreihem*). [See *Darchei Moshe ha Aroch*, ed. *Tur, Machon Yerushalayim* ed. Jerusalem, 1993, p. 10, for his expounded discussion.] And he, [i.e., Isserlein] discusses the matter at length, [see his responsum]. And it appears to me that those great authorities who permitted this did so not strictly according to the law (*lav mi-dina*), but because of the need of the hour. For the fears that if they know that they may not return to their husbands, they might well do something worse, and therefore they ruled leniently. And should you say, can one rule leniently in matters involving biblical prohibitions?! [My answer would be that] I imagine they based themselves on what we have learned in *B. Ketubot* 3a, namely that anyone who marries, does so in accordance with rabbinic permission (*a-da'ata de-Rabbanan*), and the rabbis have the authority to annul their marriage, so that they become [in effect] unmarried, so that even if they prostituted themselves, they would be permitted to their husbands . . .

(See the continuation of this passage, and the lengthy description of the Austrian decrees in the *Terumot ha-Deshen* ibid.; and R. Ovadiah Yosef, in *Yabia Omer*, vol. 2, 2nd edition, Jerusalem, 1986, *Even ha-Ezer* 9:4, p. 236.) Whether they have to remarry is an additional discussion. We are here witness to the very creative thinking of those authorities who, despite the standard formal prohibition in such cases, found a way to bypass it to the benefit of those hopeless women. Their compassion and foresight led them to their surprising conclusion.

It was, indeed, unfortunate that R. Yaakov Reischer, in his *Shvut Yaakov* no.117 did not use this argument to permit a woman who, with her husband and a group of friends, were waylaid and fell into the hands of a murderous band of brigands, who threatened to kill them all, and she saved them by prostituting herself to the leader. R. Reischer writes that despite the fact that she did the right thing by saving the lives of others, and is in no way punishable, nonetheless, she may not return to her husband, *unless she claims that her act was enforced upon her.* That is to say, that if she acted on her own free-will in order to save the company, she would be nonetheless prohibited to return to her husband. He does leave a final opening of permissibility, in his struggle between moral compassion and formulation.

See also R. Eliyahu Katz, *Beer Eliyahu, Even ha-Ezer* (*ve-Orah Hayyim* 3), Beer Sheva, 2003, no. 3, pp. 11–13, the protocol dealing with *Takkanat Agunin* after the Holocaust, in which my sainted grandfather, R. David Sperber *zt"l*, was a decisive voice. And cf. R. Yitzhak Tzvi Sofer, *Hi-Sefer ha-Sefer*, Jerusalem, 1971, part 2, sect. 9.

See further Irving J. Rosenbaum, *The Holocaust and Halakhah*, Ktav Publishing House Inc., 1967, pp. 145–147, referring to R. Ephraim Oshri, *Hi-Haamashim* vol. 1, New York, 1949, p. 151, dealing with women who had been impressed into Nazi brothels, and permitting them to return to their husbands (*Tinyana* of the *Noda bi-Yehudah*, relying on 201, *Ketav Sofer, Even ha-Ezer* 17; *Mishpetei Uziel, Even ha-Ezer* 23). This is a vast subject. Suffice it here to refer to H.J. Zimmels, *The Echo of the Nazi Holocaust in Rabbinic Literature*, Ktav Publishing House Inc., 1977, pp. 215–250. (See also Rav Kook's *Ezrat Cohen*, Jerusalem, 1969, no. 92, p. 37.)

Compassion and Casting a Blind Eye

Among the many examples that might be cited for having compassion and casting a blind eye is the case of the woman who has lived with her husband for ten years and has not given birth to a child. According to the *Gemara*, the husband is required to divorce her, even if it is against his will: "and we remove him from her, even by means of a rod" (Rif on *Yevamot* 64a). Maimonides ruled so as well (*Mishneh Torah, Hilchot Ishut* 15:7): "If he does not desire to divorce her, he should be compelled to do so; he should be beaten with a rod until he divorces her." The author of the *Shulhan Aruch* followed suit (*Even ha-Ezer* 154:6). Even in a situation where they both love each other and have lived together in love and harmony for many years, we should force the husband to divorce his beloved wife and marry another woman so that she can bear him children in order that he fulfill the commandment of procreation, which is his exclusive obligation. Is this not a tragic situation that demands an alternative halachic solution?

In fact, *Even ha-Ezer* (ibid. and also ibid., 1:3) finds that Rabbi Moshe Isserles (the Rema) commented on the ruling of the *Shulhan Aruch* as follows: "In our times, we are not accustomed to force [the

husband to divorce his wife] at all." He also adds: "The man is believed
to say that he knows that he will not have children, and we do not
force him to marry another woman." The Rema bases himself on a
responsum of R. Yitzhak ben Sheshet (the Rivash, 1326–1407), no.
45, ed. D. Metzger, vol. 1, Jerusalem, 1993, pp. 19–20. Indeed, we find
a number of reasons given to justify this lenient approach, such as the
explanation given in *Sefer Bigdei Kahunah* of Rabbi Meshullam Fiorda
(19th century) on *Even ha-Ezer*: "It is appropriate that we do not force
him [to marry another woman] in our times . . . because there is a doubt
as to whether another woman will be able to build him a family, and
there is therefore a talmudic opinion that we not use force . . . and
there is justification to remain passive (*shev ve-al ta'asheh*) and fulfill
the Divine obligation." This halachic direction reflects the sensitivity
of those authorities who wished to prevent divorce by compulsion in
these circumstances.[89] Even more significantly, the Rivash wrote in his

---

89. Similarly, when R. Eliezer Yehuda Waldenberg was presented with the same
problem, and in this case the husband wanted to force his wife to receive a bill of
divorce, or alternatively that a hundred rabbis permit him to take a second wife, R.
Waldenberg did all he could to preserve the marriage. He even exhorted the *beit din* to
be extremely cautious in their ruling, since there may be a suspicion that the husband
has other motivations that are less pure and are not merely his desire to carry out
the mitzvah of procreation. For in our generation of moral turpitude he could well
be exploiting a halachic argument for less than proper ends. (See *Tziz Eliezer*, vol. 7,
no. 48, [*Kuntres Orhot ha-Mishpatim*] chapter 1, pp. 185–192; in this responsum he
calculates that ten years have not yet gone by, because one cannot include years of
sickness on the part of both sides, and other considerations. This is despite the fact that
they had actually been married fifteen years!) He also does not permit the husband to
take a second wife (basing himself on R. Shlomo Kluger, in *Ha-Elef Lecha Shlomo*,
Even ha-Ezer no.7). However, in that same discussion, he also states that even after
twenty years of marriage without children he would hesitate "to destroy a building
over which the altar brings forth tears," despite the Talmudic ruling. (And cf. ibid.,
vol. 17, no. 55 for a similar case, this time within the Sefaradi community, which
did not accept Rabbenu Gershon's prohibition on polygamy.) However, in that same
responsum he does permit a divorce, or a second wife, after a learned, pious Jew has
been married twenty years, and his wife is now forty-four years old, and even after
medical treatment she is unable to give birth, giving a rational explanation for his
differing position in this particular case. (And cf. ibid. vol. 21, no. 34, for a similar
such ruling.) R. Ovadia Yosef is extremely lenient in this matter, permitting a second
wife, not merely for Sefardim but also for Ashkenazim. See *Yabia Omer*, vol. 7, *Even
ha-Ezer* no. 2, for the full argumentation.
    We find a somewhat similar phenomenon in the rulings of Rabbi Benzion Hai
Uziel, *Mishpatei Uziel, She'eilot u-Teshuvot be-Dinei Even ha-Ezer*, Jerusalem: Mossad

Harav Kook, 1962, section 5, pp. 22–23. The question (submitted 27 Sivan 5697) is as follows:

I find myself asked to give my opinion about a question that was posed regarding a person who had an illness affecting his testicles to the point that they swelled significantly, and the doctors said that the passage for emission had been ruined, and that there was no recourse but to remove the testicles, which was done. The rabbi of the town advocated that from a moral perspective, he should divorce his wife with a simple writ of divorce according to the laws of Moses and Israel, since he is considered a *"petzu'a daka"* and cannot be part of the community. The rabbi claimed that even if the man remains married, he will not have a marital relationship with his wife since he has lost his virility and his ability to have an orgasm. On the other hand, if he divorces her, he is likely to die from hunger from a lack of attention, for he has no one to take care of him in his old age. So, the question came before the rabbi as to whether to force him to divorce his wife.

The esteemed Torah scholar answered according to the law in the best manner enabled by God. He expanded and analyzed every detail of the law, not leaving a corner unturned, applying straight logic and deep analysis, and he drew from his vast reservoir of wonderful knowledge. in the final analysis he ruled that we should not use any pressure to force this man to divorce his wife or even separate from her, but that we are nevertheless obligated to state that there is a concern of violating a prohibition by maintaining a marital relationship with her, yet if he does not want to separate from his wife, he does not have to do so.

After a deep and detailed discussion, Rabbi Uziel agreed as follows:

I therefore agree with all of the points raised by the learned Rabbi and Posek not to use any pressure to force this unfortunate individual to divorce his wife or separate from her, and that we are nevertheless obligated to state that it is appropriate to be sensitive to the forbidden elements and to divorce, or at least to desist from marital relations, and for one who listens it will be pleasant and he will be blessed.

Compare *Mishpatei Uziel 2, Even ha-Ezer* 16, Tel Aviv: 1938, pp. 32–34, regarding the law of a *"Petzu'a Daka,"* where he was lenient and permitted the man to remain with his wife. In general, his approach is toward the lenient position. See also ibid., 11, p. 45-47, where he permitted the wife of a priest to remain with him even though she was possessed by a demon or a spirit; ibid., 15, p. 63–64, where he permitted the daughter of a Yisrael who had been raped to marry a priest based on the following reasoning: "And I further say that for the welfare of a Jewish girl, that she not become part of a wicked culture, for not everyone would agree to marry the daughter of a friend who had been raped, it is appropriate to rule permissively regarding her marriage to a priest. It would be considered the fulfillment of a commandment to save a Jewish girl from the possibility of abandonment, and by so doing to prevent promiscuity and lewdness from our streets" (p. 64); and ibid., 23, pp. 83–88, where he ruled as follows regarding the wife of a priest that was abducted by thieves in order to take her money: "This woman is permitted to her husband, the priest, and we don't say that he [the husband] is trusted to make her forbidden to himself," (p. 88); ibid., 20, pp. 49–51, where he permitted a "deadly" woman to marry a third time, and ibid., 21, pp. 51–54 (compare there to 5, pp. 20–22), on a similar matter of permitting a "deadly woman" to remarry (compare to p. 153 note 107 below). See also, ibid., vol. 5, Jerusalem, 2002 (2nd edition), section 15, on the law of allowing a questionable

Responsa Section 15 (ed. D. Metzger, Jerusalem, 1993, vol. 1, p. 20) as follows:

All of this [that we force him to give a writ of divorce] is the letter of the law. However, what can we do when we have not seen in our days or heard for several generations of a rabbinical court that compelled a man to divorce his wife when she has lived with him for ten years without bearing children . . . The sages of the generations *cast a blind eye* in matters of conjugal relations so as to not prevent them, and certainly not to separate them. It all goes according to what they want. And there is not in the marriage any element of unchastity or unholiness (*issur kedushah*). (My emphasis – D.S.)

---

bastard into the congregation, which he permitted; ibid., 16, on the issue of a "*Petzu'a Daka*"; and ibid., 17 and 18, in which he validated the testimony and matrimony of Karaites, and declared them questionable bastards. Similarly, it is of value to note the lenient tendencies of Rabbi Moshe Feinstein as reflected in his responsa, and particularly those dealing with issues of personal status in which there is an issue of great distress to a particular individual. See for example, *Igrot Moshe, Even ha-Ezer,* I, New York, 1974, sections 24, 41, 63, 65, 66, etc. This is not the place to engage in a lengthy discussion on this phenomenon.

But having mentioned R. Moshe Feinstein's sensitivity to issues of distress, we should note his "solution" to the woman who has been married for many years and has not been able to become pregnant, and it is apparent that this is due to the husband's inability. In his *Igrot Moshe*, vol. 1, no. 10 (and cf. no. 71) he makes his very famous – which some consider infamous – ruling permitting the wife to be impregnated with the sperm of a non-Jewish donor. He writes:

And concerning the woman who has been unable to give birth for over ten years, and the doctors state that it is his [i.e., the husband's] inability, and she wishes to give birth as is the desire of all women, as is stated in B. *Yevamot* 65, even though she is not obligated by law to carry out the mitzvah of "be fruitful and multiply," nonetheless we force the husband to give her a bill of divorce, and she receives no *ketubah* since it is she who demands the divorce. What will become of this woman? Does she not require a staff to lean on and a spade for my burial, [i.e., a son to support her in her old age and to provide for her burial (B. *Ketubot* 64a)]? And even without this, it is known from the holy foremothers how much they wished to have children, and so it is with all women . . .

It is out of his deep sympathy for their great distress that he finds the halachic sources to permit them to take this radical action. He was severely criticized for this ruling, and a whole spate of virulent polemic articles were published in an early issue of the journal *Ha-Maor* by prominent authorities, such as the Satmar Rebbe, R.M.Y. Breisch, and cf. *Tzitz Eliezer* of R. Eliezer Waldenberg, vol. 9, 51:4, to which R. Moshe vigorously replied.

He continues responding to a different question as to whether a man who has no children may marry a widow who is ninety years old, who the community suspects wishes to marry her only for her money and therefore objects to such a marriage, as follows:

> Therefore in this particular case that has come before you, if that old woman is pleased to be married and have a husband in lieu of children, ... and she found someone who is willing to marry her because of his straightened circumstances, and if he has no children, if you wish to turn a blind eye [to this case], as has been practiced in many fine great communities ... with scholars and distinguished people (*anshei maaseh*), you have the right to do so ...

We find the Rivash using this same phrase in a rather different context, and somewhat more surprisingly. For there were those who thought that Jewish prostitutes should not be driven out of the city, since it was better to go to a Jewish one than to a gentile one. Others strongly disagree, insisting that such wanton Jewesses be driven away from the city. (See R. Yehuda ben Asher, *Zichron Yehudah*, sect. 17, 3b.) However, the Rivash (ibid., no. 425, vol. 2, p. 645) wrote that "the great ones of the generation should cast a blind eye, lest the licentious of our people err with gentile [women], and a fire will go forth and take hold of thorns and consume the haystack" (a reference to Exodus 22:5).[90]

In three separate instances we find R. Ovadiah Yosef ruling in this direction. In the first case (*Yabia Omer*, vol. 2, Jerusalem, 2nd edition, 1986, *Even ha-Ezer*, no. 2, pp. 210–214), he was asked whether someone who had committed adultery with a married woman, and wished to repent his sin, was obliged to inform the woman's husband of his deed and bring great shame, divorce, and suffering upon her family. Since there were no witnesses to their relationship, and there is a view that in such a case she is not forbidden to her husband, he should say nothing, because of the dignity of the individual. This will also encourage repentance (*takkanat ha-shavim*). (See below section entitled "Encouraging Repentance" and also above section entitled "Human

---

90. See on this A. Grossman, *Hasidot u-Mordot*, Jerusalem, 2001, p. 240.

Dignity.") In this case, the rabbi receiving this information also felt no duty to inform the husband.

In a second case (ibid., vol. 8, Jerusalem, 1994, *Even ha-Ezer*, no. 32, pp. 350–353), he was asked about a woman who in her youth lived with someone and became pregnant and had an abortion. She then moved to a different city, became a *baalat teshuvah*, married a *yeshiva bocher* and live together with great love and happiness. She again became pregnant, gave birth to a boy, and her husband, who had no knowledge of her earlier life, wishes to have a *pidyon ha-ben*. Does she have to inform him that this is not her first pregnancy, the information of which might well destroy the marriage? After a long and detailed analysis he ruled that the *pidyon* should take place with a full *berachah*, and that the local rabbi who ministers at the *pidyon*, and who knows the whole story, should make sure that the *Kohen* receiving the *pidyon* ask no embarrassing questions, so as not to generate either lies or shame, but cast a blind eye to the earlier facts, again to save the dignity and integrity of the couple.[91]

In yet a third responsum (in vol. 9, Jerusalem, 2002, *Even ha-Ezer*, no. 10, pp. 371–372), he deals with the question of women *baalot teshuvah*, who, while they were non-religious, betrayed their husbands and had relations with other men. With tears in their eyes they now ask whether they have to inform their husbands, and perhaps be divorced from them. Again, after a careful discussion (the details of which we leave to the interested reader) he ruled:

> In sum, one should cast a blind eye from this, and they need not inform their husbands, especially now that they are repentant and have drawn close to their God, . . . and we may well rely upon those authorities who permitted this.

Here again we are witness to the wisdom and sensitivity of a great *posek* who utilized the full range of halachic principles and the vast heritage of rabbinic precedent to arrive at a legitimate compassionate conclusion.

Casting a blind eye as a legitimate halachic practice may be hinted at in a statement by R. Ilaa, in *B. Hulin* 89a, where he explains the verse in

---

91. Cf. above section entitled "Care not to Shame or Embarrass." And see also ibid., vol. 9, *Even ha-Ezer*, no. 10, p. 311.

Job 26:7, ". . . and hangeth the earth upon nothing – *al belimah.*" The world only exists because of him who muzzles him during a period of strife. Admittedly, we are not dealing with a period of strife (*merivah*) but one of tragic circumstances. But, here too, the virtue of restraint and keeping silent is emphasized. The Rashba explicitly states in his responsum to R. Yaakov ben ha-Kashaf (read: Karshaf), in vol. 5, no. 238, (ed. Machon Yerushalayim, Jerusalem, 1998) p. 159:

> And this is what I replied to the *Hacham* R. Yaakov ben ha-Kashaf, the head of the Yeshiva in Toledo, concerning [his] leadership of the community and the punishment of the transgressers:
>
> Know that a soft tongue will break bones (Proverbs 25:15). . . . And behold, listen to this, and you will also understand that it is impossible to lead all people in an identical fashion. But please remember how our master King David was wont to cast a blind eye [ignoring the actions] of Yoav and Shimi, even though they were worthy of execution. And the reason he gave was, ". . . what have I to do with you, ye sons of Zeuriah, that ye should this day be adversaries unto me? Shall there any man be put to death this day in Israel? For do I not know that I am this day king over Israel" (2 Samuel 19:23). For at any time it may be that casting a blind eye from the sinner may on occasion be a mitzvah, and it all depends on the requirements of the time. And the wise man at times very easily may cast a blind eye. And you already know that our first king, Solomon, ". . . held his peace" (I Samuel 10:27) [i.e., was silent despite the behaviour of the children of Belial]. And casting a blind eye in such a situation, until such time that the one's control be strengthened is great mitzvah. And he who fulfills this mitzvah has created a basis for positive institutions and builds a strong wall, and later on your arms will be strengthened, and you will be able to rule as you desire . . .

He continues in this style, paving the way for later authorities to adopt this path: namely, when one cannot prevent the community from carrying out certain transgressions, it is best to say nothing, rather than indulge in futile exhortation. For instance, the Radbaz writes (in his responsum, part 1, no. 187):

> The leader of the generation should be moderate in such matters, for not all people are the same and not all transgressions are identical.

How so? Some people are habituated to sinning and are confident in their position. We do not care about them, and whatever will be we will uphold the Torah. But if someone is not a habitual sinner, and it is likely that he will listen [to us], then we seek to persuade him until he starts to repent in part. And we do not hurry to punish him for his errors, etc. And everything should be in accordance with the understanding of the judge and the leader, so long as all their activities are for the sake of Heaven.

And the *Ktav Sofer*, R. Avraham Shmuel Benjamin Sofer (*Even ha-Ezer*, Pressburg, 1888, no. 47) makes a very similar statement, namely that it all in accordance with the judges discretion whether his words will be accepted or not. Likewise, the Hida writes (in *Birkei Yosef, Orah Hayyim* 608:4):

> When we are strong [and have authority] over the sinners . . . then we are obligated to rebuke. But when we know that will not accept [our authority], for they are blind to it . . . and we have not the strength to distance them [from transgressions], in such circumstances we are not obligated to rebuke them, and this is [in accordance to] what they said in *B. Yevamot* 65, "not to say that which will not be listened to."[92]

And yet another example of casting a blind eye, or refraining from revealing factual evidence, in order not to disrupt the marital framework and to avoid casting great shame upon the spouse, has been brought by Daniel Z. Feldman, in his *The Right and the Good: Halakhah and Human Relations*, 2nd edition, New York, 2005, p. 93:

> R. Shimon Greenfield [*Shut Maharshag*, Berdichev 1931, vol. 3, no. 65] considers the case of a woman who, in her youth, had given birth under circumstances less honorable than those in which she now chooses to live. Currently married, she has just borne her husband's first son. The husband, unaware of the more unsavory aspects of his wife's past, enthusiastically awaits performing the mitzvah of *pidyon ha-ben*. Is the husband to be informed that it is not necessary, irrespective of the

---

92. Cf. above section on "Care Not to Shame or Embarrass" *ad initium* on the mitzvah of *tochecha* and its limitations.

substantial damage that will be incurred to marital harmony? Or, is a sham religious ceremony to be countenanced? R. Greenfeld, cognizant of the imperative to maintain peace looming large, allows the pseudo-ritual, while providing advice on the avoidance of the transgression of pronouncing an unwarranted blessing. R. Ovadiah Yosef [*Yabia Omer*, vol. 8. *Yoreh Deah*, no. 32, cited above], in a similar instance, goes as far as to allow the blessing.

Feldman brings a wealth of additional related material (ibid., pp. 93–94, note 95), which is extremely instructive.[93]

The sensitivity of the ruling sage is expressed well in the formulation of the author of the *Aruch ha-Shulhan*, Rabbi Yechiel Michel Epstein (1828–1908), on the *Shulhan Aruch, Even ha-Ezer* 27:

> The obligation to divorce after ten years [if no children have been born] is a great stringency that the sages imposed, for in all of the commandments, a person is not obligated to do more than is required by the Divine commandment. Since this man married a woman who was not an *ailanit* (barren) . . . what more can he do? The fact that he has not had children is a "secret of G-d" (based on *Berachot* 10a).[94]

So we see how many great authorities saw fit to "look the other way" in order to avoid causing embarrassment to the other. This is surely a crucial message of essential advice to every practicing communal rabbi.

Searching a Source for an Ethical Directive

Let us point out another interesting phenomenon that strengthens our basic argument that the halachah rests on a foundation of fundamental values. There is one important commandment that is mentioned in the morning daily prayers: "the fruits of which a man enjoys in this world, while the principle remains for him in the World to Come" (*Mishnah Peah* 1:1)[95] – the commandment to visit the sick. Maimonides

---

93. See above pp. 128–130 note 88.

94. See also my *Netivot Pesikah*, pp. 160–164, and see also Moshe Kahn, "The Halakhic Parameters of Delaying Procreation," *Meorot* 8, 2010, pp. 100–101.

95. On this *Beraita* that appears in the morning prayers and its formulations, see

establishes in *Mishneh Torah, Hilchot Evel* 14:1 that "it is a positive commandment of the rabbis to visit the sick." In the *Shulhan Aruch, Yoreh Deah* 335:1, Rabbi Yosef Karo formulates it as follows: "It is a commandment to visit the sick." Yet, what is the source of this commandment? The *Gemara* in *Sotah* 14a cites the following statement of Rabbi Hama bar Hanina: "What does the text mean that 'You shall walk after the Lord your God?' (Deuteronomy 13:4). Is it possible for a human being to walk after the *Shechinah*, for has it not been said: 'For the Lord your God is a devouring fire'? But [the meaning is] to walk after the attributes of the Holy One, blessed be He. . . . Just as the Holy One, blessed be He, visited the sick, for it is written: 'And the Lord appeared unto him by the oaks of Mamre' (Genesis 18:1), so do you also visit the sick." In comparison, *Baba Kama* 100a and *Baba Metzia* 30b cite the following teaching of Rabbi Yosef: "'And you shall show them the way wherein they must walk' (Exodus 18:20) – 'wherein they must walk' refers to visiting the sick." Tractate *Nedarim* 39b provides an additional source: "Resh Lakish said: Where is visiting the sick indicated in the Torah? In the verse, 'If these men die the common death of all men, or if they be visited after the visitation of all men' (Numbers 16:29). How is it implied? – Raba answered: [The verse means] if these men die the common death of all men, who lie in a sick bed, and men come in and visit them." And *Midrash ha-Hefetz* on Genesis 48:1 states: "'And it came to pass after these things that one said to Yoef: Behold, your father is sick. And he took with him his two sons, Manasheh and Ephraim' – from here we derive the obligation to visit the sick."

Note the degree to which the sages of old made great efforts to find a source or hint in the Torah for the commandment of visiting the sick, which is such a special commandment (see Maimonides, *Sefer ha-Mitzvot* 2) to the point of blurring the boundary between halachah and *aggadah* in these teachings.[96] Apparently, the rabbis understood

---

what is written in *Siddur Tzeluta de-Avraham* of Rabbi Yaacov Werdiger, vol. 1, Tel Aviv (c. 1932), pp. 14–15.

96. On this phenomenon, see what my father and teacher of blessed memory, Rabbi Shmuel Sperber, wrote in *Ma'amarot*, Jerusalem: Mossad Harav Kook, 1978, p. 178. On halachah derived from *aggadah*, see Y. Beeri (Kolodner), *Ha-Midrash ke-Halachah*, Tel-Aviv, 1960. Prof. S.K. Mirsky wrote an interesting series of articles entitled "*Mekorot ha-Halachah ba-Midrashim*" *Talpioth* 1/2, 1944, pp. 218–247; 21/2, 1945, pp. 348–374; 2/3-4, 1946, pp. 348–374. They were according to the order of *Shulhan Aruch, Orah Hayyim*. Regretably, he did not get beyond sect. 128. R.M. Gifter,

that there must be such a commandment – because it is demanded by

---

also published there (1/3-4, 1944, pp. 551–561) an article entitled *"Ha-Halachah be-Midrash R. Eliezer Beno shel R. Yosi ha-Gelili."* See also David Sabato, *"Halachah ve-Aggadah ba-Mishnah: Tafkidan shel ha-Hatimot ha Aggadiot ba-Mishnah" Netuim* 18, 2013, pp. 39–68. R. Yeruham Leiner, in his *Tiferet Yeruham*, edited by his son Yaakov Leiner, Brooklyn, 2008, pp. 558–566, also delved into this subject. See also Avraham Arzi, *"Shiluv Aggadah ba-Halachah be-Mishnat Rabbi Eliezer ben Hurcanus," Shanah be-Shanah*, 1936. This issue was also dealt with at length by Maharatz Chajes, in his *Darkei Horaah*, part 2, chapter 7, apud *Kol Sifrei Maharatz Hayyut*, vol. 1, Jerusalem, 1958, pp. 243–252. Recently, Yair Loberbaum dealt with this subject in an article entitled "Reflections on the Halakhic Status of Aggadah," *Dinei Yisrael* 24, 2007, pp. 29–64. This is a subject that requires much further examination.

Here we may add that the rabbis made a clear distinction between halachah and *aggadah,* so much so that they ruled (in *Y. Peah* 2:6, *Y. Hagigah* 1:8) that one does not derive *halachot* for *haggahot* (and cf. *Y. Horayot* 3:5). See the exhaustive analysis of this principle in B. Lifshitz, "'*Aggada' u-Mekomah be-Toldot Torah she-Baal-Peh," Shenaton ha Mishpat ha-Ivri* 22, Jerusalem, 2001–2003, pp. 233–328.

See also responsa *Noda bi-Yehudah, Tinyana, Yoreh Deah* 161:

But the *Midrashim* and the *Aggadot* their main aim is [to teach] ethics, and their hints and parables are all for the [ethical] basis of religion *(ikar ha-dat)*, but their main intent is not for halachic rulings, and hence we do not learn from them how to rule halachically . . .

The Rivash sect. 171 (77a) discusses how the rabbis would exaggerate the punishments in order to prevent a person from sinning, bringing examples from *B. Erachin* 15b, and *B. Shabbat* 105b. And see further responsa of Rambam, ed. Blau, vol. 2, no. 458, etc.; and for the attitude of the *Geonim* to *aggadah* vis-à-vis halachah, see Lifshitz ibid., pp. 249–253.

This was also the position of the *Geonim.* See, e.g., *Sefer ha-Eshkol*, ed. Albeck, *Hilchot Sefer Torah* 60a (R. Sherira Gaon); *Otzar ha-Geonim*, ed. B.M. Levin, *Hagigah, Perushim* 14a, pp. 59–60 (Hai Gaon), ibid., p. 4, (Shmuel ben Hofni), etc. See also Rambam's explicit statement to R. Pinhas ha-Dayyan *(Igrot ha-Rambam*, ed. Blau, no. 458, p. 739) as well as his responses elsewhere (to R. Ovadiah ha-Ger, ed. Shilat, vol. 1, pp. 236–237, etc.):

All those statements are of a haggadic nature, and one does not raise questions in matters of *haggadah*. . . . For they are not a part of our tradition *(kabbalah)* and there is in themselves neither forbidden nor permitted (i.e., one cannot learn from them such rulings). . . .

The situation changes somewhat during the medieval period where we find that in the Ashkenazi tradition a sharp distinction was not made and halachot were derived from *aggadot.* (See A. Grossman, *"Kidush ha-Shem be-Meot* 11-12," *Peamim* 75, 1998, p. 39.) Again, this is too broad a field to be dealt with here.

See further on this principle, and when it is applied, in Y. Tamar, *Alei Tamar, Yerushalemi Zeraim*, vol. 1, Givatayim, 1979, pp. 373–374, on *Y. Peah; Entziklopediah Talmudit*, vol. 1, Tel Aviv, 1947, p. 62.

However, see R. Ovadiah Yosef, *Yabia Omer*, vol. 9, Jerusalem, 2002, *Yoreah Deah*, no.10:8, pp. 285–286, that this principle is only applicable in a case where the *aggadah* contradicts a Talmudic ruling. But in other cases one can certainly derive *halachot* from aggadic texts. See the numerous sources to which he refers us, especially Rabbenu Tam, in his *Sefer ha-Yashar,* ed. S.F. Rosenthal, Berlin, 1898, sect. 45:3, p. 81, who writes:

Anyone who is not conversant with *Seder Rav Amram Gaon,* and *Halachot Gedolot,* and tractate *Soferim* and *Pirke de-R. Eliezer,* and [*Midrash*] *Raba* and the Talmud, and the other books of *aggadah,* can undermine the words of [our] earlier authorities and their customs, but they must depend (i.e., accept) their words which do not contradict our Talmud and augment [it]. And, indeed, many of the customs that we practice are based on their words . . .

R. Ovadiah touched upon this subject in yet a number of additional responsa in *Yabia Omer.* See vol. 1, *Yoreh Deah* 4:8–9; vol. 2, *Even ha-Ezer* 1:6; vol. 4, *Even ha-Ezer* 8:1; vol. 7, *Even ha-Ezer* 2:10; vol. 8, *Even ha-Ezer* 21:2; ibid., *Hoshen Mishpat* 12:3; vol. 9, *Even ha-Ezer* 16; vol. 10, *Orah Hayyim* 56:4/17; ibid., *Yoreh Deah* 24.

Furthermore, there is another principle that one does not derive halachot from what happened before the Torah was given at Sinai (*Y. Moed Katan* 3:5; *Tosafot Moed Katan* 20a; *B. Yoma* 28b; and for a full discussion, see *Entziklopediah Talmudit,* ibid., pp. 296–297, but see final note, ibid., no. 35, and M.M. Kasher, *Torah Shelemah,* vol. 7, tome 8, New York, 1950, to Genesis 50:10, pp. 1872–1873, note 33).

Nonetheless, we find many examples where the halachah is derived from *aggadah,* which relates to an early biblical (pre-Sinaitic) episode. Here we shall give just two such examples to illustrate the issue.

The Talmud in *Megillah* 16b-17a states in the name of Rabah in the name of R. Yitzhak bar Shemuel bar Marta:

Greater is *Talmud Torah* than honouring one's father and mother. For all those years when our father Jacob was [studying Torah] in the house of Ever, he was not punished [even though he was not honoring his parents during that period] . . .

On the basis of this text the *Sheiltot* to *Toldot* 19, ed. S.K. Mirsky, pp. 128–9) asks:

Someone who has a father and mother and is obligated to look after them, to feed them and give them drink, to get them up and dress them . . . , and he wishes to go to his teacher to study, or to a place of Torah where he will not study alone . . . , which is more important? [Honoring one's parents or learning Torah? Do we say] learning *Torah* is more important, since it has precedence over all other acts, or perhaps honouring one's parents, since this is likened to honouring God [he quotes Exodus 20:12 and Proverbs 3:9]. What is the halachah?

The answer given is the citation from *B. Megillah* ibid. (with a small addition).

The Talmudic passage from a Babylonian Amora of the third century C.E. finds a biblical derivation as homiletically interpreted from the earlier anonymours Tannaitic statement in *M. Peah* 1:1:

These are the things whose fruits a man enjoys in the world while the capital is laid up for him in the World to Come: honouring one's father and mother, deeds of loving, kindness, making peace between a man and his fellows, and the study of Torah has precedence over [so I translate *ke-neged*] all of them.

Our Talmudic passage finds itself as the basis of a halachic ruling in a responsum of R. Yisrael Isserlein's *Terumat ha-Deshen,* New York, 1958, sect. 40:

The question: A student wishes to leave his country to learn Torah from a certain rabbi in whom he has confidence that with him he will see success [in his learning], but his father objects, telling him, "My son, if you leave for that country where the rabbi is to be found, you will cause me much pain, for I will constantly be worrying about you, lest you be taken into captivity or they will plot against you as is common in that country . . ."

The answer: It would appear that under these circumstances he does not need to listen to his father. . . . For the study of Torah takes precedence, for our father Jacob was not punished for [not] honouring his father all those years that he studied Torah in the house of Ever. And it does not seem to be the case that one should distinguish between [not] honoring one's father, and the father's claim that his leaving will pain him, for both honoring [his father] and fearing him [*morao*, i.e., holding him in awe, so that one refrain from hurting him in any way] are both positive commandments of equal status (and hence, of lesser status than *Talmud Torah*).

Isserlein here uses the Talmudic precedent to rule in a practical issue, presumably with a fine psychological understanding that emotional manipulation on the part of the parents' pressure will ultimately have its backlash on the son, and therefore the son should study where he feels most comfortable and have most confidence in his chances of success. Indeed, this was already clearly stated by R. Yossi (in *B. Eruvin* 47b), that "not from everyone does a person successfully study (*zocheh lilmod*)", a statement cited by the *Terumat ha-Deshen* in that responsum.

With this background in mind we can understand the reasoning of R. Ovadiah Yosef, in his *Yehaveh Daat*, vol. 5, Jerusalem, 1983, sect. 56, pp. 251–258, who rules in a lengthy and complex responsum that a student who wishes to learn in a Yeshiva, while his parents want him to study in a *Yeshiva Tichonit* – a Yeshiva high-school – does not have to follow his parents' desire. However, he does add that one should try to persuade and to conciliate the parents, so that this will also be according to their will. Here R. Ovadiah's ideological "bias" comes to the fore, but his sympathy and understanding for the parents' position is also articulated. (See further R. Yehuda Ayash, *Beit Yehudah*, Livorno, 1746, *Yoreh Deah*, sect. 54; *Pithei Teshuvah*, *Yoreh Deah* 240.)

Yet another somewhat remarkable example of the use of homiletic *aggadah* for determining halachah may be seen in the development of the early praying of *maariv*. This subject was treated exhaustively in a seminal essay by Yaakov Katz, which first appeared in *Zion* 35, 1970, p. 60 et seq., entitled "*Maariv bi-Zemano ve-she-lo bi-Zemano* . . ." There he demonstrated how the northern European communities, where during the summer sunset and nightfall is very late indeed, had a custom of praying *maariv* on Friday several hours before the onset of Shabbat, i.e., before nightfall. We shall not repeat his arguments, neither shall we duplicate the sources that he brought, but merely point to an aspect of this issue with which he did not deal.

The *Mishnah* at the beginning of *Berachot* states clearly that *shema shel aravit* is read after the stars appear. Yet the custom was in Ashkenaz and France, in accordance with the ruling of Rabbenu Tam, to recite the evening prayer much earlier (See *Tosafot Berachot* 2a). The Tosafot raises a question against the *Mishnah* from *B. Hulin* 91b, when we read the following:

R. Akiva said, I once asked R. Gamliel and R. Joshua in the meatmarket of Emmaus where they had gone to buy a beast for the wedding feast of R. Gamliel's son. It is written: "And the sun rose upon him." Did the sun rise upon him only? Did it not rise upon the whole world? R. Yitzhak said, it means that the sun which had set for his sake now rose for him. For it is written: "And Yaakov went out from Beer-Sheba, and went toward Haran" [Genesis 28:10]. And it is further written: "And he lighted upon

basic ethics – and that it is thus impossible that it not be implied in

---

the place [ibid., 11]. When he reached Haran he said [to himself], 'Shall I have passed through the place where my fathers prayed and not have prayed too?' He immediately resolved to return, and no sooner had he thought of this than the earth contracted and he immediately lighted upon the place. After he prayed, he wished to return [to where he was], but the Holy One, blessed be He, said, 'This righteous man has come to my habitation; shall he depart without a night's rest?' Thereupon the sun set.
(Modified from E. Cashdan transl. in Soncino ed.)

And we have learned from *Y. Berachot* 4:1 and *B. Berachot* 26b that the "[daily] prayers were derived from the forefathers' [prayer activities], and that Yaakov instituted the *aravit* (*maariv*) prayer, deducing this from the verse in Genesis 28:10 'and he lighted upon the place' – ויפגע במקום, *va-yifga ba-makom. Pegia* [here] means prayer." A number of verses are cited to prove this interpretation of *pegia* as prayer, such as Jeremiah 27:18, ibid., 7:16, etc.

However, according to R. Yitzhak, Yaakov prayed before the sun set, and only after praying went to sleep to dream his "ladder dream." On the basis of this interpretation, Rabbenu Tam reached his conclusion, adding (Tosafot ibid.) "and our custom is fine, and indeed, it is good to pray [*maariv*] while it is still day." As to the *Mishnah*'s dissenting view, this is explained that we rule in accordance with the opinion of R. Yehudah (*Berachot* 26b) "that the time for *minhah* is up until *plag ha-minhah*, that is to say up until the nine and three quarters hour of the day, immediately after which we may pray *maariv*. The *Mishnah*, on the other hand, is in accordance with the view of R. Yehoshua ben Levi (ibid.) that *minhah* can be recited until nightfall (*ad ha-erev*), just as the sacrifice was offered until nightfall, and the prayers were based on the daily sacrifices (*temidin*).

However, what is most surprising, and in my opinion most significant, is the interpretation of the verse in Genesis ibid. For a plain and simple meaning of the word *va-yifga* is "and he alighted upon," or perhaps more literally "bumped into." The interpretation that "he prayed" is wholly homiletic. Furthermore כי בא השמש – *ki va ha-shemesh* plainly means for the sun had already set, and therefore he tarried there, as he could not continue his journey in the dark. That the "earth contracted" and he went backwards and forewards to Haran and Bethel is wholly midrashic. Yet this apparently justified and legitimized the northern European custom of early *maariv*, though it stood in opposition to an explicit *Mishnah*. (See also *Genesis Rabba* 68:10, ed. Theodor. Albeck, pp. 780–781, and the editor's long note, ibid.) And on the relationship between *P'shat* and *Derash* – plain reading and homiletic interpretation – see David Weiss Halivni, *Peshat and Derash: Plain and Applied Meaning in Rabbinic Exegesis*, New York and Oxford, 1991, and especially Chapter 3, entitled "The Meaning and History of the Plain *Peshat*," ibid., pp. 52–88.

At all events, here we have a clear example of the interplay between halachah and *aggadah*, and even ritual practice being derived from the acts of the forefathers prior to Sinai. We could bring numerous additional examples, but we have already strayed far beyond the compass of this study, so let the above suffice.

These are but two of many examples of how aggadic homiletic sources are used in halachic decision-making. However, this somewhat lengthy note also demonstrates how the decisor's understanding of the issue, whether educational, psychological, or ideological, is reflected in his halachic formulations. He may appear superficially to be

one way or another in the biblical text. And so, they sought to reveal the source of the commandment in those teachings, which are certainly not clearly derived from the biblical text. Indeed, according to some opinions, the commandment is even a Torah obligation (see *Halachot Gedolot*).

---

following a Talmudic precedent in a somewhat formal almost artificial manner, but in point of fact we see his deep inner understanding of the issue at stake.

Finally, I should like to give some brief examples to characterize the difference between halachah and *aggadah*. In Numbers 21:26 we read, "For Heshbon was the city of Sihon the king of the Amorites, who had fought against the former king of Noah, and taken all his land out of his hand, even unto Arnon." And on the words "out of his hand" the *Yerushalmi Gittin* 8.1 remarks in the name of R. Yishmael: And did he take it "out of his hand"? [No.] Then what does "out of his hand" mean? Out of his possession (*mi-reshuto*). See parallels in *B. Baba Metzia* 56b and cf. *Mechilta Mishpatim, Massechta de-Nezikin* chapter 5, on Exodus 21:16, Genesis 24:10; *Sifrei Matot* 157 to Numbers 31:6, on "in his hand" equals possession. See further M.M. Kasher, *Torah Shelemah Hukkat*, vol. 41, Jerusalem, 1989, pp. 251–252, note 182, ibid., *Mishpatim*, vol. 17, New York, 1956, p. 90, note 313, ibid., vol. 18, New York, 1958, p. 16, notes 38–40. (And see also *Havat Daat*, by R. Yaakov of Lyssa, to *Yoreh Deah* 87:1.)

On the other hand, the verse in Genesis 23:17, "And the field of Ephron, which was in the Machpelah which was before Mamre, rose . . . (*va-yakam*)" is usually translated as "was made sure." The *Midrash Aggadah* explains that it was "half a cubit higher than the surrounding land in order to distinguish it from the other fields" (*Torah Shelemah Hayyei Sarah*, vol. 4, Jerusalem, 1934, p. 936, no. 80). The standard translation-interpretation is that this constituted a confirmation of the conveyance (*kinyan*) (cf. ibid.).

And in *Genesis Rabba* 69:4, on the verse in Genesis 28:13, ". . . the land whereon thou liest to thee will I give it and to thy seed," we read:

R. Shimon ben Lakish in the name of Bar-Kappara: He (i.e., God) folded [the land of Israel] like a *pinax* (a writing tablet) under his head.

And in *B. Hulin* 91b we read even more explicitly:

Said R. Yitzhak: We learn that the Holy One blessed be He folded all of the Land of Israel and placed it under his head, so that it would be easy for his offspring to conquer it.

(See *Genesis Rabba* ed. Theodor Albeck, 2nd edition, Jerusalem, 1965, p. 794, note 1; parallels in *Tanhuma Buber, va-Yeitzei* 9; *Zohar-Hadash* 28b; see also *Torah Shelemah*, vol. 5, Jerusalem, 1935, p. 1136, note 92.)

The above examples demonstrate how sometimes the Aggadists take the text literally in a homiletic fashion, while the halachists are less literal, broadening the semantic range of meanings to a biblical word in accordance with accepted legal practice. (And see the discussion on whether *bishool*-cooking includes frying in *Yoreh Deah* 87:1; *Meorot ha-Daf ha-Yomi* 842 to *Nedarim* 49–55, 2015, pp. 1–2.)

Encouraging Repentance

The requirement of mercy expresses itself in the rabbinic ruling of *takanat ha-shavim*.[97] This is basically an amendment to a biblical command. The source of this ruling is in a *Mishnah* in *Gittin* 5:5:

> R. Yohanan ben Gudgada testified . . . that if a man built a stolen beam into a structure he need only repay its value as a precaution for the benefit of the penitent . . . (*mi-penei takanat ha-shavim*).

That is to say he need not pull apart his structure (*birah*, house) in order to restore the actual beam. This is despite the explicit biblical command that a thief return the actual object he had stolen (Leviticus 5:23). The rabbis realized that a person would not tear apart his house in order to return a theft. They therefore gave him an additional chance to remedy his transgression by permitting him to reimburse the original owner of the beam. This concern for the "benefit of the penitent" is a true expression of the rabbinic requirement of merciful consideration in halachic legislation.[98]

Actually, they went even further and applied this rule to a stolen *sukkah* – i.e., the *schach* or the walls – even if the stolen elements were not actually firmly fixed, i.e., built into the *sukkah*. The rabbis did so, even though a stolen *sukkah* is invalid by biblical law based on the verse in Deuteronomy 16:13, "The feast of tabernacles you should make for yourself," which the rabbis interpreted that the *sukkah* should be yours (*lach*), and not stolen. (See *Shulhan Aruch, Orah Hayyim* 637:3; *Mishnah Berurah* ibid., no. 18; based on M. *Sukkah* 31a.)

However, there is an even further extention of this principle among some of the *Rishonim*. Thus, the Baal ha-Itur (in *Hilchot Sukkah* 85d, cited in the Tur *Orah Hayyim* 637 ad fin.) writes that only if the thief has intentions of returning the value of the theft, may he sit in the *sukkah*. However, if he does not, then the *Sukkah* is a stolen one (*Sukkah*

---

97. Cf. above sections on "Care Not to Shame or Embarrass" and "Human Dignity."

98. For another, perhaps more radical examples of the use of this argument, see the Rambam's responsum in *Pe'er ha-Dor*, sect. 132, ed. David Yosef, Jerusalem, 1984, pp. 260–261 (ed. Blau, vol. 2, Jerusalem, 1960, pp. 373–375), and the extent to which his ruling was accepted in note 15 ibid. And see below Appendix 6, ad fin.

gezulah) and disqualified (*pesulah*), and he may not sit in it. However, the *Beit Yosef* states that since we have not found in Rashi, the Tosafot, or the Ran (Rabbenu Nissim) an example of a stolen *sukkah* other than the one on a carriage, it would seem clear that *even if he had no intention of making a recompence, nonetheless, his sukkah is not a sukkah gezulah*, and he merely owes the value of the theft to the original owner by virtue of *takanat ha-shavim*. Indeed, so ruled the *Mishnah Berurah* (ibid. note 15, and cf. *Shaar ha Tziyyun* ibid., note 21).[99]

These extentions of the original mishnaic enactment further reflect the remarkable emphasis on benevolent legislation. This is most eloquently expressed in the statement in B. *Shabbat* 133b, "Just as He (God) is merciful and gracious, so you too shall be merciful and gracious." Going back to the verse in Exodus 34:6, "The Lord, the Lord, merciful and gracious . . ." this is the classical example of *imitatio dei*.[100]

This same principle is to be found in *Sefer Hasidim*, sect. 594, ed. S. Gutman, Brooklyn, N.Y. (c. 2013), p. 540, which reads as follows:

> He who stole or robbed, and [the rabbis] declared a ban on whosoever should have [the theft] so that he return it to its owner, and indeed, it was returned [to its owner], and even if no ban was declared, but there are witnesses that he stole and returned [the theft], one may not speak badly of him or publicize his unlawful activities]. Even if he swore [falsely] and afterwards returned [the theft], we may not embarrass him, so that we not close the door before repentents.

A very significant extension of this principle is found in a responsum of

---

99. See R. Ovadiah Yosef's extended discussion in his *Hazon Ovadiah, Sukkot,* Jerusalem, 2005, pp. 58, note 27; and note the responsum of the Rivash (R. Yitzhak ben Sheshet), no. 417, p. 639.

100. See on *Takanat ha-Shavim* the detailed analysis in N. Rakover, *Takanat ha-Shavim – Avaryan she-Ritzah Et Onsho*, Jerusalem, 2007, pass., but especially pp. 112–119 who also on p. 119, note 49, refers to R. Moshe Feinstein, *Igrot Moshe, Yoreh Deah*, part 2, sect. 46, pp. 64–66, for an example of the extended use of this principle – coupled with additional considerations; Aaron Kirschenbaum, *Equity in Jewish Law. Vol. 15: Halakhic Perspectives in Law – Formalism and Flexibility in Jewish Civil Law.* Hoboken N.J. and New York, 1991, p. 35, as an example of "equitable legislation"; Yitzhak Brenner, "*Takanat ha-Shavim*" *Dinei Yisrael* 20–21, 2000–2001, pp. 437–473; and also most recently Barry Selman, "*Mipnei Takanat ha-Shavim*: Outreach Considerations in Psak Halakhah," *Milin Havivin* 3, 2007, pp. 85–91.

the Rambam in his *Peer ha-Dor*, no. 132 (ed. David Yosef, Jerusalem, 1980, p. 261, ed. Blau, vol. 2, Jerusalem, 1960, pp. 374–375, with variations), where he was asked concerning a young man, who was said to have maintained relations with a non-Jewish maid-servant, whether, inter alia, he could release her from servitude, convert her, and marry her. Although this would appear to be contrary to Talmudic ruling (*B. Yevamot* 21b), he permits such a marriage, concluding:

> And so when we ruled in such cases that she should be released from servitude and he should marry her, we ruled thus because of *takanat ha-shavim*, and [in addition] we said better that she eat gravy and not the [forbidden] fat itself (based on *B. Kiddushin* 21b and *B. Yoma* 82a, i.e., this be the lesser evil), and "It is time for Thee, Lord, to work: for they have made void Thy law" (Psalms 119:126, and cf. *M. Berachot* 9:5, i.e., sometimes it is necessary, and also legitimate, to transgress the law under special circumstances. See also *B. Gittin* 60a, *Soferim* 16:10, etc.).

The Rambam here gives three reasons for his unusual rulings, but the first listed, and perhaps of the primary priority, is that of *takanat ha-shavim*. Indeed, in a variant reading of this responsum, cited by Yosef in his note 10 on p. 261, the text states "and we have ruled thus on many occasions in cases similar to this one."

R. Uziel used this responsum of the Rambam in his seminal responsum in *Mishpetei Uziel*, vol. 1, *Yoreah Deah*, no. 14, in the case of a Jew in Saloniki who married a gentile woman and lived with her many years, had children with her, and she afterward decided to convert to Judaism, permitting her to convert, him to marry her in a Jewish manner, etc. The Rambam's argument formed a significant element in his ruling. In this ruling, he also relied partially on R. Shaul Elyashar (1817–1906), in his *Yisa Ish*, 1986, *Even ha-Ezer* no.7, and disagreed with R. Shmuel Matalon, from Saloniki, in his *Avodat ha-Shem*, Saloniki, 1893, *Even ha-Ezer* no. 4.[101]

An extension of *Takanat ha-Shavim* is to ensure that the penitent

---

101. See the extensive analysis of Tzvi Zohar, *Conversion (Giyyur) in Our Times: A Study in the Halakhic Responsa of Rabbi Uzziel*, Jerusalem, 2012, [Hebrew], pp. 35–54 (especially pp. 50–51.) R. Uziel used this principle with the Rambam's responsum as a precedent in a number of additional responsa, as Zohar has so masterfully demonstrated (ibid., pp. 89–92, 96, 108–109, 131–133, 158, 166, 302).

baal teshuvah does not continue to hear the stigma of his past, for that would surely deter him from repenting his sins and correcting his aberrant behavior. To this end we read what R. Hai Gaon wrote in one of his responsa:

> If a person left the faith, and he is senior and great [i.e., important], and then he repented openly, not secretly nor hiddenly, he has the status of a kosher [Jew]. He may pray among the multitude on Yom Kippur and at any time, and if he is a *Kohen* he may bless the people, and no one has the right to argue with him or prevent him from that to which he is suited, [and he is] like all other kosher Jews . . . And even if he ate carrion on the meat of camels and pigs unwittingly, one may not shame him for this, nor prevent him from praying in the community (*be-rabim*). And he who shames him over these things . . . one is deligated to place a ban upon him, and keep him away from the community of God, for he is standing against the blood of his neighbour [reference to Leviticus 19:16]. And one must be very careful in this matter, and act with stringency against anyone who shames such a person, and prevent any such occurrence. . . .[102]

This position goes back to a passage in *Tosefta Demai* 2:8 (cited in *B. Avodah Zarah* 7a, *B. Berachot* 31c), where R. Shimon and R. Yehudah rule "that all those who do repent are received, as it is written, 'Return, ye backsliding children, [and I will] heal your backslidings. Behold, we come unto thee, because that art the Lord our God' (Jeremiah 3:22)." And the Talmud in *Avodah Zarah* ibid. states:

> R. Yitzhak from Kfar Akko said [in the name of] R. Yohanan: The halachah is in accordance with [the view of] that couple [i.e., R. Shimon and R. Yehudah].[103]

And we find a clear expression of this position in the liturgy of the *Kol Nidrei* ritual on the night of Yom Kippur, where it is publically announced that sinners [i.e., those against whom bans were initiated] are permitted to join in prayer with the general community.

---

102. See M.A. Friedman, "*Mi-Shut Rav Hai Gaon: Ketaim Hadashim min ha-Genizah*," *Teudah* 3, 1983, p. 79; Rakover, ibid., pp. 139–140.

103. See Rakover, ibid., pp. 132–145.

This principle also finds its use in certain cases of leniency in personal status law. See e.g., Rambam's responsum in *Peer ha-Dor*, ed. David Yosef, Jerusalem, 1984, no. 132, p. 261, and closer to our times in R. Eliezer Waldenberg, *Tzitz Eliezer*, vol. 16, Jerusalem, 1988, no. 65, pp. 168–170.[104]

But perhaps even more remarkable is the statement in B. *Baba Kama* 94b (whose source is in *Tosefta Sheviit* 8:12):

> We have learned: The robbers (*gazlanim*) and usurers who wished to return (the theft or the money), one does not accept this from them. And he who does accept, the rabbis are dissatisfied with him. Said R. Yohanan, "In the days of Rabbi [Yehudah HaNasi] this passage was formulated. For we have learned: It once happened that a certain person wished to repent. His wife said to him, "Oh empty one, if you repent, even your girdle will not be yours, (i.e., if you return everything you stole, you will be left with absolutely nothing)." And he desisted and did not repent. At that hour they said: The robbers and the usurers who wished to return, one does not accept from them, and he who does accept, the rabbis are dissatisfied with him.

This is, of course, an extension of *takanat ha-shavim*, the details of which are discussed among the *Rishonim*, and brought in the *Shulhan Aruch, Hoshen Mishpat* 366:1 as follows:

> A well-known robber who wishes to repent, if what he stole no longer exists, one does not accept from him, so that he desist not from repenting. But if he wishes to atone before heavens, and return [what he had taken], we do not stop the one whom he robbed from accepting from him.[105]

---

104. See also *Sefer Hasidim* ibid., sect. 597. See above section on "Care Not to Shame or Embarrass." This principle appears frequently in *Sefer Hasidim*, see index in ed. Gutman, ibid., p. 50a s.v. *busha ve-bizionot*.

105. See the extended discussion in Rakover, ibid., pp. 120–231 with additional bibliographic references.

A remarkable example of the halachah's willingness to forgive and accept may be found in *Shulhan Aruch, Hoshen Mishpat* 34:22. There we read concerning those who are acceptable as witnesses – in a section that lists those who are not acceptable – in the Rema's annotation, as follows:

An apostate who was remorseful and took upon himself to be a penitent, is immediately accepted, even though he has not yet began his penitence.

Finally, see *Derashot ha-Hatam Sofer* 407, cited by Y. Weiss, in his *Rabbanut u-Kehillah be-Mishnat Maran ha-Hatam Sofer zt"l*, Jerusalem, 1987, pp. 50–51, beginning, "It is well known that the leader in Israel must be a person of mercy who gives direction to his people with compassion . . ." and consequently must do all, within the parameters of the halachah, to encourage people to rectify their wrongs and ease their way to this end.

Summary of the "Friendly" *Pesak*

These are but some of the many examples of how ethical foundations direct the methods of halachic teaching and create a halachic reality. Let us end this section by citing the words of Maimonides in *Mishneh Torah, Hilchot Shabbat* 2:3: "This teaches that the judgments of the Torah do not [bring] vengeance to the world, but rather bring mercy,[106] kindness, and peace to the world." This is a clear and decisive formu-

---

The supercommentaries (*Shach* ad loc. 21, *Sma* ad loc. 54) cite the *Terumat ha-Deshen* of R. Yisrael Isserlein (1390-1460), responsum 198, who explains that:

Since the apostate was living among gentiles who have all sorts of lusts (*taavot*), and he wishes to distance himself from all of them and be repentant, they – i.e. the Rabbis – were not stringent with him and accepted that he would indeed be completely repentant.

We see how remarkably generous and permissive the Rabbis were even so far as to accept and encourage an apostate in his initial stage of repentence. It is interesting to compare this with the statement of R. Yoel Sirkes (the *Bah* to *Yoreh Deah* 268:13:

It is common knowledge at present that the majority of apostates have converted out of their lust for robbery, promiscuity, and consuming ritually forbidden foods in public.

Cf. idem, ibid. 340:35:

Probably all apostates in our times have not [really] converted except for reasons of lust (*lo nishtamed ela le-teiavon*).

See further Shlomo Eidelberg, *Jewish Life in Austria in the XVth Century*, Philadelphia, 1962, pp. 27–31.

106. See Y.I. Herzog, *Heichal Yitzhak Even ha-Ezer* 2, Jerusalem, 1967, sections 85–86, pp. 305–315 on the following case: A priest married a widow on the assumption that she was available, but afterwards it became known that her first husband had a brother and that she was thus beholden to perform a levirate marriage with the brother, who publicly profanes the Sabbath and eats non-kosher meat. While the woman was living with her first husband, she underwent very difficult surgery in which they removed her uterus and her reproductive organs, and the doctors indicated that her reproductive organs were faulty from birth and that it was obvious from the start that she would never have children. The woman and her husband are very attached to each other, and they say that were they to be separated, it would be at the expense of

lation of the fact that those basic values constitute the foundation for halachic decision-making. How much the scholars of our generation could learn from these words of the great teacher of the complexity of the halachah.[107]

---

their lives. Rabbi Herzog was asked if a permit could be found to allow them to remain together, and he found a permit which he explains in a lengthy and detailed discussion.

107. As another example, we mention the case of the "deadly woman" – Katlanit (two of her husbands have died), about whom the Rosh ruled (Ketubot 4:3) that we force him (her new husband) to divorce her. The Ritva also ruled (Yevamot 64b) that we excommunicate him until he divorces her, an act that was actually employed by Maimonides. This approach was also cited in the name of the Nimukei Yosef, ibid. It is also implied in Sefer Hassidim (107–108), and is the opinion of the Tur (Even ha-Ezer 9) and Shiltei Giborim, ibid. However, Maimonides in responsa Pe'er ha-Dor 146, wrote: "And the prevailing custom with us is that we don't marry one who has this presumption before we ask her if she wants to, and him if he wants to, for maybe she has found another man who wants to marry her, and if she with the best of intentions accepts matrimony before two witnesses, we then bring her to the rabbinical court where they write a ketubah for her, bring her under the marriage canopy, and recite the seven blessings. This is what was done in the court of Rabbenu Yitzhak, author of the Halachot (the Ritz), in the court of his student Rabbenu Yosef Halevy, and in all subsequent courts, as we ruled and performed in practice in Egypt from the time that we arrived there." This is apparently in opposition to explicit sections of the Gemara, such as Yevamot 64b and Niddah 64a. See what is written in Yevamot 24a: "To a third she may not get married?" in the language of the questioner. Yet Maimonides ruled that she should not marry, "whether because it is actually forbidden (because of a concern for saving a life), or because there is a general concern." (See responsa Pe'er ha-Dor, Rabbi David Yosef edition, vol. 1, Jerusalem, 1984, pp. 282–287, which brings voluminous additional sources in its rich and fascinating notes.) The Noda bi-Yehudah also discussed this question (Even ha-Ezer 9, Machon Yerushalayim edition, Jerusalem, 1994, pp. 27–28) with regard to his beloved student whose "soul I see longs to cling, but wants to receive permission from me." He continues: "Know my dear that the words of the Shulhan Aruch, Even ha-Ezer, are open before you, and you see that it is impossible to issue a permit a priori, and while his rabbi can be permissive without protest, it is enough that I not protest, since I see that your desire and yearnings to say this, I will copy the words of Maimonides in a responsum." He then cited the responsum mentioned above, but subsequently he writes: "But the Rosh was very stringent in this matter." A decision in opposition to the Rosh was very difficult for him, but apparently because of his mercy and pity for his student, he continued as follows: "And know that I can issue one leniency," but after doing so, he concluded: "Nevertheless, since I did not find this reasoning in any of the former scholars, I could not bring myself to permit explicitly, but it is sufficiently clear to anyone who wants in any case to act, that he has a small peg upon which to hang his actions and to remove the fear from his heart." We see the ambivalence of this great halachic authority, and his great desire to find an opening for a permit to lighten the emotional burden of his beloved student, as well as the spirit of mercy that beats in his heart. And note the ambivalent attitude of the Hatam Sofer, in his responsum no. 22 to Even ha-Ezer, where he writes that it

is dependent upon whether the groom fears marrying a *katlanit* or not (*talia be-man de-kapid*, and if the groom came to the rabbi asking him whether or not to marry, presumably he is fearful, and should therefore desist from such a marriage. (See most recently, Y.A. Schwartz, *Tzava'at R. Yehudah le-Hassid le Shiduchim ve-Nisuin*, Bnai Brak, 2016, pp. 184–185.) And the Rivash, R. Yitzhak ben Sheshet, in his responsum no. 241 (ed. D. Metzger, Jerusalem, 1993, vol. 2, pp. 304–305) rules that if nonetheless someone married a *katlanit*, we do not demand a divorce. See also *Beit Yosef* to *Even ha-Ezer* 9. (See responsa *Sho'el u-Meishiv*, *Tinyana* edition, vol. 1, 14, *Likutei ha-Edot*, p. 371, which finds support for the *Noda bi-Yehudah* from the *Tanhuma*, end of *Parshat Ha'azinu*, according to which it would appear that she is a *katlanit* only after *three* husbands died.) The story in the *Tanhuma* is a tale and abbreviated version of *Maasei-Tuviah*. See A.H. Fraenkel, *Simhah Temimah*, Jerusalem, 1986, pp. 267–269. For bibliographic references on the Tuviah story, see M.M. Kasher and Y.D. Mandelbaum, *Sarei ha-Elef*, 2nd edition, Jerusalem, 1979, vol. 1, p. 52, no. 21, vol. 2, p. 563. See also Frank Zimmerman's introduction to his edition and translation of *The Book of Tobit*, New York, 1985. See also the book of Rabbi Aryeh Leib Gelman, *Ha-Noda bi-Yehudah u-Mishnato le-Or Pesakav u-Drashav*, Jerusalem, Mossad Harav Kook, 1962, Chapter 5, pp. 43–59, "*Rahamin be-Din: Al Meafyen Zeh be-Psikotav*," and the following chapter (pp. 51–52) in which he discussed the power of leniency as the guiding principle in his rulings. This issue is also discussed in R. Tzvi Hersch Chajes, apud *Kol Kitvei Maharatz Chajest*, Jerusalem, 1938, *Darkei Horaah*, chapter 4, p. 229, on leniency with regard to the *katlanit*. See further A. Grossman, "*Mi-Morashto Shel Yahadut Sefarad: Ha-Yahas El ha-Ishah ha-'Katlanit bi-Yemei ha-Beinaim*" *Tarbiz* 67, 1998, pp. 531–561; idem, *Hassidot u-Mordot*, 2nd edition, Jerusalem, 2003, pp. 474–493; idem, *Ve-Hu Yimshol Bach*, Jerusalem, 2011, index "*Katlanit*," p. 617. Aviad ha-Cohen, "*Shikulim Meta-Hilchatiim be-Pesikat ha-Halachah*," *Filosofiah shel ha-Halachah*, Jerusalem, 2008, p. 299. And see most recently Shoshana Razel Gordon Guedalia's essay in *Keren* 1, 2013, pp. 85–97, entitled "'The Pesaqratic Oath': Good Faith Presumption in the Spirit of Religio-Legal Rulings" for an analysis of R. Yaakov Ettlinger's position of the *katlanit* in his *Binyan Tzion*, no. 131. On the Rambam's position on the *katlanit*, see what Yaakov Blidstein wrote in his article "*Ha-Emet shel ha-Dayan ke-Chli Pesikah*," *Dinei Yisrael* 24, 2006, pp. 148–149, and see M.A. Friedman, "Tamar: A Symbol of Life: The Killer-Wife Superstition in the Bible of Jewish Tradition," *AJS Review* 15:1, 1990, pp. 50–54.

See further the many responsa of R. Ovadiah Yosef in his *Yabia Omer* (see index in vol. 11), but most especially in vol. 3, 2nd edition, Jerusalem, 1986, *Even ha-Ezer* no. 5, pp. 220–225, and ibid., vol. 10, Jerusalem, 2004, *Yoreh Deah*, no. 9, p. 217, that according to some authorities this law no longer applies. See above p. 122 note 81.

To the above we may add a reference to R. Tzvi Pesach Frank's *Har Tzvi*, *Even ha-Ezer* vol. 1, Jerusalem, 2004, no. 31, p. 69, where we find a whole series of detailed reasons for permitting a *katlanit* to remarry.

However, the most remarkable approach to the prohibition of the *katlanit* is that of the Rambam, in his *Pe'er ha-Dor*, no. 146, ed. David Yosef, Jerusalem, 1984, pp. 284–285. First he is amazed at learned rabbis who do not distinguish between prohibitions of biblical authority and those of rabbinic status. He then continues to explain that there is no actual *issur* (prohibition) for the *katlanit* to remarry; rather, it is merely advice because of possible danger. Furthermore, if we forbid it, she may well

What emerges from all of the above is that innovative halachic creativity must include enhanced sensitivity to the demands of ethical values, which should be the central factors in determining the halachah. (See infra note 168.)

---

act in a transgressionary way and fall into the hands of sinners. He brings testimony that they used to carry out full wedding ceremonies to *katlaniot* in the *beit din* of the *Rif* (R. Yitzhak Alfasi) and his disciple R. Yosef ha-Levi, and were followed by other religious courts and "such is [the] ruling in Egypt from the day I arrived. For can one reject a mitzvah of the Torah because of mere suspicion (or apprehension) (*hashasha be-alma*)? We have never heard of such a thing!" (This responsum is cited in brief in the *Noda bi-Yehudah Kama, Even ha-Ezer*, no. 9, by R. Yehezkel Landau, ed. *Noda bi-Yehudah ha-Shalem, Even ha-Ezer*, vol. 1, Jerusalem, 1994, pp. 27–28.)

However, this is contrary to the ruling of the Rosh, *Ketubot*, chapter 4, sect. 3, who obligates a divorce. So too the *Ritba* to *Yevamot* 64b and the *Nimukei Yosef*, ibid., *Sefer Hasidim* nos. 477–478, Tur *Even ha-Ezer* 9, and cf. *Shulhan Aruch*, ibid., that if she got married we do not force a divorce. See the extensive discussion in the editor's notes to *Peer ha-Dor*, ibid., no. 23, pp. 285–286.

II. THE "FRIENDLY" POSEK

The Unfriendly Rabbi

After trying to uncover and delineate directions and trends in methods of halachic *pesak*, we will try to identify the appropriate personal qualities of the rabbinic *posek*. We will begin by citing six stories[1] from the *Gemara*, all six demonstrating negative qualities that should be avoided.

First Story: The Winds of Man

The first story appears in *Gittin* 31b:

> Rav Huna and Rav Hisda were once sitting together when Geniva passed by them.[2] One of them said: "Let us rise before him,[3] for he is a learned

---

1. On Talmudic stories in general, see Yona Fraenkel, *Iyyunim be-Olamo ha-Ruhani shel Sippur ha-Aggadah*, Tel-Aviv, 1981: idem, *Sippur ha-Aggadah-Ahdut shel Tohen ve-Tzura: Kovetz Maamarim*, Tel Aviv, 2001; Jeffrey L. Rubinstein, *Talmudic Stories: Narative Art, Composition, and Culture*, Baltimore and London, 1999, etc.

2. Geniva was a scholar, as we see in the *Jerusalem Talmud Avodah Zarah* 2:8; *Gittin* 7a, as well as from the continuation of our story in *Gittin* 62a. See an in depth discussion on this point in the article of Moshe Beer, "*Rivo Shel Geniva be-Mar Ukva*," *Tarbiz* 31(3), 1962, pp. 281–286, who explains the nature of Geniva's "quarrelsomeness" within historical political context concerning the status of the Reish Galuta.

3. Compare to *Shabbat* 31b: "Let us arise before him, because he is a sin-fearing man" and *Kiddushin* 33b: "Rabbi Yehezkel was different for he had many good deeds to his credit, so that even Mar Shmuel stood up before him."

See Y. *Bikkurim* 3:3 for an extended discussion on before whom one should rise, and also before whom one should not rise. Thus, for instance, R. Yoshiah says concerning a judge or rabbi who is appointed for monetary reasons that "the *tallit* that is upon him is like the pack-saddle of an ass." Another authority, R. Shayn, declares that for such a person "one does not rise before him, neither does one address him [as rabbi]," etc. See Yisachar Tamar, *Alei Tamar* ad loc., Givataim, 1980, *Zeraim*, vol. 2,

man." Said the other: "Shall we rise before a quarrelsome man?" When he came up to them he asked them what they were discussing, they replied: "We were talking about the winds (ruhot)." He said to them, "Thus said Rav Hanan b. Rava in the name of Rav: Four winds blow every day and the north wind blows with all of them, for were it not so the world would not be able to exist for a moment. The south wind is the most violent of all, and were it not that the Son of the Hawk keeps it back, it would devastate the whole world; for so it says, 'Does the hawk soar by thy wisdom, and stretch her wings towards the south?' (Job 39:26)."

It has been questioned how these two scholars could give a non-truthful response to Geniva, as if they were speaking about the winds when they were not. One of the proponents of *mussar* answered by quoting the following *Mishnah* from *Pirkei Avot* (3:10): "He [Rabbi Hanina ben Dosa] would also say: One who is pleasing to his fellow men [*ru'ah habriyot noha heimenu* – the word *ru'ah* also means wind], is pleasing to God. But one who is not pleasing to his fellow men, is not pleasing to God." They were speaking about these *ruhot*,[4] or in other words, they

---

pp. 247–249 (that this refers both to judges as well as rabbis). See further *Or Zarua, Alfa Beta*, no. 37, *Midrash Shemuel* 7:6, ed. Buber, Cracow, 1893, p. 68. And see the various commentaries to Exodus 18:21, on those who "hate covetousness." See further M.M. Kasher, *Torah Shelemah*, vol. 16, New York, 1953, p. 37, note 136 to that verse.
See also B. *Ta'anit* 7a, where we read:
Rava pointed out an incongruity: It is written, "My doctrine shall drop (*yaarof*) as the rain," and then "My speech shall distil as the dew" (Deuteronomy 32:2). The explanation is that for a scholar who is worthy, the Torah will distil on him like dew, but if he is not, it will drop on him like rain (*orfehu ke-matar*)."
These latter two words have been variously interpreted. Pseudo-Rashi ad loc. explains "kill him" – *orfehu* – means something like "chop off his neck" or "break his neck" form *oref* – neck. However, this seems a little extreme, to say the least. Henry (Tzvi) Malter, in his translation to *Ta'anit*, Philadelphia, 1967, p. 80, in a footnote writes: "the learning will harm him, as heavy rain harms the crop." The author of *Tzror ha-Kesef ve-Tzror ha-Hayyim*, R. Hayyim ben Shmuel (a disciple of the Rashba), in his notes to B. *Ta'anit* 28, offered a different interpretation. However, the Maharsha, ad loc., suggests the meaning to be "turn your back (literally neck) on him." This seems to be the more likely explanation, i.e., ignore him, which is what Rav Huna and Rav Hisda did.
See also R. Hayyim Yaakov Sofer, *Ner Yehudah*, Jerusalem, 1992, chapter 13, pp. 208–210.
4. A very nice short article was written by Rabbi Isaac Klein of Temple Emmanuel in Buffalo, New York: Isaac Klein, "The Rabbi and his Family," in Jules Harlow (ed.),

were saying that it is not enough to be a great and enlightened scholar, but a scholar must also be pleasing to other people. If he is pleasing to his fellow men, he will also be acceptable before God. Similarly, we find the following formulation in *Avot de-Rabbi Natan* (Version 1, Chapter 22):

> He would also say: One who has good deeds and learned much Torah, what is he comparable to? To a tree that stands on water with few branches and many roots, whom all the winds in the world cannot budge from its place, as is stated, "He shall be as a tree planted upon water . . ." (Psalms 1:3). One who has no good deeds but has learned much Torah, what is he comparable to? To a tree in the desert with many branches and few roots; comes a storm and uproots it, and turns it on its face, as is stated: "He shall be as a lone tree in a wasteland . . ." (Jeremiah 17:6).[5]

The Rabbinical Assembly Proceedings, New York: The Rabbinical Assembly, 1974, pp. 163–165. In this article, which discusses this section of *Gittin*, he brings the words of Rabbi Shimshon of Shpectiva, which connects to what appears in *Pirke Avot*. In fact, he brings the following saying of the *Jerusalem Talmud* without citing its place: "One who is pleasing to God is pleasing to his fellow man," and writes his explanation of it. Nevertheless, I have yet to find this quote in the *Jerusalem Talmud* or in any other place.

See also Daniel Z. Feldman, *The Right and the Good: Halakhah and Human Relations*, 2nd edition, New York, 2005, pp. 73–95, a chapter entitled "Not to be Brutally Honest: Lying for the sake of Peace."

And here we may recall that which is stated in a *beraita* in B. *Yoma* 86a: "And thou shalt love the Lord your God" (Deuteronomy 6:5) – that the name of God become beloved through your [behaviour]. He should read [Torah] and study [*Mishnah*] and serve learned rabbis, and his relationship towards people be gentle. What will people say about him? "Blessed be his father who taught him Torah." For this person who learned Torah, how pleasant are his ways, how correct his behaviour. Concerning him the verse writes, "And he said unto me, Thou art my servant, O Israel, in whom I will be glorified" (Isaiah 49:3). However, he who reads [Torah] and studies [*Mishnah*] and serves learned rabbis, but his relationship towards people is not one of honesty and his conversation is not gentle, what will people say about him? "Woe unto him who studied Torah; woe unto him whose father taught him Torah; woe unto his teacher who taught him Torah. This individual who studied Torah, see how spoiled are his actions, how ugly is his behaviour." Concerning him the verse writes, ". . . these are the people of the Lord, and are gone forth out of His Land" (Ezekiel 36:20).

See Rashi ad loc. explaining that they were driven out of their land, dispersed among the nations, and were beyond redemption.

5. And see what I wrote in my *On the Relationship of Mitzvot between Man and his Neighbor and Man and his Maker*, Jerusalem and New York, 2014, pp. 133–137, on one who *only* learns and does not teach and engage in civic affairs.

It is clear that one who cannot attain the respect of others cannot be a communal leader, and one who is quarrelsome and contentious cannot be a halachic authority in the Jewish world. We learn from this that a rabbinic authority must be not only a scholar who exhibits fear of Heaven, but also one who makes certain that his rulings are to the good of his constituents. If so, he will be pleasing to God.

Second Story: A Stained Reputation

The second story is found in *Massechet Moed Katan* 17a:

A certain student of the scholars[6]

---

6. It should be noted that this scholar's name is not mentioned. (See above near note 32, on the Yehudah and Tamar story.) It was a policy in Talmudic times to safeguard the honour of a sage who had sinned. "They would rarely publicize his name, nor would they openly discuss the nature of his transgression. He would, however, be judged according to the fullest severity of the law by an internal tribunal, thereby precluding any calumny." They based themselves on biblical precedents, such as the anonymous "Wood-gatherer," whom the rabbis identified as Tzelofhad, but whose name is not mentioned in the biblical source; see *B. Shabbat* 96b–97a; *Sifrei Ba-Midbar* no. 113, ed. Horovitz, Leipzig, 1917, p. 122, according to R. Akiva, (and parallels), and see M. Beer's article, in *Zion* 53/2, 1988, pp. 155–166 (English summary V – VI), entitled "*Al Likudam shel Hazal*" ("On Solidarity Among the Sages"). See, for example, the case he brings from *B. Sanhedrin* 11a, where we are told that a woman came to the *beit midrash* of R. Meir, and said to him, "Rabbi, One of you married me through intercourse." Immediately R. Meir wrote out a *get* (bill of divorce) and gave it to her. Then all the members of the *beit midrash* did the same. They each did this in order not to embarrass the individual who had committed intercourse.
    And so too in the following tale cited ibid:
    It once happened, that while Rabbi [Judah the Prince] was giving a lecture, he smelled garlic in the room. "The person who has eaten garlic must leave," he announced.
    Rabbi Hiyya stood up and left, and then all the other scholars followed him out.
    In the morning, Rabbi Simeon, the son of Rabbi, met Rabbi Hiyya and said, "Was it you who caused that annoying odor?"
    "Heaven forbid!" said Rabbi Hiyya, [but he and the other scholars wanted to keep the culprit from humiliation].
    Interestingly enough Alfred Cohen, in his article "Privacy: A Jewish Perspective" *Journal of Halacha and Contemporary Society* 1:53, 1981, pp. 74–78, (cited by Michael J. Broyde, *The Pursuit of Justice in Jewish Law*, 2nd edition, New York, 2007, p. 24), writes as follows:
    Our research shows that the majority of halachic authorities accept the position that a person whose livelihood depends upon maintaining the confidentiality of revelations made to him, need not jeopardize his position by telling those secrets. Although

keeping silent might violate the negative *mitzvah* of not standing by and allowing another Jew to be harmed, yet as long as he is not violating the commandment by *doing* any action and, were he to act he would endanger his own livelihood, then he is permited to remain silent.

Indeed, R. Hayyim Halberstam of Tzanz (1793–1876), when asked whether to reveal to a husband that his wife had had an extra-marital affair, and whether the adulterer is obliged to tell the husband so that they be divorced, ruled that he did not need to reveal his actions to the husband. See responsa *Divrei Hayyim*, vol. 1, Lvov, 1875, *Orah Hayyim*, sect. 35, for the reasoning. (And see further R. Ovadiah Yosef, *Yabia Omer*, vol. 2, *Even ha-Ezer*, sect. 2:10; N. Rakover, *Gadol Kevod ha-Briyot*, Jerusalem, 1998, p. 95, note 312, and p. 134.) On the other hand, R. Menachem Merzburk (in his *Nimukim* at the end of *Shut Mahari Weil, Dinei Boshot*) ruled in the case of a husband who slandered his wife and there was need to receive testimonies from those who heard the slander, even though they had been ordered by the husband not to reveal that which he had told them, were obligated to give evidence of the slander, for "the words of the master (i.e., the Torah) and the words of the servant – to whom do we listen [and obey]?"

See *Otzar ha-Geonim* to *Sanhedrin*, ed. Hayyim Tzvi Taubes, Jerusalem, 1967, p. 86, sect. 197. Beer also brings our stories, ibid., p. 161–162, along with a number of additional illuminating sources. As to this individual's sin, the commentators suggest he was a fornicator or adulterer (*noef*). See Beer ibid. note 44. See further Beer's article in *Tarbiz* 33/4, 1964, pp. 354–355, on the story about Rahbah bar Nahmani.

The source for this policy of preserving anonymity is, of course, in the biblical text cited above (near note 32), namely that Tamar did not reveal Yehudah's name, but merely said, "By the man whose these are, I am with child" (Genesis 38:25). From this the rabbis learned that, "Better for a man to cast himself into a fiery furnace rather than shame his fellow in public" (*B. Sotah* 10b, and *B. Berachot* 43b, *B. Ketubot* 67b). I mentioned there that my father discussed the question whether this is actual halachah or merely *aggadah*. (See e.g., R. Kook, *Daat Cohen*, sect. 84.) This issue, of the prohibition against embarrassing others, was discussed in considerable detail in David Z. Feldman, *The Right and the Good: Halakhah and Human Relations*, 2nd edition, Brooklyn, N.Y., 2005, pp. 1–36, and on the specific Tamar story, see especially ibid., pp. 2–3, note 5, with a wealth of additional sources from a wide spectrum of rabbinic literature. See also my *On the Relationship of Mitzvot between Man and His Neighbor and Man and His Maker*, Jerusalem and New York, 2014, chapter 15, p. 103 et seq.

Here we merely add, basing ourselves on M.M. Kasher, *Torah Shelemah 6/7*, Jerusalem, 1938, pp. 1472–1473, note 106, who pointed out that the derivation of this rabbinic statement "Better for a man to cast himself into a fiery furnace . . ." seems to be based on a variant reading in the biblical text, a *ketiv haser*, a *defective* reading. Our text has היא מוצאת – *hi mutzeit*, "She was led out [to judgement . . .]" But some early authorities, (such as *Tosafot Ketubot* 67b, R. Hananel, *Aruch* s.v. צת. Sechel Tov, Rif, Rashba apud *Shitah Mekubetzet*, etc.) had an alternative reading, מוצת – *mutzat*, i.e., she was being ignited! Hence, their derivation. If this is indeed a halachic statement, and not just *aggadah*, then we have here once again an example of halachah derived from (biblical, pre-Sinaitic.) *aggadah*. See above note 104. Indeed, Feldman (ibid., pp. 3–5), after surveying the different views of the various *Rishonim* who discussed this *sugya*, summarizes as follows (p. 5):

What emerges, then, is a dispute among *rishonim*, with the Rif, the Tosafot, and Rabenu Yonah taking the Talmud at its face value and obligating self-sacrifice before shaming another, and the Meiri and the Rambam apparently, unwilling to allow so drastic a notion into practical *halachah*.

See continuation of his discussion.

Here is the place to add that R. Yaakov baal ha-Turim to the verse in Genesis 28:34 states in the name of R. Yehudah ha-Hasid that (the biblical) Yehudah never intended that she be burned but that she be branded on her face as a sign that she acted as a prostitute. And R. Eliezer Ashkkenazi, in his *Gedolim Maasei ha-Shem*, Venice, 1583, *Va-Yeshev*, chapter 36, adds that this indeed is the practice among the Moslems to brand a prostitute on her forehead. (See *Prostitution: Islamic Law and Ottoman Societies*, www, z, Wurwick. ac. v.k. baldwin; William L. Andrew, *Bygone Punishments*, London, 1899. This is still practiced nowadays among the Taliban. Further on mutilation of prostitutes, see responsa of Rosh, *Klal* 18 sect. 13, on cutting off noses, Rema in *Shulhan Aruch, Even ha-Ezer* 177:5; Z.W. Zicherman, *Otzar Plaot ha-Torah*, vol. 2, Brooklyn, 2013, pp. 521–523; and on medieval Jewish prostitutes see A. Grossman, *Hasidot u-Mordot*, Jerusalem, 2001, index s.v. *zenut, zonot*, p. 545b.)

We may add in passing that the fact that Yehudah admitted his guilt served him well, for in reward he was awarded kingship. See M.M. Kasher *Torah Shelemah*, vol. 7, New York, 1850, p. 1796, note 106; cf. ibid., pp. 1799–1800, note 125.

For a different aspect of this whole issue, see Michael J. Broyde, *The Pursuit of Justice and Jewish Law; Halakhic Perspectives on the Legal Profession*, 2nd edition, New York, 2007, chapter 3, entitled "Professional Confidentiality," pp. 21–25. There (p. 24) he quotes Rabbi Alfred Cohen, "Privacy: A Jewish Perspective," *Journal of Halacha and Contemporary Society* 1, 1981, p. 84; also idem, "On Maintaining A Professional Confidence," ibid.,7, 1984, pp. 74–78; and see also the material in *Crime and Punishment in Jewish Law: Essays and Responsa*, eds. W. Jacob and M. Zemer, New York and Oxford, 1999, pp. 34–44, 81–92, 99–100.

There are additional sources in rabbinic literature from which was derived the prohibition to publicize names of sinners, so as not to shame them. See Y. *Yevamot* 8:3, where R. Levi in the name of R. Shimon ben Lakish learns from Leviticus 10:17, that the sin offering is sacrificed in the same place of the burned offering in order not to reveal the identity of the sinner. Similarly, according to B. *Sotah* 32b the *Amidah* prayer is said *silently* for the same reason. And see Y. *Bikkurim* 3:4, that the declaration of Deuteronomy 26:13 is said *silently* for this reason. Cf. M. *Sotah* 9:10 (Tosefta, ibid., 13 ad fin). See also *Shulhan Aruch, Orah Hayyim* 139:3, in the Rema; *Noda bi-Yehudah Tinyana, Even ha-Ezer* 1; B. *Ta'anit* 27b, etc.

However, we also find other approaches in rabbinic literature. Thus, the Midrash in *Numbers Rabba* 21:4 that the reason the Bible reveals the name of Zimri ben Salu (Numbers 25:14) is that:

Just as the Holy One blessed be He involves Himself in the praise of righteous people to publicize [their name] in the world, so too does He involve Himself in publicizing the shamefulness of the evil. Thus, he made public the name of Pinhas in praise, and that of Zimri in disgrace. And concerning them it is written, "The memory of the just is blessed; but the name of the wicked shall rot" (Proverbs 10:7).

And Rambam, in his commentary to *Avot* 1:16 (and cf. *Hilchot Deot* 6:8), follows this directive, ruling that one despises the wicked in order that people keep away from

obtained an unseemly reputation.[7] Rav Yehudah said: "What should we

---

them and not follow in their ways. That is to say, this is more an educational policy than a form of punishment. And Rabbenu Yonah of Gerona (13 cent.) in his *Shaarei Teshuvah* (sect. 3, nos. 147, 199, 219) states explicitly that unrepentant sinners may be shamed and one may speak openly of their disgraceful behaviour. However, these views must be treated with caution and perspicacity. Because some offenders are nonetheless positive, moral individuals who may have, as it were, one strike against them, they should be treated with respect, though this must not be taken in such a manner as to give apparent legitimacy to their errant conduct. So R. Moshe Feinstein (*Igrot Moshe Orah Hayyim*, vol. 2, sect. 51) permits honoring a Jewish doctor of fine medical repute, who is very helpful towards his patients but is married to a gentile, with the opening and closing of the ark. Other such examples could be given, but rather see N. Rakover's fine summarizing presentation in his *Gadol Kevod ha-Briyot*, Jerusalem, 1998, pp. 33–40 (and see above pp. 59–60).

On this issue of privacy, there is a considerable literature. See, for instance, N. Rakover's pamphlet *Haganah al Tzinat ha-Perat* (privacy), Jerusalem, 1970 (published by the Ministry of Justice); idem, the expanded version in his *Ha-Haganah al Tzinat ha-Perat* (Protection of Privacy in Jewish Law), Jerusalem, 2006; idem, "The Protection of Privacy in Jewish Law," *Israel Yearbook of Human Rights*, vol. 5, pp. 169–180; idem, *The Multi-Language Bibliography of Jewish Law*, Jerusalem 1990, nos. 7367–7368, 7379, 7380 7436,7438. (I have only referred to those studies in English).

See also the statement in *Zohar ha-Azinu*, vol. 3, 294b: He who reveals a secret transgresses "Thou shalt not murder," [and it is] as though he worshipped idols! R. Hayyim Palache, in his *Tochahat Hayyim*, Jerusalem (1994), vol. 2, p. 484, among his ten directives to a judge, lists one that if he finds some wrong-doing in the defendant, and the defendant accepts the judgement, the judge may not reveal the wrong-doing lest it generate hate. See further ibid., p. 186, not to reveal secrets even to your wife.

Of related interest is the very fine comment made by R. Yaakov Hayyim Sofer, in his booklet *Lecha Naeh le-Hodot*, Jerusalem, 2010, p. 113, namely that the *Hafetz Hayyim*, in his *Mishnah Berurah*, when he rejects the view of R. Shneur Zalman mi-Ladi author of the Tania, (in three places) in his *Shulhan Aruch ha-Rav*, never calls him by his name, but merely "One of the *Aharonim*." And in parenthesis he suggests that "One" – *Ehad* – hints at what is stated in B. *Megillah* 28a [B. *Yoma* 34b, ibid. 70b], and B. *Hulin* 28a, "Ehad Meyuhad" – the one special one – thus indicating his enormous respect for the Baal ha-Tania.

7. See *Shulhan Aruch, Yoreh Deah* 246:8: A teacher who does not go in the proper way – even though he is very learned and every one is dependent upon him – one should not learn from him until he repents. Cf. Rambam, *Hilchot Talmud Torah* 4:1; Shach, *Yoreh Deah* ad loc.

Of tangental interest in the chapter in Jeffrey L. Rubinstein, *Talmudic Stories: Normative Art, Composition and Culture*, Baltimore and London 1999, entitled: "Torah and the Sinful Sage," pp. 64–104. R. Ovadiah Yosef, in *Yabia Omer*, vol. 7, *Yoreh Deah*, sect. 19, pp. 242–244, and again in a somewhat abbreviated form in his *Anaf Etz Avot al Pirkei Avot*, Jerusalem, 2011, pp. 232–236 rules that one may not learn from a *Talmid Hacham* who is tainted in some form, discussing how R. Meir studied under Aher, Elisha ben Avuyah, according to B. *Hagigah* 15b, and explaining why that was acceptable.

do? Excommunicate him? The rabbis need him. Not excommunicate him? It would be a profanation of the name of Heaven." He said to Raba bar Bar Hana: "Have you heard anything on this point?" Raba bar Bar Hana replied: "Thus said R. Yohanan: What is the meaning of the verse 'For the priest's lips should keep knowledge, and they should seek the law at his mouth; for he is the messenger of the Lord of hosts' (Malachi 2:7)? If the rabbi is like a messenger of the Lord of hosts, they should seek the law at his mouth, but if he is not, they should not seek the law at his mouth." So Rav Yehudah excommunicated him. In the end, Rav Yehudah became sick. The rabbis came to inquire about him and that man came along with them. When Rav Yehudah saw him, he laughed. The man said to him: "It is not enough that he put upon me excommunication, but he even laughs at me?" Rav Yehudah replied: "I am not laughing at you, but as I am leaving to the world beyond, I am happy to think that I did not indulge even such a person as you." Rav Yehudah's soul came to rest. The man then came to the House of Study and said to them: "Absolve me." The rabbis said to him: "There is no man here of the standing of Rav Yehudah who can absolve you, but go to Rabbi Yehuda Nesiah that he may absolve you." He went to him. He [Rabbi Yehuda Nesiah] said to R. Ammi: "Go forth and look into his case, and if it is necessary to absolve him, absolve him." R. Ammi looked into his case and was disposed to absolve him. Rabbi Shmuel bar Nahmani stood up and said: "Even the severance of a maid servant was not treated lightly by the rabbis for three years, how much more so one imposed by our colleague Rav Yehudah." R. Zeira said: "The fact that this scholar happened to come to the House of Study now after not having come for so many years, informs us that he should not be absolved." He [Rabbi Yehuda Nesiah] did not absolve him. [The man] cried and left. A wasp then came and stung him in his private parts and he died. They brought him to the burial cave of the pious, but they did not accept him. They brought him to the burial cave of the judges, and they did accept him. Why so? Because he acted in accordance with the dictum of Rabbi Illai, for Rabbi Illai said: "If one sees that his evil inclination is gaining sway over him, he should go to a place where he is unknown, put on black clothes and wrap himself in a

---

These texts have been further analyzed and discussed by Malka Puterkovsky, in her *Mehalechet be-Darka* (Following her Halakhic Way), Tel Aviv, 2014, pp. 482–496.

black garment, and do what his heart desires, but not publicly profane the name of Heaven."[8]

We can compare R. Yohanan's statement cited above with another of his statements in B. Ta'anit 7a:

This is what R. Yohanan said: ". . . For the man is [like] the tree of the field" (Deuteronomy 20:19). And is a "man the tree of the field"? But the verse says, "for thou mayest cut of them, and thou shalt not cut them down" (ibid.), and it is says "that one thou shalt destroy and cut down" (ibid., 20:20) . . . How (do we solve this apparent contradiction)? If he is a decent scholar, "for him may you eat [the fruits, i.e., benefit from his learning], and not cut [him] down; but if not, that one thou shalt destroy and cut down."

(Rashi explains that this means to keep away from him.) See further the various statements of Rav Hanina bar Papa, Rav Aha bar Rav Hanina, and Rava (ibid.) all of whom contrast the worthy scholar, basing themselves on the verse in Deuteronomy 32:2 that one keep away from the unworthy scholar and seek one's learning elsewhere. (Rava's derivation is problematic; see H. Malter, *The Treatise Ta'anit of the Babylonian Talmud* [the critical edition, in Hebrew], New York, 1930, p. 19, to line 13, and *Torah Temimah* ad loc.)

Indeed, R. Ovadiah Yosef, in his *Yabia Omer*, vol. 7, Jerusalem, 1993, *Yoreh Deah* 19, pp. 242–244, and again in vol. 9, Jerusalem, 2002, *Orah Hayyim* 76:6, p. 115, rules that one may not learn Torah nor cite halachic rulings from a rabbi whose behaviour is questionable.

---

8. The difficulty in this story lies in the fact that Rav Yehudah lived in Babylonia, and R. Yehuda Nesiah lived in Eretz-Yisrael. How likely is it that a person would travel from Babylonia to Palestine to have his excommunication absolved? The solution would seem to be that we know there was considerable traffic between the two countries during this period. See, for example, my article in *Archiv Orientalni* 34, 1966, pp. 54–66, entitled "The Inflation in Fourth Century Palestine" and ibid., 38, 1970, pp. 1–25, "On Social and Economic Conditions in Third Century Palestine." It may well be that the man was one of the *Nehutei*, a travelling salesmen who moved regularly between these two countries. On some such occasion he could have sought the aid of Rabbi Yehuda Nesiah. But since he is not identified in our text (and understably so as explained above), all this remains within the realm of conjecture. On the *Nehutei* see, for example, M.A. Tennenblat, *Perakim Hadashim le-Toldot Eretz-Yisrael u-Bavel bi-Tekufat ha-Talmud*, Tel Aviv, 1966, p. 290, 354, 365.

This means that a rabbi who serves as a guide for others must be free of any stain on his reputation[9] and be punctilious in his personal qualities.[10] This is reminiscent of the statement cited in *Yoma* 86a:

---

9. See Rambam, *Hilchot Sanhedrin* 2:6. See the comments of the *Maharik* (Rabbi Yosef Colon) on rabbis who "have a bad reputation, and through them the divine name is desecrated," in the responsum of the *Maharik* 161. Great rabbis were particularly punctilious about distancing themselves from any trace of sin. It is told about the Holy Saba, Rabbi Yisrael of Viznitz, that if he sent a letter through a courier and not through the postal service, he would tear a stamp. See the book of Natan Eli Roth, *Sefer Kadosh Yisrael*, Bnei Brak: The Institute for the Distribution of Hassidic Teachings Nahalat Tzvi, 1976, p. 247-248.

Cf where R. Shmuel David ha-Cohen Munk relates in his responsa *Peat Sadcha* (vol. 2, sect. 149) that he once received a letter in the post with a stamp that by mistake was not franked by the postal authorities, and he was not certain if this was considered to be a loss of the non-Jewish postal authorities or a theft. Theft from a non-Jew (*gezel akum*) is forbidden (Rambam, *Hilchot Gezeilah ve-Aveidah* 30:2, *Shulhan Aruch, Hoshen Mishpat* 348:2, 359:1), whereas there is no obligation to return a non-Jewish lost object (*B. Sanhedrin* 76b). The question was posed to the Hazon Ish whether this unfranked stamp could be used again, or would this be considered theft. His reply was that reuse of the stamp would be considered theft from the postal authorities and therefore prohibited. (See *Meorot ha-Daf ha-Yomi*, vol. 6, Bnei Brak, 2006, p. 69, to *B. Sanhedrin* 57a, citing *Maaseh Ish*, vol. 5.) R. Yehuda Leib Maimon, in his *Sarei ha-Meah*, vol.1, 6th edition, Jerusalem, 1961, p. 283, tells a similar tale relating to R. Akiva Eiger:

It is related that (after he had saved many people during a plague) [R. Akiva Eiger] was sent a special letter of thanks from the king in the hand of a noble messenger. He, of course, welcomed the nobleman warmly and most respectfully, taking him into his inner sanctum. The nobleman saw on the table a small box full of unusual torn stamps. Expressing his surprise he asked R. Akiva Eiger the meaning of these torn stamps. R . Akiva answered, saying, "From the neighbouring cities I receive by special messengers many questions which require my opinion. I write my answers and hand them over to the messengers to bring back to the questioners. And each time I do this I buy a stamp and tear it so that the government should not be caused a loss of income."

See also the book of *Meir Eini Yisrael* (on the *Hafetz Hayyim*), Bnei Brak, 1951, p. 291 ff., regarding his punctiliousness on anything that involved a suspicion of thievery, etc. See also Rabbi H.D. Halevi, vol. 1, *Asei lecha Rav*, vol. 3, p. 72, that a rabbi should never accept a gift. See also Y.L. Maimon, *Sarei ha-Meah*, Jerusalem, 1961, vol. 2, p. 274, on R. Tzvi Hirsch Rabinowitz's description of the requirements of a rabbi. (He was the son-in-law of R. Yitzhak Elhanan Spektor.)

10. Compare to the responsum attributed to Rav Amram Gaon that is cited in the responsa of Rabbi Yoel ha-Cohen Miller, *Halachot Pesukot Min ha-Geonim*, Cracow, 1853, Section 92, pp. 51–52: "A cantor about whom there was bad gossip, they must get together to get rid of him and bring in another in his place, for anyone whose role is to conciliate between Israel and their Father in heaven must be righteous, straight, and free of any blemish. If he is not so, the rabbis said: 'My heritage has become unto me as a lion in the forest; she has uttered her voice against me; therefore have I hated her.' This refers to the cantor who goes before the ark when he is not worthy" (*Ta'anit*

15b). (This responsum appears in *Sefer Rav Amram Gaon* 2:55 [Goldschmidt edition, Jerusalem, 1972, p. 94]: "They asked before the *metivta* . . ." and in *Sefer ha-Manhig*, at the beginning of *Hilchot Ta'anit* [Rafael edition, Jerusalem, 1978, p. 269]: "As Rav Natronai . . . ." For remaining references, which are primarily related to the *Rishonim*, see note 15 of the editor and the comment of Goldschmidt there. See also Rabbi Binyamin Menasheh Lewin [ed.], *Otzar ha-Geonim, Ta'anit*, Jerusalem, 1933, section 55, pp. 27–28, and *Sha'arei Teshuvah* 51, in the name of Rav Hai.)

We may further compare this with a similar responsum possibly of Rav Natronai Gaon, Gaon of Pumbedita in Babylonia c. 938–1038), found in *Teshuvot Geonei Mizrah u-Maarav*, ed. Y. Miller, Berlin, 1888, no. 132, fol. 30b–31b (cited in Avraham Yaakov Finkel's *The Responsa Anthology*, New Jersey and London, 1990, p. 9, but misleadingly referring to *Teshuvot ha-Geonim mi-Toch ha-"Genizah"* ed. S. Assaf, Jerusalem, 1929, where it is not to be found. Furthermore, he attributes it to Rav Hai Gaon). We cite Finkel's translation (though it is not an accurate translation but more an abbreviated paraphrase, which gives a fair rendering of the contents):

Question: concerning a Kohen who is a Torah scholar and has objectionable character traits. He regards himself as a wise man and has contempt for everyone. . . . He often publicly insults people, telling them what fools they are. He even curses his aged mother. He has a bad temper and would think nothing of killing a man. Most people know that he has these qualities, yet he pretends to be a virtuous man. He lectures people on the values of modesty and humility, on respecting the truth, and the like. Everyone says that he is a disgrace to God's name and that he is not qualified to be a Kohen. We have found precedents in the writings of the rabbis where kohanim were disqualified. [Is this man unfit to officiate as a kohen?]

Responsum: This is most certainly a case of desecration of God's name. A Torah scholar who does not act properly is discussed in (an external) Mishnah, (i.e., *Pesikta Rabbati*, ed. Ish Shalom, Vienna, 1880, chapter 22, fol. 110b–114b), where Rabbi Shimon interprets the verse "Do not take the name of God your Lord in vain" (Exodus 20:7) to mean, "Don't wrap yourself in a tallit while you violate the Torah." . . .

This kohen, by engaging in repulsive behavior, has tainted his holy calling and placed a blemish on himself (a reference to Leviticus 21:180, which states that any blemished priest may not offer a sacrifice). He should not be first to be called to the Torah, nor should he bless the congregation, even if there is no other kohen present. He should be content not to be considered a Yisrael. . . .

(See editor's notes ad loc., and compare no.171, ibid., fol. 41b–42a, a similar responsum of R. Yosef [Tuv Elem]. Note editor's note ad loc. Note further that this responsum is not brought in Y. Brody's edition of *Teshuvot Rav Natronai bar Hilai Gaon*, Jerusalem, 1994, 2 vols. Presumably he was not convinced as to the attribution.)

Furthermore, in a responsum of Maimonides (*Teshuvot ha-Rambam* [Friemann edition, Jerusalem: *Mekitzei Nirdamim*, 1934, Section 18, pp. 16–17, and Blau edition, 1, Jerusalem: *Mekitzei Nirdamim*, 1958, Section 111, pp. 191–194] that is cited in the Radbaz, 2 *Alafim* 78, and in *Orah Hayyim* 53:9) relating to the question whether "A well known person who was appointed to be a cantor and he is a student, has a rumor circulating that he performed a sin that cannot be mentioned, but this has not been verified by legitimate witnesses . . . should he be removed from his appointment or not?" And he responded: "A person should not be removed from an appointment based on rumors, even if he has no enemies." Apparently, he based himself on the statement of Rabbi Eleazar in the *Jerusalem Talmud, Sanhedrin* 2:1: "'A high priest who sinned is given lashes [apparently in private], but is not removed from his high position.' Rav Mana said that it is written: '[Neither shall he go out of the sanctuary, nor profane the sanctuary of his God,] for the consecration of the anointing oil of his God is upon him' (Leviticus 21:12). As if, just as I am in my state of holiness, so Aharon is in his state of holiness." (Perhaps the words "nor profane the sanctuary of his God" indicate a concern for desecration of the divine name.) So the Rambam ruled in *Mishneh Torah, Hilchot Sanhedrin* 17:8: "When a High Priest sins, he is lashed on the basis of the judgment of a court of three like people at large. Afterwards, he returns to his position of eminence." Yet, in 17:9 he wrote: "When, by contrast, the head of the academy transgresses, he is given lashes in the presence of a court of three but does not return to his position of authority. He is also not reinstated as one of the other judges of the *Sanhedrin*. The rationale is that we ascend higher in matters of holiness, and do not descend." (See the continuation of the *Jerusalem Talmud*, ibid.) Indeed R. Huna reports that "In Usha, they made a regulation that if the Head of the Court committed an offense, he was not to be formally excommunicated, but they would say to him: 'Save your dignity and remain at home' (2 Kings 2 14:10). If he committed another offense, they would excommunicate him because of the desecration of the divine name." This is at variance with Resh Lakish, for Resh Lakish said: "A scholar who committed an offense is not excommunicated in public, as it says: 'Therefore shall you stumble in the day, and the prophet will also stumble with you at night,' (Hosea 4:5) – i.e., keep it dark like the night" (*Moed Katan* 17a). And compare the *Jerusalem Talmud, Moed Katan* 3:1, in the name of Rabbi Shmuel in the name of Rebbe Abbahu: "If an elder committed an offense, he was not to be formally excommunicated , but they would say to him: 'Save your dignity and remain at home.'"

Rambam, *Hilchot Talmud Torah* 7:1, ruled like Resh Lakish, rejecting the regulation passed by the Elders of Usha, according to R. Huna. The *Beit Yosef*, by R. Yosef Karo, follows Rambam's ruling. (See below where we refer to the *Shulhan Aruch*'s similar ruling.) The difficulty posed by following Resh Lakish as opposed to the Elders of Usha, according to Rav Huna, has been carefully analyzed by R. Yaakov Hayyim Sofer in his article "*Hiddushei Torah*," no. 12, in *Mekabtziel* 17, 1992, pp. 78–80. He points out that Resh Lakish's opinion is cited by *B. Menahot* 99b, without mention of the Usha ruling, but rejects this as an explanation for Rambam's position. The *Beit Yosef* had already noted that the Yerushalmi in *Moed Katan*, (called *Mashkin*) 3:1, 81d, seems to support the view of Resh Lakish. (See Yisachar Tamar, *Alei Tamar, Moed*, vol. 3, Alon Shvut, 1992, pp. 322–323.) But this too is insufficient reason to reject the Elders of Usha's ruling. Sofer (ibid.) solves this problem by pointing out that whenever we find the Talmudic formula "*u-pliga a-de-Rabbi X*" (and this is in opposition to [the view of] Rabbi X), Rambam rules in accordance with "Rabbi X." And since the Talmud in *B. Moed Katan* ibid. after citing the opinion of the Elders of Usha, writes "*u-pliga de-Resh Lakish*," the Rambam ruled according to the view of Resh Lakish. This principle, he demonstrates, is already to be found in the writings of R. Saadia Gaon, R. Hananel, cited in the *Or Zarua* (*Hilchot Tefillin*, sect. 588), the *Hida* (in his *Yair Ozen* 6:20), etc. See his copious bibliographic references ibid. and also his discussion of the variant readings in *B. Moed Katan* ibid.

See also the *Shulhan Aruch, Orah Hayyim* 53:25, and the *Magen Avraham* there. See *Alei Tamar* ibid, *Seder Nezikin*, on *Sanhedrin*, ibid.; Israel, 1983, p. 101; and on

"What constitutes profanation of the Name? – Rav said: 'If I were to take meat from the butcher and not pay him immediately.'"

Third Story: Halachic Morality

The third story is found in *Ta'anit* 23b-24a:

> Rav Yossi bar Avin used to attend the lectures of Rav Yossi of Yokeret. Later, he left him and went to those of Rav Ashi. . . . [Rav Ashi] said to him: "Did you not frequent the lectures of Rav Yossi of Yokeret?" He replied: "Yes." [Rav Ashi] said to him: "Why did you leave him and come here?" He replied: "How could the person who showed no mercy to his son and daughter show mercy to me?" What happened to his son? Once, Rav Yossi had laborers in the field. When night fell, no food was brought to them, and they said to his son: "We are hungry." They were sitting under a fig tree, and he said: "Fig tree, fig tree, bring forth fruit so my father's workers can eat." It produced fruit and they ate. Meanwhile, his father came . . . and said to him: "My son, just as you have troubled your Creator to cause the fig tree to produce fruit before its time, may you also be taken before your time." What happened to his daughter?

Horayot 3:1, pp. 302–303. See also the responsa of *Hatam Sofer, Orah Hayyim* 41, where he discusses this matter and writes in the conclusion of his discussion: "Nevertheless, to the heart of the matter, on the issue of removing a rabbi from his position if he sins, I am perplexed." And he turned to Rabbi Zalman Margolis, requesting: "Inform me of your exalted opinion on this." There is more to discuss on this issue, yet it seems that in our times it is clear that a rabbi who committed an offense must be removed from his position because of the resulting desecration of the divine name, for these things are publicized immediately in the media and it becomes a public issue.

Further on the Hatam Sofer's position on this issue, see Y. Weiss, *Rabbanut u-Kehillah be-Mishnat Maran ha-Hatam Sofer zt"l*, Jerusalem, 1987, pp. 191–192, note 17, bringing a number of sources also from his disciples, and concluding that even if in Talmudic sources it is stated that one does not dismiss an errant rabbi (see *Hatam Sofer, Hoshen Mishpat*, sect. 162, *Maharam Schik Yoreh Deah* section 220). Nonetheless, nowadays the situation may be different (*Maharam Schik* ibid., sect. 221; *Hatam Sofer Hoshen Mishpat* 162, 163, 207), and the congregation may be permitted to desist from paying him his wages.

See further the responsum of R. Yehudah Altaretz, on corrupt judges, in *Seridei Teshuvot mi-Hachmei ha-Imperiah ha-Otmanit*, ed. S. Glick, Jerusalem, 2013, vol. 1, pp. 316–322.

A full discussion of the different aspects of spiritual leaders of various status, rabbis, judges, kings, cantors etc., may be found in N. Rakover, *Takanat ha-Shavim: Avaryan she-Ritzah et Onsho*, Jerusalem 2007, pp. 151–305.

He had a beautiful daughter. One day he saw a man boring a hole in the fence to get a glimpse of her. He said to the man: "What is this?" [The man] said to him: "Master, if I am not worthy enough to marry her, may I not at least be worthy enough to get a glimpse of her?" [Rav Yossi] said to [his daughter]: "My daughter, you are a source of trouble to mankind. Return to the dust so that men not sin because of you."

In other words, one who exaggerates his piety[11] and is so radical in his

---

11. On excessive piety, see the comments of Maimonides, *Mishneh Torah, Hilchot De'ot* 3:1: "Lest a person say, 'Since envy, desire, [the pursuit] of honor, and the like, are a wrong path and drive a person from the world, I shall separate from them to a very great degree and move away from them to the opposite extreme' to the point that he will not eat meat, nor drink wine, nor live in a pleasant home, nor wear fine clothing, but, rather, [wear] sackcloth and coarse wool and the like. . . . This, too, is a bad path and it is forbidden to walk upon it. Whoever follows this path is called a sinner. . . . Our Sages have forbidden a man to mortify himself by fasting. Of all the above, and their like, Solomon directed and said: 'Do not be overly righteous and do not be overly clever; why make yourself desolate?' (Ecclesiastes 7:16)." See also what I have written in my *Minhagei Yisrael*, vol. 2, Jerusalem, 1991, pp. 127–128, note 1:

See, for example, the words of Refael Mordechai Malki about a person who creates bundles and bundles of stringencies and adopts each: "One who adopts stringencies in this and in that, not only do we not permit him to do so, but he is considered like a fool who goes in the dark, who tries to improve things, but actually causes damage. One who does so is a foolish righteous person, about whom the verse says: 'Do not be too righteous.' (Ecclesiastes 7:16)." (Cited by M. Benayahu, *Sefer Zikaron Le-ha-Rav Yitzhak Nissim*, Jerusalem, 1985, p. 295.)

See also *Yam Shel Shlomo, Baba Kama* 7:41 (on *Baba Kama* 81b):

. . . And if so, it is proven from here that it is appropriate to excommunicate Bar Bei Rav who was arrogant in his rulings and was stringent on laws in which a permissive approach prevailed in the entire Jewish community. . . . And even where a permissive approach has not completely prevailed, a person should not adopt a position that is more stringent than that of his teacher if he has no proof to refute his words.

(And see the comments of J. J. Schacter, *The Neglected Mitzvot*, 1990, pp. 40–47.)

See also the responsum of the *Radbaz*, R. David ben Zimra, no. 444, concerning R. Yitzhak ben Asher (the Riva) who who fasted on Yom Kippur against the advice of the doctors – did he act correctly? The Radbaz seeks to justify his actions, but says clearly that for lesser persons this would not be permissible. (See also *Seridei Teshuvot mi-Hachmei ha-Imperiah ha-Otmanit*, ed. S. Glick, Jerusalem, 2014, pp. 536–538.)

It is also worth paying attention to the language of the Maharshal, in his responsa, 27 (on the question of whether it is permissible on the Sabbath before *Tisha B'Av* to wear a garment that was laundered, or if it relates to asceticism), where he wrote: "This therefore seems to me to be foolish piety if one is stringent in this matter and negates the enjoyment of Shabbat." (Cited in *Mateh Moshe*, section 736 and in *Magen Avraham* 551:4.) It is also worth mentioning the language of Rabbi Eliezer Papo, *Hesed le-Alafim*, Salonika, 1841, 135:9: ". . . In anything like this, one needs a level spirit and balanced judgment so as to not perpetrate extreme piety and an act of arrogance"(referring to kissing the Torah with one's hand rather than with one's mouth). On the question of when one who is stringent is an idiot and when he glorifies the commandments, see *Shulhan Aruch ha-Rav, Orah Hayyim* 32:8. See also my *The Relationship between Man and His Neighbor and Man and His Maker*, Jerusalem and New York, 2013, chapter 10.

And in *Minhagei Yisrael*, vol. 4, Jerusalem, 1995, pp. 285–286, I cited additional sources on this subject:

This type of opposition to excessive piety comes to sharp expression in the words of Rabbi Yosef Karo, in the *Kessef Mishneh* on *Hilchot Terumot* 1:11, in opposition to "another scholar" who is identified as Rabbi Yosef Ashkenazi (see the *Drishah* on *Yoreh Deah* 331:11), who wanted to rule stringently regarding the taking of *terumot* and *ma'asrot* on fruits that were grown, completed, and stored by non-Jews on land that they had purchased in the Land of Israel. On this, Rabbi Karo wrote: "And the prevailing custom in the Land of Israel is in accordance with the words of our teacher (Maimonides). And we have not heard on his right a dissenting opinion. And now, another scholar arises to whom it seems appropriate to self-righteously overturn the prevailing custom, and to require tithes for produce grown on the land of a non-Jew, . . . and he goes and entices others to accept this upon themselves and to act in accordance with his words. It seems clear to me that it is appropriate to prevent them from doing so in order to prevent disunity, and furthermore because in all of these countries, they have accepted upon themselves to follow the teachings of our teacher, except in situations that involve giving respect to earlier scholars whose teachings had already been accepted (see *Minhagei Yisrael*, vol. 2, p. 119, end of note 169). It is therefore appropriate to issue a decree that they not adopt this practice, and if they refuse to do so, they should be compelled. . . . And subsequently, the practice (i.e., the stringency) spread to the point that the sages of the city had to enact decrees of excommunication that a person should never tithe produce purchased from a non-Jew, but should maintain what was practiced until now according to the ruling of our teacher . . ." (The controversy on this issue is ably described in the book of S. A. Horodetsky, *Olei Tziyon*, Tel Aviv, 1947, in the chapter on Rabbi Yosef Ashkenazi, and especially p. 67.)

The reaction of Rabbi Karo is similar to that of the Mabit to the same group in Tsefat of "well known and capable scholars" who exaggerated in their stringencies. See the article of C. Horowitz that is cited in *Minhagei Yisrael* 2, p. 139, note 27, and the other sources cited there, as well as the words of the Mabit that are cited, including his accurate admonition: "Do not be too righteous – what the Torah prohibited is enough." See also the responsa of Maharshdam, *Yoreh Deah* 193. As a sort of continuation of this note, see the Meiri, *Magen Avot*, in the 20th topic (toward the end) [Rabbi Yekutiel Cohen edition, Jerusalem, 1989, p. 237]: "And so the matter for me of assumed piety that goes beyond all boundaries, even though they become pious in the recitation of prayers that they attribute to be for the need of performing a commandment, relates in my opinion to what was stated in the *Jerusalem Talmud* [*Pesahim* 4:1] the custom of women not to work on after the conclusion of the Sabbath – i.e., every Saturday night – is not a custom, i.e., that this is only piety that is beyond what is appropriate, and we do not take it into account, until they create an order – i.e., until they complete a set order of what is to be recited after the conclusion of the Sabbath, which is a custom – i.e., even though it is beyond the regular obligation, it cannot be nullified . . ."

See also what I wrote in the continuation there (and add a responsum of the *Radbaz*, R. David ben Zimra, vol. 4, no. 1139 [242], p. 28). In this case, however, I am just drawing a drop from the ocean of possible examples. I will nonetheless bring one last example from the multitude of possibilities from *Shibolei ha-Leket* of Rabbi Tzidkiyah ben Rabbi Avraham ha-Rofeh (13th century), section 194 (Buber edition, p. 151):

It happened that Purim fell on Sunday, and the community observed the fast [of Esther] in advance on Thursday, as is customary. One woman who had to ride to the government came to ask our teacher [R. Yitzchak – i.e., Rashi] if she could fast the next day and eat today [Thursday] because of the difficulty of traveling. Our teacher said: "This fast is not from the Torah, nor is it a rabbinic enactment, but just a custom. . . . Nevertheless, I will not allow a person to separate from the community as we say: '*lo titgodedu*' - you should not make separate groups within the community. There are *Perushim* who fast on Thursday with the community and fast as well on Friday so that the fast be closer to Purim, and our teacher [Rashi] said about them: 'The fool walks in darkness' (Ecclesiastes 2:14) – and the essence of the fast is only a custom and these people who are stringent make it as if it is from the Torah. And since the majority has the custom to fast on Thursday, that is the law."

(On "*Lo titgodedu*" see Y. D. Gilat, *Bar Ilan* 18–19, 1981, pp. 78–98, and what I wrote in *Minhagei Yisrael*, vol. 3, pp. 108–112; Moshe Walter, *The Making of a Halachic Decision*, Brooklyn, 2013, pp. 134–147; David Z. Feldman, *The Right and the Good: Halakhah and Human Relations*, 2nd edition, New York, 2005, pp. 55–61.)

Most recently Berel Wein and Warren Goldstein, in their book *The Legacy: Teachings for Life from the Great Lithuanian Rabbis*, Jerusalem, 2012, pp. 76–78, discussed the issue of "the damaging impact of extra piety," basing themselves on the case found in *B. Baba Kama* 81b. I shall cite them verbatim:

The great Tannaim, Rabbi Yehudah HaNasi and Rabbi Chiya, were walking together on private property adjacent to the public road. They were allowed to do so because of a special dispensation given by Yehoshua when he originally conquered and divided the Land of Israel. In the days of dirt roads, the winter rains made the roads of Israel difficult to walk on because the mud dries in such a way that there are hard spikes left behind. Yehoshua decreed that in such circumstances one could walk on private property adjacent to the public road. Since the land was given to the people with this decree in place, walking on private property in this instance is not regarded as a violation of private property rights.

While walking, Rabbi Yehudah HaNasi and Rabbi Chiya noticed that Rabbi Yehudah ben Kenusiah refused to rely on Joshua's dispensation and, instead, was walking in the middle of the public road, despite the spikes in the road. Not realizing the stature of Rabbi ben Kenusiah, Rabbi Yehudah Hanasi was outraged at the violation of *yuharah* and wanted to impose an excommunication ban on Rabbi Yehudah ben Kenusiah. Rabbi Chiya endorsed the outstanding character of Rabbi Yehudah ben Kenusiah, who was his student, assuring Rabbi Yehudah HaNasi that his intentions were purely for the sake of Heaven. This endorsement saved him from the ban.

There follows the explanation of the Maharshal (R. Shlomo Luria) to this passage, and they end with the following statement:

The Maharshal derives another principle from the case of Rabbi Yehudah ben Kenusiah: in the absence of a clear indication of the greatness of the individual (and his halachic opinions[12] is not suitable to serve as a guide or educator. Since every rabbi must inherently be an educator; one who is exceedingly radical is not suitable to serve as a rabbi.[13] In the words of Rabbi Avraham Yitzhak Ha-Kohen Kook (*Orot Ha-Kodesh*, Part 3, p. 27): "It is prohibited for the fear of Heaven to push aside a person's natural morality, for then his fear of Heaven would no longer be pure."[14]

Fourth Story: The Ugly Man

The fourth story comes from *B. Ta'anit* 20ab. There we are told how

R. Elazar ben R. Shimon from Migdal Gedor [or Eder, according to a different reading] was once riding a donkey alongside the river fealing

---

exceptional dedication to God) anyone who performs an act of extra piety by acting stringently in the case of a well-established and well-accepted lenient halachic ruling dispensation, contravenes the *yuharah* principle and is liable to an excommunication ban. The Maharshal explains that the sanction for *yuharah* is actually part of a broader category of the sin of arrogance, which the *Gemara* elsewhere says is punished by excommunication (*B. Sotah* 5a).

A remarkable case of extreme piety is cited by R. Ovadiah Yosef, in his *Yabia Omer*, vol. 5, Jerusalem 1986, no. 28:3, pp. 102–103. He cites the *Helkat Yaakov* vol.2, no.132, who, when asked whether one would walk on Shabbat in shoes that have letters on their soles, permits it, (though they may leave their imprint on the ground, and this may be regarded as writing on Shabbat). But he adds that he heard in his youth that his father-in-law the *Tzaddik*, the Belzer Rebbe, would cut or peel off those letters which protruded from the soles of his shoes before Shabbat. But, he states, this extraordinary case was fitting for such a great man.

R. Ovadiah then proceeds to demonstrate that this was quite unnecessary from a halachic point of view, giving a whole list of reasons. He also gives additional examples of such super-stringency, concluding that we should not learn practical halachah from such stories. And further on excessive piety and stringency, see most recently Lior Silber, *Milei de-Hassiduta*, 2nd edition (c. 2014), pass.

Finally, there are, indeed, some rules as to when it is more advisable, or even permissible, to rule stringently, and when not. These have been conveniently summarized in a clear fashion – though perhaps over-simplified , in Moshe Mendel Shklarsh's *Hayyei Moshe*, Bnei Brak, 2001, pp. 274–280, with copious sources. See also B. Braun's important article, "*Ha-Hahmarah: Hamishah Tipusim min ha-Et ha-Hadasha*" apud *Iyyunei Halachah u-Mishpat le-Chvod Prof. Aharon Kirshcenbaum*, ed. A. Edrei, *Dinei Yisrael* 20–21, 2000–2001, pp. 123–237; Daniel Goldstein, "The Role of Humrot," *Hakirah* 1, 2004, pp. 11–24.

12. See the words of Rabbi Yisachar Tamar, *Alei Tamar la-Yerushalmi, Shabbat* 13b, p. 155.

13. Compare p. 170 note 11 above.

14. See the comments of Shifman, *supra* p. 120 note 81.

full of joy and overly proud of himself because he had learned much Torah. He came upon a fellow who was exceedingly ugly. The person said: "Peace be upon you, Rabbi," and [Rabbi Elazar] did not respond to him. [On the contrary], he said to him, "Worthless one, how ugly you are.[15] Are, then, all the members of your town as ugly as you?" He replied, "I do not know; but go tell the craftsman who made me, 'how ugly is the vessel you created.'" When [Rabbi Elazar] realized that he had sinned, he got off his donkey, prostrated himself before him, and said to him, "I submit myself to you [i.e., I beg your pardon], forgive me." "I shall not forgive you," the ugly man replied, "until you go to the craftsman who made me and say to him, 'How ugly is this vessel you created.'" So Rabbi Elazar continued to follow him until they came to his town. The townsfolk came out to greet him, calling out "Peace be upon you, our Rabbi, our Rabbi, our Teacher, our Teacher." "Who are you calling 'Our Rabbi, Our Rabbi'?" he asked. "He who is walking after you," they replied. He said to them, "If this is your Rabbi, may there not be many like him in Israel." They asked him, "Why?", and he told them, "Such and such did he do to me." "Even so," they responded, "forgive him, for he is a person great in Torah." He replied, "For you I will forgive him, on condition that he not make this his practice." Thereupon, Rabbi Elazar

---

15. We may perhaps be reminded of the passage in B. Ta'anit 7ab. (I have used M. Malter's translation in his *The Treatise Ta'anit of the Babylonian Talmud*, Philadelphia, 1967, p. 84.):

R. Osha'ya said: "Why are the words of the Torah likened unto these three liquids: water, wine and milk? – As to water, it is written (Isaiah 55:1): 'Ho, every one that thirsteth, come ye to the waters'; as to wine and milk, it is written (ibid.): 'And he that hath no money come ye, buy, and eat; yea, come, buy wine and milk without money and without price?' – To indicate to you that just as these three liquids can be preserved only in the cheapest kind of vessels, so will the words of the Torah be preserved only in him whose mind is lowly." This explains the story of the daughter of a Roman emperor, who said to R. Joshua b. Hananiah: "What brilliant wisdom in such an ugly vessel!" Whereupon he exclaimed: "Oh, you daughter of a man who puts wine in vessels of clay!" "Wherein should he put it?" she asked. "You nobles should put it in vessels of gold and silver!" Whereupon she went home and told her father, who ordered the wine to be put into vessels of gold and silver, and the wine became sour. They then went to R. Joshua and asked him, "Why did you give her such advice?" "As she spoke to me, so I spoke to her," R. Joshua replied. "But there are also handsome people that are learned!" they said. "If the same people were ugly, they would be still more learned," was R. Joshua's answer.

Here, of course, the message, which is different, was stated at the outset. (And cf. B. Nedarim 50b.)

entered [the house of study] and preached, "May a person always be pliant like a reed and not unbending like a cedar."

This tale is also found in *Derech Eretz Rabba* 2:1 (*Massechtot Derech Eretz*, ed. M. Higger, Brooklyn, 1935, pp. 166–171), and *Avot de-R. Natan*, ed. S. Schechter, Vienna 1887, 1, p. 131. The Tosafot (*Ta'anit* ad loc.) suggest that the ugly person was actually Elijah the Prophet, who came to test and to teach Rabbi Elazar how to behave. (They refer us to *Derech Eretz*, however, this detail is not to be found in our versions.)

The clear message of this tale is twofold. Firstly, the dangers of excessive pride for one who knows himself to be well versed in Torah, and more so than most others. Secondly, to respect every person, despite his outward appearance, and to refrain from judging him on this basis. On the contrary, one should show sympathy for those whom misfortune has visited, for they too are the creatures – i.e., creations – of God, and clearly shaming such a person shows an utter lack of sensitivity to the unfortunate.

A somewhat different formulation, but with much the same basic message, may be found in *B. Berachot* 17a:

> A favorite saying of the rabbis of Yavneh was:
>
> I am a creature of God and my neighbor is also a creature of God. I work in the city and he works in the country. I rise early for my work and he rises early for his work. Just as he cannot excel in my work, I cannot excel in his work. Will you say that I do great things and he does small things?
>
> We have learned that it does not matter whether a person does much or little, as long as he directs his heart to heaven.

To this we may add the statement of Ben Azzai in *Avot* 4:3:

> He used to say: Despise no man . . . for there is not a man that has not his hour.

To which R. Yonah ad loc. adds: "no man" – even if he is base and contemptible (*pahut ve-nikleh*).

This is surely the meaning of R. Hanina ben Dosa's statement in *Avot* 3:9:

He whose works (*maasav*, i.e., good deeds) exceed his wisdom, his wisdom endures; but he whose wisdom exceeds his works, his wisdom does not endure.

And in a similar spirit he stated (ibid., 3:10):

He in whom the spirit of mankind finds pleasure, in him the spirit of God finds pleasure; but he in who the spirit of mankind finds no pleasure, in him the spirit of God will find no pleasure.

So even one who is endowed with great learning, but is not involved in interacting positively and sympathetically with people, and certainly one who acts negatively towards those who may appear to be ignorant, empty-headed and visibly repulsive, all his learning is virtually worthless, and outweighed by withdrawn, or worse still inhuman behavior.[16]

Fifth Story: The Ignorant Jew

A person may well be ignorant and boorish but nevertheless have admirable qualities, as we learn from a fifth passage found in *Leviticus Rabba* 9:3, ed. Margaliot p. 176-179, which teaches us how one must be all too careful not to judge from outward appearance alone.

It happened that R. Yannai was walking along when he met a man who looked well-dressed and most respectful (*meshupa be-yoter*). He said to him, "Will you be willing to be a guest in our house?" The man replied, "If this pleases you." He took him into his house and examined him [to know whether he was versed] in Bible and found he was not. In *Mishnah* he was not, and in Talmud and in Aggadah he was not. R. Yannai said to him, "[Kindly] make a blessing [over the food]," to which [the guest]

---

16. For a further (literary) analysis of this story, see Yonah Fraenkel, *Sippur ha-Aggadah-Ahdut shel Tochen ve-Tzurah: Kovetz Maamarim.* Tel-Aviv, 2001, pp. 189–197; Shulamit Valler, Shalom Ratzabi, *Sihat Hulin be-Talmud ha-Bavli,* Tel-Aviv, 2007, pp. 89–99; and cf. Y.L. Levin, *Maamad ha-Hachamim be-Eretz-Yisrael bi-tekufat ha-Talmud: Hebeitim Historiim,* Jerusalem, 1986, pp. 79–80.

And in the world of Hassidut, the *Tamim*, "the Simple Person," is a beloved figure who appears in numerous stories in a very favorite light. See Gedalyah Nigal, *The Hasidic Tale,* (translation, Edward Lewin), Oxford and Portland, Oregon, 2012, pp. 257–263.

replied, "May Yannai make the blessing in his own house." He asked him whether he could repeat after him what he would say to him. And he replied, "Yes." R. Yannai said, "Say: The dog ate Yannai's bread." The guest rose up and seized hold of him, saying, "Is my heritage [only] with you that you mock me?" "What is this heritage of yours that you claim is mine?" asked R. Yannai. "Children," he replied, "say, 'Moses commanded us a law, even the heritage of the congregation of Jacob' (Deuteronomy 33:4) – the congregation of Yannai is not written here, but the congregation of Jacob.'" After they placated one another [R. Yannai asked his guest], "Why did you merit to eat at my table?" [The guest] replied, "I never heard something bad and passed it on to him [about whom it was said]; and wherever I saw two people quarrelling amongst themselves I always made peace between them." [R. Yannai] responded, "Such fine deeds (*derech eretz*), and I called you a dog!"

This tale has multiple messages. First, we learn how R. Yannai judged his guest by his outward appearance alone, assuming that since he was dressed in a highly respectable fashion, he must be a learned person. As soon as he discovered he was actually an ignoramus from a Torah perspective, he mocked him directly to his face, again not realizing that this person may have other positive attributes. It was only when he learned of his fine moral qualities that he felt regret at his own behaviour towards him. So he first misjudged him on account of his outward appearance. He then misjudged him on account of his apparently boorish behaviour, and reacted to it in a totally unacceptable fashion. Hardly the way to treat a guest, and hardly an example of rabbinic discernment![17]

I am reminded of the passage in *Seder Eliyahu Zuta* chapter 2 (ed. Meir Ish Shalom, Vienna, 1901, p. 175), where we read that "even if a person sits all day reading just one, apparently insignificant, verse, namely *Genesis* 36:22 'and the sister of Lotan was Timna,'even so he has the Torah reward in his hand." This, I would suggest, may be interpreted to mean that even a person who has only minimal Torah knowledge, and has to struggle a full day on a single verse which has

---

17. See for a detailed analysis of this passage in Yonah Fraenkel, *Darkei ha-Aggadah ve-ha-Midrash*, Givataim, 1991, pp. 245–247, and most recently R. Shmuel Lewis, *Ve-Lifnei Kavod Anavah* [*And Before Honor-Humility*], Jerusalem, 2013, pp. 243–246.

no obvious halachic or moral significance, merits divine reward. And if he is, as it were, valued by God sufficiently to merit His reward, surely he deserves our respect.

Sixth Story: Charcoal and Distress

We are further reminded of yet the following sixth story related in *Berachot* 28a that when Rabban Gamliel decided to go pacify R. Yehoshua, and he came to his house, he found the walls of his humble abode blackened. He then said, "The walls of your house testify to your being a charcoal worker." To which R. Yehoshua retorted, "Woe is the generation who has you as their leader; for you are quite unaware of the distress of *Talmidei Hachamim*, and [the hardships they endure] to make ends meet and to find sustenance." Here, too, the disconnect between the spiritual leader and members of his "flock" is very severly criticized. A rabbi must have a deep knowledge, acquaintance, and involvement with all members of his constituency.[18]

---

18. Furthermore, he must not steep himself so much in his learning that he has little or no involvement with his community. Thus we read in *Yalkut ha-Machiri* , ed. Greenhut, (to Proverbs 82b):

"[The king by judgement establisheth the land,] but he that receiveth gifts over-throweth it" (Proverbs 29:4). This refers to the scholar who knows *halachot, midrash* and *aggadot*, and when an orphan or a widow go to him so that he pass fair judgement between them, and he replies, "I am busy with my learning", God says to him, "I view you as one who has destroyed the world."

Similarly, we hear of R. Asi who wept on his death-bed. When asked why, surely he had studied and been involved in good deeds all his life, he replied that he was fearful because he had not been involved in judgement, i.e., rabbinic leadership. However, compare *B. Shabbat* 10a, where we are told that R. Ami and R. Asi used to sit and study between the columns of the *beit midrash*, and at periodic intervals they would interrupt their studies and call out to anyone who required some kind of judgement (*dina*), perhaps also meaning that they would answer halachic queries. See Moshe Beer's fascinating article in *Ish al ha-Edah: Ha-Kinus ha-Shenati le-Machshevet ha-Yahadut*, 13, 1973, pp. 110–111, entitled "*Al Mekomam shel Talmidei Hachamim be-Hanhagat ha-Tzibbur*," and the whole article, pp. 105–120, where he demonstrates how well-known rabbis of the Talmudic era devoted themselves to the needs of the community, alongside their intensive learning. And see further my *On the Relationship of Mitzvot between Man and his Neighbor*, chapter 4, p. 47 et seq. There I bring the following story related in Yehezkel Shraga Fraenkel's *Rabbenu ha-Kaddosh mi-Shin-yeve*, Ramat-Gan, 1992, pp. 256–257. He relates that once the Rabbi of Warsaw came to visit the *Divrei Hayyim*, R. Hayyim of Tzanz. The Tzanzer Rebbe asked him, "Do you learn?" "Yes," the Warsaw Rabbi replied. The Rebbe replied, "Do you always learn?" The reply was, "When someone who is embittered and needs help comes to

But the criticism leveled against Raban Gamliel is even more severe. For on the previous page (ibid., 27b) we are told that during a controversial dispute between Rabban Gamliel and R. Yehoshua (concerning whether the evening prayer is elective or mandatory), Rabban Gamliel, after rejecting R. Yehoshua position, continued to sit and preach, while R. Yehoshua remained standing before him:

> Until all the congregation began to murmur, and told Hutzpit the translator to stand up (i.e., stop explicating Rabban Gamliel's sermon). He did so, and they said, "Till when will we continue to cause distress [to R. Yehoshua]? He [Rabban Gamliel] did so last year in the issue of *Bechorot*,

---

me, I close my *Gemara* and deal with him, to help and encourage him." "That is what I wanted to hear," said the Tzanzer. "Whether you have the good sense to close your *Gemara* when someone needs your help, both in word and in deed, and in any case to encourage him and bolster his spirit."

There is yet another example where the plaintif asks is this is the law. See the story in *B. Baba Metzia* 29b, *B. Ketubot* 17b:

There came a brother to Mari b. Isak from [the town of] Be Hozai, saying to him, "Divide [my father's estate] with me."

"I do not know you," he replied. So they went to R. Hisda.

R. Hisda said to the plaintiff, "He [Mari] may be speaking the truth to you, for it is written, '*And Joseph knew his brethren, but they recognized him not*' (Genesis 42:8), which teaches that he had gone forth without a beard and now appeared before them with one. [So Mari may not recognize you, too, even if you are his brother.] Go then," he continued, "and produce witnesses that you are his brother."

"I have witnesses," he replied, "but they are afraid of him because he is a man of violence."

Thereupon R. Hisda turned to Mari, "Go you, and bring witnesses that he is not your brother."

"Is that the law?" he exclaimed. "The onus of proof lies on the claimant?"

"Thus do I judge in your case," retorted R. Hisda, "and for all other men of violence of your like."

"But after all," he argued, "witnesses will come and not testify [the truth]."

"They will not commit two wrongs," he rejoined.

R. Hisda did not answer the basic questions. He merely stated that that was his ruling. Did R. Hisda deviate from the law, or did he fulfill it? In its general formulation he, perhaps, deviated from it. But in the particular circumstances his ruling achieved an equitable fulfillment. Is this another example of *lifnim mi-shurat ha-din*?

See Aaron Feldman's analysis of this text and how it was understood by the Rambam and differently by R. Yitzhar Arauro, in his article "Maimonides and Equity" apud *Din ve-Yosher be-Torat ha-Mishpat shel ha-Rambam*, eds. H. Ben-Menahem B. Lipshitz. (*On Law and Equity in Maimonidean Jurisprudence: Reading the Guide for the Perplexed III*), Jerusalem, 2004, pp. 143–153.

and also in the case of R. Tzadok. Now here again he is doing so. Let us remove him from his office . . ."

And so they did, placing R. Eleazar ben Azariah in his place. (Whether as *Nasi* or *Rosh Yeshiva* is a question we cannot deal with here.) The lack of respect that the leading rabbi had for his colleagues was a fault that could not be overlooked, and, in this case, was ample reason to "demote" him.[19]

This is echoed by the Rambam in *Hilchot Sanhedrin* 25:1, where he writes:

> It is forbidden for a person to act high-handedly and abusively towards the community; but he should act in humbleness and fear. And any leader who causes fear unwarrantedly over his constituents and not for the glory of heaven, will be punished . . .

He must then command respect of the community but also be respectful of its members.

---

19. See Elisha Alterman, *Binyano shel Olam*, Jerusalem, 2010, p. 79, for a summary of the reasons for removing a rabbi from office.

III. THE FRIENDLY RABBI

THE BEST EXAMPLE FROM WHICH WE CAN LEARN THE POSITIVE
qualities that a halachic authority should emulate is Hillel the Elder,
both in his personal life and in his halachic rulings and enactments.
Hillel serves as the archetype for appropriate behavior by a rabbinic
leader. In *Avot* 1:12, he establishes the fundamentals for relating to
others: "Be of the disciples of Aharon: loving peace and pursuing peace,
loving his fellow man, and drawing them near to Torah." From a series
of stories recorded in *Massechet Shabbat* 30b-31a, we learn about his
unlimited tolerance.

First Story: Hillel

Here let us cite perhaps the most famous of them.

> We have learned: One should always be humble like Hillel, and not
> severe and exacting (*kapdan*) like Shammai. It once happened that two
> people wagered with one another. They said, "Anyone who can go and
> anger Hillel will receive four hundred zuz." So one of them said, "I will
> anger him." That day was shortly before Shabbat and Hillel was washing
> his hair. [We may note parenthetically, that Hillel was very careful as to
> his personal cleanliness, as we learn from *Leviticus Rabba* 34:3, ed. M.
> Margaliot, vol. 4, Jerusalem, 1958, p. 776, and most especially before
> Shabbat. See editor's note 2, ibid.; and S. Lieberman, *Tosefta Ki-fshutah*,
> vol.1, New York, 1955, p. 56.] [The fellow] went and stood at [Hillel's]
> doorstep, and called out, "Is Hillel here? Is Hillel here?" Hillel cloaked
> himself and came out to greet him, saying to him, "My son, what do you
> want?" He replied, "I have a question I wish to ask [of you]." "Ask my
> son, ask," replied [Hillel]. "Why are the heads of the Babylonians oval?"

"My son," said Hillel, "you have asked a most important question. It is because they do not have intelligent midwives." He went away, waited an hour and then came back, calling out, "Is Hillel here? Is Hillel here?" [Again] Hillel got dressed and came out to greet him, saying, "My son, what do you want?" "I have a question I would like to ask you," he replied. "Ask my son," replied [Hillel]. "Why are the eyes of the Tadmorians slanted?" He answered him saying, "My son, you have asked a most important question. It is because they live among the sands." He went away, and waited an hour, and then returned, calling out, "Is Hillel here? Is Hillel here?" He [again] got dressed, and came out to greet him, asking, "My son, what do you want?' "I have a question to ask," he replied. "Ask my son, ask," [said Hillel]. "Why are the feet of the Africans wide?" "My son, you have asked a most important question. [It is] because they live among the swamps." "I have many questions to ask, but I fear that you may get angry [at me]." [Hillel] cloaked himself, sat before him, and said, "All the questions you may have, please ask them." He said to him, "Are you the Hillel who is called the Nasi of Israel?" "Yes," he replied. "If you are he, may there not be many like you in Israel," said [the fellow]. "Why, my son?" asked [Hillel]. "Because," he replied. "I have just lost four hundred zuz because of you." Hillel responded, "Take care of your temper. Better that you loose four hundred zuz on account of Hillel, than that Hillel be angered."

(And cf. the version in *Avot de R. Natan*, ed. S. Schechter, Vienna, 1887, p.60.) This tradition teaches us the relationship between restraint and humbleness.

We read there how he drew converts near and brought them under the wings of the Divine Presence.[1] In the enactments that he instituted

---

1. This again is in contradistinction to the behavior of *Shammai*. See the analysis of Yonah Frankel, *Sippur ha-Aggadah – Ahdut shel Tochen Ve-Tzurah: Kovetz Ma'amarim*, Tel Aviv, 2001, pp. 296–302.

Here I would like to cite two anecdotes that Rabbi Shlomo Riskin related in *The Jerusalem Post Magazine*, February 21, 2014, p. 42. He titled his article, "A tale of two rabbis."

There was a young man studying in the famed Yeshiva of Volozhin, bright and especially gifted of mind and pen, who began to go "off the derech" (lose his way religiously). He was discovered smoking a cigarette on the holy Shabbat. The head of the yeshiva, Rabbi Naftali Zvi Yehuda Berlin, asked to see the errant student, urging him to mend his ways. The young man audaciously responded that he was merely

"for the general welfare" (*Mishnah Gittin* 4:3), there is an evident

exercising his gift of free will. The yeshiva head, who had given his life and finances to the institution – and who continued the difficult task of teaching and fund-raising to maintain his yeshiva even in his later years – was overcome with anger. He slapped the student on the cheek.

The mortified young man left the yeshiva and made his way to America, where he became a well-known author and editor of Yiddish newspaper *The Jewish Daily Forward*. He was for many years bitterly antireligious, and under his watch, the famous (or infamous) "Yom Kippur Eve parties" were held in the *Forward*'s building on the Lower East Side.

In the early 1970s, my family and I would vacation in Miami Beach, Florida, where on Shabbat afternoons I would give *shiurim* (Torah classes) at the Caribbean Hotel. On one particular Shabbat, I was speaking about the Mussar (Ethicist) Movement and specifically about the famed Rabbi Yisrael Meir Kagan, known as the Hafetz Haim after his book against slander. I invoked a passage in the Talmud (B.T. Arachin 16b), in which Rabbi Tarfon maintains that "no one knows how to properly rebuke in our times; if one person says to another, 'remove the flint from between your teeth,' the other will respond, 'remove the bean from between your eyes.'"

However, I added, apparently the Hafetz Haim, who lived 2,000 years after Rabbi Tarfon, did know how to rebuke, and how to bring an errant Jew back to God. It is told that a student in the Yeshiva in Radin (the city of the Hafetz Haim) was caught smoking on Shabbat. The Hafetz Haim spoke to him for two minutes, and the student not only repented, but even received rabbinical ordination from the Hafetz Haim.

As I concluded my lecture, an elderly gentleman, who had been visibly agitated as I spoke, grabbed my arm and urgently whispered, "Where did you hear that story?" I told him I didn't remember, and I didn't even know if it was true. "It is true," he said. "I was that boy; I was smoking on Shabbat and I have *semicha* from the Hafetz Haim."

We were both overcome with emotion. We left the hotel and silently walked along the beach. Finally, I couldn't restrain myself. "What did the Hafetz Haim tell you that changed your life in two minutes?" Here is what the elderly man responded, and his words remain inscribed on my soul.

"I was standing in front of the yeshiva with my belongings, ready to leave for home. Standing in front of me was the Hafetz Haim, who took my hand in his and politely asked if I would come to his house. I felt I couldn't refuse. We walked the two blocks in silence, hand-in-hand, until we reached his home. I entered a very small, dilapidated but spotlessly clean two-room hovel, in which not one piece of furniture was whole. The Hafetz Haim, who was quite short, looked up at me and said only one word: 'Shabbes.'

"He gently squeezed my hand as an embrace, and there were tears in his eyes. He repeated again, 'Shabbes,' and if I live to be 120 I will never stop feeling the scalding heat of his tears as they fell on my hand. He then guided me to the door. At that moment, I felt in my soul that there was nothing more important than the Shabbat, and that – despite my transgression – this rabbinical giant loved me. I took an oath not to leave the yeshiva without rabbinical ordination from the Hafetz Haim."

On the Hafetz Hayyim, see what I wrote in my *On the Relationship of Mitzvot between Man and his Neighbor and Man and His Maker*, Jerusalem and New York, 2014, pp. 159–160 (with bibliography), 167–169, and index s.v.

There is in these two anecdotes as certain parallelism to the Hillel and Shammai trend to accommodate the law to the changing demands of life so that the changing circumstances not distance the people from the Torah.[2] These included enactments to help women collect their *ketubot* (widows' benefits) from the assets that are transferred to the orphaned children (*Gittin,* ibid.), the aforementioned *prozbul* (ibid.), and the enactment enabling a person to exercise his right to redeem a house in the city wall that he had sold (*Erachin* 9:4). Hillel's personal qualities were summarized in his eulogy: "Alas, the pious man! Alas, the humble man! Disciple of Ezra!" (*Tosefta Sotah* 13:3; *Sotah* 48b). These qualities were transmitted to his students, who were also "kindly and modest" (*Eruvin* 13b), and who, as opposed to the School of Shamai, usually ruled leniently, (with the exception of those cases listed in *M. Eduyot,* chapters 4 and 5).

Benevolence can express itself in a number of ways. Sometimes it requires courage, humbleness, and a willingness to forgo one's dignity. Let us take two examples from the life of R. Meir. The first was already referred to above note 121, as found in *B. Sanhedrin* 11a, where R. Meir, out of care not to embarrass any member of his *beit midrash,* acted as though he might be the guilty party.

Second Story: R. Meir

This story may be found in *Y. Sotah* 1.4, and runs roughly as follows:

> R. Meir used to preach in the synagogue at *Hamah* every Shabbat eve, and a certain woman would come regularly to hear him. Once it happened that by the time she came home, she found that the candle had burned out. Her husband demanded to know "Where have you been?" She replied, "To hear the sermon [of R. Meir]." He said, "I swear that you will not come back into this house, until you go and you spit in the preacher's eye." R. Meir became aware of what was going on through divine inspiration. He pretended to have an illness in his eye, and announced, "Any woman who knows to treat eyes, should come and do

---

themes though here it is kindness and empathy, certainly coupled with restraint that is the main emphasis.

2. See Mordechai Margaliyot (ed.), *Entziklopedia le-Hakhmei ha-Talmud ve-ha-Geonim,* vol. 1, Jerusalem and Tel Aviv (Fourth Edition), p. 248.

so." The lady's neighbour [heard this and] said to her, "Go and say you have a cure for his eye by spitting into it." She went to [R. Meir], and he said to her, "Do you have a cure for my eye?" But she fearfully answered, "No." He said to her, "Spit into [my eye] seven times, and it will be cured." She did so, whereupon he told her, "Go, tell your husband: 'You told me to spit once, and I did it seven times.'" R. Meir's disciples said to him, "Rabbi, so do you shame the Torah! Had you told us, we would have brought him [i.e., the husband] and beaten him until he made up with his wife." He answered them, "The honor of Meir cannot be greater than that of his Maker. If the Torah commanded us to obliterate His holy name in order to bring peace between a man and his wife, how much more so the honor of Meir!"

R. Meir was willing to be publically shamed in order to help mend the relations between the wife and her husband, and enable her to go back to her home.[3]

The quality of benevolence is very evident in a famous responsum (no. 125) of R. Moshe Isserles (the Rema) (Cracow, c.1520–1572). Solomon Freehof in his *A Treasury of Responsa* (Philadelphia, 1955), p. 113, called it "A Radical Decision," and indeed it was so. For he ruled that though normally marriages may not take place on Shabbat (*Shulhan Aruch, Orah Hayyim* 339:4), in cases of emergency, and in order to protect the honor of human beings, it may be permitted. He tells the story of what impelled him to make such a decision (Freehof's translation, pp. 115–117):

There was a poor man in our land who had betrothed his elder daughter to a suitable mate. During the period of the betrothal, which was of considerable duration, the girl's father died.[4] (Isserles uses the classic phrase: the father went to his world and left life to all of Israel.) The daughter was left bereaved, without father and mother, except for relatives who lived far from her. They shut their eyes to her plight, all except one relative

---

3. See my discussion of this text in my article entitled "*Zutot*" in *Sidra* 24–25, 2010, pp. 475–478. See above near note 101, the responsum of R. Shimon Greenfield.

4. See my forthcoming book, *The Jewish Life Cycle: Custom, Lore and Iconography: Jewish Customs from the Cradle to the Grave*, vol. 2, chapter 17, on the long time-interval between engagement and marriage in medieval times, and its often negative results.

(literally, one redeemer), the brother of her mother, who brought her into his house, for she had no relative nearer than he. Then when the time came for her marriage and it was time to prepare for the feast and the requirements of the *huppah*, she did not see anything of the dowry and the other needs (which the relatives had promised her). But she was told to take her ritual bath and prepare herself for the marriage, and that the dowry would be forthcoming. This maiden then did as the women neighbors commanded her. They decked her with the veil on the sixth day, as virgins are decked. When the shadows of evening began to fall and the Sabbath was approaching, her relatives who were to give the dowry closed their fists and refused to give a sufficient amount, so that at least a third of the dowry was still lacking. Then the groom absolutely refused to marry her. He paid no attention to the pleas of the leaders of the city that he refrain from putting a daughter of Israel to shame for the sake of mere money. He refused to listen to them, *as a deaf serpent does not hear the voice of a charmer* [a phrase from Psalms 58:5]. Nor did the voice of the rabbi move him. Because of these quarrels, time drew on; as the saying goes, "There is no marriage settlement (*ketubah*) without dispute," and the work of Satan prompted them until the time mentioned above came. Then they finally agreed and the groom consented to enter under the *huppah* and no longer to shame a worthy daughter of Israel. Thereupon I arose and conducted the marriage at that hour.

Now, since people are complaining against me, I have come now to remove their complaints from me and to bring the proof and the reasons upon which I relied in this matter, saying: In this way behold and sanctify. . . .

He does so at length, citing Talmudic sources and leading medieval authorities (Rabbenu Tam and Moshe of Coucy), discussing the various ways in which old rabbinic restrictions were set aside under changed circumstances. He concludes as follows:

But the truth is that the need of the hour leads us to be lenient in such matters which are only an additional prohibition of the rabbis. The rabbinical prohibitory decrees were not meant to apply in times of emergency, and on this we stand (literally, "On this I go down and on this I come up," a familiar Talmudic phrase found in *Pesahim* 87b). To be sure, one must be strict in urging people to be energetic (efficient) before the Sabbath, so that they should not have to face such an emergency. But when it has occured, what can be done if the hour has moved along until darkness, and there is ground for concern that the match may be broken or the maiden put to shame? Under such circumstances, he who relies on the above arguments to be lenient has not lost (has not done harm).[5] May he enjoy in peace the joy of the Sabbath thereafter. The good deed that he has done will atone for him, if his intention was for the sake of Heaven and of peace.

Thus sayeth Moses, the son of my father and teacher, Israel of blessed memory, the one called Moses Isserles of Cracow.[6]

---

5. On the principle of *Kocha de-heteira adif,* the primacy of lenient ruling and its parameters, see E. Shochetman, "The Power to Render a Lenient Ruling, *Koah De-hetera Adif,*" *Jewish Law Association,* vol. 1, 1992, pp. 126–155; Hirschenson, *Malki Ba-Kodesh,* vol. 6, Siaini, 1928, p. 161; *Darkah shel Halachah,* pp. 138–140. This is a very important principle which requires a deeper and more detailed examination, which is beyond the scope of this study. However, we may point out that the *Shlah ha-Kadosh,* R. Isaiah Horowitz (1570–1628), a halachic authority of tremendous influence, in his *Shnei Luchot ha-Brit (Shlah),* Amsterdam, 1649, part 1, p.184b, he declares "*Koah de-heteira* [should be applied] . . . in all rulings, even for oneself," and "greater is the one who is tireless in the study of the Torah in order to find a reason for permitting" (ibid.) Also, "though it is a sign of piety to adopt a stricter ruling for oneself, this is only right when there is a reason for stringency. But if not, doing so only because of lack of knowledge and had one studied properly and penetrated more deeply into the matter, one would have seen that there is no reason for stringency and yet one takes a stringent position, then one is a foolish man" (ibid.). (See Eugene Newman, *Life and Teachings of Isaiah Horowitz,* London, 1972, p. 123.)

And the Meiri, to *Hulin* 49b, Masorah edition, New York, 1945, p. 91, wrote: Wherever an issue comes before a Rabbi, and he finds a way to rule leniently without conflict (*be-lo mahloket*), he upon whom one may rely, it is not right (*raui*) that he should act with false piety (*lo-hithased*) and search out excessive stringencies, but have compassion [to prevent the loss of] finances of Israel, for the Torah too was compassionate [in its relationship] to the finances of Israel . . .

R. Baruch Halevi Epstein, in his *Mekor Baruch* vol. 3, Vilna, 1928, p. 1174, 1183 (already referred to in passing at the end of note 11) has a section on *Koah de-Heteira* in which he shows how his father, following the directives of R. Hayyim of Volozin (cf. above pp. 41–42) always strove to find lenient solutions, giving several examples. R. Baruch himself (ibid., pp. 1176–1177) brings sources to justify such an approach. He cites the Rosh in his *Responsa* (*klal* 2. *siman* 17) that "he who wishes to forbid *halah* must bring strong and clear proofs, for the Torah was compassionate [not to cause] loss to Israel." And he suggests a source for this approach in *M. Yadaim* 4:3. He brings further the ruling of the *Bah* to *Yoreh Deah* 374, that one need not pay attention to the stringent ruling of the author of the *Levushim* – R. Mordechai Yoffe – without evidential proof. And so too the *Bah* to *Yoreh Deah* 187, (and see the note 1 ad loc), and see his additional reference on p. 1177, note 1.

6. See further *Shut ha-Rema le-Rabbenu Moshe Isserles z"tl,* ed. Asher Ziv,

Accordingly, we read in *Shulhan Aruch, Orah Hayyim* 339:4 as follows:

> . . . And one does not get married [on Shabbat] (R. Yosef Karo, the *Mehaber*). To which the Rema adds: And some permit getting married [on Shabbat], in a case when he [the bridegroom] has no wife and children (Rabbenu Tam). And possibly it is also the case that to hold the wedding ceremony [on Shabbat] is permitted (*Sefer Mitzvot Gadol*), even though we do not follow this opinion, nonetheless, we may follow it in a crisis situation (*shaat ha-dehak*), for great is the dignity of the individual (*Gadol kevod ha-Briyot*) [cf. above section on Human dignity], so, for example, we are sometimes accustomed to do when the marital parties are unable to come to an agreement as to the value of the dowry on a Friday afternoon until nightfall, and then one carries out the wedding ceremony on the night of Shabbat (i.e., late Friday night, since they have already prepared the banquet and it would be a great shame for the bride and bridegroom if they could not consummate the marriage. But, in the first instance one must take care not to reach such a situation.[7]

This sense of compassion for the penniless maiden and her difficulties in obtaining the dowry required for a wedding is expressed incidentally in a passage in R. Yosef Juspa Neurelingen's *Yosef Ometz,* Frankfurt a M., 1928, p. 314. The issue under discussion is whether one is obligated to act as a guarantor so that a poor man can take a loan. He writes as follows:

> And it would appear to me that just as it is a great mitzvah to grant a loan to a poor man, so too is it a great mitzvah when in a case of one who has no means to take a loan and there are rich people who are only wishing to give loans if they are certain [to get it back], then one who acts as a guarantor is doing almost as great a mitzvah as one who actually lends [money]. And even though the rabbis said that a person should always distance himself from surety, [B. *Yevamot* 109a, in the name of

---

Jerusalem, 1970, pp. 488–495, and his copious editorial comments. The actual event was observed by Maharam mi-Tiktin, who recorded it in his *Hidushei Anshei Shem* to *Mordechai Beitzah* ad fin. See A. Ziv, *Rabbenu Moshe Isserles,* (Rema), New York, 1972, pp. 215–216.

7. See *Mishnah Brurah*'s note ad loc. and for the concept of *shaat ha-dehak*, see below Appendix 2, note 2.

Bar Kappara], nonetheless we must find a way not to "close the door before" those who require loans. . . . And if a person will not act as a guarantor for those who require it, then we fear that the borrower will sink [into debt and poverty] and no one will raise him up, and he will have no bread nor clothing in the icy [weather]. *And at times his daughter will sit in spinsterhood until her hair be white, and her countenance will be covered in shame because her nuptials were cancelled since her father could not pay for her dowry in cash.* . . . (My emphasis – D.S.)

Here again we hear the note of humane commiseration for the dismal outlook of the daughter of an impoverished family. This was probably a common phenomenon with which the rabbis were well acquainted.

We should, however, point out that the rabbis of Cracow, where the Rema's event took place, disagreed with the Rema's ruling, and enacted a resolution forbidding weddings on Friday in Cracow. Anyone who wished, or needed, a Friday wedding would have to do so outside Prague, such as the neighbouring city of Podgorze.[8]

Power of Leniency

This quality of *hesed* (charity, benevolence) toward others – "Alas, the pious man (*hasid*)! Alas, the humble man!" – found expression in the halachic rule that "the power of leniency is preferable."[9] Let us mention here what was written in this regard by the Taz on *Yoreh Deah* 141:2:

---

8. See Hayyim Natan Dembitzer, *Kelilat Yofi*, Cracow ,1888–1893, part 1, 17a, in a note; and see also Z.W. Zicherman, *Otzar Plaot ha-Torah*, vol. 1, Brooklyn, 2013, pp. 429-430.)

On a wedding on Shabbat before Shavuot, see *Hilchot u-Minhagei R. Shalom mi-Neustadt* (died 1413), ed. Shlomo Y. Spitzer, Jerusalem, 1997, no. 470, p. 142, and cf. ibid. no. 339, p. 104, with editor's note 2; Maharshal (R. Shlomo Luria), *Yam Shel Shlomo* to *Ketubot*, chapter 1, sect. 18; *Sefer ha-Minhagim le-Rabbenu Issac Tyrnau*, ed. Spitzer, Jerusalem, 1979, p. 164, in *Hagahot ha-Minhagim* no.13, and editor's note 2, ibid., and ibid., p. 166.

9. See below Appendix 2; *Berachot* 60b; *Eruvin* 72b; *Gittin* 41b, 74b; *Kiddushin* 60b; *Hulin* 58a; *Nidah* 59b. See also Pinhas Shifman, "*Hirhurim Al ha-Humra*" *Turei Sinai* 35 (Shvat-Adar 5733), pp. 10–11; and Eliav Shochetman, ibid., pp. 125–155. See also Rabbi Hayyim Hirschenson, *Malki ba-Kodesh* 6, Saini: 1928, p. 161:

Yet this is their way – to fear every bit of light that penetrates the camp of Israel, as if our Torah was God forbid not a Torah of life and light. And in particular, they do not know that the power of leniency is not only preferable, but it is essentially the power of

The Tur wrote on this matter: "Since it might have been used for idolatry, it is prohibited. . . . And one could wonder – since it was apparently so, what is his basis for adopting a stringency in a case of doubt? Even more difficult is what he said subsequently about something that is found in a city, that we assume that it was certainly made as an adornment [and not used for idolatry]. Why is that certain? Perhaps it was also made for idolatry. And it appears that even though we are stringent with something

---

our Torah and our religion to permit the many terrible prohibitions imposed on every step of the idolaters, so that they not anger their gods, and to find favor with them. The Torah only prohibited the things that introduce a bad nature into life, and its ways are ways of pleasantness, designed to give us conditions to proceed in every matter and not disturb life, and if you know them well, it is very clear that nothing can stand in the way as a stumbling block to life, as I have discussed at length in other places.

We should add to this discussion the issue of stringency, for it states explicitly in the *Jerusalem Talmud, Sotah* 8:2 that just as it is prohibited to decree as pure that which is impure, so too it is forbidden to decree as impure that which is pure. It says in the *Babylonian Talmud, Berachot* 28b regarding Rabbi Nehunia ben ha-Kanah: "When he entered [the study hall] what did he say? [. . .] And let me not say that something impure is pure or that something pure is impure." And see the words of the Shach, *Kitzur Hanhagot Issur ve-Heter*, Section 9, *Yoreh Deah* 245, who expanded on the point: "Just as it is prohibited to decree as permitted that which is forbidden, so too it is forbidden to decree as forbidden that which is permitted, even because of idolatry and even when it is not a situation of excessive loss, because for the most part, there is an element of leniency that will come to expression somewhere else because of the prohibition and it will be a stringency that brings about a leniency. And even if it seems that it will not lead to a prohibited leniency, it is possible that it will indeed evolve into a leniency after one hundred steps." Similarly, in the *Rokeah*, section 29, he wrote: "The sin of permitting things that are prohibited is just like the sin of prohibiting things that are permitted." (See below next chapter.) See also Rabbi Shalom Messas, responsa *Tevuot Shemesh, Yoreh Deah* 275, Jerusalem, 1980, section 72, where he discusses this at length and cites from the book *Sdei Hemed, Hilchot Hametz u-Matzah* 8:8, in the name of Rabbi Eliezer Fleckeles, *Teshuvah Me-Ahavah*, sections 180–181: "For the punishment of one who is unjustifiably stringent is greater than one who is unjustifiably lenient, for one who is unjustifiably stringent must placate his friend, as hinted in the case of the great scholar Rabbi Tarfon who was stringent and declared food to be not kosher," (See *Berachot* 4:4). See also my article in *Akdamot, supra* note 9, p. 131, note 6. Rabbi Messas added that it is permissible for a person to be stringent on himself "particularly in the confines of his own house, but in public, where there is a concern for arrogance, he is not permitted to be stringent" (ibid., p. 153). He discussed this further at length there. This means that not only is the power of leniency preferable, but there is a severe prohibition against ruling stringently when there is a possibility of being lenient. See also Lior Silber's *Milei de-Hassiduta*, 2nd edition (c. 2014), a collection of sources on the negative aspects of stringency in halachah, and Appendix 2 below. See further the important article by B. Brown, *Hahmarah: "Hamishah Tipusim min ha-Et Hadashah"* apud *Derech ha-Ru'ah – Sefer Yovel le-Eliezer Schweid, Mehkerei Yerushalayim* 19, Jerusalem, 2005, pp. 537–600.

that might have been used for idolatry, nevertheless, in a situation where there is a basis to either permit or prohibit, it is appropriate to be lenient, for we establish that in any circumstance of doubt we do not impose an assumption that something is prohibited, and we only are stringent in a case of doubt when there is a previous assumption that it is prohibited."[10]

It was well known that Rabbi Salant was a lenient *posek*[11] and that he always sought a way to permit,[12] when challenged that he was too

---

10. See below Appendix 2.

However, note the *Aruch ha-Shulhan*'s revelatory characterization of the Rema (*Orah Hayyim* 553:11):

And our teacher the Rema, *the lover of Israel,* struggled to justify the custom . . . (My emphasis – D.S.)

This passage was brought to my attention by reading Haym Soloveitchik's "Rupture and Reconstruction: the Transformation of Contemporary Orthodoxy" (supra p. 15 note 1), p. 107, note 7. See also *Minhagei Yisrael*, vol. 3, Jerusalem, 1994, pp. 53–54, on Rema's tendency in certain areas to *kula* (leniency).

11. Yaakov Rimon and Yosef Zundel Wasserman, *Shmuel be-Doro: Rabi Shmuel Salant, Rabbah Shel Yerushalayim 1841–1909 – Hayav u-Pe'ulato, Maslul,* 1961, pp. 122–126.

12. As an example, we bring the following citation from Rimon and Wasserman's book, ibid.:

A woman came to the home of Rabbi Shmuel on the eve of the Sabbath in the afternoon with a very sour face and shaking from her great distress. "Rabbi," she said in a tearful voice. "I cooked some meat for my family for the Sabbath and to my great anguish, a little bit of milk fell into the dish, and what am I to do? It is too late to prepare another dish." Rabbi Shmuel questioned the woman about the size of the pot, the amount of meat, the water, the spices and the amount of milk that had been mixed in. When it was unclear from her answers whether the amount of milk that fell in was 1/60 of the amount of the dish, he asked her for the name of her dairy man. He then advised her to go home and to return in an hour because he had to think about the matter. In the meantime, he sent his aid to urgently summon the dairy man to him. The dairy man came, and Rabbi Shmuel in his wisdom and intelligence extracted from the dairy man the amount of water that he adds to the milk that he sells. Based on this, he calculated that the dish was far more than 60 times the amount of milk [that fell into the dish]. The woman returned at the appointed time and Rabbi Shmuel preempted her saying: "It is kosher, it is kosher. Go home and enjoy the Sabbath food with your family." The woman cried and praised the rabbi incessantly. The sayings "the Torah has pity on the money of the Jewish people" and "the power of leniency is preferable" were guiding principles for him, and he always strove to find the permissive argument, and found it. He would always say to those who questioned him: "This way I can be certain that they will not punish me in the afterworld on the stringencies, just as they will not punish me for the leniencies (in the name of Yisrael Bar-Zakkai, the grandson of Rabbi Shmuel Salant)."

See above supra p. 170 note 11, and see my *The Relationship between Man and*

lenient, he would respond as follows: "I rule according to the halachah. A *posek* must learn much and must understand what he is saying. In order to be stringent, one does not need to learn much."

Not to Prohibit the Permitted and the Sin of Indolence in Adjudication

A further element to be taken into account in order more fully to understand the significance of these stories is the very pivotal halachic principle that it is forbidden to forbid the permitted. And because of its paramount importance, we shall take a closer look into this principle (which was briefly referred to above note 143).

Its source appears to be in *Y. Terumot* 5:3:

> Said R. [E]lazar: Just as one may not declare the impure pure, so too one may not declare the pure impure.

Compare this to *B. Beitzah* 16b:

> that you forbid that which is forbidden to him, and do not forbid that which is permitted to him.

On the basis of this Yerushalmi text the Shach in *Yoreh De'ah* 242, *Kitzur Hanhagot Issur ve-Heter* sect.9, ruled:

> Just as it is forbidden to permit the forbidden, so it is forbidden to forbid the permitted.

(Rav Kook cited this in his responsum in *Orah Mishpat*, Jerusalem, 1979, no. 112, p. 126.)

The commentary to *Y. Terumot* ibid., *Mareh ha-Panim*, explains:

> He should not say [to himself] I shall not trouble myself to fully clarify the issue, and as I am uncertain [as to the correct ruling] I will declare it impure, he is forbidden to do so.

His Neighbor and Man and His Maker, chapters 24, 27, and 28. I have heard similar formulations of this story with reference to a different Torah sage.

Yisachar Tamar, in his comments to *Y. Terumot* ibid. (*Alei Tamar*, vol. 2, Givataim, 1980, pp. 116–118), examined extensively this principle. He pointed to the *Vidui ha-Gaddol of Seder Yom Kippur ha-Katan*, by Rabbenu Nissim, in which, inter alia, the seriousness of the sin of forbidding the permitted is characterized as "the revolt of the servant against his master" and likened to the "stubborn and rebellious son" (Deuteronomy 21:18) – who, incidentally, the Bible tells us, should be stoned to death (ibid., verse 21). See also *Teshuvot R. Yishayah di-Trani* (ha-Rid), ed. A.Y. Wertheimer, Jerusalem, 1967, no. 55, p. 263 ad fin.; and additional sources and discussions in Y.Y. Bronstein, *Avnei Gazit*, Jerusalem, 2002, pp. 181–183. Tamar also cites the *Pithei Teshuvah* to *Yoreh Deah* 116 sect. 10, ad fin., who cites the *Solet le-Minhah* (by R. Yaakov Reischer, Dessau, 1696) in the name of *Torah ha-Asham*, that he who wishes to rule stringently and to forbid that which we do not find forbidden among the *Amoraim*, it is like *epikorsut* (heresy!), and he will lose more than he will merit.

See further the *Korban ha-Edah* to *Y. Sotah* 8:2, who states that one may not forbid the permitted out of a tendency to stringency without a real reason, and certainly not as a result of unwillingness to delve deeply into the issue to find the correct solution, and merely to forbid or to declare impure because of uncertainty (*mi-safek*). He also draws our attention to the passage in *Va-Yikra Rabba* 3:6, ed. Margaliyot, p. 71):

> "The Law of truth was in his mouth" (Malachi 2:6) – that he did not say that the impure was pure, nor that the pure was impure. "And iniquity was not found in his lips" (ibid.), – that he did not forbid the permitted, nor permit the forbidden.[13]

We may further recall the words of R. Dimi in the name of R. Yitzhak in *Y. Nedarim* 9:1, that the judges exhort one who takes upon himself another prohibition of something that is actually permitted, saying, "Is it not sufficient for you that which the Torah prohibited, but that you wish to prohibit additional things!"[14]

---

13. And see Tamar's examination to the correct version of this passage, which, however, has no effect on our discussion. See the continuation of his comments, and what he wrote in vol. 1, Givataim, 1979, p. 149, to *Y. Berachot* 4:2.

14. See also, Baruch Halevi Epstein, *Mekor Baruch* to *Avot*, 2nd edition, Tel Aviv, 1965, pp. 72–73.

From the above, we see the extreme seriousness of the indolent decisor, who through negligence and lack of a real sense of responsibility does not exert himself sufficiently to find the truth, and "covers himself" with stringencies that actually forbid the permitted.

In point of fact, in the stories related above, the rabbis did not rule stringently with regards to *kashrut*, but rather leniently so as not to cause monetary loss and distress to the client.[15] Indeed, this is similar to that which is related of R. Hayyim, the Brisker Rav, who was well known for ruling leniently on fasting on Yom Kippur. He was wont to explain his position saying:

> I do not rule leniently concerning Yom Kippur (etc.), but stringently concerning the law, "take ye therefore good heed unto yourselves" – ונשמרתם מאד לנפשותיכם (Deuteronomy 4:15).[16]

So a rabbi's lenient approach should not be merely the result of his sensitive empathy toward the questioner, but also resulting out of real *yirat shamayim*, fear of heaven, not to give an incorrect response by "forbidding the permitted." This is especially the case where such an incorrect response, due to the lazy "short-cut" of declaring *assur* rather than toiling to resolve the *safek*, will cause harm and damage to the questioner. It is true that it takes a graver effort and a greater burden of responsibility to rule leniently, but the added sensitivity to the plight of the client should counterbalance any "fear of judgement" (*yirat horaah*), and meticulous study and research should assure the *posek* that he is ruling in the correct direction.

This grave burden of responsibility is expressed brilliantly by J. David Bleich, in his *Contemporary Halakhic Problems*, vol. 4, New York, 1995, p. xi, where he writes:

> Halakhic pronouncements should bear a Surgeon General's warning that they may be dangerous to spiritual health and well-being. The onus of error is entirely analogous to that which in the realm of the physical

---

15. See above p. 37 and *Alei Tamar*, vol.1, ibid.

16. See the discussion in my *On the Relationship of Mitzvot between Man and His Neighbor and Man and His Maker*, Jerusalem and New York, 2014, pp. 98–101, and especially note 101, ibid.

accompanies the granting of a seal of approval or the issuance of a public warning of impending danger. An erroneous endorsement can easily lead to serious danger, an unwarranted interdiction can wreak havoc with human lives.[17]

Sensitivity to the "Have-Nots"

Sensitivity to the poverty of the "have-nots" is a common theme throughout rabbinic literature. We are well-acquainted with the famous *Mishnah* in *Keritot* 1:7, which we read as follows (in Herbert Danby's translation, Oxford, 1933, p. 564):

> If a woman suffered five issues that were in doubt or five miscarriages that were in doubt, she need bring but one offering, and she may then eat of the animal-offerings; and she is not bound to bring the other offerings. If she had suffered five miscarriages that were not in doubt or five issues that were not in doubt, she need bring but one offering and she may then eat of the animal-offerings; and she is bound to bring the other offerings. Once in Jerusalem a pair of doves cost a golden *denar*. He went into the court and taught: If a woman suffered five miscarriages that were not in doubt or five issues that were not in doubt, she need bring but one offering, and she may then eat of the animal-offerings; and she is not bound to offer the other offerings. And the same day the price of a pair of doves stood at a quarter-*denar* each.

And based on this text the *Beer Haiteiv* to *Shulhan Aruch, Orah Hayyim* 242:1 cites a number of authorities (such as *Pri Hadash, Minhagei Issur*, sect. 15, etc.) who rule that even though there is an obligation (according to *Tikkunei Shabbat*) to eat fish at each Shabbat meal, if the price of fish went up steeply, one should desist from doing so until the price drops down again. As we have seen elsewhere, in *B. Moed Katan* 27ab, there were a number of rabbinic enactments which instituted taking account of the plight of the poor. Indeed, the Torah was keenly aware of the economic stratification of society, as is evident from the

17. See what I wrote in my introduction to *Darkah shel Halachah*, Jerusalem, 2007, pp. 7–10, and see also R. Shalom Messas' responsum cited above p. 190 note 9 ad fin.

gradiated sacrifices (*korban oleh ve-yoreid*) listed in Leviticus 5:6, 7, and 11:

6. And he shall bring his trespass offering unto the Lord for his sin which he hath sinned, a female from the flock, a lamb or a kid of the goats, for a sin offering; and the priest shall make an atonement for him concerning his sin.

7. And if he be not able to bring a lamb, then he shall bring for his trespass, which he hath committed, two turtle doves, or two young pigeons, unto the Lord; one for a sin offering, and the other for a burnt offering.

11. But if he be not able to bring two turtle doves, or two young pigeons, then he that sinned shall bring for his offering the tenth part of an ephah of fine flour, for a sin offering; he shall put no oil upon it, neither shall he put *any* frankincense thereon: for it *is* a sin

There are numerous additional examples of this special consideration for the impoverished.[18]

This meticulousness on interpersonal matters and exceptional sen-

---

18. See, e.g., what I wrote in my *Darkah shel Halachah,* Jerusalem, 2007, pp. 98–99, etc., and see above section entitled "Beyond the Letter of the Law." We could, for instance, point to the *Mishnah* in *Eruvin* 4:9, where special consideration was afforded to poor people with regard to the complex laws of *Eruvin,* according to R. Meir. (However, there are a variety of interpretations of the term *ani,* a poor person, in the *Rishonim,* such as that of Rabbenu Hananel (to B. *Eruvin* 51b) who remarks that "all travelers may be regarded as poor people, since normally they do not have a loaf [for the *eruv*] available to them." Nonetheless the simple understanding of the Talmud's explanation in B. *Eruvin* 51b, is that "it was for the poor person the Sages ruled with this leniency." See also the well-known Talmudic dictum, "He who has a loaf in his basket is in no way similar to him who has no loaf in his basket" (B. *Yoma* 18a, 67a, 74b, B. *Yevamot* 37b, B. *Ketubot* 62b). This is a broad topic that requires its own treatment.

Indeed, the Torah is replete with mitzvot relating to charity (*tzedakah*) to the poor, (e.g., *leket, shikhah* and *peah,* etc.), and clearly takes into account different social classes (e.g., *korban oleh ve-yoreid,* Leviticus 5:7-22), etc. But this is a field beyond the scope of this study on which there is, in any case, a considerable literature. See, e.g., Yehuda Bergman, *Ha-Tzedakah be-Yisrael: Toldotav u-Mosdotav,* Jerusalem 1943; Betzalel Landau, "*Ha-Tzedakah be-Hayyei ha-Tizbbur,*" *Mahanayim* 1961, etc.

And see, for example the very moving passage in Deuteronomy 15:7-14:

7. If there be among you a poor man of one of thy brethren within any of thy gates in they land which the Lord thy God giveth thee, thou shalt not harden thine heart, nor shut thine hand from thy poor brother:

sitivity to the poor came to expression in halachot defined as *hesed* – kindness – related, such as charity, loving kindness, visiting the sick (see above), etc. Thus, for example, with regard to charity, in addition to giving money or other help to the poor and hungry, the halachah states (Maimonides. *Mishneh Torah, Hilchot Matnot Aniyim* 7:3): "Even if the personal habit of this poor person was to ride on a horse and to have a servant run before him and then he became impoverished and lost his wealth, we should buy a horse for him to ride and a servant to run before him, as it is said (Deuteronomy 15:8) [provide him with] 'enough to [fill the] lack that he feels.' You are commanded to fill his lack . . ." (based on *Ketubot* 67b).

In a like manner, the Rambam, in *Hilchot Yom Tov* 6:17-18, writes:

A person is obligated to be happy and of good spirits, he, his children and his wife and all those with him during Israel's festivals, as it is written "And thou shalt rejoice in thy feast" (Deuteronomy 16:14), and there is no happiness without meat and wine. And when he eats and drinks he is obligated also to feed the stranger, the orphan and the widow together with the other unfortunate poor. But he who locks the doors of his courtyard [to keep out the poor] and eats and drinks, he, his wife and children, and does not give food and drink to the poor and bitter souls, this does not constitute the happiness of the mitzvah of the festival, but rather the pleasure of his stomach, and concerning him who acts

---

8. But thou shalt open thine hand wide unto him, and shalt surely lend him sufficient for his need, *in that*, which he wanteth.

9. Beware that there be not a thought in thy wicked heart, saying, The seventh year, the year of release, is at hand; and thine eye be evil against thy poor brother, and thou givest him nought; and he cry unto the Lord against thee, and it be sin unto thee.

10. Thou shalt surely give him, and thine heart shall not be grieved when thou givest unto him: because that for this thing the Lord thy God shall bless thee in all thy works and in all that thou puttest thine hand unto.

11. For the poor shall never cease out of the land; therefore I command thee, saying, Thou shalt open thine hand wide unto thy brother, to thy poor, and to thy needy, in thy land.

12. And if thy brother, and Hebrew man, or a Hebrew woman, be sold unto thee, and serve thee six years; then in the seventh year thou shalt let him go free from thee.

13. And when thou sendest him out free from thee, thou shalt not let him go away empty;

14. Thou shalt furnish him liberally out of thy flock, and out of thy floor, and out of thy winepress; *of that* where-with the Lord thy God hath blessed thee thou shalt give unto him.

in this fashion is it said, "their sacrifices shall be unto them as bread of mourners; all those eat of them shall be polluted . . ." (Hoshea 9:4), and this happiness is shameful to them, as it is said, "and [I will] spread dung upon your faces, even the dung of your solemn feasts" (Malachi 2:3).

Compare this to *Zohar-Exodus* (*Yitro*) 88b, that at every festival a person must seek to include a "wretched person" (*miskein*), otherwise he may be punished. (The *Zohar* quotes the same verse from Malachi.) How much did the rabbis trouble themselves and extend themselves in order to preserve the dignity of a poor person to help him in his hour of need, and certainly not to humiliate him?[19]

I remember my father telling me the following story that actually took place: Once, my father saw his father, the Gaon Rabbi David Sperber, without the large silver watch that was always hanging from his vest by a silver chain (my grandfather, who was very poor and sufficed with very little, had received the watch as a gift from a member of the community). But he did not say anything to him. Some time later, my father saw the same watch in the possession of one of the wealthy residents of the village. My father asked his father to explain why he had given the watch to the rich man? My grandfather answered that this rich man had lost his wealth, and his situation was so bad that he had to sell his own watch in another city. Since it was beneath this man's dignity to be seen without the watch, and it would reveal his condition, he gave him his watch. In my father's bewilderment, he asked – "We need to help him to that extent?" My grandfather explained that this is an explicit halachah: "If the personal habit of this poor person was to ride on a horse and to have a servant run before him . . . we should buy a horse for him to ride and a servant to run before him."[20]

---

19. See the book of Nahum Rakover, *Gadol Kevod ha-Briyot: Kevod ha-Adam ke-Erekh Al*, Jerusalem, 1989, pp. 145–150, (and many other examples could be added to his words, but this is not the place to expand on this). See also Yehuda Bergman, *Ha-Tzedakah be-Yisrael: Toldoteha u-Mosdoteha*, Jerusalem, 1944, pp. 138–140 (on giving secretly, or perhaps we should say discreetly). For further bibliographic information see Rakover, *supra* note 10, pp. 317–318, nos. 7888–7911. See above section entitled "Human Dignity" (especially pp. 59–61 note 17) and the preceding section entitled "Care Not to Shame or Embarrass."

20. See the remarkable story told of R. Yehoshua Yehuda Leib Diskin, in Yosef Scheinberger, *Amud Aish: Toldot Hayyav ve-Poalav Shel Maran Moshe Yehoshua Leib Diskin*, Jerusalem (1955), pp. 145–146, which bears many similarities to the above.

The halachah took great cognizance of the poor and the starving. So we find that a tailor who is poverty-stricken and hungry, is permitted to ply his trade after the first of Av, and even during *Tisha b'Av*, if this be the only way he can support himself. So ruled R. Yosef Hayyim, the *Ben Ish Hai*, despite the fact that the Rema, in *Shulhan Aruch, Orah Hayyim* 551:7, as explained in the *Mishnah Berurah* ibid. note 51, and the *Kaf ha-Hayyim* ibid. notes 109, 110, forbade this. This was already the opinion of R. Yisrael Bruna (c.1400–1480), in his responsa no. 10, where he wrote that:

A Jewish tailor is permitted to sew new clothing if he has not what to eat, just as a mourner [may] after the [initial] three days [of mourning].[21]

R. Ovadiah Yosef, in his *Halichot Olam* vol. 2, Jerusalem, 1998, pp. 140–143, goes so far to permit this even on *Tisha b'Av* itself, and even when there is pleasure involved (*ve-afilu be-binyan shel simhah*), comparing this situation with that of a poor worker who needs to earn a living on *Hol ha-Moed*. He further cites R. Moshe Coucy *Sefer Mitzvot Gadol, Lo Taaseh* 75, ed. Machon Yerushalayim, vol. 1, Jerusalem, 1993, p. 320:

[And we learn from there (*B. Moed Katan* 12a etc.) that whatever is forbidden during *Hol ha-Moed*, one may also not ask another Jew to do it. And all that is forbidden on *Hol ha-Moed*, if he has not what to eat, he may do for his livelihood. And he may do business for his livelihood.] And it is permitted for a rich man to hire a poor worker who has not what to eat to carry out such work for him which is [normally] forbidden on *Hol ha-Moed*, in order that he may receive a wage for his livelihood. And one may purchase things not needed for the festival in order to help the vendor who has not what to eat.[22]

---

21. This is also cited by the *Kaf ha-Hayyim*, ibid., note 104.

22. And see R. Ovadiah's additional references, ibid., p. 141, and his extended discussion on the poor man's work on *Tisha B'Av* with the usual wealth of sources.

To this we may add that though the *Shulhan Aruch, Orah Hayyim* 551:2 rules (on the basis of M. *Ta'anit* 1:7) that during the "nine days," after the first of Av till *Tisha B'Av*, one minimizes one's business activities, the *Mishnah Berurah* (ad loc. note 11) notes that:

In our times they were accustomed to be lenient in all these affairs, because nowadays all [business] is considered for one's livelihood (*kedei parnasato*).

A famous example of rabbinic concern for the poor is to be found in the changing rules of burial. For the Talmud in *B. Moed Katan* 27b tells us how, because of the great financial outlay involved in using costly burial shrouds, the relatives of the deceased, upon whom these expenses devolved, would leave the body and run away! There upon

> Rabban Gamliel set an example of disregard of custom through himself [inaugurating simplicity at burial] when [according to his request] they buried him in linen garments, and the people followed his practice (cf. *B. Ketubot* 8b).

The Talmud continues that Rav Papa (in Babylonia) added that nowadays the practice is for people to use for their shrouds "even rough cloth worth a *zuz*." Even though the *Beer Heiteiv*, in *Yoreh Deah* 352:1, stated that one should take care not to change the customs of dressing the corpse in a shroud (i.e., the quality of the shroud, the loss of linen shrouds), "because the dead are particular on this issue." When types of linen became too expensive, the rabbis suggested using cheaper materials.[23]

(See his references there in *Shaar ha-Tziyyun*, pp. 43–45 note 5. And cf. above note 12, and what I wrote in my *Minhagei Yisrael*, vol. 3, Jerusalem, 1994, pp. 50–59.)

Similarly, a mourner during the *shiva*, the first seven days of mourning, is not permitted to do any kind of work (*B. Moed Katan* 21b; *Shulhan Aruch, Yoreh Deah* 380:1-2) or trade (*Semachot* 9:14 and 5:1). However, if the mourner is a pauper and has not what to eat, he may work (i.e., earn) after the first three days of mourning, but discreetly in his own house (ibid.) However, the Sages said: "May his neighbours be cursed that they made this necessary for him." (See ibid. and *Y. Moed Katan* 3:5, where the curse is mentioned, and where work *on the third day* is permitted. See further *Genesis Rabba* 100:7, ed. Albeck, p. 1290. In his note ad loc. he refers us to *Ben Sira* (Hebrew) 38:16–17, the first *two* days are days of crying – *bechi*, not three.)

On the nature of this curse, see Yisachar Tamar, *Alei Tamar, Moed*, vol. 3, Alon Shvut, 1992, p. 332. Incidentally, the reference in the *Tosafot* to *Moed Katan* ibid. s.v. *Mi-Kaan*, is somewhat misleading, as the "curse" is not mentioned in *Semachot*, only in the *Yerushalmi*. The further and clearer formulation may be found in *Shitah le-Talmido shel R. Yehiel mi-Paris* to *Moed Katan*, ed. M.Y.L. Sachs, and F. Friedman, Jerusalem, 1936, p. 85, and so too in *Perush Massechet Mashkin le-Rabbenu Shlomo ben ha-Yatom*, ed. H.P. Chajes, Berlin, 1909, p. 107. See further, *Entziklopedia Talmudit*, vol. 1, Tel-Aviv 1947, p. 31, and idem, vol. 27.

23. See, e.g., *Shut ha-Rival*, R. Yehuda Leib Friedman, Preshburg, 1822, sect. 64, discussing the use of "*papierleinwand*," some sort of cheap linen made of recycled old clothes. See *Meorot ha-Daf ha-Yomi* 798, to *Moed Katan* 27 – *Hagigah* 5, 12 Elul 5774, p. 1. And cf. above section entitled "Care Not to Shame or Embarrass."

The concern for the welfare of the poor emerges from an interesting story related in *Y. Shekalim* 5:4. There we read how:

> R. Hanina bar Papa used to distribute charity at night. One time he encountered the leader of the [evil] spirits, [whose realm is during the night]. He said to him, "Have you not taught, our Master, 'Thou shalt not remove thy neighbour's landmark' (Deuteronomy 19:14) [meaning: do not trespass into the domain of another, i.e., and night is our domain, and human beings should not enter into it]." He replied, "And is it not written, 'A gift in secret pacifieth anger' (Proverbs 21:14)?" And [the evil spirit] shrank away in fear of him and ran away from before him.

The *Korban he-Edah* ad loc. explains why he would distribute charity to the poor at night, namely that he did so as not to embarrass them.[24] Indeed, this explanation is in harmony with what we read in the *Mishnah* in *Shekalim* ibid.:

> There were two chambers in the Temple: one the Chamber of Secrets and the other the Chamber of Utensils. In the Chamber of Secrets the devout used to put their gifts in secret and the poor of good family received support therefrom in secret.

And in that same *Yerushalmi* section, we read how R. Yonah used to distribute charity:

> When he saw a poor person of good family who had lost his [family] fortune, he would say to him, "My son, I have heard that you just received an inheritance from somewhere else; take [this money], and you will repay it." After he received it, he would say to him, "It is a gift" (i.e., you do not have to pay it back).[25]

Concern for the poor even had its influence on the development of the liturgy. Thus we learn from *Sefer ha-Pardes*, ed. Ehrenreich, Budapest,

---

24. On the question as to whether one may give charity at night, and the kabbalistic reasons for not doing so, see R. Ovadiah Yosef, *Yabia-Omer*, vol. 10, Jerusalem, 2004, *Yoreh Deah*, no. 48, p. 299, for a full discussion.

25. See above section on "Care Not to Shame or Embarrass."

1924, p. 306, and likewise from *Shibbolei ha-Leket*, ed. Buber, Vilna, 1987, sect. 44, pp. 37–38, in the name of Rashi, that, in the past, the practice was that every day after the *Shaharit* prayer there would be a reading from the Torah, the Prophets, the *Mishnah* and the *Gemara*. However, over the years this practice was abandoned because of the spread of poverty, and people were forced to leave the synagogue early in order to get to their jobs to work for their sustenance. As a memory of this early practice they established a daily recitation of two verses from the Prophet Isaiah 59:20–21, "And the redeemer shall come to Zion (*U-va le-Tziyyon*). . . . As for Me, this is My covenant . . ." It is for this reason that on Shabbat, when we do have a *haftarah*, meaning a reading from the Prophets and additional readings from the *Mishnah* and *Gemara*, we do not say "And the redeemer shall come to Zion . . ." Nonetheless, in order that this practice be not completely forgotten, these verses were moved to the Shabbat *Minhah* service.

Whether this is the true explanation for the evolution of the *U-Va le-Tziyyon* prayer, or rather that of R. Natronai Gaon, as found in *Teshuvot ha-Geonim*, ed. Mussafiah, Lyck 1864, no. 90, pp. 29–30, where the explanation is quite different, is perhaps not so important for our purpose. What is significant is that in the school of Rashi they were willing to explain a development in the liturgy, and an abbreviation thereof, as caused by the community's poverty, and that the shortening of the service was to help the poor to be able to work longer and earn more.[26]

We may recall the passage in *Zohar Exodus Va-Yakhel*, vol. 2, 198a, in the name of R. Yehudah, beginning with a homily on the verse in Isaiah 58:7, "Is it not to spread out thy bread to the hungry . . ."

> Come and see he who takes pity on the wretched (i.e., poor), and restores his spirit (i.e., by helping and feeding him) the Holy One blessed be He credits him as though he had recreated his spirit. And for this reason Abraham, who took pity on all people, was regarded by the Holy One blessed be He as though he had created them, as the verse says "and the

---

26. For a detailed discussion of this issue, see Y.M. Elbogen, *Ha-Tefillah be-Yisrael be-Hitpathutah ha-Historit*, ed. Y. Heineman, Tel-Aviv, 1972, pp. 62, 403–404, note 23. And on shortening the service because of lack of time in the synagogue, see my *On Changes in Jewish Liturgy: Options and Limitations*, Jerusalem and New York, 2010, p. 72 and note 2, ibid.

souls that they had made in Haran" (Genesis 12:5) "Is it not to spread out . . ." – what is "to spread out"? To spread out before him bread and food to eat.[27]

Indeed, in *Zohar Genesis, Va-Yera*, 104a, we read (in a version similar to that found in *Va-Yakhel* ibid.):

> . . . For we have learned, that when the Holy One blessed be He loves someone, he sends him a gift. And what is that gift? A wretched person, so that he can give him charity. And as soon as he gives him charity, a thread of favour is drawn over his right side and covers his head and is written upon it, so that when he comes before the divine court, the [angel of] destruction will beware of him, and cast his eye to see that sign and leave him . . .[28]

We could greatly multiply such examples of how the halachah and the kabbalah paid special attention to those in penury and found all manner of leniencies, perhaps even making changes in the liturgy, to emeliorate their plight, but let us end with the following beautiful passage by R. Yosef Yaavetz ha-Hasid, in his commentary to *Avot* 1:5:

> The Holy One blessed be He is very very far away in the heavenly heavens and [yet] close to the wretched poor. And it is for this reason that the Sages said [*B. Shabbat* 127a], "Greater is the hosting of guests even than welcoming the *Shechinah* itself." For the *Shechina* (Divine Presence) is to be dwelling between the shoulders of the poor, so that the mitzvah of hosting them is most elevated, and it does not constitute a barrier before welcoming the *Shechinah*. On the contrary it is inestimably greater. And if this were not the case, as I have stated, what would be the meaning of that statement of the Sages? For surely the ultimate goal is welcoming [and cleaving to] the *Shechinah*, and how could it be pushed aside for something else?![29]

---

27. See continuation and the many parallels referred to in Margaliot's edition, notes 1–3.

28. See also *Sefer ha-Yashar*, attributed to Rabbenu Tam chapter 13, for a parallel version, in the name of "a wise man said."

29. There is a considerable body of literature on the Subject of *Tzedakah* – charity. We shall only mention a few important works:

Knowing the Needs of Others

Since I have mentioned my wonderful paternal grandfather – who is to me, alongside with my sainted father, the archetype of a rabbi who was dedicated and true to his community, one who combined wisdom and kindness – I cannot refrain from citing the words of my father from his introduction to my grandfather's book, *Michtam le-David Al ha-Torah*:[30]

> This empathy for the distress of other Jews was a great and emphatic quality of his, and there was no Jew who was not important enough for him to participate in his distress. He viewed every individual from the perspective of "I found Israel like grapes in the wilderness" – as a real find. And he would dedicate his soul and be softened by his distress, and try to help and aid him to the best of his ability, and even beyond his ability. I was very much amazed and in awe of his quality of perfect innocence that knew no bounds, and even with his great wisdom and intelligence, he remained with this childlike innocence. It seems that this is the sign of a person's greatness. There is no personal or spiritual greatness that is not accompanied by innocence. It was a favorite saying of his: "I will go in my innocence," (Psalms 26:11). And the rabbis already discussed at length the severity of one who has the capability to pray for mercy for his friend and doesn't do so. Our father would say: "Who can say: 'I have made my heart clean' and how can it be known who is worthy of that?" And he would say: "The distinction is clear – one who feels the pain of his friend is also able and obligated to pray for mercy on his behalf."

Martin Buber, in his *Tales of the Hasidim*, New York, 1991, Part 2, p. 86, tells a wonderful story of "How the Rabbi of Sasov [Reb Moshe Leib of Sasov, died 1807] Learned How to Love":

Naftali Tzvi Yehudah Bar-Ilan, *Nitkadesh bi-Tzedakah*, Rechovot, 1991, provides a fine comprehensive discussion of this subject; the anonymous *Le-Hair Hilchot Tzedakah be-Or Yakrut*, Jerusalem, 2010, is another good source; and, of course, the classic text on this subject, is R. Yisrael Meir ha-Cohen of Radin (the *Hafetz Hayyim*), *Ahavat Hesed*, Warsaw, 1988–1993, reprinted numerous times.

30. Rabbi Shmuel Sperber, "Introduction: The Spiritual Personality of the Author, of Blessed Memory" [Hebrew] in Rabbi David Sperber, *Michtam le-David Al ha-Torah*, B. Sperber (ed.), Jerusalem, 1965, (2nd edition, Brooklyn, 2014).

Rabbi Moshe Leib told this story:

"How to love men is something I learned from a peasant. He was sitting in an inn along with other peasants, drinking. For a long time he was as silent as all the rest, but when he was moved by the wine, he asked one of the men seated beside him: 'Tell me, do you love me or don't you love me?' The other replied: 'I love you very much.' But the first peasant replied: 'You say that you love me, but you do not know what I need. If you really loved me, you would know.' The other had not a word to say to this, and the peasant who had put the question fell silent again.

"But I understood. To know the needs of men and to bear the burden of their sorrow – that is the true love of men."

Buber continues to relate:

Whenever the rabbi of Sasov saw anyone's suffering either of spirit or of body, he shared it so earnestly that the other's suffering became his own. Once someone expressed his astonishment at this capacity to share in another's troubles. "What do you mean 'share'?" asked the rabbi, himself replying, "It is my own sorrow; how can I help but suffer it?"

Of course, not everyone is expected to have such a degree of empathy, but a degree of sensitivity for the distress of the other and for his needs is a primary requirement. While one cannot necessarily sense all a persons' needs, one should be able to sense his personal distress. Indeed, the following is told of the Hozeh of Lublin (R. Yaakov Yitzhak of Lublin, 1745–1815). When R. Mordechai of Pinchov, who was very poor, came to visit him after many previous visits, he poured his heart out to the Hozeh, explaining that he could no longer bear his poverty and that of his family. The Hozeh asked him why he had not mentioned this earlier, and Reb Mordechai replied that he did not wish to trouble the Rabbi with material issues. And then he added in a quiet voice, "I said to myself, 'Surely the Rebbe, with his divine inspiration, knows what goes on in my house.'" The Hozeh answered with a smile.

"In the biblical chapter dealing with leprosy there is a difference between leprosy in a man and that in houses. Concerning the former it is said, 'When a man shall have in the skin of his flesh a rising, a scab, or a bright spot . . . And the priest shall look on the plague in the skin of the flesh. . . .' (Leviticus 13:2-3). While concerning leprosy in the house it is written, 'And he that owneth shall come and tell the priest, saying it seemeth to me that there is as it were a plague in the house' (Leviticus 14:35). Apparently," explained the Hozeh, "for people's leprosy (i.e., personal, physical distress), one does not have to inform the priest. It is enough to come to him, and he, without listening to any complaint, sees it, and will know how to deal with it. But as to material and financial troubles (the house leprosy), one has to report it to the priest so that he be able to advise how one might remedy the matter."

Now the plain and simple *pshat* meaning of these verses is really quite clear. The *Kohen* can see at first sight the overt signs of leprosy upon the person facing him. But he needs to be taken to the house to examine the leprous signs on the walls before he can broach an opinion.

Nevertheless, the message of the Hozeh is also quite clear. In his own homiletic style he states that the rabbi should be able to sense obvious signs of physical distress in his congregant. However, he should not necessarily be expected to be able to discern the inner financial trouble of his house and family. Thus, it is encumbent upon the congregant to offer the plain facts before the rabbi, should he seek his help and advice.

Indeed, it is often necessary to interrogate the congregant in order to get a fuller picture of the question he is bringing before the rabbi. For all too often the congregant does not know how fully to formulate his question, or at times he may be embarrassed to reveal certain aspects of it, or even be unaware of them and their implications. This point was made by R. Moshe Walter, in his *Making a Halachic Decision,* Brooklyn, 2013, pp. 107–109, noting that the Rav has to know to distinguish between *le-hitchilah* and *be-di-avad,* to take account of the religiosity of the questioner, in order to intuit the appropriate decision for [the] particular individual. (See *Pri Megadim, Hanhagat ha-Nishal im ha-Shoel* 1:1.) A fine example of this may be found in Malka Puterovsky's *Mehalechet be-Darkah,* Tel-Aviv, 2014, pp. 189–221, a chapter dealing with the question of the degree to which children are obligated to love and respect parents that are mentally abnormal.

To be aware of the needs of others, both physical and psychological, a rabbi has to be something of a psychologist. See, for instance, the story told in *Y. Yoma* 6:4:

R. Hanina sat before R. Haggai on Yom ha-Kippurim. He said to him: "I am very thirsty." He replied, "Go drink." A while later he found him, and said to him, "What did you do for your thirst?" He replied, "Since you permitted me to drink, [my thirst] passed."

The text continues to relate that R. Hiyya bar Aba would relate the following tale:

It happened that a certain person was walking along in the market-place with his daughter. "Father, I am thirsty," said the daughter to her father. "We have but a little way to go," he replied. "But father, I am thirsty," she said. [Again] he replied, "We have but a little way to go." And she died.

R. Aha, when the congregation had finshed the *Musaf* service, would announce, "My brothers, whosoever has a small child, go home [i.e., to feed him, lest he comes to a state of danger]."

The first R. Hanina and R. Haggai story is cited in the *Beit Yosef,* to *Orah Hayyim* 618:1, who added on the basis of an earlier statement in the *Yerushalmi* ibid.:

From here we learn that the evil inclination only craves that which is forbidden, and hence this was the right way in which to act.

R. Haggai surely knew that by permitting R. Hanina to drink, his thirst would be abated even without his drinking. R. Yisachar Tamar, in his *Alei Tamar Moed,* vol. 1, Alon Shvut, 1992, p. 337, comments that:

The rabbi who permits eating [under such circumstances] should not feel pangs of doubt lest he did not rule correctly . . . for had he not permitted it, he might have brought the requester to a state of danger.[31]

Incidentally, this *Yerushalmi* text served as a source for a *psak halachah* of the Rogotzover, in his *Tzofnat Paneah* section 39, where he talks of the subjective feeling of fear as a justification for certain permissiveness (*heterim*). See also the responsum of R. Yitzhak Zilberstein, in *Kovetz*

---

31. See his additional pertinent comments on the story of the dying daughter, pp. 377–379.

Torani Even Yisrael, Bnei Brak, 1991, pp. 175–177, dealing with "fear of the fast." There, too, we see the perspicacity needed of a rabbi to see in-depth the inner needs of his congregants in order to arrive at the right halachic rulings.

Surely this is what the *Gemara* in *B. Hagigah* 3b meant when stating that the judge must:

> Make your ear like a hopper (*afarkeset*), and develop a heart that un-
> derstands (*lev meivin*) to hear the words of those who declare impure
> and those who declare pure, those who forbid and those that permit. . . .

Thus the *lev meivin*, the understanding heart, is a quality required of the rabbi to *posek*.

The *lev meivin* is wonderfully exemplified in a story told of R. Ye-hoshua Yehuda Leib Diskin, in R. Yosef Scheinberger's biography *Amud Aish*, Jerusalem, 1954, pp. 148–149:

> It happened that once on the night after Yom Kippur, when our Master
> was sitting in his house [with his disciples], that he noticed that one of
> those present was steeped in worry and distress. Our Master conjectured
> that probably he had had a seminal emission on Yom Kippur, and the
> Sages said that if that happened one should be concerned a whole year. At
> that moment our Rabbi raised his eyes, gazing at the company that encir-
> cled his table and said simply: "Our Sages said that he who has a seminal
> emission on Yom Kippur, that is an evil omen for him, and he should
> be concerned a whole year. But that is only if we say that the various
> prohibitions (*inuyim*) [of Yom Kippur] are all of biblical status. But if it is
> our opinion that all of them, with the exception of fasting, i.e., eating and
> drinking, are only of rabbinic status (Tur *Orah Hayyim* 811 and Rosh in
> the name of the Rivash) then it is likely that this is not an evil omen and
> one need not be concerned. And proof of this," continued our Master,
> "is from the Tosafot in *B. Sukkah* 2a (s.v. *Ki Avid Lei*). For the Tosafot
> explains that if the prohibition to use planks (*nesarim*) for schach is only
> of rabbinic status, then the lack of rain on Sukkot is not an evil omen,
> since the whole prohibition is only of rabbinic status, and consequently
> there is no relevance to evil omens. From this we may learn that since
> the other prohibitions on Yom Kippur are also only of rabbinic status, a
> seminal emission on the holy day does not constitute an evil omen."

When our Master ended his talk, that individual could no longer control himself, and he jumped up from his place and shouted out to our Master in a loud voice, "The Rabbi has removed a heavy stone from my heart."

Perhaps this is also subtly indicated in B. *Shabbat* 138b. On the verse in *Amos* 8:10, "And they shall run to and fro to seek the word of the Lord, and shall not find it," the Talmud asks:

And what does it mean that "they shall run to and fro to seek the Word of God . . ."? They replied: It will come to pass that a woman shall hold a loaf of bread of *terumah*, and go from synagogue to synagogue and from *beit midrash* to *beit midrash* seeking to know whether that loaf is ritually pure or not. And no one will understand [her question] (*ve-ein meivin*)!

The text does not say "and no one will *know* the answer" (*ve-ein yo-dea*), but rather "no one will *understand*." The Talmud then discusses that text in detail, examining the minutiae of its meaning. But perhaps we may infer, that our text wishes to indicate to us, that in addition to no one having the answer to this halachic question, no one even understood (*ein meivin*) the personal dilemma facing this woman, who goes running from one place to another to find out whether she can alleviate her hunger, and that of her family, with this problematic loaf of bread. "The Word of God" requires not only the correct knowledge of the halachah, but also deep understanding of the personal needs of the individual.

And at times, with such insight he may well require a careful interrogation of his congregant in order to avoid a mistaken ruling, as already stressed above. (See B. *Sanhedrin* 32b: *din merumeh*, and *Torah Temimah* to Deuteronomy 16:20, note 83, pp. 209–210.)

The *lev meivin*, empathy and understanding, that a rabbi requires is to be reflected in a remarkable responsum of R. Yaakov Weil (died 1450), no. 12. (ed. Y.S. Domb, Jerusalem, 2001, vol. 1, pp. 14–16). Concerning a young married woman who had indulged in an adulterous affair and gave birth to a *mumzer*, he was asked what her punishment should be. He begins by saying that she should receive very severe punishment by law. However, he notes, she may not have the strength to suffer them, and be truly repentant, since she is "young and tender in years." Also, since she has become habituated to her sinful practices, it will be difficult to turn her away from them. One must think deeply at all aspects of the case, and how to draw her back with the ropes of love (cf. Hosea 11:4), and with words of encouragement and appeasement. It would seem best to explain to her all that she is obligated to do [in order to achieve true repentence] bit by bit, not in one go, such as "what to do during the first three months, and if she carries that out, then turn her for another three months, till the end of the first year . . ." We see in this response a very caring and understanding approach to the issue of punishment and repentence for very serious halachic offence.

Yet another poignant example is the case brought in R. Hayyim Sofer's *Mahaneh Hayyim* to *Even ha-Ezer*, part 3, Muncacz, 1872–1875, no. 55, concerning a married woman who had repeated sexual relations with a demon. The question was if this is considered adultery to forbid her to her husband. A similar case was brought before R. Aharon Wertheimer, in his *Sheelat Shlomo*, Jerusalem, 1932–1934, no. 82, when the wife of a *Kohen* came in tears, claiming she had been raped by a demon, again asking whether she is permitted to her husband. R. Ovadiah Yosef, in his *Yabia Omer*, vol. 9, 2nd edition, Jerusalem, 2002, *Even ha-Ezer*, no. 16, p. 379, brings a variety of sources that discuss this issue (going back to a responsum of Maharam mi-Lublin nos. 116–117), and, inter alia, brings the reason for leniency.

> It is by no means clear that a demon actually raped her, and it is possible that this was merely her imagination, and as the result of many dreams and stupid folk-beliefs (*havalim*), this imaginative notion took a firm hold over her, for it is in the nature women . . . to be seduced by fanciful imagination that leads them astray, so much so that they really believe it happened. But this will not prohibit her to her husband. . . . One should therefore rely on the fact that this is the result of imagination and [sense-less] thoughts, and therefore she is permitted to her husband, and one may not call with doubt the presumption of her *kashrut*.

Here, again, rationality coupled with psychological insight solved these hapless women's plight. Such examples can be greatly replicated, but these should suffice.

This kind of empathetic sensitivity, *lev meivin*, to the needs and wellbeing of others is beautifully illustrated in a series of tales told of

R. Yisrael (Lipkin) Salanter (1810–1883). R. Yehuda Leib Maimon in his *Sarei ha-Meah*, vol. 2, Jerusalem, 1961, pp. 272–273, relates the following:

And it once happened that Reb Yisrael Salanter, during his stay in Kovno, lived for a while in the house of a wealthy pious man, Reb Yaakov Karpas, and would dine at his table. Members of the household noted that when he washed his hands before the meal, he would do so with a minimal amount of water, even though a bucket full of water was prepared for him. They wondered in amazement: Should not a *tzaddik* like Reb Yisrael rule more stringently (*mehadrin*) to wash his hands with a plentiful amount of water? They went and spoke to Reb Karpas, who examined the matter and found that indeed Reb Yisrael would wash his hands with no more than a *reviit ha-log*. He too was most surprised, and when they sat together at a meal, he asked Reb Yisrael: "Forgive me, our Master, but this is a matter of Torah, and I must learn about it. Why then does it suffice you to wash your hands with a *reviit*? Surely, it is a clear ruling in the *Shulhan Aruch, Orah Hayyim* 155:10, 'even though the amount (for handwashing) is a *reviit*, one should wash more plentifully.' Why then do you, sir, not do so?"

Reb Yisrael answered as follows: "I have seen that the maid brings the water from afar, from a well in the valley. Your house is situated high on the hill, and the maid almost collapses under the weight of her burden, when she brings up the pail of water on her shoulders. *It is forbidden for a person to be overly religious* (להדר) *at the expense of others.*" (My emphasis – D.S.)

Indeed Reb Yisrael was wont to say:

"At times, out of excessive zeal to carry out a mitzvah between man and his Maker, people err and transgress a much more serious mitzvah between man and his neighbor. As, for example, is the case of the days of *Selichot*: If someone rises very early to recite the *Selichot* in the synagogue, and in doing so causes discomfort to the maid in his house, who, generally speaking, is a poor orphan girl who hires herself out to serve in the house of strangers, and she has to get up early in order to prepare a hot drink in the morning, then the sin of 'distressing an orphan' outweighs all of the mitzvah of reciting the *Selichot*." . . .

It is further related of R. Yisrael Salanter that he once visited the *Hiddushei ha-Rim*, R. Yitzhak Meir Alter, the Gerer Rebbe. The latter paid him great respect and accompanied him to the nearby synagogue. It quickly became known to the *Hasidim* that R. Yisrael was in town, and as he came to the synagogue a huge crowd thronged around waiting to see how the great visitor prayed. How deep was their disappointment when they saw, that, rather than praying lengthily as expected of a *tzaddik,* he prayed very briefly. At the end of the service, R. Yisrael sensed the peoples' disappointment and bewilderment at his unexpected behavior. He explained to them as follows: "I saw that because of my presence so many people have interrupted their work: the tailor – his cutting; the shoemaker – his last; the blacksmith – his bellows. They left their work in order to see me. I therefore felt that if I would pray at length I would be causing them a financial loss. And therefore I prayed speedily."[32]

An additional story told of R. Yisrael (in Immanuel Etkes, *Rabbi Yisrael Salanter ve-Reishitah shel Tenuat ha-Musar,* Jerusalem, 1982, p. 181) concerns his supervision over the preparation of *matzot* for Passover in the city of Salant. For on one occasion he found himself too busy to be able to stay present during the actual baking of the matzot. His disciples asked him with what should they be most concerned in order to receive his approbation (*hashgahah*). His reply was, "The only thing I request of you is to be most careful lest through your being overly stringent in your inspection, you will cause pain and anguish to Tzipah who kneads the dough. She may fear that she is not kneading it quickly enough. Do not forget she is a widow, and one may not cause grief to a widow."

In fact, we can more fully understand his concern when we read descriptions of *hand matzah* baking in the mid-19th century. Thus, in the *Bitul Modaah* by R. Mordechai Brand, (cited in *Modaah le-Beit Yisrael* and *Bitul Modaah,* Jerusalem, 1973, 23b), we read as follows:

> All the work of kneeding, rolling, and perforating the *matzah* is done in a single room in which the stove is also found. The room is overflowing with men, women, and children who summoned the tables, some twenty-five of them to role out the *matzot,* not including some perforators and bakers, and *matzah*-owners, and all sorts of loyal onlookers, coming to over forty people in one room. And the helpers, who roll out the *matzot* do so by hand from morning to night, while the palms of their

---

32. *Maaseihem shel Tzaddikim,* by Ma-Tov Getz, Jerusalem: 1986, vol. 3, 191–192.

hands are burned from the amount of labour, and their flesh is scorched by the intense heat . . . , and it is impossible that these helpers who are exhausted from this extrme labour will not flag a little in the middle of their work to rest their hands aching from the non-stop rolling. . . . And without a doubt some spittle from their mouthes will fall on the dough. [All of which will make the *matzot* not kosher] . . .

We can also imagine the sweat dripping off their bodies onto the *matzot* from the swellering heat of this grossly overcrowded room with its burning furnace.

Another version of this tradition tells that he was asked to certify the *kashrut* of a certain *matzah* factory. The owner had recently opened the factory and proudly led Rav Salanter through his factory, showing off his highly efficient, scrupulously regulated *matzah* baking operation. At the end of the tour, the owner asked Rav Salanter, "So? Will you give us your *hashgahah*?" Rav Salanter said quietly, but firmly, "No." "No?" The owner asked. "But everything here is so clean, so efficient, *mehadrin min hamehdrin*! What's the problem?" Rav Salanter replied, "You have created a very efficient plant, but the women producing the *matzot* are strained beyond their limits under the burden you have placed on them. Your workers are suffering. We have been accused of using the blood of Christian children in our *matzah*. While this is clearly untrue, in this case the blood of your workers is in these *matzot*. I cannot, therefore, give my *hashgahah*."

But perhaps one of the most remarkable tales told of Reb Israel is that related by R. Yishayah Steinberger, in an article (in the *Makor Rishon* newspaper, January 28, 2011, Shabbat Supplement, 10):

When Reb Israel was on his death bed, there was a simple person who remained with him to minister him during his last hours. And after his decease, the great disciples, who were not with him at that time, the Saba of Kelm (R. Simchah Zissel mi-Kelm), the Saba Novardok (R. Yosef Yoizel Horowitz), Reb Naftali Amsterdam, Reb Itzele Blazer and others, all sought to hear from the attendant what were his last words, his last acts, his final communications. Surely at such a crucial juncture of his life, he must have expressed deeply meaningful statements. "Did he say the *vidui*?" (confession at the death-bed), they asked. "Certainly," replied the attendant. "Did he say it at length?" "He seemed to murmur some such prayers," was the reply. The disciples remained dissatisfied with these neutral responses. They were convinced he must have done something of much greater significance on the eve of giving up his soul to his Creator. So they continued to press the attendant, until suddenly he remembered something else. "Several times before his death the Rabbi repeated a strange statement," said the attendant. "Dead people are not dangerous. There is no reason to be afraid of them." The disciples instantly understood what was Reb Yisrael's intention with this statement. He knew that this simple person would have to spend a long night alone with a dead corpse, and very likely he would have an attack of panic. He wished to assure him that there was no reason for fear.

Thus at the very last moments of his life, his main concern was for the mental and emotional well-being of his attendant.

Earlier on we cited one of his aphorisms, namely that:

> Even at the hour when one stands in fear and trembling before the awesomeness of judgment, one is not free from the obligation of taking care not to tread on one's neighbor's foot.

And here it should be stressed that all R. Yisrael's *musar* ideology was fully embedded in his understanding of the halachah.[33]

This deep concern for the wellbeing of others and awareness of their possible distress is not only an approach of great piety (*hassidut*), or the mark of the *Musar* movement, but as Rabbi Joseph B. Soloveitchik wrote in his classic work *Ish ha-Halakhah: Galu'i ve-Nistar (Halakhic Man)*: "My uncle, Rabbi Meir Bar-Ilan, told me that he once asked Reb Hayyim of Brisk: "What is the profile of the Rabbi?" Reb Hayyim answered him: "To prosecute offenses against the lonely and forsaken, to protect the dignity of the poor, and to save the businessman from the exploiter."[34]

---

33. I discussed these tales in greater detail in my *On the Relationship of Mitzvot between Man and His Neighbor and Man and His Maker*, Jerusalem and New York, 2014, chapter 23, pp. 150–158, with full bibliographic references and an analysis of the halachic aspects of these and other tales cited there, told of R. Yisrael Salanter.

34. Yosef Dov Halevy Soloveitchik, *Ish ha-Halachah: Galu'i ve-Nistar*, Jerusalem, Ha-Histadrut ha-Tziyonit, 1992, p. 80. This latter requirement goes back to Rambam, *Hilchot Sanhedrin* 2:7, where he derives it from the verse in Exodus 2:17, where we are

Communal Involvement

The relationship between the rabbi and the general public finds interesting expression in the words of Resh Lakish in *Massechet Hulin* 92a:

This people is like a vine: Its branches are the aristocracy, its clusters are the Torah scholars,[35] its leaves are the common people, and its twigs are

---

told how Moshe saved Yitro's daughters from the shepherds at the well. See Tur and *Beit Yosef, Hoshen Mishpat* 7:11. See further the discussion of Aviad ha-Cohen, in his article *"Shikulim Meta-Hilchatiim be-Pesikat ha-Halachah" Filosofiah Shel Halachah: Iyyunim Hadashim be-Filosofiah Shel ha-Halachah*, ed. A. Ravitzky and A. Rosenak, Jerusalem, 2008, pp. 284–289.

A wonderful example of this is related of R. Yosef Dov Halevy Soloveitchik in H. Karlinsky, *Ha-Rishon le-Shushelet Brisk,* Jerusalem, 1984, pp. 172–174.

A person approached R. Yosef Dov on the eve of Pesach asking whether it was permitted to use milk for the four glasses (*arba kosot*, usually of wine). R. Yosef Dov inquired as to the nature of the questioner, his profession, and his state of health. He replied he was a blacksmith; he was healthy and this was not why he had asked whether he could use milk. But of -late snow and floods affected [his] livelihood, as the farmers have not been able to reach [him], because the roads are unpassable. He had a family of six. R. Yosef Dov offered him twenty five rubles, but the blacksmith refused to take them, saying he never accepted charity. R. Yosef Dov assured him this was not charity but a loan, to be repaid whenever he could do so. He then urged him to take the money, buy wine for the *arba kosot* and all other requirements for the festival. When the blacksmith left, R. Yosef Dov's wife asked him why he gave him so much money that would suffice for wine for as many as ten people. R. Yosef Dov smiled and replied, "If he asked me whether he could use milk for the *arba kosot*, obviously he could not afford to buy meat for the meal either, and probably not even fish. For a family of six, how could I give him less than twenty-five rubles?"

It is told of R. Hayyim that once he was approached by a coachman who asked him: "I am a *Kohen*. Can I take a widow?" "Yes, you may," answered R. Hayyim. Those surrounding him were very surprised. "Surely a *Kohen* cannot take a widow in marriage!" R. Hayyim smiled. "He is a coachman. He asked whether he could take her in his carriage. He did not understand that the prohibition was only related to marriage, and not to transporting a widow in his carriage." The rabbi-*posek* has to understand the nature and circumstance of the questioner. See above in the preceding section.

It is further related that R. Hayyim told his disciple, R. Baruch Ber Leibowitz, that one of the prerequisites of being a *Rav* is "not to be a fool." (See M. Walter, *The Making of a Halachic Decision,* Brooklyn, 2013, p. 107, note 15.) For further example of R. Hayyim leniency, see Asher Ziv, *Rabbenu Moshe Isserles (Rema),* New York, 1972, p. 376. For the background, see ibid., pp. 373–376. See further my *On the Relationship of Mitzvot between Man and His Neighbor and Man and His Maker,* Jerusalem and New York, 2014, pp. 149–150, on R. Hayyim Brisker.

35. Compare to the end of *Mishnah Sotah* 9:9: "They nullified the clusters," and in the *Gemara* there (47b): "What are the clusters? Rabbi Yossi bar Hanina said, 'The

those in Israel that are empty of commandment. And this is what was meant when the word was sent from there [the Land of Israel]: "Let the clusters pray for the leaves for were it not for the leaves, the clusters could not exist."

And Rashi explains there:

Its branches are the aristocracy: Just as this branch gives forth the *lu-lavim*, the leaves, and the fruit which is the essence of the vine, so too the aristocracy are kindly, support the poor, and dispense money to the government on behalf of their brethren, who are sustained by them.

Its leaves: For on the vine, they suffer the wind and protect the clusters, so that they not be stricken by the sun and winds. So too, the common people plow, sow, and harvest what the Torah scholars eat.

This allegorical image establishes that there is a certain inter-dependence between the rabbi and his congregation, and more significantly, a responsibility of the rabbi for all elements of his congregation. Therefore, he must pray for mercy even for the common people, for without them, he could not exist.

This inter-dependence is expressed in the statement found in *B. Sanhedrin* 8a (and from there to Rambam, *Hilchot Sanhedrin* 25:2):

"And I charged your judges at the time [saying 'Hear the causes between your brethren, and judge righteously between every man and his brother, and the stranger there is with him]'" (Deuteronomy 1:16), and it says, "And I commanded you [plural] at that time [all the things which you should do]" (ibid. 18). Said R. Eleazar, said R. Simlai, "A warning to the community that the fear of the judge be upon them, and a warning to the judge that he should be supportive (*she-yisbol*) of the community." "To what extent [should he be supportive, or perhaps suffer acceptingly]?" Said R. Hanan, and some say R. Shabtai, ... "[Carry them in their bosom], as a nursing father bears the sucking child ..." (Numbers 11:12).

---

person who has everything in him.'" On this word, see my article "Greek and Latin Words in Rabbinic Literature" *Bar Ilan Annual* 16–17 (1979), p. 18, note 43, and again (expanded) in my "*Greek in Talmudic Palestine*," Jerusalem, 2012, p. 96, note 52.

Just as the father will bear (in both of its meanings) his sucking child, so must the rabbi-teacher bear his community, respecting its needs and desires, while preserving his self-respect, i.e., the community's respect for him.

See Rashi to Numbers 27:16, who writes: "Appoint over them a leader who *suffers* (*sovel*) each and every one in accordance with his understanding." Again, the message is clear: the congregation must respect its rabbi, judge, or leader, just as the rabbi, judge, or leader must respect, "suffer," and "support" his congregation.

Based on the aforementioned *Gemara* in *Hulin*, Rabbi Hayyim Hirschenson demanded of the rabbis that they make an effort to find solutions through enactments for "those who are under financial strain and their souls are embittered,"[36] who have become profaners of the

---

36. I recall a story that my father told me about once, at the end of the 1930s, late on Shabbat afternoon, he was walking through the market in Petticoat Lane (in London) on the way to the shtiebel of my great uncle, the Trisker Rebbe, and one of the street vendors at his stall turned to him and asked him, "When does Shabbes go out?" My father, somewhat surprisedly responded, "Why is this important to you? Surely you are selling and handling money throughout the Shabbat!" The man answered, "I work to earn a living and support my family. But I do not smoke on Shabbat, only after the Shabbat ends." My father tearfully embraced him, saying, "O, what a good Jew [*taire yid*] you are." (This was at a time when there was no Sabbath Observation Bureau, and there was great poverty among the immigrant Jewish population.)

See R. Efraim Greenblat's *Rivevot Efraim, Orah Hayyim*, vol. 4, Brooklyn, New York, 1985, p. 94, no. 70, who was asked whether one could include a Shabbat defiler as making up a quorum, *minyan*. In his reply he refers to a number of sources permitting this, adding:

Those who do so out of pressures of gaining a livelihood, but in other matters act like kosher Jews, and whenever there are ten [Jews] the *Shechinah* is in their midst . . . And we see how great scholars are hurt to the heart and seek to find some sort of justification and rely upon the broad shoulders [of the authorities] in this issue, and blessed be he who is lenient with the Children of Israel, the Children of God, of whom it is written that He resides with them in their impurities – even though they are impure, the *Shechinah* is among them . . . And may the Merciful One save us [from error] . . .

I am reminded of the story that Simhah Raz, in his classic *Ish Tzaddik Hayah: Massechet Hayyav shel R. Aryeh Levin*, Jerusalem, 1980, pp. 196–197, tells of Reb Aryeh's relationship to Sabbath desecrators:

On one Sabbath eve, after candle-lighting, Reb Aryeh was walking slowly on his way to the synagogue, when a Jew turned to him with a lighted cigarette in his mouth, and asked him the way to a certain hotel. Reb Aryeh was hesitant as to whether to show him the way accompanying him while he smoked his cigarette. On the other hand, this was a stranger who did not know his way about Jerusalem, how could he leave him alone? So Reb Aryeh decided to accompany him all the way to the hotel right up to the front entrance. They strode together side by side, the one short with a long white beard dressed for the Sabbath, the other tall and aggressive-looking, completely secular. Reb Aryeh did not make a single comment to him on his smoking, merely asking him how he was, how he felt, and hoping he would enjoy his stay in the *Holy City*. The stranger walking alongside the Rabbi became aware of the strange situation, and when they reached the hotel, they looked at one another. The stranger threw away his cigarette and turned to Reb Aryeh very emotionally saying, "Rabbi, I am not religious, and I am very obstinate, and I have never given in to anyone. But you broke me down. Before you I have the greatest of respect. Now I have thrown away my cigarette, and I have taken upon myself never to smoke on the Sabbath."

In those same pages Raz tells additional heart-warming tales of how Reb Aryeh related to criminals sinners and Sabbath desecrators. His tales can serve as a lesson to us all.

Here, I cannot resist bringing a tradition attributed to R. Avraham Abele in his response to the ultra-Orthodox of Vilna, who had demanded that he issue a *herem* (ban, excommunication) against the local *maskilim* (reform-type intellectuals). He refused, records Y.L. Maimon in his *Sarei ha Meah*, Jerusalem, 1961, vol. 2, p. 175, and responded as follows:

In the beginning of *Parshat Kedoshim* (Leviticus 19:2–4) it is written, ". . . Ye shall be holy: for I the Lord your God am holy. Ye shall fear every man his mother, and his father, and keep my Shabbaths; I am the Lord your God. Turn ye not unto idols nor make yourselves another gods: I am the Lord your God."

Surely this is strange. Why did the Torah repeat the words "I am your God" three times? Surely He could have included all three sentences in one, ending in the words "I am your God." However, the Torah wishes to teach us a lesson, namely that there are three classes of Jews, each less than its neighbour, but for each and every one of them God is their God. "Ye be holy" refers to the pious Jews who live a life of holiness. For them, God is surely their God. There are those of lesser piety, but they still keep the mitzvot, for they keep the Sabbath as did their parents and grand parents. For them, too, God is their god. But there are those who do not keep those mitzvot, and you might think they are rejected by God, and should be rejected by us – the Torah teaches us that they also must be respected, for they are not idolaters, and God is their God too. It is forbidden to scorn and show contempt and to dishonour any single Jewish person.

Perhaps here we should further recall the tale told of the father of the Baal Shem Tov (1700–1760), as recorded in Martin Buber's *Tales of the Hasidim: The Early Masters*, New York, 1947, pp. 35–36 (also cited in my *On the Relationship of Mitzvot between Man and His Neighbor and Man and His Maker*, Jerusalem and New York, 2014, p. 106):

Rabbi Eliezer, the Baal Shem's father, lived in a village. He was so hospitable that he placed guards at the outskirts of the village and had them stop poor wayfarers and bring them to his house for food and shelter. Those in Heaven rejoiced at his doing, and once they decided to try him. Satan offered to do this, but the prophet Elijah begged to be sent in his stead. In the shape of a poor wayfarer, with knapsack and staff, he came to Rabbi Eliezer's house on a Sabbath afternoon, and said the greeting. Rabbi Eliezer ignored the desecration of the Sabbath, for he did not want to mortify the man. He invited him to the meal and kept him in his house. Nor did he utter a word of reproof the next morning, when his guest took leave of him. Then the prophet revealed himself and promised him a son who would make the eyes of the people of Israel see the light.

Of course, this is also a lesson in *hachnasat orhim*, welcoming and hosting guests. At times it is absolutely essential, and also legitimate, to cast a blind eye and, as it were, overlook the actions of non-observant Jews. See above section entitled "Compassion and Casting a Blind Eye," where we brought he remarkable statement of the Rashba in his responsum to R. Yaakov Karshaf of Toledo. Incidentally, this passage is (partially) quoted by R. Ovadiah Yosef, in his *Yabia Omer*, vol. 8, section 12/2, p. 289. In that responsum we see that the rabbi has to know when to exercise restraint and wisdom especially vis-à-vis non observant Jews.

Another great American posek of the 20th century, R. Yosef Eliyahu Henkin (1881–1973), had a special view on how to regard Sabbath desecration in his day. Thus in his *Gevurot Eliyahu*, Lakewood, 2013, 38:1, p. 81 he rules that they may be accepted to make up a *minyan*, as they may be regarded as *anusim* and should not be driven away from Orthodox congregations. (And cf. ibid., 38:3, p. 82.) He adds that:

However, in a place where the sinners are numerous, and we have not the strength [to influence them] and we need every Jew who comes to our synagogues to pray, we do not make inquiries [as to his religious status], and many of them return to the fold . . .

(This responsum is from 1961.) He, too then, counsels "casting a blind eye" to a certain extent, believing that drawing them close and including them in the congregation might well encourage them to repent. (See above sections on "Compassion and Casting a Blind Eye," and "Encouraging Repentence.")

Here is not the place to enter into the complex discussion of how one views a secular Jew, and more specifically the Sabbath desecrating Jew, from a halachic point of view. (See above pp. 182–183 note 1.) A useful summary of this question may be found in Avraham Wasserman's *Reiacha ka-Mocha: Biur Hilhati be-Sugiot she-bein Datiim ve- Hilonim*, Petah Tikvah (c. 2007), in his opening chapter, pp. 31–44. His conclusion is that most authorities see secular Jews as coerced by circumstances – *anusim* – and should therefore halachically be viewed leniently. How much more so regarding those who are really coerced and compelled by economic circumstances to desecrate the Shabbat, that from a halachic viewpoint they should be regarded leniently, with all the implications involved. See further, David Zohar, *Mehuyavut Yehudit, supra* note 20, pp. 140–150, on Hirschensohn's position on this issue, and especially pp. 144–145. See his *Malki ba-Kodesh*, vol. 2, St. Louis, 1921, Responsum 3, pp. 135–139. See also Yosef Eliyahu Henkin, *Shut Gevurat Eliyahu*, Lakewood, 2013, sect. 38, pp. 81–82.

In point of fact, he developed a very interesting and innovative argument in this regard. Firstly, he describes the situation of those shopkeepers (in America, where he was living) who kept their shops open on Shabbat. They did so because of severe financial pressures, and were plagued with guilt for the Sabbath-desecration. Beginning with the accepted premise that prohibitions of biblical authority must be treated with greater stringency, and the prima facia assumption that salesmanship is prohibited by biblical law, he argues that actually the biblical prohibitions proscribes *buying* on the Sabbath, rather than selling. It is, then, the *purchasors* who are sinning seriously, while the vendors, if they are careful not to transgress major Sabbath proscriptions (*avot melachot*), err only in lesser rabbinic prohibitions, such as *muktzah* when they handle money (*Malki ba-Kodesh* ibid., pp. 141–142). He supports his novel argument by citing the verse in Nehemiah 10:32, "And if the people of the land bring ware of any victuals on the Sabbath to sell, that *we should not buy it of them on the Sabbath, or on the holy day* . . ." We see here the stress on buying rather than selling. As a consequence, he concludes that we may regard these compelled salesmen in a more lenient light. We are witness to a great and unique inventive creativity used in the confrontation of a serious contemporary halachic challenge. I have somewhat belaboured this point, because I see it as an exemplary lesson as to how a *posek* should function, with sympathetic concern and innovative thinking.

We may further compare this with R. Moshe Feinstein's responsum in *Igrot Moshe* vol.4 *Yoreh Deah* section 52, who, in discussing a somewhat similar case, states that "basically a *hechsher* is given regarding the food" and not those that sell it. See further *Yabia Omer*, ibid., p. 290, who, as one might expect of him, brings a wealth of references to bolster this argument. And cf. *Yabia Omer* 4. *Yoreh Deah*, sect. 52.

On the subject of drinking wine touched by a Sabbath-desecrator there is a considerable literature. See most recently David Bigman's discussion in his article entitled "Secular Jews and Forbidden Wine," *Kerem* 1, 2013, p. 67–84, in which he concludes that "we may drink of wine poured by modern-day Sabbath-violating Jews ..." (ibid., p. 84).

Of very special interest are the remarkably insightful and sympathetic arguments expressed by R. Joseph Messas (1892–1974) in his *Otzar ha-Michtavim*, vol. 2, no. 1302 (as cited in Zvi Zohar's article entitled "What all Jews can learn from the Great Sephardic Rabbis of Recent Authorities," *Conversations* 21, 2015, pp. 40–41):

Many of the *Amei haAretz* publicly desecrate the Sabbath, some in order to make a living. But there are also rich people who have been accustomed to this from their youth. However, they all believe in God, and perform philanthropic mitzvot. Does their touch render wine prohibited ...

But, we can mend their situation on the basis of another consideration, namely: Because of our many sins that prolong our exile, the *Amei haAretz* who desecrate God's Sabbath and Holidays are numerous. Most of our give and take is with them, and they are in continuous social contact with us: they enter our homes, and we enter theirs. And there is not one banquet, whether mandatory or optional, in which we do not sit with them, in their own homes, such as Zeved ha-Bat, circumcision, redemption of the first born, marriages, and so forth.

So, if we came to forbid wine they have touched, by even the slightest gesture or hint, we would rapidly become involved in conflict and would fan the flames of controversy to the heart of the heavens. By doing so we would be causing ourselves great injury, though their enmity and hatred; and it is possible that as a result they would spurn even the few commandments that they do fulfill, and totally reject everything, God forbid ...

Therefore, it is right to be lenient in this matter, even for the sake of Peace alone, whose power is great. For the sake of Peace they [i.e., the rabbis, Hazal] permitted the performance of acts that are rabbinic prohibitions, and the non-performance of acts mandated by positive commandments of the Torah [see: *S'deh Hemed, Pe'at Ha'Sadeh*, section Gimmel, paragraph 36]. This is all the more so with respect to this prohibition, which is quite light, for even the Christians and Muslims of our time are not worshippers of other gods, and therefore if they accidentally touch our wine it is permitted even for drinking [as our teacher, Rabbi Joseph Karo, wrote in *Yoreh Deah*, section 124, clause 7].

For a synopsis of Hirschensohn's arguments concerning Sabbath desecrators, see the new edition of *Malki ba-Kodesh*, vol. 2, ed. D. Zohar, Jerusalem, 2012, David Zohar;

English abstract, pp. XVII–XXIV. See further Y. Ettlinger, *Binyan Tziyon ha-Hadashot*, Vilna, 1873, sect. 23, on the status of Sabbath desecrators in our days, (i.e., his days); the summarizing volume by Menachem Adler, *Bina ve-Daat: Hilchot Mehalalei Shabbat bi-Zemaneinu, Biur Gidrei Tinok She-Nishba*, Jerusalem, 2008, especially the introduction on pp. 7–39. See further A.S. Ferziger, *Exclusion and Heirarchy*, Philadelphia, 2005, pp. 103–109 on Ettlinger's attitude to Sabbath desecrators, and ibid., index s.v. Sabbath desecrators for a fuller discussion of the issue. See also S.Z. Leiman, *Rabbinic Responses to Modernity*, New York, 2007, pp. 50–57, and the various articles in *Jewish Tradition and the Nontraditional Jew*, ed. J.J. Schacter, Northvale, New Jersey, and London, 1922, pass., most especially Ephraim Kanarfogel's "Rabbinic Attitudes towards Nonobservance in the Medieval Period," ibid., pp. 3–35, and Judith Bleich in "Rabbinic Responses to Nonobservance in the Modern Era," ibid., pp. 37–115, for fine overviews on the subject. (And cf. above pp. 182–183 note 1 ad fin.)

In my *Darkah shel Halachah*, p. 55, note 68, I referred to the ruling of Rav Kook, in *Daat Kohen*, Jerusalem, 1969, sect. 131, p. 245, that one gives charity also to a community that does not keep the Torah and mitzvot, for "we should, in all probability, regard them as unwhitting *(shogeg)*, and one must feed him without examining [him]. . . . And in general, in these days one must extend compassion to all Israel, because due to their tribulations they appear to be [sinning] intentionally *(ke-mezidin)*, but we should regard them as [acting] without intent [to sin]." See further, Neriah Gotel, *Bi-Netivei Mishnato ha-Hilchatit ha-Hagutit shel ha-Rav Kook*, Jerusalem, 2005, pp. 57–58. But also see the painful words of Rav Kook in *Afikim ba-Negev*, Jerusalem, 1872, p. 23: "How hard, how very hard it is to love a person from Israel who rebelliously transgresses the laws of our holy Torah." See M. Tz. Nehorai's important article in *Tarbitz* 59, 1990, p. 486 et seq., entitled "*Hearot le-Darko shel ha-Rav Kook be-Pesikato*."

For an example of brilliant innovative halachic reasoning in order to find a solution to a serious question, I cannot refrain for calling attention to the *Noda bi-Yehudah*'s (R. Yehezkel Landau's) responsum no. 20, in his *Orah Hayyim Kama* (ed. Machon Yerushalayim, Jerusalem 1994, pp. 32–41).

The question facing him was as follows:

Someone died on the eve of Pesach after midday, and had not sold his *hametz* before his death, neither did he do relinquishment *(bitul)*, and a large amount of *hametz* of great value passed as inheritance automatically to his heirs. The questioner asked: What is the status of this *hametz*, whether the heirs are obligated to destroy it before nightfall so as not to transgress the law of *baal Yeraeh* (that it may not be seen in your property), since the deceased they inherited as heirs, or not. And also he asked: If they did not destroy it and left it till after Pesach what is its status: is it permitted or does it have the status of *hametz* which existed throughout Pesach [from which one may have no benefit according to rabbinic decree].

A simple reading of the question would lead to a straightforward conclusion, that it had forthwith to be destroyed, and if not, it would have forbidden status after Pesach.

In a very long and involved response he nonetheless reaches the conclusion that the *hametz* does not have to be destroyed, and one may benefit from it after Pesach. To simplify his argumentation we may briefly summarize that he argues that since he died after midday on the eve of Pesach, according to R. Shimon he has not yet transgressed the prohibition of *bal yeraeh*. And since on Pesach, *hametz* is considered *assur be-hanaah* and therefore has no [monetary] value, the heirs could not inherit something of no value. Only after Pesach it comes into their possession, but since neither they (who did not possess it before Pesach) nor the father (who died before he could do *bitul*) can be said to have consciously and negligently omitted to do *bitul*, the *kenas* – fine, forfeiture, that the rabbis enacted for negligence in not performing *bitul*, (expressing itself by declaring the *hametz assur be-hanaah*, forbidden to receive benefit therefrom) is no longer applicable. Hence the *hametz* is permissible to be sold, and its considerable value was saved.

See further *Orah Hayyim Tinyana*, sect. 60–63, 65, 75–77, 90–91.

However, the question as to whether *issurei hanaah* can have ownership is not straightforward. Thus, the *Ketzot ha-Hoshen* 406:1–2, while showing both sides of the argument concludes that they can be owned, though they cannot be sold since they are not in his possession (*bi-reshuto*), but they are in his ownership (*be-baaluto*). Furthermore, there are opinions that *issurei hanaah* can be transmitted as inheritance, (such as the Meiri, and in modern times R. Elhanan Wasserman, but this issue is beyond the scope of this study. See, for example, R. Elhanan Wasserman, *Kuntres Divrei Sofrim* [first published Baranowitz, 1924, ed. with *Iturei Sofrim*, 2004, pp. 20–23]).

See further the remarkable responsum of R. Joseph Messas (Moroccao, 1892–1974) in which he permits eating of meat slaughtered by a butcher who desecrate the Sabbath (*Shut Mayyim Hayyim*, Fez 1934, vol.1, sect. 143), although here the reasoning is very different. It is not out of sympathy for the poor tradesmen, but in order to find a solution for the community of meat-purchasers.

See Marc B. Shapiro, "Rabbi Joseph Messas," *Conversations* 21, 2015, pp. 49–51, where he also discusses his permitting carrying on Shabbat in a public domain, claiming there is no *reshut ha-rabim* in his cities, and he does not even require an *eruv*, since the decree againt carrying in a *carmelit* is no longer applicable. This, of course, was a very radical view, which is difficult to accept.

And, a propos of slaughterers, R. Yosef Patzanofsky, in his *Pardes Yosef*, Pietrokov-Lodz, 1931–1939, to Leviticus 26:6, relates of R. Hayyim of Volozhin that he recommended dispensing with a controversy concerning a slaughterer suspected of not properly inspecting an animal's lung, observing that inspection of the lung is a rabbinical requirement, while strife is a biblical prohibition. (See Daniel Z. Feldman, *The Right and the Good: Halakhah and Human Relations*, New York, 2005, p. 53).

And note also Messas' permissive feelings towards Sabbath desecrators in general in his *Otzar Michtavim*, Jerusalem, 1969, vol. 2, no. 1302. And also his remarkable responsum permitting married women to go out in public without hair-covering (*Otzar ha-Michtavim*, no. 1884, vol. 3, Jerusalem, 1975, p. 211). I was surprised that Ilan Fuchs in his article entitled "Hair covering for Simple Women: A New Reading of Mizrahi Halachic Rulings," which appeared in *Nashim*, 2012, pp. 35–59, makes no mention of Messas' ruling on this issue. For yet another example of creative halachic thinking, see what I wrote in my *Netivot Pesikah*, Jerusalem, 2008, pp. 139–140, on the use of *schach* from trees growing in a cemetery.

The need to understand when "to cast a blind eye" and when *not* to say anything, when *not* to give a ruling, is of great importance. (Cf. above section entitled "Compassion and Casting a Blind Eye.") We may perhaps learn this from a passage in the *Yerushalmi Kilaim* 9:1, in a totally different halachic context. There we read how R. Imi (Ami) was studying in the *beit midrash*, and one of his students was wearing a cloak that had *kilaim* (a garment that has both wool and linen in the same web, which

Sabbath "with regard to rabbinical prohibitions because of the pressure to make a living . . . , and it is appropriate to try to improve the lot of these people for they are our brothers, our flesh and blood, and they should not be among us as a dead body which is half eaten. Let the clusters pray for the leaves, for were it not for the leaves the clusters could not exist."[37] In this statement, Rabbi Hirschenson interprets the

---

it is forbidden to wear). The student was unaware that he was wearing a forbidden garment, and R. Ami refrained from remarking to him on this. However, his fellow student did call his attention to the fact, *only after which R. Ami told him to remove the garment.* R. Ami initially said nothing, admittedly because of the principle of *kevod ha-briyot* – perhaps the *kilaim* was only *de-Rabanan.* But it would seem, according to the Rosh's opinion (*Piskei ha-Rosh* to *Niddah,* chapter 9, *Hilchot Kilaei Begadim,* sect. 6) that the fellow student should have known better than to tell him in a public place – the *beit midrash* – thus forcing him to remove his cloak, and shaming him before his fellow students. Here, there would have been more virtue in his silence. Similarly, in *B. Menahot* 37b–38a we read how Ravina and Mar Bar Rav Ashi were walking together on the Sabbath, and Mar bar Rav Ashi's *tzitzit* tore. Ravina refrained from calling his attention to this until they came home, again for the same reason. (This is according to one of the versions in the Talmud.)

See also *Shulhan Aruch, Orah Hayyim* 13:3 in the Rema, that:

If one of his *tzitziot* was separated (i.e., torn off) and he is embarrassed to sit [in the synagogue] without a *tallit,* he can wear it without a *berachah,* because of *kevod ha-briyot.*

To which the *Shiyarei Keneset ha-Gedolah* by R. Hayyim Benvenisti, Constantinople and Smyrna, 1603–1673 (cited in *Beer Heiteiv* ad loc., sect. 8) adds:

For it depends on the will (or perhaps: the nature) of the person wearing [the *tallit*]: if he is embarrassed, he may wear it without a *berachah,* but if he is not embarrassed, there is no reason to invoke the principle of *kevod ha-briyot.*

This suggests the somewhat relative nature of this principle of *kevod ha-briyot.*

Yet another fascinating example of "casting a blind eye" on the part of the halachists is to be found in a response of Isserlein's *Terumot ha-Deshen* (1390–1460), no. 16. There he is asked how come we ignore the Talmud's ruling (in *B. Berachot* 24b) that a person who is praying and needs to break wind must move away four cubits and then break wind and then wait until the smell has evaporated. His reply is that indeed there is no real reason to ignore this explicit ruling; however, since his move would be a source of embarrassement as his fellow synagogue goers would become aware of what is going on, the halachah is ignored. On this basis the Rema (in *Orah Hayyim* 103:1) ruled that the Talmud's statement only applies to one praying in his own house, i.e., in privacy, but not when he is in a public place – there he does not need to move backwards at all.

37. Responsa *Malki ba-Kodesh,* ibid., p. 129; and ibid., p. 111, on his relationship to secular Sabbath-desecrating Jews, and David Zohar, *Mehuyavut Yehudit be-Olam Moderni: Harav Hayyim Hirschensohn ve-Yahaso la-Moderna,* supra note 20, pp. 123–130.

Indeed, we may well recall Rambam's exhortation in his *Epistle on Martyrdom* (*Iggerot ha-Shemad*), edited and translated by A. Halkin and D. Hartman, apud *Cri-*

Gemara in a way that diverges from the way we think it should be interpreted – i.e., that the rabbis should pray for mercy from God for them, because without them the rabbis could not exist – but rather that the rabbis should see the distress of these unfortunate common people and should seek the necessary enactments in order to provide them with some halachic relief out of feelings of pity. Rabbi Hirschenson faulted the rabbis for not having done enough, or not doing enough, in this regard:

> Fifty years ago in America, we did not have rabbis who were considered among the great sages of the generation as we have today, whose eyes were toward the future and who could predict that which was about to occur, who would seek various ways to permit things based on the foundations of the *Shulhan Aruch* and the Codes . . . for had we, we would not have gotten to the negative situation that we have today.

His halachic approach was based on rabbinic sources. Thus, for example, we learn in *Mishnah Shabbat* 24:4: "If darkness falls upon a person on the road, he entrusts his purse to a Gentile. And if there is no Gentile, he places it on a donkey. When he reaches the outermost courtyard, he removes the objects which may be handled on the Sabbath, while for those that may not be handled on the Sabbath, he unties the cords and the sacks fall off by themselves." The *Gemara* there (*Shabbat* 153a) explains: "Why did the rabbis permit him to entrust his purse to a Gentile? The rabbis knew for certain that no man will restrain himself where his money is concerned, so if you do not permit it to him, he will come to carry it four cubits in public property."

---

sis and Leadership Epistles of Maimonides, Philadelphia and New York, Jerusalem, 1985, p. 33:

It is not right to alienate, scorn, and hate people who desecrate the Sabbath. It is our duty to befriend them, and encourage them to fulfill the commandments. The rabbis regulate explicitly that when an evil-doer who sinned by choice comes to the synagogue, he is to be welcomed and not insulted (*Tosefta Baba Kama* 7:8; *Mechilta* to Exodus 22:3) .In this ruling they relied on Solomon's counsel: *A thief should not be despised for stealing to appease his hunger* (Prov. 6:30). It means do not despise the evildoer in Israel when he comes secretly to "steal" some observance.

The editors add (ibid., p. 81) that:

Even though Maimonides equates the desecration of the Sabbath with the sin of idolatry [see Rambam *Hilchot Shabbat* 30:15] one must treat the desecrator of the Sabbath with compassion.

Rabbi Hirschenson commented on this *Gemara* as follows:

> The rabbis understood the soul of the individual – that it would be im-
> possible for him to stand by and lose his money even if it meant violating
> a Torah prohibition. His inability to forfeit his money is not based on
> evil intentions or denigration of the Torah, but rather only because of
> personal weakness. They sought an enactment to permit him to violate
> rabbinic prohibitions so that he not come to violate Torah prohibitions.
> (*Malki ba-Kodesh*, ibid.)

Indeed, Rabbi Hirschenson's suggestions are far reaching to the point
of finding points of permission for rabbinic prohibitions. Yet, we see
the degree to which he felt the pain of his fellow Jews, and how much
love he had for the unfortunate people who were forced to profane
the Sabbath, reflected in his suggestions. How great was the degree
of responsibility that he felt toward them, and how strong the need
to find leniencies to lighten their distress.[38] This again brings to mind
the comments cited above in the name of Reb Hayyim in the lecture
of Rabbi Soloveitchik: "To prosecute offenses against the lonely and
forsaken, to protect the dignity of the poor . . . ." (based on Ramban
to Deutronomy 1:17). What a great degree of courage was required to
make the radical suggestions that he proposed and to go against the
accepted halachic stream.

However, one of the serious problems facing a communal rabbi is the
fact that his duties to the community leave him little time to continue
his Torah studies. On the other hand, a *posek* cannot be lax in his
learning regimen, but has to keep up to date in halachic publications,
and must constantly review and revise his knowledge and competence
in practical halachah. It is by no means simple to find the right median
between these two pressing and time-consuming requirements. See, for
instance, R. Aharon Lichtenstein's very comprehensive study entitled

---

38. This whole subject is discussed at length in the book of Sagi and Zohar, *Giyyur
ve-Zehut Yehudit: Iyyun bi-Yesodot ha-Halachah*, Jerusalem, 1995, p. 148 ff. For more
on this unique personality see Zohar, *supra* p. 53 note 12, and on this particular topic,
see p. 140 ff. See also Zohar's introduction to Hirschenson's *Sefer Malki ba-Kodesh*,
vol. 1, 2nd edition, Jerusalem, 2007, pp. 13–56, and *Ha-Rav Hayyim Hirschenson:
Ha-Torah veha-Hayyim*, Yehezkel Cohen (ed.), Ha-Kibbutz ha-Dati –Neemanei Torah
ve-Avodah, 1988.

"Does Involvement in Torah Study Exempt One from Mitzvot?" which appeared in *Alei Etzion* 16, 2009, pp. 71–107. I also addressed this issue of the the tension between learning and communal involvement in my *On the Relationship of Mitzvot between Man and His Neighbor and Man and His Maker*, Jerusalem and New York, 2014, chapter 4, pp. 44–54. And there (p. 47) I quote a story related in Yehezkel Shraga Fraenkel's *Rabbenu ha-Kaddosh mi-Shinyeve* (Ramat Gan: 1991, 256–257). He relates that once the Rabbi of Warsaw came to visit the *Divrei Hayyim*, R. Hayyim of Sanz. The Sanzer Rebbe asked him, "Do you learn?" "Yes," the Warsaw Rabbi replied. The Rebbe repeated, "Do you always learn?" The reply was, "When someone who is embittered and needs help comes to me, I close my *Gemara* and deal with him, to help and encourage him." "This is what I wanted to hear," said the Sanzer, "whether you have the good sense to close your *Gemara* when someone needs your help, both in word and in deed, and in any case to encourage him and bolster his spirit."

Surely this is the meaning of what we find in *B. Avodah Zara* 17b in the name of R. Haninah ben Tradyon and, later, Rav Huna, namely that:

> Anyone who is engaged solely in Torah, it is as though he has no God, as it is written, "Now for a long season Israel hath been without the true God . . ." (II Chronicles 15:3). What is the meaning of "without a true God"? It is [because] anyone who is engaged solely in Torah it is as though he has no God.

One's Torah learning must always been coupled with positive communal activities, in that *sugya* called *gemilut hasadim*. Without such involvement, that Torah learning is close to being worthless.

Indeed, he must be always ready to serve the members of his community, and even not delay responding to their requests. There is a very powerful and poignant passage in the *Mechilta, Mishpatim, Massechta de-Neziqin* 18, (ed. And transl. J.Z. Lauterbach, vol. 3, Philadelphia, 1935), pp. 141–142, on the verse in Exodus 22:22:

> "If Thou Afflict in Any Wise" – This tells us that one becomes guilty of oppression only after he has repeated the act. At the time when R. Simon and R. Ishmael were led out to be killed, R. Simon said to R. Ishmael: "Master, my heart fails me, for I do not know why I am to be killed." R.

Ishmael said to him: "Did it never happen in your life that a man came to you for a judgment or with a question and you let him wait until you had sipped your cup, or had tied your sandals, or had put on your cloak? And the Torah has said 'If thou afflict in any wise' – whether it be a severe affliction or a light affliction." Whereupon R. Simon said to him: "You have comforted me, master."

Of course, here we are speaking of great pious sages; but the overall message is clear. And see Ramban to Exodus 18:22, who writes:

That having many judges, the oppressed will go to the judge at any time his wishes and find him readily available.

Subsequently I found a passage in R. Hayyim Palache's *Tochahat Hayyim*, Jerusalem (1999), vol. 2, (*Pinhas*), p. 202:

And *Maran he-Habiv* (R. Hayyim Benveniste) in his *Knesset ha-Gedolah*, *Yoreh Deah* sect. 246, *Hagahot Tur* no.7 [fol. 302], wrote concerning Maharik [R. Yosef Colon], that when he was involved in communal affairs, and he had no time to study, he would open a book and read one or two lines, and so too at night, in order to fulfil [the mitzvah of] "but thou shalt meditate therein day and night" (Joshua 1:8).

He continues to demonstrate from a rich variety of sources, as is his way, that one who is involved in communal activities – *tzorchei rabbim* – it is as though he is engaged in learning Torah (pp. 303–304). He very strongly warns and chastises those who seek to distance themselves from such involvement, claiming that it is beneath their dignity, or that it does not allow them to steep themselves in their studies and diminishes their spiritual stature etc., stating forcefully that the Divine Creator also involves Himself in "worldly affairs" (*kiyyum ha-olam*). Since we must follow in His footsteps, it is incumbent upon us to do all that we can to deal with the needs of the community, both those of the individual and those of the masses.

Finally, I should like to quote what I wrote in my *On the Relationship of Mitzvot between Man and his Neighbor and Man and his Maker*, Jerusalem and New York, 2014, p. 91, namely that the rabbi must always be deeply aware of his community and its needs:

Perhaps this is, as it were, encapsulated in a little-known halachah which may be seen as a metaphor for our overall theme, namely that true piety cannot admit isolation from the outside world. It is most eloquently expressed by Eugene Korn in a recent review essay entitled "Windows on the World – Judaism Beyond Ethnicity," *Meorot* 8, 2010, he wrote. Towards the end of that essay he writes (on p.9):

> There is an often overlooked *halachah* that the room in which one prays must contain a window. This requirement is not the result of imitating the stained-glass window décor of grand cathedrals, but reflects the healthy spiritual outlook of *Hazal*. For prayer and piety to be something significant they must connect to the world outside. They must transcend technicalities and provide a view to culture and its enduring human issue. If that is true about the single *mitzvah* of tefillah, it is all the more so about the entire enterprise of *shemirat ha-mitsvot* and our covenantal commitment to a life of Torah.[39]

How true this should be for the Rabbi.

An Independent Stance

The rabbi must be an independent thinker and have the courage to stand firm by his opinions. (See below Appendix 4.) This we learn from the Hatam Sofer in his responsum (*Orech Hayyim* 208) to Rabbi Tzvi Hirsch Chajes. In the introduction to his book *Torat ha-Nevi'im* (Zholkva, 1836), Chajes expressed his concern "that those who check for blemishes will come, seek, and find" a variety of blemishes in his book. After heaping great praise on his book, the Hatam Sofer responded to him that it is recorded in *Massechet Beitzah* 38a–b that "Rabbi Aba prayed before his *aliyah* to the Land of Israel: 'May it be his will that I say things that will be accepted.'" (Rashi interprets this to mean "by the local sages, that I not be embarrassed.") Yet, the *Gemara* tells that when he arrived at the study hall of Rav Yohanan, the

---

39. On this halachah, see R. Yaakov Hayyim Sofer, *Menuhat Shalom* 12, 2003, pp. 77–79. And on *tzorchei rabbim*, see *Shulhan Aruch, Orah Hayyim* 38:8, and *Beur Halachah*, ibid. On the difference between *tzorchei rabbim* and *tzorchei tzibbur*, see Zvi Polin, *Sefer ha-Mitzpeh al ha-Rambam*, vol. 2 (on *Hilchot Kriyat Shema*), Jerusalem, 2007, pp. 93–100, and what I wrote in my *On the Relationship between Man and His Neighbor and Man and His Maker*, pp. 28–29.

students laughed at him because of the proof that he wanted to bring to the discussion of the day. In comparison, the prayer of Rabbi Nehunya ben ha-Kanah recorded in *B. Berachot* 28b reads: "May it be your will … that no offence may occur through me, and that I may not err in a matter of halachah, and that my colleagues may rejoice in me." The Hatam Sofer asks: "What is the difference between these two prayers?" He answers that the difference lies in the fact that Rabbi Aba asked to find favor and agreement among those who would hear him, and he therefore did not achieve it. "What does it matter to me if it is well received or not? You should state your position for the sake of Heaven. Therefore, he failed." Rabbi Nehunya ben ha-Kanah, on the other hand, prayed that he would arrive at the truth of the halachah, and did not focus on obtaining the agreement of his colleagues: "Rather, the debate should be that I present my contention and my position according to my thinking in a manner that when my colleagues challenge me, I will examine my thoughts. If their words are truthful and convincing, I will retract, but if they do not seem correct in my eyes, I will maintain my position. It doesn't matter to me if he agrees with me or not, as my intent is not to change his opinion to my opinion." He therefore achieved his goal. The Hatam Sofer stated that "Anyone who himself knows that his whole approach is for the sake of Heaven and the proliferation and glorification of the Torah, transgresses if he restrains himself only out of concern for those who seek blemishes, mockers, and those who offend the angels of God. Just as he receives punishment for the teaching, so too he is punished for his withdrawal."

My grandfather, Rabbi David Sperber, followed the path of the Hatam Sofer. My father, in his introduction to my grandfather's book, wrote about my grandfather's personal qualities as follows:

> He had the quality of a Torah scholar and could be hard as steel when necessary. He was an expert judge on both public issues and monetary matters. He was invited to sit on rabbinical courts as a selected member of the tribunal or as its head on complex communal or individual matters. These discussions were at times stormy, and there were those who tried through various means to influence him or to reject his decision. I remember once after he issued a ruling in a matter that involved a very large loss of money to one of the litigants, they tried to attack him in a variety of ways. He said: "Why did they apparently choose me to head

this tribunal? If because of my Torah knowledge, there are certainly others who are greater than me in Torah. If because of wisdom based on life experience, there are others who are wiser than me. There is, however, one quality that I have in my soul – 'You shall not recognize faces in judgment' (Deuteronomy 1:17), i.e., you should not be influenced by the litigants' status."

My mother, Rabbanit Miriam Sperber, wrote in her book *Mi-Sippurei ha-Savta* that after having removed the kashrut certification of a particular butcher, a stone was thrown through the window of the home of my grandfather, Rabbi David Sperber, almost injuring a baby grand-daughter who was lying near the window. My father, Rabbi Shmuel Sperber, asked: "Is it worth it to be a rabbi, dedicating so many years to the community and then getting a stone through the window?" My grandfather replied: "It is certainly worth it. Know, my son, that a rabbi who is not the focus of controversy is not a rabbi, and a rabbi who bends to pressure is not a person."[40]

---

40. Miriam Sperber, *Mi-Sippurei Ha-Savta*, Jerusalem, Imrei Shefer, 1986, pp. 70–71: "*Ma'aseh Be-Ba'al Ha-Atliz*" (*Grandmother's Tales*, Jerusalem, 1990). The baby was my cousin, the Rabbanit Shaindy Deutch-Hager – the Viznitzer Rabbetzen! A similar tradition is told of R. Yisrael Salanter. See Y.L. Maimon, *Sarei ha-Meah*, Jerusalem, 1961, vol. 2, p. 275; and see also ibid., vol. 3, p. 48.

See also S.S.S. Laufer, *Maaseh ve-Nizkar Talmid*, vol. 2, Israel, 2006, p. 41, who relates that R. Moshe Teitelbaum, author of *Yismah Moshe*, is said to have collected all the stones that were hurled through his windows by his opponents, such as the *shochtim* and others who objected to the regulations he had enacted, and when his *beit midrash* was being built in Sighet, he fitted them into the walls. See my *Netivot Pesikah*, Jerusalem, 2008, p. 169, note 257.

A spiritual leader must not be afraid of criticism, and when necessary must speak up and voice his views. (See the statement of Rav Kook, in his *Orah Mishpat*, Jerusalem, 1979, p. 24, "Pay no attention to the complaints of the masses.") Eventually, this will benefit him. So we learn from a passage in *Midrash Lekah Tov* to Exodus 6:2 (*Va-Era*), ed. Buber, Vilna, 1880, p. 30:

"Anger is better than laughter: for by the sadness of countenance the heart is made better" (Ecclesiastes 7:3). Better the anger that the Holy One, blessed be He, directs against the righteous in this world . . . than the laughter that the wicked laugh in this world . . . Come and see: from the hour that the Holy One blessed be He spoke to Moshe at the [burning] bush, as it is written, "and He said: Moshe, Moshe" (Exodus 3:4), there were sixteen times that God spoke to him with the verb *amar*, and in none of them was the term *dibur* used, just, *Va-Yomar, Va-Yomer* ("and He spoke and He spake"). And when Moshe came before the Holy One blessed be He and said, "[For since I came to Pharaoh to speak in Thy name, he hath done evil to this people;] neither hast thou delivered the people at all" (Exodus 5:23). Immediately, the aspect of stern judgement (*Middat ha-Din*) began to accuse him, as it is written, "And God (*Elokim*) spoke (*Va-Yedaber*) to Moshe" (ibid., 6:2). And the use of the term *dibur* represents harsh speech, as it is written, "The man, who is the lord of the land, spake (*dibber*) harshly to us" (Genesis 42:30), and *Elokim* is the aspect of stern judgement; until the aspect of divine mercy (*Middat ha-Rahamium*) interceded on his behalf, as it is said, "and He said (*Va-Yomer*) to him, I am the Lord (*ani ha-Shem*) – that is the aspect of divine mercy. . . . I am the Lord (*ha-Shem*) who will exact punishment to Pharaoh and his servants, I am the Lord who rewards the righteous in the Kingdom to Come, I am the Lord, I am He and no other."

(On *dibbur* as harsh speech, see *B. Makkot* 11a, *Y. Makkot* 2:6, and *Sifrei Be-Haalotecha*, sect. 99, *Sifrei Va-Ethanan* sect. 27. And see also M.M. Kasher, *Torah Shelemah Va-Era*, vol. 9, New York 1944, pp. 1–2, note 2.)

This passage tells us that Moses did not hesitate to criticize God for worsening the situation of the Children of Israel, even though by doing so he invoked against himself the *Middat ha-Din*. But shortly afterwards his actions were justified and he was rewarded by the *Middat ha-Rahamim*. This is a true mark of courageous leadership.

We should also note that the Talmud in *B. Ta'anit* 4a brings a statement in the name of R. Aba, as follows: Any scholar who is not hard as iron is not a scholar, as it is stated, "whose stones (*avanehah*) are iron" (Deuteronomy 8:9). Do not read *avanehah* – "her stones," but *bonehah*, "her builders," (i.e., her scholars, cf. *B. Berachot* 63a). The *Torah Temimah* (ad loc., p. 84, note 12), after explaining the nature of the homily, then asks: Surely this is not the characteristic required of a *Talmid Hacham*? Are we not told that "a person should always be pliant as a cane and not hard as a cedar" (*B. Ta'anit* 20a)? (This aphorism was cited above in the fourth story, "The Ugly Man".) The *Torah Temimah* offers a different interpretation of the meaning that the *Talmid Hacham* should be hard as iron. His suggestion is that it means he should be intellectually as sharp as iron, referring us to *B. Menahot* 95b, as interpreted by Rashi. However, I think that his interpretation is unnecessary, and that there is no real contradiction between the various statements. For at times a rabbi must be resolute and unbending, and at other times pliant and flexible – all depending upon the circumstances. Certainly, this was the case with my grandfather, who combined both characteristics without any internal contradiction. Indeed, it is just this ability to be multifaceted that is the requirement of a good Rav and *posek*. (See, however, *B. Ketubot* 46a, explaining the verse in Leviticus 19:16, as teaching that a court of law should not be soft and tender [*rach*] to one and hard [*kasheh*] to another. For an understanding of this ruling, see Rambam, *Hilchot Sanhedrin* 21:1, and we shall not elaborate on this issue.) On the *Talmid Hacham* being as hard as iron, see *B. Ta'anit* 7a on Proverbs 27:12; and *B. Menahot* 75b, Rashi s.v. *Adam Kasheh*.

See further, Moshe Lowenthal, *Serarah she-Hi Avdut: Sugyot be-Rabbanut ha-Kehillah*, Jerusalem 2007, pp. 537–557, on examples of rabbis taking a firm stand in the presence of extreme pressure, and Y. Amital, *Jewish Values* (supra note 8), pp. 217–220.

Apropos of being "hard as iron," we should further reflect upon what is stated in *B. Yoma* 22b–23a:

Said R. Yohanan in the name of R. Shimon ben Yehotzadok: Any scholar who is not vengeful and grudge-bearing like a serpent is not a [true] scholar.

R. Shimon ben Yehotzadok was indicating that at times a rabbi has to be relentless in persuing the truth, and even punishing those whom he regards as evil doers.

This was indeed the way of the *Rishonim*. See, for example, the comments of Rabbi Yeshayahu di-Trani:[41]

But this is my way: Anything that doesn't appear correct to me, I do not obey even if it was said by Yehoshua bin Nun, and I do not refrain from speaking about it as I see it within my limited intelligence. . . . But I judge myself according to the parable of the philosophers . . . that if the midget is riding on the shoulders of the giant, who sees a greater distance? In other words, the eyes of the midget are now higher than the eyes of the giant. So too are we midgets who ride on the shoulders of giants.[42] . . . In a situation where we see a controversy in which one prohibits and one permits, what are we to do? . . . We can only examine their words, for both are the words of the living God, and to debate and study in depth the power of their words to determine in what direction the law tends.

However, R. Avraham Hayyim Hirsch cautions that one must be careful to find no personal pleasure or satisfaction in such uncharacteristic behavior. (See R. Avraham Hayyim Hirsch's comment in *Moriah* 7–9 (391–392), 2014, p. 269.)

41. Cited in the *Responsa of the Rid*, 62, 1. His words are also quoted in the introduction of the book *Shibolei Ha-Leket*, and in the introduction to the commentary *Megilat Esther* on Maimonides' *Sefer ha-Mitzvot*. More recently, it was cited in the important article of Rabbi Eliyahu Soloveitchik, "*Hirhurim Al Mahapechat ha-Sifrut ha-Toranit ha-Hadashah*" *Ha-Ma'ayan* 43(2) (Tevet, 5763), p. 78.

42. This parable of the midget on the shoulders of the giant has been discussed frequently. For the history of the parable, see Robert K. Merton, *On the Shoulders of Giants*, New York, 1965. On its permutations in Hebrew literature, see Dov Zlotnick, "The Commentary of Rabbi Abraham Azulai to the *Mishnah*" *PAAJR* 40 (1972), pp. 147–168; idem "*Al Mekor ha-Mashal 'ha-Nanas Veha-Anak' ve-Gilgulav*" *Sinai* 77 (1945), pp. 164–189. A comprehensive article on this topic was written by my late friend, Israel Ta-Shma, "*Hilchata ke-Batrai – Behimot Historiyot Shel Klal Mishpati*" *Shenaton ha-Mishpat ha-Ivri* 6–7 (1979–1980), pp. 405–423 (where he even cited on pages 418–419 the citation brought above). Subsequently, my friend Avraham Meir Rafeld wrote: "*Hilchata ke-Batrai Etzel Hachmei Ashkenaz ve-Polin be-Me'ot ha- 15-16*" *Mekorot ve-Sefihin, Sidra* 8 (1992), pp. 119–140, and again in his *Netivei Meir: Assufot Maamarim*, Israel, 2013, pp. 351–368, 439–442; and my friend Yosef Wolf, "*Ha'omnam Massoret Halachah Italkit?*" *Sidra* 10 (1994), pp. 57–59. Recently, a book was published on this subject by Professor Avraham Melamed: Avraham Melamed, *Al Kitfei Anakim: Toldot ha-Pulmus Bein Aharonim la-Rishonim be-Hagut ha-Yehudit bi-Yemei ha-Beinayim ube-Reishit ha-Eit ha-Hadashah*, Ramat Gan, 2004. On the limitations of this principle see *Teshuvot Maharam* (R. Moshe be-R. Yitzhak) *Alashkar*, sect.53–54: *Seridei Teshuvot mi-Hachmei ha-Imperiah ha-Otmanit*, ed. S. Glick, vol. 2, Jerusalem, 2013, pp. 688–700; (and see ibid., p. 685, note 2 for additional bibliography). See also my *Legitimacy and Necessity: Scientific Disciplines and the Learning of Talmud*, Jerusalem, 2006, pp. 60–62, note 54.

For this is what the scholars of the *Mishnah* and the Talmud did, and the *Ahronim* never hesitated to speak about the opinions of the *Rishonim*, and to rule in contradiction to their words. . . .[43]

---

43. This is also the approach of Rabbi Moshe Feinstein in *Igrot Moshe, Yoreh Deah* 88, p. 329, where he concludes his responsum as follows: "And if so, how very much more so should we not be concerned about disagreeing with the great sages of our generations, even the greatest, but in a respectful manner." Examine there his proofs for this assertion, and see also, *Yoreh Deah* 2, 45, p. 61: "The fact that the honorable Torah scholar apologized because he did not hold as did I, I don't know why he needs to apologize. Clearly, every person needs to clarify the truth according to his understanding, whether it be lenient or stringent, even if it is the opinion of a student versus that of his teacher, and even more so anyone who are not students. See also *Igrot Moshe, Orah Hayyim* 109, [p. 173] where I discussed this at somewhat greater length." See there, where after a discussion of the matter, he wrote: "Even if the honorable Torah scholar considers me a great sage, he is allowed to disagree with me, and *he is required to express his opinion*, and he need not apologize." (My emphasis – D.S.) See also *Igrot Moshe, Even ha-Ezer* 1:63, p. 152, where he writes: "How much more so that he not be concerned about respect for the great sages even though they are our teachers and the geniuses of the world if it prevent him from writing what is correct in his humble opinion in law and in practice." See also the important article of Eliav Shochetman, "*Ha-Hashash Be-Hotza'at La'az Al Ha-Rishonim Ke-Shikul Be-Pesikat Halachah*" *Shnaton Bar-Ilan* 18–19 (1981), pp. 170–195. See also the formulation of Rabbi Benzion Meir Hai Uziel, *Mishpetei Uziel* 4, 2nd edition, end of section 5, p. 33, regarding a judge whose qualities were: "Men of valor, great in wisdom, endowed with spirit, who fulfill the verse: 'You shall not respect persons in judgment . . . for the judgment is God's' (Deuteronomy 1:17)."

This view that posits the legitimacy of halachic innovation in changing circumstances of necessity, permitting disagreement with earlier authorities (see above pp. 18–26), has clear precedent in earlier sources. Thus, we read in b. *Hulin* 6b as follows:

Rabbi [R. Judah the Prince] permitted all of Beit Shean [to eat its produce in an untithed state, meaning that he considered it outside of the halachic Land of Israel], and they said to him, "In a place where our fathers and our father's fathers were accustomed to observe a prohibition, are you being lenient?" So he expounded to them the following verse: 'And he [Hezekiah] ground up the bronze serpent which had been made by Moses, for until those days the children of Israel were offering incense and called it Nehushtan' (2 Kings 18:4). Is it conceivable that Asa came and did not destroy it? That Yehoshafat came and did not destroy it? Did not Asa and Yehoshafat destroy every object of pagan worship in the world? Rather, his fathers left a place for him to make himself distinguished. So too, my fathers left me some place in which to act."

Regarding this, Rashi comments: "When our children shall come after us, if they will not find anything to correct, how can they distinguish themselves?" Similarly, in Y. *Demai* 2:1 (22c): "Rabbi allowed them to take vegetables at the end of the sabbatical year, and everybody spoke against him. He said to them: Come let us discuss it. It is written: 'And he ground up the bronze serpent.' Was there not any righteous man who rose up between the time of Moses and that of Hezekiah to destroy it? Rather, he said: 'A crown has been left me by the Holy One, blessed be He, with which to crown myself. We too have been left this crown to crown ourselves.'" We find that with a

Summary: The Requirements of the Contemporary Rabbi

I should like to stress that one who takes upon himself the position of a rabbi, and who wishes to see himself also as a *posek*, takes upon himself an enormous responsibility. The *Hida*, in his *Shem ha-Gedolim* (*Maarechet Gedolim* 10, sect. 254), relates that the *Yaavetz*, R. Yaakov Yisrael Ashkenazi Emden, did not want to take upon himself the position of a rabbi, and used to say in the morning benediction *shelo asani abad* (spelled with an *aleph*) instead of *shelo asani eved* (who has not made me a slave) – a pun on the word *eved* (spelled with an *ayin*). Instead of *eved*, a slave, he said *abad, av beit din*, i.e., head of a rabbinic court. Indeed, he himself reports this in his *Shut Sheelat Yaavetz*, vol. 2, sect. 153. R. Hayyim Berlin is said also to have pronounced the Yaavetz's blessing.[44] The burden of the rabbinate is already clearly spelled out in *B. Berachot* 55a, where we read that "three things shorten the life of a person," one of which is "he who serves as a rabbi" (*Manhig Atzmo be'Rabbanut*). Here *rabbanut* may mean leadership, since R. Hama bar Hanina derives this from the fact that "Yosef died earlier than his brothers, because he held a position of leadership" (Exodus 1:6). Similarly, in *B. Pesachim* 87b we read, "Woe to the rabbinate which buries its bearer." And cf. *M. Avot* 1:10 when Shemayah says: "Hate

---

change in situation and circumstance, there is room in the halachah to "distinguish oneself." See my detailed discussion in "Congregational Dignity and Human Dignity" *supra* note 3, pp. 86–106. See also, Rabbi Ovadiah Yosef's (rightly reserved) statement in *Yabia Omer*, vol. 2, pp. 12–13:

Even though we have been permitted to disagree with the statements of latter-day decisors (*ahronim*) when we have clear-cut proofs, and [our] rulings are very firmly based on sound foundations, nevertheless, we must control ourselves and speak with great humbleness, holy fear, and great humility.

So, while he fully legitimates involvement in halachic innovation, he also very rightly cautions us to do so with the greatest attention and deepest respect toward earlier generations. (Cf. Meiri to *Sanhedrin* 17a.) This again is a very broad and serious subject that merits a separate study. However, see, for example, the discussion in A. Yehuda Warburg, *Rabbinic Authority: The Vision and the Reality*, Israel, 2013, pp. 45–53. See further my discussion in my *Legitimacy and Necessity: Scientific Disciplines and the Learning of Talmud*, Jerusalem, 2006, pp. 23–24, 60–62, notes 54–58. And see the comment of R. Abraham Bornstein of Sochotchov, *Avnei Naizer, Orah Hayyim* 362, on the influence of the publication of the second half of the *letter*, Lvov 1860, on certain earlier halachic decisions.

44. See Zeev Wolf Zicherman, *Otzar Plaot ha-Torah, Shemot*, Brooklyn, New York, 2014, p. 21 note 54.

the rabbinate." Hence, the need for great motivation in taking up this path as a career.

Having said that, there is a list of ideal requirements for the prospective rabbi: a broad general education enabling him to be halachically creative and innovative,[45] pleasant relations with other people, purity of one's personal qualities, sensitivity and tolerance for others, moderation in one's approach to the community, the wisdom to know when to be assertive and when to exercise restraint and self control, empathy for the pain and joy of others, independent thinking and the courage to stand by one's convictions even in the face of pressure and criticism,[46] and the deep and truthful desire to improve the lot of others from a perspective of *tikkun olam* (perfection of the world) and draw them near to the Torah and its commandments to a life of pleasant behavior. These are all demanded of the contemporary rabbi, along with a broad and deep knowledge of the Written Torah and the Oral Law.[47] In the

---

45. See my study entitled *Legitimacy and Necessity: Scientific Disciplines and the Learning of Talmud,* Jerusalem, 2006, and in an expanded form in Hebrew, in my *Netivot Pesikah: Kelim ve-Gishah le-Posek Halachah,* Jerusalem, 2008.

46. For additional material on this point, see Marc D. Angel, "Authority and Dissent: A Discussion of Boundaries," *Tradition* 25(2), 1990, pp. 18–22. In addition, I again turn the reader's attention to the article by Shifman, *supra* p. 120 note 81, which deals entirely with this subject. See below Appendix 6. And on assertiveness coupled with self-control, see Y.L. Maimon, *Sarei ha-Meah,* Jerusalem, 1961, vol. 2, pp. 281–282.

47. See *Seder Eliyahu Rabbah* (Ish Shalom Edition, Chapter 14, p. 67): "From here they said: A person should not teach Torah publicly unless he has learned the Torah, the Prophets, and the Writings, and studied the *Mishnah* and the *Midrash,* as it says: 'Who can express the mighty acts of the Lord, and make all His praise to be heard?' (Psalms 106:2)" Compare this with *Makkot* 10a: "For whom is it proper to teach the masses? One who has all of the produce, which is what R. Eliezer said: 'Who can express the mighty acts of the Lord, and make all His praise to be heard?' For whom is it proper to express the mighty acts of the Lord? One who is able to make all of his praises to be heard." (So too, in *B. Horayot* 13b.) Also compare to *Pirke de-Rabbi Eliezer,* beginning of chapter 3, in the name of R. Eliezer b. Hyrkanos, and see the comment of the *Redal* there, note 2; See also the *Jerusalem Talmud, Berachot* 9a, in the name of R. Shmuel bar Nahman, and in the *Midrash Shoher Tov,* chapter 9, etc. See also what was written by Rabbi Yisachar Tamar, *Alei Tamar,* vol. 1, Givataim, 1979, pp. 279–280. This is not the place to discuss this at length.

But "a broad and deep knowledge of the Written Torah and the Oral Law" is in itself not sufficient. For as Rabbi J.D. Bleich wrote so eloquently in his "Lomdus and Psak: Theoretical Analysis and Halakhic Decisions-Making" apud *The Conceptual Approach to Jewish Learning,* Orthodox Forum Series, ed. J. Blau, New York, 2006, p. 88:

Halakhic decision-making is indeed an art as well as a science. Its *kunst* lies precisely

characteristic language of Maimonides (*Mishneh Torah, Hilkhot San-hedrin* 2:7): "Although we are not careful to demand that a judge for a court of three possess all of these qualities, he must, however, possess these seven attributes:[48] wisdom, humility,[49] the fear of God, a loathing

---

in the ability to make judgment calls in evaluating citations, precedents, arguments etc. It is not sufficient for a halakhic decisor to have a full command of relevant sources. If so, in theory at least, the decisor *par excellence* would be a computer rather than a person. The decisor must have a keen understanding of the underlying principles and postulates of Halakhah as well as of their applicable ramifications and must be capable of applying them with fidelity to matters placed before him. No amount of book learning can compensate for inadequacy in what may be termed the "artistic" component. The epithet "a donkey carrying books" is the derisive reference employed in rabbinic literature to describe such a person.

48. The Mabit (Rabbi Moshe of Trani), Responsa 1, Venice edition, 389, Lvov, 1861, section 280, held "that they are all mandatory prerequisites," but the *Hida* disagrees with him in *Birchei Yosef, Hoshen Mishpat* 7:33: "These were not mentioned to disqualify, as was stated by the *Lehem Mishnah, Hilchot Sanhedrin*, Ch. 2, in his holiness. . . . Clearly, if only one is not found, it does not prevent him from serving . . . and I felt it necessary to say this to the exclusion of someone who tended in the other direction in understanding the intent of the Mabit." See also, Rabbi H. D. Halevy, *supra* note 15, p. 269.

49. Cf. *Midrash Tannaim*, Deuteronomy 1:15, ed. D. Tzvi Hoffmann, Berlin, 1908, pp. 8–9, and M.M. Kasher, *Torah Shelemah, Yitro*, vol. 15, New York, 1953, pp. 38–39, note 138. See also *Y. Sanhedrin* 1:4, and Y. Tamar, *Alei Tamar, Nezikin*, Givataim, 1982, pp. 98–99.

On these seven virtuous qualities, see below pp. 239–240 note 53. There is considerable literature on humility. Moses, who is always a role-model for everyone, is said to have been "the most humble of all men" (Numbers 12:3). *Mishnah Avot* 4:4 counsels in the name of R. Levitas of Yavneh that one should "be exceeding lowly of spirit." Indeed, *Avot* is replete with state merits counseling humility. And see *Derech Eretz Zuta* 7:2, on how a scholar should behave. See my *A Commentary on Derech Erez Zuta: Chapters Five to Eight*, Jerusalem, 1990, pp. 116–130, and my *Massechet Derech Eretz Zuta u-Perek ha-Shalom*, Jerusalem, 1994, pp. 65–68, and pass. R. Saadia Gaon, in his *Emunot ve-Deot, Maamar Yod*, s.v. *ha-Teshii*, has an informative passage on the negative consequences of pride. See J.D. Eisenstein, *Ozar Musar U'midot*, New York, 1941, p. 111, citing a variety of sources: M.Y. Halevy Weiss, *Beit Yehezkel: Hilchot Deot*, Bnei Brak, 1970, pp. 204–239; Menachem Trevish, *Orah Mesharim*, Magenza (Mainz) 1878, chapter 7, pp. 44–54, especially 7:15, p. 51, etc. The Hillel stories are, of course, exemplary of this characteristic, (see *B. Shabbat* 31a); A. Tobolsky, *La-Anavim Yitein Hen*, Bnei Brak, 1979, pass., a large collection of statements and stories on pride and humility from the whole range of rabbinic literature. As stated above this is a vast subject dealt with in innumerable tracts of the *Musar* literature. However, a fine example of humility may be found in the unique statement of the great Babylonian sage of the early 4 cent. c.e., Rav Nahman bar Yitzchak, who said of himself (*B. Pesahim* 105b):

Ana La Hakimah, Ana La Hozaah, ve-La Yehidaah Ana, Ela Gemarna ve Sadarna, ve-Chein Morin be-Veit Midrasha Kavati.
I am not a Sage, nor am I a Seer, and I am not a unique individual, but merely one who studies and orders [material], and in the academy they take note of my opinion.
(See the brilliant interpretation of this passage in R. Meir Simhah of Dvinsk's *Or Sameah: Hilchot Shabbat* 29:12.)

See also Berel Wein and Warren Goldstein, *The Legacy: Teachings for Life from the Great Lithuanian Rabbis,* Jerusalem, 2012, pp. 70–72, on the statement in B. *Baba Batra* 98a, "Whosoever takes pride in wearing the cloak of a *talmid hacham,* and is not a *talmid hacham,* will not be allowed into the inner partition of the Holy One, blessed be He." They mention that the Hafetz Hayyim was not recognized in public because he wore a simple worker's cap, and not a rabbinic hat.

See also what the Rambam wrote of himself in his epistle to R. Yosef ben Yehudah:
Know that I have set myself the goal of behaving humbly in every action, and even though it damages me in the eyes of the crowd. If someone wishes to flaunt his own excellence by demonstrating my failings, then I forgive him, even though he may be one of the most insignificant students. . . .

(See *Birkat Avraham,* by R. Baer Goldberg, Lyck, 1860, p. 15, from Munk, "Notice sur Josef ben Jehuda" *Journal Asiatique,* 3rd ser. vol. 14, 1842, p. 68.) This statement reflects, of course, Rambam's bitterness at the criticisms leveled at his writings. See, e.g., *Igrot ha-Rambam,* ed. Y. Shilat, vol. 1, Maaleh Adumim 1987, epistles 15, 20, 22, 25, and especially p. 300, 304, and his advice on p. 308, etc. This is a subject which is beyond the bounds of this study.

See also the remarkable statement of the Hida in his *Shem ha-Gedolim ha-Shalem,* ed. M.M. Krengil, vol. 2 *Maarechet Sefarim,* Brooklyn New York, 1965, p. 18b s.v. *Beit Yosef:*
Know that I received [a tradition] from a person, great in learning and fear [of heaven] who received it from a great rabbi who received it from Elders, that in the generation of *Maran the Beit Yosef* – i.e., R. Yosef Karo, [in which generation] there were R. Moshe Cordovero, and the Ari (R. Yitzhak Luria) and all the holy [Sages] with them, that it was revealed from heaven that the Jewish people needed a book which would collect all the laws, uncover their sources in order to clarify practical rulings of halachah. And in that generation there were three individuals who were fit [to carry out such a project], namely, R. Yosef Taitachik, *Maran* and *Maharivel* (R. Yosef ben Levi). And each of them was fit [to carry out] this work. And from the heavens it was unanimously decided and the order was given that it should be *Maran* the holy one, because of his extreme humbleness, as is evident from his holy books. . . .

He then refers back to the Hida's *Shem ha-Gedolim ha-Shalem,* vol. 1, *Maarechet Gedolim* s.v. *Maran R. Yosef Karo* (p. 87a) where he wrote that:
. . . I saw that R. Eliyahu Alfandari in *Kuntres Iguna* (apud *Michtav me-Eliyahu,* Constantinople 1723) 29a, wrote that it was not the practice of *Maran* to say anything negative about anyone who ruled contrary to his opinion, and his *Mishnah* (i.e., his learning) is the *Mishnah* of the Hasidim.

And finally, a truly remarkable testament of humility may be found in the Hafetz Hayyim's introduction to his *Likkutei Halachot,* Warsaw, 1899:
I, the lowly and poor in good deeds, do not know anything in the area of Torah, not even a single halachah [do I know] properly, nor even a single mitzvah with perfection,

for money, a love for truth;[50] he must be a person who is beloved by people at large, and must have a good reputation. All of these qualities are mentioned explicitly in the Torah." He continues these wonderful words, where he adds that they should be beloved by all, have a good eye, and be humble, socially friendly, and genteel in their dealings with others. He relates these qualities to biblical verses, such as Exodus 18:21, where Moshe is counseled by Yitro to choose men that "fear God, men of truth, hating covetousness."[51] One who encompasses all

---

am as nothing a thousand-fold, compared to the *Rishonim*, and am but like a little beadle in the *beit midrash* who brings the books of the Rif, the Rambam, and the other books to the table to study from them.

This from the author of the *Mishnah Berurah* (and his other writings) which shows a complete grasp of the whole spectrum of rabbinic writings, and the ability to analyze this huge body of literature and to come to accepted conclusions. (See also R. Ovadiah Yosef, *Anaf Etz Avot al Pirkei Avot*, Jerusalem, 2001, p. 389.)

50. See the words of Rabbi Uziel, *Mishpatei Uziel 1*, Tel Aviv, 1935, pp. x–xi in the introduction: "In all of my responsa, I did not intend to be lenient or stringent based on my own opinion and my judgment. Rather my intent and direction was to search for and find the truth. I went in the light of our rabbis, the *Rishonim*, to the extent of my understanding, for from their waters we drink and from their light we are enlightened; and from this holy light that is emitted from the hidden light I enlightened my eyes." See also the article of Tzvi Zohar, "*Atazma'ut ha-Poseq be-Yahas le-Pesiqa be-Avar*" in Sagi and Zohar, *supra* note 172, pp. 308–310. Similarly, we should note the words of Rabbi Yitzhak Yaacov Reines (1839–1915) in his book *Orah Ve-Simhah*, Vilna, 1895, pp. 119–120: ". . . For the search for the truth is beloved before the Lord, and is as dear as the truth itself. For truth is not limited by natural limitations and independent boundaries, and a person cannot hold the truth in his hand, but his goal in life is simply to seek the truth." See also the book of Avi Sagi, "*Elu Ve-Elu*" – *Mashma'uto Shel ha-Si'ah ha-Hilchati: Iyun be-Sifrut Yisrael*, 1996, Chapter 9, pp. 143–158, "*Ha-Erekh ha-Dati Shel Bakashat ha-Emet.*"

51. The characteristics of kindness and mercy are absolutely essential. It for this reason that the *beraita* in B. Sanhedrin 36b states that "We do not appoint the *Sanhedrin* an old man, or a eunuch, or one who is childless." Rambam (*Hilchot Sanhedrin* 2:3) explains:

We do not appoint to any *Sanhedrin* a very old man or a eunuch, for they possess the trait of cruelty, nor one who is childless, so that the judge should be merciful.

It is interesting to note the use of non-halachic biblical verses to support a rabbinic halachic statement. A fine example of this, albeit a random one, is to be found in a responsum of the *Tashbetz*, R. Shimon ben Tzemah Duran (14 cent.) who was asked concerning a women whose husband was causing her much anguish, by starving her so that she hated her life, (*Sefer ha-Tashbetz*, ed. Yoel Katan, vol. 2, Jerusalem, 2002, sect. 8, pp. 19–20). In his response he writes:

It is almost certain that she should be divorced and receive her *ketubah*, for it is our principle that [marriage] was given for [a good] life and not distress, as we have

of these qualities to a degree[52] can be considered among "the disciples of Aharon."

And finally we may recall the statement of Rav Zutra bar Tuvia in the name of Rav in *B. Hagigah* 12a:

> The world was created on [the basis of] ten principles: wisdom, intelligence, knowledge, strength, courage, justice, law, kindness, and mercy.

A rabbi should combine these characteristics in his rabbinic practice,[53]

---

learned from the verse in Genesis 3:20 "because she [Eve] was the mother of all living" (see *B. Ketubot* 61a).

He continues to discuss the issue citing the verse in Proverbs 17:1, "Better is a dry morsel, and quietness therewith, than a house full of sacrifices with strife." Ibid., 15:17, "Better is a dinner with herbs where love is, than a stalled ox and hatred therewith." All these are non-halachic verses cited to support a halachic ruling forcing the husband to divorce his wife, in which he also gives full expression to his deep compassion.

Numerous additional examples could be cited, but let this one suffice. On this phenomenon, however, see Y.D. Gilat, *Perakim be-Hishtalshelut ha-Halachah*, Jerusalem, 1992, pp. 374–393 (first published as an article entitled "*Midrash ha-Ketuvim ba-Tekufah ha-Betar-Talmudit*," apud *Michtam le-David: Sefer Zikaron le-ha-Rav David Ox*, Ramat-Gan, 1978, pp. 210–231).

52. See Lowenthal, *Serarah she-hi Avdut*, Jerusalem, 2007, pp. 173–200, on the rabbi's personal behavior as an example to others.

53. One might argue, as a certain reviewer did in commenting on my *Netivot Pesikah*, that this is a "mission impossible." However, I believe that, however daunting the challenges may appear to be, the goal is reachable. It requires a careful selection of suitable candidates, a vigorous training, which includes real *shimush* – a sort of apprenticeship to an experienced *posek* – and the understanding that while one does not have to, nor indeed can, answer every question posed; one does need to know where to look and whom to ask. Given a high degree of intelligence, a warm and engaging nature, and a willingness to commit to a long and arduous journey of study and self-discovery, I believe that we can aim for, and look foreward to, a future cadre of "good rabbis."

(See Rava's statement in *B. Berachot* 6a, and R. Kook's comment on it in his *Ein Ayah* ad loc. Sect.45.)

We should also take note of the passage in *Deuteronomy Rabba* 1:10:

R. Berechiah in the name of R. Hanina said: Judges have to have seven virtues and these they are: "Wise men, and understanding, and known . . ." (Deuteronomy 1:13), and another four [qualities] as is written (in Exodus 18:21), "Moreover than shalt provide out of all the people able men (*anshei hayyil*) such as fear God, men of truth, hating covetousness." And if you do not find [people with] all seven [virtues], then four [will suffice]; and if you do not find four, bring three; and if not even three, bring one, for so is written in Proverbs 31:10 "Who can find a woman of valour?" (which R. David Luria, the Redal, explains to mean that even that single quality of

and above all be a mench."[54]

---

anshei hayyil [able men] is difficult to find, just as the *Eshet Hayyil*, the woman of valor, is difficult to find).
Cf. *Midrash Tanaim* to Deuteronomy ed. D.Z. Hoffmann, Berlin 1908–1909, p. 8, 95, on these "seven virtues."
We should note that Rabbenu Bahya, in his commentary to Exodus 18:21, ed. H.D. Chavel, vol. 2, Jerusalem, 1967, p. 165, states that "all these qualities are all included in *anshei hayyil* [following the Ramban], for *anshei hayyil* are those who know to lead the people in justice, and it is impossible to do true justice without these qualities . . ."
However, if we do not find individuals with all these qualities, let us hope we will be able to find (and train) at least some of them to serve as competent rabbis.
54. Here we may quote Rabbenu Bahya, ibid., p. 165, who writes:
Come and see, how great is the power of [these] virtues: for the righteous one (*tzaddikim*) and the prophets in the Torah, such as Noah, Abraham, Yaakov, and others, were not given their titles for their wisdom, understanding, and knowledge, but for their virtues. Concerning Noah it is said, [that he] "was a just man and perfect – *tamim* – [in his generation]" (Genesis 6:9); and of Abraham it is said, "And be perfect – *tamim*" (ibid. 17:1); and Yaakov [is called] "a perfect – tamim – man" (ibid. 25:27); and Moshe was "very humble" (Numbers 12:2). And all this is to teach that what is most important is not wisdom but the qualities of honesty (*yosher*, or straightness) . . . And so the rabbis interpreted the verse in Psalms 111:10, '". . . a good understanding have all that do [his commandments]' – that study [his commandments]" is not stated, but [rather] "that do them" (*B. Berachot* 17a).
It is not sufficient merely to theoretically know how to be good; one has to carry out that knowledge and actually be a "mench."

APPENDIX I: THREE EXAMPLES
OF SENSITIVITY AND COMPASSION
IN *PSAK*

Introductory Note

Aviad Hacohen, in his *The Tears of the Oppressed*, Jersey City, 2004, p. 86, wrote the following very succinct and illuminating statement that may serve as an introductory note to this section.

> Every judicial system uses conventional legal categories to establish norms and principles that enable decision-making in cases where conflicting considerations need to be resolved. In addition, alongside these standard legal principles, in every system there also are unconventional frameworks which establish special norms, *lex specialis*. In Jewish jurisprudence as well, such special norms serve the rabbinic scholar when he searches for a solution to a question on his docket that is not soluble by standard halakhic methodologies. In some cases, this entails advancing a completely new halakhic claim. But more often, it refers to reliance on a legal argument which is well-known from other sources, and which the halakhic scholar extends in usage. Whereas in the original source the legal argument is used only for a specific matter, the halakhic scholar utilizes it and, either by force of analogy or by force of logic, extends its application to cover a different situation . . .

In this appendix we shall try to demonstrate how the halachic scholar threads the element of compassion into the web of his complex argumentation. It may not necessarily be the only – or even the main – thrust of his analysis, but it does reflect the direction, aim, and "tendenz" of his ruling.

The Dumb*

In the journal *Moriah* (8–10, 344–346, 2009, p. 185), Rabbi Moshe Barzilai of Modiin expresses uncertainty as to whether a dumb person,[1] who prays merely through thinking or listening to his neighbor, has to have a fixed place in the synagogue at which to pray in accordance with the ruling found in *Shulhan Aruch, Orah Hayyim* 90:19. For there it is written that a person should establish a permanent place for prayer. The reason for his uncertainty, he explains, is because the *Tzlah* (*Tziyyun le-Nefesh Hayyah*, by R. Yehezkel Landau, Prague, 1783) to *Berachot* 6b wrote that the reason for fixing a place is because the place acquires holiness, and as he prays there an additional time the holiness of the place helps his prayers be accepted. Rabbi Barzilai suggests through verbal expression the place acquires holiness, but not if his prayer is only in thought or through listening. He leaves this question unsolved; but what seems to emerge from this way of thinking is that in his opinion a dumb person is not duty-bound to have a permanently fixed place in the synagogue. The corollary of this view is that the congregation is not obligated to give the dumb member a permanent fixed seat in the synagogue, even if he comes regularly to prayers. Needless to say, if he purchased a place the situation would be different. (See *Shulhan Aruch, Hoshen Mishpat* 235:18, and *Even ha-Ezer* 121 ad fin., and cf. the responsum of the Rosh, *Klal* 85:17.) The effect of such a halachic position is to cast a great affront upon one whom nature has treated so harshly, and is, as such, constitutes a humiliation of his dignity. Hence, it is halachically unacceptable, since it constitutes an offence to *kevod ha-briyot*, the honor and dignity of the individual, this principle being a key element in the ethical foundation of the halachah.

Furthermore, in R. Michael Menahem Shiloni's exhaustive study entitled *Shome'a u-Mashmia*,[2] Jerusalem, 2006, p. 163, there is a lengthy

---

* This is a reworking of an article I published in Hebrew in *Pesach Sheni: Sovlanut min ha-Torah*, pp. 22–24.
  1. On the status of the dumb in the halachah, see Avraham-Sofer Avraham, *Nishmat Avraham*, vol. 1, Jerusalem, 1983, index s.v. (p. 358a); Tzvi Marx, *Halakha and Handicap: Jewish Law and Ethics on Disability*, Jerusalem-Amsterdam, 1992–1993, pp. 411–436.
  2. This is a very broad and complex subject which touches upon a variety of different halachic issues, which are dealt with in Shiloni's book. See, for example, Yitzhak

discussion on the subject of "hearing is speaking (or answering)." He writes as follows

> The Rosh to the first chapter of *Hulin* sect.3 wrote that the deaf the Sages always spoke of is one who neither hears nor speaks. The Rambam (*Hilchot Shechitah* 4:9) wrote that an expert [slaughterer] who was struck dumb but both understands and hears may slaughter in the first place (*le-chithilah*), and so too he who is deaf may serve as a slaughterer. [The Rambam] wrote of the person that was struck dumb that he could slaughter *le-chithilah*, but of the deaf man he did not write *le-chithilah*, because he cannot hear the benedictions, and so he should not slaughter in the first place, as those who have learned from the beginning of *Terumot* that a deaf person who can speak but not hear should not offer [the *terumah* title], but if he offered it, his offering is accepted. And so wrote the Tur, *Yoreh De'ah* ad fin.: that a deaf person, who speaks but cannot hear, even if he speaks, should not slaughter in the first place, because he cannot hear the benedictions. But if he slaughters, even alone, his slaughtering is kosher. However, he who hears but does not speak, if he is an expert, he may slaughter in the first place, if someone else makes the benedictions.
>
> From the words of the Rosh and the Tur, unlike R. Avraham ben Shlomo, (in *Shibolei ha-Leket, Hilchot Tefillah* 20), who is of the opinion that he who cannot make a benediction by himself, his listening to that of another will not avail . . . , we learn that a dumb person, even though he cannot make a benediction on his own, can slaughter in the first instance if another makes the benediction and he hears it . . .
>
> Behold, in *B. Berachot* 21a, in the discussion of one who had a seminal emission (*baal keri*), in relation to that which Rav Hisda said, that even though thinking is not the same as speaking, nonetheless, the *baal keri* thinks (i.e., does not speak out loud) so that the public be not aware and involved in his state. And the question was raised that surely prayer is something in which the public is involved, and we have learned in a *Mishnah* that if he was standing in prayer and suddenly remembered that he was a *baal keri* he should not interrupt his prayer, but merely shorten it. That is the case, when he already began to pray; but if he had not yet

Reitfurt, *Kuntres be-Din Motzi et ha-Rabim yedei Horatam* (*Kuntres* 21), Brooklyn, N.Y., 1998, who discusses *megillah* reading for others on the part of a blind man.

started, he should not begin. See the Ritva ad loc. . . . The answer given
is that since he hears the benedictions from the *hazzan*, it is as though
he articulated them. . . . From which we may conclude that the Ritva is
clearly of the opinion that a *baal keri* can regard himself as 'one who
has heard it is as though he has spoken,' even though he himself is not
actually permitted to answer himself . . .

He continues his complex discussion, rejecting the view of *Hagahot
Asheri* (cited in *Beit Yosef, Yoreh Deah 1*) who expresses doubt as to
the ability of the dumb to fulfil his obligation through hearing, since, as
noted above, the *Shulhan Aruch* does not hold this position of doubt.
Furthermore in *Orah Hayyim* 104:7, R. Yosef Karo ruled like Rashi
that if one is standing at prayer and hears *kedushah* or *kaddish*, he
should be silent, direct his thought to what the *hazaan* is saying and is
as a responder (*oneh*). There again we see that even if one only hears
and does not actually speak, according to the *Shulhan Aruch* he has the
status of *shome'a ke-oneh* (listening is like responding).

We may further call attention to what R. Yaakov Emden wrote in
his *Siddur, Hilchot Keriat ha-Torah*, sect. 20 (p. 752):

> Someone who was struck dumb and so can no longer speak, because of
> his sickness, but all his other limbs and capacities are in working order,
> and he can read in his mind, one may [call him up to the Torah] when he
> is an important person . . . and someone else will make the benedictions
> for him. In our days doctors have found cures for dumb people, even for
> those who were born deaf, so that they can read and write and under-
> stand what they read and write and even speak in an incoherent fashion,
> and surely respond to their teachers' questions intelligently. Such people
> know there is a God above who created all things, and can therefore
> say in the morning a benediction in Hebrew like any other person, and
> anything else required by the religion, and think and calculate. Therefore,
> he can be called up to the Torah.

(See further Akiva Meller, *Ha-Keriyah ba-Torah ve-Hilchotehah*, Jerusalem, 2009, p. 272, sect. 5, note 11.)

In light of the above, it is clear that, coupled with the principle of "the
dignity of the individual" – *kevod ha-briyot*, any question of doubt can
be cleared up, and any point of uncertainty as to which opinion (in the

controversy of the *Rishonim*) should be followed, which leads us to the clear conclusion that dumb persons should be treated by the congregation as any other congregant and afforded a fixed place of his own and given *aliyot* to the Torah. Our sympathy and compassion should go out to him, making him feel a fully-fledged member, rather than a deficient outsider. This compassion is not just a subjective emotional response to seeing a "challenged" individual, but mandated by the halachah.[3]

The Blind

R. Moshe Feinstein, one of the leading decisors of the last generation, was asked (*Igrot-Moshe*, vol. 1, *Orah Hayyim* 45, pp. 104–105) whether a blind man could enter into a synagogue with his dog. Surely this would be seen as disrespect to the sanctity of the synagogue. (See *Shulhan Aruch, Orah Hayyim* 151, on the sanctity of the synagogue, and the prohibition to desecrate it.) Furthermore, it is by no means clear that a blind man is obligated to attend synagogue services. Indeed, the halachic status of the blind is extremely complex and subject to considerable controversy among the authorities.[4] Should then a blind

---

3. I sent a fully documented and detailed study as a response to Rabbi Barzilai's article in *Moriah* (see my article in *Pesach Sheni*, ibid.), but they did not publish it. However, they did publish a brief note by someone else, which reached much the same conclusion.

4. This again is a multi-faceted issue, which has its origins in a controversy between R. Yehudah and the Sages in B. *Baba Kama* 87a; see *Rashba* to *Megillah* 24a; *Shulhan Aruch, Orah Hayyim* 139:3. *Rema* ibid. basing himself on the *Maharil*, etc. See, for example, Tzvi Marx's very important (though somewhat rare) book *Halakha and Handicap*, pp. 377–396, 509–516, 527–530, 540–542, 545, 544, 553, 571–575, 578–580, 585, 619, etc. In addition, see Yom Tov Zanger, *Kuntres Pokeah Ivrim*, Bnei Brak, 1992, and Arieh Rodriguez, *Sefer ha-Suma*, Jerusalem, 2002; *Nishmat Avraham*, vol. 1, index s.v. *suma* (p. 370); all of which have comprehensive summaries of all the various halachic issues relating to the blind.
See also Akiva Meller, *Ha-Kreyah ba-Torah ve-Hilchotehah*, Jerusalem, 2009, pp. 267–272, 768–774, on whether a blind man can be called up to the Torah.
See also R. Ovadiah Yosef, *Yalkut Yosef*, vol. 1, 2nd edition, Jerusalem, 1985, pp. 84–87: idem, *Yabia Omer*, vol. 9, Jerusalem, 2002, *Orah Hayyim* 88:1, that a blind man can be a *shaliah tzibbur* even on the *Yamim Noraim*. But cf. Yaakov Yitzhak Weiss, *Minhat Yitzhak*, vol. 3, 2nd edition, Jerusalem, 1979, no. 12, pp. 23–26. However, he too, who was normally *mahmir* (stringent) in his rulings, after much inner discussion, permits a blind boy to reach the *haftarah* (with special reservations), adding to the various reasons and views he had cited and analyzed that this is:
In order somewhat to lessen the distress of these unfortunate youngsters, who

man enter the synagogue, hear *kedushah*, *kadish*, and the Torah reading
etc., while all the time his dog sitting at his side in the precinct?
In his response, R. Moshe writes:

> There can be no greater example of "hour of need" (*sha'at ha-dehak*);
> for if we do not allow him [to enter the synagogue with his guide dog],
> during his whole life he will be unable to participate in communal prayer,
> to hear the Torah reading, and the reading of the *megillah*,[5] and he will
> have a very great measure of emotional Holidays distress (*agmat nefesh*),
> such as during the High Holy days where the masses join together [in
> prayer]. (See Rema *Orah Hayyim* 88 ad fin.) Therefore there is consider-
> able evidence to allow the blind person to enter into the synagogue with
> his guide dog which has to be at his side permanently in order to pray
> and hear the holy Torah etc . . .

[would otherwise] not be able to act like other [normal] youths who are used to
reading their *haftarot*.

See above sections entitled "Sensitivity to Personal Feelings," "Care Not to Shame
or Embarrass," and "Leniency to Prevent Stress and Suffering."

5. We find a similar argument in a responsum of the *Rema*, no. 98, ed. Asher Ziv
(*Shut ha-Rema*), Jerusalem, 1971, pp. 228–229. Tzvi Marx, ibid., p. 156, uses this
text in his sub-chapter (d) entitled "Human Dignity and Physical Ailment." I quote
him verbatim:

R. Moshe Isserles (Rema, 16th C.) was especially daring in a case involving a man
who has a chronic kidney problem resulting in loss of bladder control which led to
him involuntarily discharging urine. He inquired about his eligibility for donning the
phylacteries and reciting the Shema, two Scriptural precepts. The Talmud is meticulous
in requiring personal hygiene as a prerequisite in the discharging of these religious
precepts. His medical condition could very easily have been taken as grounds for
exemption, or even prohibition from discharging these precepts. R. Moshe Isserles
allows him, nevertheless, to engage in the mitzvot of donning the phylacteries and
reciting the Shema, combining the grounds that it is a case of inadvertence – אונס – and
that he has a special garment to catch the drops. *It is inconceivable, given his chronic
condition*, argues the Rema, *to prevent a Jew from fulfilling these mitzvot all his life.*
(My emphasis – D.S.)

He continues his discussion with the following emphasis:

Beyond that, the Rema, in a continuation of the last case, ruled that the man may
even enter the synagogue, though there were separate grounds to prohibit it on the
basis of the sanctity of the synagogue. For the Rema, the man's claim to human dignity
carried more weight, so justifying the dispensation for him to enter the synagogue
and participate in the life of the worshipping community. For the sake of preventing
personal humiliation, he does not even require him to sit segregated from others.

See also his note 210, on pp. 774–775.

His reference to the Rema in *Orah Hayyim* 88 is to be understood as follows: There was a view,[6] according to which a "menstruating woman, on the days when she has a flow, should not enter the synagogue, pray, mention God's name, or touch a scroll" (*Hagahot Maimoniyot*, cited by the Rema, *Orah Hayyim* ibid.).

However, continues the Rema:

> But during the days of purification [i.e., the seven days counted between the end of the menstrual flow and the time that the woman immerses herself], the practice is to permit it. And even where a stringent practice is followed, they are permitted to attend the synagogue on the High Holidays like other women, and as occasions when the multitude gather in the synagogue, *for it would cause them great distress to remain outside when everyone else assembles* [there], (*Piskei Marai* sect. 132). (My emphasis – D.S.)[7]

Thus, "hour of need" and "extreme distress" constitute halachic norms permitting a position of leniency. However, R. Moshe does not rely merely on this argument. He brings added support to his decision by citing a passage in the *Yerushalmi* (*Megillah* 3:3, 74a), where we read as follows:

> R. Ivri ordered the scribes [as follows]:
> If someone who has in him the flavor of Torah comes to you, receive him with his donkey and his tool-kit.

This passage comes after a series of discussions on how in synagogue one must behave with decorum, and *kalut rosh* – levity, frivolity – is not permitted. Nonetheless, since the workman is connected to his donkey[8]

---

6. I discuss this in detail in my study on "Congregational Dignity and Human Dignity," apud *Women and Men in Communal Prayer: Halakhic Perspectives*, ed. Chaim Trachtman, Jersey City, N.J., 2010, pp. 67–68.

7. See my extensive discussion of this ruling ibid., pp. 68–72, 162–177; Yaakov Blidstein "Great is Human Dignity" [Hebrew], *Shenaton ha-Mishpat ha-Ivri* 9–10, 1982–1983, p. 167, note 90; *Sefer Pardes Eliezer*, on *Aseret Yemei TeShuvah – Yom Kippur*, Brooklyn, N.Y., 2000, pp. 161–163, and note 18, ibid., and the discussion on *Magen Avraham* to *Orah Hayyim* 610:5.

8. In this he follows the interpretation of the *Pnei Moshe* and the *Korban ha-Edah* ad loc, understanding *hamrai* as "his donkey." However, R. Yisachar Tamar, in his

great commentary to the Yerushalmi, *Alei Tamar*, to *Megillah*, ad loc. (vol. 3, Alon Shvut , 1992, pp. 118–119), refers us to *Mi-Yakirei Yerushalayim*, by A.Y. Dzubas, vol. 1, Pietrokov, 1932, sect. *Beit ha-Knesset*, who "correctly interprets *u-le-hamrai* as meaning 'and to his servant' who 'leads a donkey' [*ha-mehamer*] who is called a *hamar* – a donkey driver." (See M. Sokoloff, *A Dictionary of Jewish Palestinian Aramaic of the Byzantine Period*, Ramat-Gan, 1990, p. 207b s.v.) However, later on he argues that even if we are talking of a donkey, surely it was only brought into an outer courtyard. Be that as it may, R. Moshe's argument is not based solely on this source.

Here I would like to add the following comments. R. Breisch argues that a dog in the synagogue would distract the people's attention from their prayer. He refers us to *Orah Hayyim* 90:21–22. However, in subsection 21, the *Mehaber* states that:

There must be nothing obstructing between him [who is praying] and the wall, and a permanent fixture, like a cupboard and the *teivah* do not constitute an obstruction. . . . And animals do not obstruct, even people are not an obstruction.

On this the *Rema* comments:

In my opinion animals are an obstruction, but people are not. And so appears to be the opinion of the *poskim*, and perhaps there is a mistake in our books, [i.e., we should really read: and animals *do* obstruct . . .]

Strangley enough the *Mishnah Berurah* ad loc. has no comment on this issue. We may also note that the *Mehaber*'s reading is as it is in our books in the first edition of the *Shulhan Aruch*, Venice, 1565. However, the *Kaf ha-Hayyim* (12b, note 134) shows that there was a major controversy among the *poskim* as to whether there was a mistake in the *Shulhan Aruch* or not. The *Rema* thought there was, as we have seen, and so too the *Levush* and the *Maamar Mordechai*, (although an emendation would be quite difficult and require restructuring the whole phrase). But the *Shiyarei Kenesset ha-Gedolah*, the *Pri Hadash*, and the *Nahar Shalom* accept the original reading. Whichever reading be the correct one, the passage presupposes that animal did come into the synagogue during times of prayer, and that this was allowed.

As to the following subsection (23) which talks of colored clothing causing a distraction, so that one should not face them when praying, and the super commentaries discuss the fact that one should not have pictures in the synagogue for that reason, or pray with an illustrated *siddur*. The *Aharonim*, basing themselves on the *Zohar* (*Deut.* 72) state that one should look downwards, or close one's eye when praying (especially the *Amidah*), consequently one would not see these "distractions." (See *Kaf ha-Hayyim* ibid., 12b–13a, no. 137 for full references.)

On the subject of art in the synagogue, see the comprehensive discussion of Y.Z. Kahana, in his *Mehkarim be-Sifrut ha-Teshuvot*, Jerusalem, 1973, pp. 349–394.

And as to the evidence he cites from *B. Berachot* 62a, which he himself admits is somewhat questionable, see David Yoel Weiss, *Megadim Hadashim* to *Berachot*, Jerusalem, 1989, p. 293, where to harmonize contradictory statements concerning Abbaye's relationship to animals, it is suggested that the text in *Berachot*, which talks of his being in constant contact with a lamb, (which R. Moshe suggests must have also been with him in the *beit midrash*), was when he was still young, while later, as in *B. Kiddushin* 81b, he kept away from animals. (He cites the Malbim's *Artzot ha-Hayyim*, sect. 3, subsection 2. We may add that the contradiction was also noted by R. Reuven Margaliot, in his *Nitzotzei Or*, Jerusalem, 1965, to *Berachot* ibid., p. 29, who points our attention to *B. Baba Metziah* 30b.)

However, R. Yaakov Breisch, the Chief Rabbi of Zurich, in his *Helkat Yaakov*, vol. 3, Bnei Brak, 1966, no. 87, pp. 193–194, rejects R. Moshe's ruling, stating that it is strange (referring to *Rema* in *Yoreh Deah* 10), and is "a structure based on a weak foundation." He argues that the *Yerushalmi* is not referring to a time when the congregation is praying, for a dog in the synagogue would distract their attention (referring to *Rema Orah Hayyim* 90:21–22, that even colorful clothing is distracting, and should not be in a synagogue at prayer times). Can one imagine a donkey or a dog in the middle of the synagogue not causing a distraction? He brings additional evidence to refute R. Moshe's ruling, explaining that the *Yerushalmi* is talking of someone who comes to spend the night, but not during the times of prayer. He further questions the identification of *hamrei* with "his donkey," suggesting, as we have seen above, that maybe it means his "donkey driver." And even if *hamrei* means his donkey, dogs are far wiser than donkeys, he argues, bringing additional sources to validate this contention. After seeking to disprove other elements in R. Moshe's argument, he ends by saying that surely the blind man can find alternative ways of attending the service, having a friend lead him in and take care of him, etc. So the argument that he can never hear the Torah reading is far-fetched. And, if this were the case, he would be exempt, in any case, by reason of "compulsion" (*ones*). Now while it is true that all these are powerful arguments, R. Breisch takes little account of the blind man's feelings. The fact that he may be exempt from these *mitzvot*, because he is simply *unable* to carry them out, does not necessary reduce his *feelings of distress*. It is this element, I believe, that drove R. Moshe to his conclusion. See further R. Shlomo Zalman Braun, *Shaarim Metzuyanim be-Halachah*, vol. 1, Jerusalem, 1978, 12 note 2, pp. 73–74, who also expresses his surprise and disagreement with R. Moshe's ruling, quoting the *Helkat Yaakov*, and adding his own additional comment, that since gentiles would not suffer a dog to come into their Church or Mosque, to do so in a synagogue is certainly a form of desecration, and we must at least observe the same standard of respect to our places of worship as they do to their's (referring to *Hatam Sofer, Orah Hayyim* no. 31). (The above is also cited in Zanger's *Pokeah Ivrim* pp. 25–26, note 33.) Avraham-Sofer Avraham, in his *Nishmat Avraham*, vol. 1, *Orah Hayyim*, Jerusalem, 1983, p. 132, note 11, further refers us to M.M. Kasher's *Torah Shelemah* vol. 15, New York, 1953 (*Yitro, Miluim*) p. 147, who also raises a series of objections to R. Moshe's ruling.)

However, the greatness of R. Moshe's ruling is that he rejects a merely formalistic approach and argues that the act of helping and allaying the distress of a blind person cannot be regarded as an act of desecration of a holy place. Thus his ruling serves as testimony to the courage, individuality, and creativity of thought of this great *posek*. (See above section entitled "Conflict Between Legal Formalism and Morality.")

Again we may add to bolster R. Feinstein's ruling – though he does not require it – that the *Shulhan Aruch, Orah Hayyim* 151, that discusses the sanctity of the synagogue, and as a consequence the prohibition to act frivolously in it or in any way belittle its sanctity, rules that, for this reason, one does not sleep in a synagogue, (section 3). But, if for the benefit of the synagogue itself and our praying in it, we may do so (section 4). And therefore on the night of Yom Kippur we may sleep in it, or when people gather together to intercalate the year one may eat in it (ibid.); (and see *Kaf ha-Hayyim* ibid. 155a, notes 32–34). We see from the above that when the intent of such normally forbidden behavior is spiritually positive and supports the basic aim and function of the synagogue, it is permitted. Surely, then, the deep desire of the blind

as indeed he is to his tools, the R. Imi permitted him to enter with it, and did not see this as violating the sanctity of the synagogue. So too, argues, R. Moshe if a blind man needs his dog to be at his side, always relying on its guidance, this is not to be regarded as violating the sanctity of the synagogue. However, the main element of R. Moshe's argument is not based on this *Yerushalmi* source, but the halachic weight of the need to express sympathy with the blind man's distress and anguish.[9]

---

man to pray in a synagogue with a *minyan* cannot serve as a reason to exclude him because of his guide dog (as indeed R. Moshe wrote towards the end of his responsum).

9. For a continuation of this discussion, see B. Lau, "Access of People with Guide Dogs to the Western Wall Prayer Plaza," *Human Rights Responsa Online* 2013. A related issue is the question whether a blind man can go in a public place with his guide dog on Shabbat, or whether this is *tiltul bi-reshut ha-rabim*. *Lev Arieh*, by R. Dov Arieh Klig, Lvov, 1936, vol. 2, no. 2, permits this, since both the person and the dog are "carrying" the dog's lead (or leash), and even though two who did an act (*melachah*) is prohibited by rabbinic law, in this case it is permitted in accordance with B. *Shabbat 153b*, that any act that is forbidden by his neighbor but not punishable (*patur aval asur*) is permitted to an animal ab initio. However, other authorities are doubtful as to the permissibility. See Avraham-Sofer Avraham, *Nishnat Avraham*, vol. 1, *Orah Hayyim*, Jerusalem, 1983, 301 note 11, p. 131, citing (himself) in *Lev Avraham*, vol. 2, Jerusalem, 1978, p. 18, that R. Shlomo Zalman Auerbach expressed his doubts on this issue. (See *Kuntres Pokeh Ivrim*, p.36.) R. Moshe's responsum on entering the synagogue with the guide dog posits a premise that one could bring the dog to the synagogue through a public area. And since we are talking about carrying in a *reshut ha-rabim*, there is also the issue of the blind man's cane. Here there are a variety of opinions, but what seems to be the majority position is that if he is totally reliant on his cane, he may use it in a public place. See *Kuntres Pokeah Ivrim*, pp. 36–37, no. 42, and note 64. Tzvi Marx, in his *Halakha and Handicap*, p. 561, has little doubt as to its permissibility, unlike Zanger (above), and he brings an illuminating anecdote, recorded by C. Actor, *What Makes People Different*, New York, 1985, pp. 105–106:

A young Bobover Hassid . . . instinctively retrieved the fallen crutches to its young handicapped owner who lost his cool when they fell out of his grasp, sitting down to cry in his misery. The Hassid dealt with technical restrictions of the Shabbat thus: "If the Talmud forbids us to taunt the lame and the impaired, so much more does it forbid us to celebrate the holiday while this young man sits crying on the stairs."

On the use of a cane (and a battery operated chair) for the lame, see further Tzvi Marx ibid., pp.561–562.

Here I would like to call attention to a very interesting controversy. In *Shulhan Aruch, Even ha-Ezer* 142:11, there is a discussion concerning a totally blind man's inability to bring a *get* (bill of divorce) from another country, because he cannot say "it was written and signed in my presence," but in certain cases he may do so as long as he recognizes the voice of the woman being divorced (on the basis of B. *Gittin* 23a – *tviat eina de-kala*). The *Beit Shemuel* (by R. Shmuel Feibush), ad loc (note 18) writes:

See above 132:6 what I wrote in the name of the *Magid* [*Mishnah*, to Ramban, *Hilchot Gittin* 3:9], that in our days no man can be believed on the basis of such a form

A further example of R. Moshe's compassion in *psak* is to be found in Tzvi Marx ibid., pp. 346–348, and because of the importance and relevance I shall quote it in full:

Kohen with a Prosthesis – A contemporary case addressed by R. Moses Feinstein concerns the religious obligation of an amputee; a kohen who has prosthetic legs, (*Igrot Moshe, Orah Hayyim*, vol. 2, no. 32). When he removes his shoes, as required by the Halakha, the congregation is likely to be distracted. Though the community may have foreknowledge of his condition, that knowledge is not the same as directly experiencing this fact. May the kohen be permitted to offer the priestly benedictions with his prosthesis visible, or should he disqualify himself? [See *B. Sotah* 40a for the reason the kohen has to remove his shoes.]

He permits the kohen's participation, on the grounds that it is not a significant detail that will distract the community, since they understand that it is because of his disability. Seeing him this way will not be especially novel for the community used to seeing him with his prosthesis. If effect,

of recognition (i.e., of the voice), even a scholar, and one cannot make a distinction between visual recognition and aural recognition . . .

The implication of this statement is that in our days, even a scholar would be prohibited from having relations with his wife, since he cannot be certain who she really is! (See Aryeh Rodriguez, *Sefer ha-Suma*, p. 458.)

However, R. Meir Posner, in his *Beit Meir*, Frankfurt, 1787, to *Even ha-Ezer* 142:11, rejects the view of the *Beit Shemuel*, arguing that the *Magid Mishnah* was only referring to visual recognition, but did not deal with the issue of aural recognition. Consequently, a totally blind man who recognizes the voice of his wife may have normal marital relations with her (Rodriguez, ibid.). In this way Posner found a persuasive halachic solution permitting the blind to have a normal married life style. In order to give a somewhat fuller picture of the halachic status of the totally blind, we should note that there is a serious controversy among the *Rishonim* as to whether such a person is obligated to keep *mitzvot* or not. Rabbenu Yeruham follows the opinion of R. Yehudah in *B. Baba Kama* 87a that he is not obligated by biblical law, but by rabbinic law he is (cf. *Tosafot* ibid. and in *B. Eruvin* 96a). So too, the *Ritba* in his response no. 97, and others. But the majority view is that he is obligated to keep all *mitzvot*, and see the summary in R. Hayyim Hezkiah Medini's *Sedei Hemed*, vol. 4, *samech klal* 66, vol. 9, sect. 69, and Rodriguez ibid., pp. 263–279. The son of the *Klei Hemdah* (by R. Meir Don Plotzki), Cracow, 1888–1893, wrote a special section in his father's book (143a), in which he demonstrated that even according to R. Yeruham, in *mitzvot* between man and his neighbor the blind person has complete obligation.

See further A. Lichtenstein, Regarding a Blind Person's Obligation in Mitzvot," *VBM Halakha* sects. 1, 2.3; David H. Tov, *Halachic Rulings Relating to the Blind: A Compendium of Jewish Law, Responsa and Tradition Affecting the Blind and Visually Impaired*, Brooklyn, N.Y., 1997.

then, R. Moshe rules that he is to be considered sufficiently familiar, so as not to require disqualification, out of a concern that he will be distracting. This solution is both humane and satisfies the technical requirements of the Halakha, relying on the issue of familiarity just discussed.

He extends this reasoning further to a kohen who wears his shoes while participating, on the grounds that the removal of his shoes is either impossible or makes his prosthetic limbs visible. Were he to remove his shoes, the congregation would be distracted and that would constitute a more serious breach than disregarding the rabbinical ordinance about the removal of shoes. Therefore, he is instructed by R. Moshe not to remove his shoes and is not disqualified, (*Nishmat Avraham, Orah Hayyim*, pp. 70–74).

The force of this responsum is in its seeking to include the disabled *Kohen*, enabling him to fulfill a religious obligation. R. Feinstein never mentions this as the explicit motivation behind his ruling. It is based on formal halachic and technical grounds pertinent to the issues connected to the precept. *I suggest that compassion for the disabled Kohen's exclusion is nevertheless implicit in the discussion, since he could just as plausibly have argued for the Kohen's disqualification.* A *Kohen* with prosthetic legs, conspicuously wearing shoes, could easily be said to attract the community's attention if one were seeking a way to exclude this disabled person. R. Feinstein's arguing for an alternative that minimizes these problems demonstrates an inclination to rule in favor of the inclusion of the disabled. The responsum sympathetically extends the concept of "familiarity" for the inclusion of the *Kohen*. (Compare in a somewhat different context the discussion of R. Yehuda Henkin, in his *Understanding Tzniut: Modern Controversies in the Jewish Community,* Jerusalem and New York, 2008, pp. 73–84, in a chapter [2] entitled "The Significant Role of Habituation in Halachah.") See also "The Physically and Mentally Disabled: Insights Based on the Teachings of Rav Moshe Feinstein," Moshe D. Tendler and Fred Rosner, *Journal of Halacha and Contemporary Society*, 22, 1991, pp. 91–92, and on the deaf, see below, ibid., pp. 92–93).

The Deaf

A third example of the humanitarian element which is found in a hala-chic responsum, refers to the question of whether a deaf person[10] can wear his hearing aid on Shabbat. Since a hearing aid is an electronic de-vice, and therefore would seem to come under the category of *muktzah*, surely it cannot be moved on Shabbat (*mi-shum tiltul*). Furthermore, usually one does not sleep with a hearing aid, so one would have to put it into one's ear on Shabbat, which means holding and moving it. Consequently, it would appear that a deaf person cannot use such an instrument on Shabbat, and for example, will never be able to hear the Torah reading in a synagogue on Shabbat, *Barechu, Kedushah*, or *Kaddish*. R. Eliezer Waldenberg, a great *posek* who only recently passed away and published, inter alia, fifteen wonderful volumes of responsa on the whole range of halachic issues, deals with this question at great length (in his *Tzitz Eliezer*, vol. 6, no. 6, pp. 24–28 . (The responsum is dated 7 Tishri 1957, and is a reply to another great authority, R. Baruch Yashar Shlichter. He returned to this issue in vol. 9, no. 21.)

First he analyzes at length the status of *muktzah*, which is a rabbinic prohibition, arguing from well-known Talmudic sources that the "dig-nity of the individual" –*kevod ha-briyot* can override the prohibition of *muktzah*. He continues to examine a variety of different aspects related to this issue, such as the status of electricity, the effect of carrying the

---

10. On the status of the deaf in the halachah, see Avraham-Sofer Avraham, *Nishmat Avraham*, vol. 1, Jerusalem, 1983, index s.v. *heresh* (p. 363b). And see R. Shlomo Zalman Auerbach, *Minhat Shlomo*, vol. 1, Jerusalem, 1986, no. 34, pp. 187–188; *Petichah Kollelet* by the author of the *Pri Megadim*, R. Yosef Teomim, ed. Yitzhak Leib Talesnik, Jerusalem, 1893, pp. 79–85. See further Meller, ibid., p. 272, sect. 4, and note 10, ibid.

We may add that deaf mutes according to biblical law cannot marry one another, but, nonetheless, the Sages instituted marriage for them. (*Shulhan Aruch, Even ha-Ezer* 44:1, based on *M. Yevamot* 14:1, *B. Yevamot* 112b; Rambam, *Hilchot Ishut* 4:9; and see super commentaries to the *Shulhan Aruch*, ibid.). We shall not expand on this issue, but refer the reader to Avraham Hayyim Fraenkel, *Simhah Temimah*, Jerusalem, 1986, pp. 134–135, references in notes 19–21.

On the question whether a deaf person can act as a *shaliah tzibbur* (*hazan* or cantor), see most recently Shaul Wieder, *Shaliah Tzibbur ho-Shalem*, Haifa, 2016, 1:31, pp. 32–34, who shows there is a difference of opinion on this issue between the Tashbatz (3:113) and R. Akiva Eiger (to *Berachot* 15a); the Tashbatz permitting and R. Akiva Eiger forbidding. The accepted ruling is that one may if there is no one else available (*Mishnah Berurah* 53:41, *Shaar ha-Tziyyun* 38; *Kaf ha-Hayyim* 43:67, etc.).

instrument, the use of batteries and the various discussions concerning *muktzah*, and so forth, and then summarizes his (interim) findings as follows:

> We have learned from the above that the prohibition of moving *muktzah* is annulled . . . when [it conflicts with] the dignity of the individual, such as if a person would be shamed in his own eyes and in the eyes of the public if he were not permitted to use this *mukzah* object. If this be the case, surely there is no greater case [for the use of the principle] of "the dignity of the individual" than to avoid the shame and disgrace of the deaf person, who cannot hear what people say to him. One can hardly imagine the magnitude of the abuse (*herpah*), shame, and discomfort when he comes among people in the synagogue and he is alone and solitary, not hearing what is going on, unable to reply to those that question him, such that there is a far greater [affront to] his dignity than the cases discussed earlier [in his response from the Talmud]. Furthermore, his shame is combined with distress that he is unable to participate in public prayer, hearing the Torah reading, responding *Amen Yehei Shmei Rabba* [in the *kaddish*], and the *kedushah*, etc., in effect his inability to carry out [*bitul*] a whole host of both light and weighty mitzvot.
>
> Therefore, clearly it is better to permit the use of the *muktzah* because of [the principle of] the dignity of the individual, and thus to permit the deaf person to make full use of his hearing aid on Shabbat.

This is not the only reason for his permitting the use of this instrument, because, he clearly points out, that for this reason alone, it would not be simple to permit the use of *muktzah*; but again he adds, that not using the hearing aid on Shabbat would mean that "he would never be able to hear the Torah reading on Shabbatot," a very perplexing halachic situation. Clearly the elements of shame, distress and affront to his dignity, alongside an understanding of the nature of electricity, the use of batteries, the way the hearing aid should be carried (worn) in a public place[11] constitutes a very important component in his total argument.

---

11. However, there is an additional issue involved, namely whether one is allowed to wear (carry) the hearing aid in a public place – a *reshut ha-rabim*. See *Nishmat Adam*, vol. 1, pp. 128–129, note 5, who brings the relevant material on this subject. The early hearing aids had a device which was carried in one's pocket and attached with a wire to the actual aid placed in the ear (or behind it). Hence, part of the discussion is

Indeed, I would suggest, it is this issue which moved him to search out the solution through defining the other halachic factors involved.[12] This issue is further discussed in an interchange of letters between R. Yosef Eliyahu Henkin and R. Shlomo Zalman Auerbach, in R. Auerbach's *Minhat Shlomo*, vol. 2, Jerusalem, 1999, no. 18, pp. 67–70. R. Auerbach reaches much the same conclusion as R. Waldenberg, through

---

how one carries this device (discussed by the *Tzitz Eliezer*). R. Yaakov Yitzhak Weiss, in his *Minhat Yitzhak*, vol. 1, Jerusalem, 1979, no. 37, pp. 85–86, at first ruled that if the device was stuck deeply in the ear so that it was clear that it could not fall out, one could wear it in a public place, provided the deaf man really could not manage without it. But in vol. 2, Jerusalem, 1975, nos. 112–113 he recanted, taking a more stringent position after learning a responsum of R. Zvi Pesach Frank. (*Har Tzvi, Orah Hayyim*, vol. 1, no. 173, pp. 177–179). However, others permitted it. Nowadays, there are a variety of different models, connected to spectacles, for example, each of which require a separate analysis (e.g., *Shmirat Shabbat ke-Hilchatah*, by R. Neuwirth, 34 note 108, *Nishmat Avraham* ibid.). See further, R. Ovadiah Yosef, *Yabia Omer* vol. 1, 2nd edition, Jerusalem, 1986, no. 19, ad fin., p. 70a, who, as is his custom, brings a wealth of material on this subject. Tzvi Marx, ibid., p. 678, writes as follows, citing *Yair Moshe* p. 41 as follows:

Yair Moshe adds additional halachic reasons to support dispensations for the deaf regarding Shabbat: "In addition to his humiliation, there is also the great distress entailed in the loss [of fulfillment] of communal prayer, hearing the Torah read, responses to the Kaddish and Kedusha etc. Therefore, it is better to permit the carrying of that which is only prohibited rabbinicly for the sake of this great human dignity, in permitting the deaf person to carry a hearing aid."

And on p. 892, note 80, he adds in the name of the same *Yair Moshe* that:

He also cites Tos. (*Shab.* 50b, s.v. בשיל) in rejecting the proposal that the deaf can avoid humiliation by not mixing with others. This is intolerable for "there is no greater travail than this" isolation.

12. See further R. Ovadiah Yosef, *Yabia Omer*, vol. 7, Jerusalem, 1993, *Orah Hayyim* no. 38:3, p. 113, who agreed with R. Waldenberg, and cites additional authorities who rule accordingly, such as R. Yosef Eliyahu Henkin, *Edut le-Yisrael*, p. 122; R. S. Z. Auerbach, *Minhat Shlomo* no. 9. Cf. *Yabia Omer* vol. 1, *Orah Hayyim* no. 19, ad fin. Idem; *Yehaveh Daat*, vol. 2, no. 49; R. Yaakov Breisch, *Helkat Yaakov*, vol. 3, no. 186; R. Yaakov Yitzhak Weiss, *Minhat Yitzhak*, vol. 1, no. 37; vol. 2, no. 17:4. (R. Ovadiah in *Yabia Omer*, vol. 7, ibid., also refers us to those who are dubious as to this leniency, and tend to prohibition, such as R. Ovadiah Hedaya, *Yaskil Avdi*, vol. 5, no. 38:4, and vol. 6, no. 15:10.) In a different halachic context R. Joseph Messas (in his *Otzar Michtavim* vol.1, sect. 420) ruled that a deaf person getting married says the benedictions under the *huppah*, even though he does not hear what he says. Likewise if the bride is deaf and she does not hear the benedictions , they are said with the full name of God (*be-shem ve-malchut*) because of the dignity of the individual (*kevod ha-briyot*), and also so that there may be no future acts of licentiousness with the excuse or legitimation that the *kiddushin* (marriage ceremony) was not really valid (cf. *Pithei Teshuvah, Even ha-Ezer* 44:1; see also Zechariah Zarmati, *Hod Yosef Hai*, Jerusalem, 2008, p. 277).

slightly different argumentation. But here again, his final words are most significant. For on p. 70 he writes:

> And it would appear to me that it is a great mitzvah to lean towards leniency and to alleviate the great suffering of the deaf, concerning whom the Sages said "to the deaf one gives full compensation. . . ."[13]

Tzvi Marx (ibid,. p. 677) refers us to a statement in *Yair Moshe* p. 412:

> It seems to me that there is no greater [issue] of human dignity than the prevention of humiliation to the deaf in not being able to hear those addressing him. It is hard to describe the shame, embarrassment, and discomfort caused him in his social intercourse with people and in the synagogue, when he is isolated, cannot attend to what is going on, and cannot respond to what is asked of him. In this there is a greater urgency for human dignity than in other subjects spoken of already.

The preceding three cases are but a mere sampling of the numerous examples of the element that compassion can play within the area of psak, and further emphasizes the need to find humane solutions to distressing halachic issues.[14]

---

13. See also idem, vol. 1, Jerusalem, 1986, no. 9, p. 65, 67, 74. And for a contrast, see R. Yaakov Yitzhak Weiss, *Minhat Yitzhak*, vol. 1, Jerusalem, 1979, no. 37, p. 86: "And he who hears with difficulty without a hearing aid, he should not use it, because, besides the possibility (*hashash*) of the prohibition of Shabbat, there are those who say if it like hearing an echo, and so he cannot fulfil the obligation of Torah reading, the *shofar* blousing, and *megillah*-reading . . ." (unlike the position of R. Ovadiah Yosef, *Yabia Omer*, vol. 7, *Orah Hayyim* no. 18:2, p. 43). But cf. ibid., vol. 2, Jerusalem, 1975, no. 17, p. 37, and no. 113, p. 230, etc. There is considerable literature on the subject, which we cannot possibly deal with within this context.

14. Just one final example from an essay by Benjamin Lau, "The Challenge of Halakhic Innovation," *Meorot* 8, 2010, pp. 55–56 (This is a translation of his original article in Hebrew in *Akdamot* 23, 2009.) It concerns the status of the deaf-mute:

Some three hundred fifty years ago, Rabbi Jacob Hagiz, [in his *Halachot Ketanot* section 22, no. 38] considered the halachic status of the deaf mute, particularly the question of whether the Sabbath might be desecrated to save his life. In his responsum, one can discern the distress of a great man who senses that the mute is possessed of the divine image yet is of uncertain halachic status; numerous sources treat him as "not a life." His distress led him to pray that the mute not suffer a dangerous illness on the Sabbath, for people might be unwilling to desecrate the Sabbath in order to treat him. Some two hundred years later, Rabbi Israel Meir Kagan of Radin (known as the

Hafetz Hayyim) [in his *Beur Halachah* to *Orah Hayyim* 329:4] read that responsum with surprise: "I don't know what it was that caused the author of *Halakhot Qetanot* [that is, Rabbi Hagiz] to have doubts about whether to desecrate [the Sabbath, if needed to treat his illness] or kill [to defend him from murderous attack] on his behalf; and his words are hard to understand." But the *Hafets Hayyim* needn't have been surprised: during the two centuries that separated his time from that of Rabbi Hagiz, the attitude toward the disabled had undergone a revolutionary change. During the nineteenth century, the abilities of deaf mutes were discovered and schools for them began to be opened. Great Torah scholars, among them Rabbi Hayyim of Sanz, were asked about the status of the deaf in light of these changes, and their rulings effected a total change in their status. Rabbi Azriel Hildesheimer expressly addressed the issue in a responsum to the rabbis of Germany:

That was the perspective regarding deaf mutes in those times, and it is so stated in medical books of the period. Only later did they change their minds and reach the conclusion that deaf mutes have mental capacity (though it is difficult for them to express it), and that is certainly shown by experience today. And this does not at all contradict the words of our sages of blessed memory, for they were speaking of a mute for whom use of his mental capacity was impossible.

[Responsa of Rabbi Azriel Hildesheimer, part 2, *Even ha-Ezer, Miluim*, sect. 58. In that responsum, he sets forth the change in the attitude toward the deaf of society overall and discusses the difference between those who are willing to recognize a changed reality and those who entrench themselves in the understanding reflected in the Talmud.]

It should indeed be stressed that in bygone times deaf people were often deaf mutes, since they could not be taught to speak, and blind people often were not really educated, so that those physically impaired in this manner were given a different halachic status and usually treated as inferior beings. So a *heresh* is not merely a deaf person, but is coupled with the *shoteh*, the idiot. But nowadays such people can function in regular society, can communicate, study, hold positions of authority, involve themselves in sophisticated research etc. So clearly their status must be differently viewed. And this is actually what Rav Hildesheimer was saying, when he wrote:

It would appear to me that the main issue is dependent upon the degree of understanding of the deaf person, whether he is completely infirm or that he is personally normal, and is on it were a hidden treasure.

In other words, we have to unlock the treasures hidden in him, reveal them to himself and to ourselves, recognize his basic normalcy and accord him the respect and dignity he deserves.

A somewhat similar situation may be seen in the changing societal and halachic attitudes of the leprous and the mentally disturbed. As medical knowledged advanced their status changed. See, e.g., *Ephraim Shoham-Steiner, Harigim Baal Korhan: Meshugaim u-Metzoraim ba-Herra ho-Yehudit be-Uropah bi-Yemei ha-Beinayim*, Jerusalem, 2008, pass.

For further discussion of the status of the blind and the deaf vis-à-vis the declarations of certain *berachot* (e.g., "who opens [the eyes of] the blind," and "who gave intelligence to the hen" etc.), see R. Ovadia Yosef, *Halichot Olam*, vol. 1, Jerusalem, 1998, p. 51; idem *Yabia Omer*, vol. 5, *Orah Hayyim* 10:3, idem, *Yalkut Yosef*, vol. 1, p. 53), and the many sources he cites.

APPENDIX 2:
ON LENIENCY IN HALACHAH

O NE OF THE THEMES THAT RUNS LIKE A LEITMOTIF THROUGH-
out this study is the need to find halachically acceptable methodologies
to be able to reach a lenient solution when it is clear that such is
required, or in the language of *Hazal, Koah* (or *Koha*) *de-Heteira Adif,*
(*B. Berachot* 60a, *B. Beitzah* 2b, *B. Kiddushin* 60b, *B. Gittin* 41a, *B.
Hulin* 58b, *B. Niddah* 59b).

It is well-known that the Hida stated that Sefardim tend more to leniency, because they are more bound to the aspect of *hesed* (charity), while
Ashkenazim, who are more bound to the aspect of *gevurah* (might),
have a tendency towards stringency. (These are kabbalistic notions.)

A fine characteristic example of the Sefardi mode of lenient adjudication may be seen in the voluminous writings and rulings of the
late R. Ovadiah Yosef, who openly declared that it was his dominant
intent to seek solutions in this direction. And so he wrote in his characterization of R. Yaakov Shaul Elyashar, in his article in *Shevet ve-Am*
95, 1971, entitled *"Mishnato shel ha-Yisa Berachah,"* p. 97, and in his
declaration of intent when he presented himself as a candidate to be the
Chief Rabbi of Israel, (Dunash, *"Ha-Rabbanim ha-Roshiim le-Yisrael,"*
Shanah be-Shanah 1974, pp. 280–282). For there he states explicitly
that "he will aim to rule *be-koha de-heteira*, according to the line of
thought of Beit Hillel, in accordance with the rules of adjudication of
our rabbis the decisors . . ."

Indeed this halachic direction was the main thrust of my two books,
Darkah shel Halachah, Jerusalem, 2007, and *Netivot Pesikah,* Jerusalem, 2008. One of the methodologies employed, when there are issues
such as severe loss of income (see above notes 10 and 11), welfare of
the community (above note 11), tragic situations (above Appendix 1),

etc., is to have resort to minority opinions, despite the general normative principle that we follow the majority opinion. However, this methodology is well-founded in our early sources. Thus the *Mishnayot* in *Eduyot* 1:5–6 teaches us the following:

> 5. And why do they [the Masters of the *Mishnah*] record the opinion of the individual against that of the majority, whereas the halachah [ruling] may only be according to the opinion of the majority? That, if a court approves the opinion of the individual, it may rely upon him . . .
>
> 6. R. Yehudah said: If so, why do they record the opinion of the individual against that of the majority when it does not prevail? That, if one shall say [i.e., at a later date], "I have received such a tradition," another may answer, "Thou did not hear it [only] as the opinion of such a one."

To this we should add the text found in the Tosefta *Eduyot* 1:4, where we read:

> The halachah is always in accordance with the opinion (*divrei*) of the majority; the opinion of the individual as opposed to that of the majority is only cited to be rejected. R. Yehudah says: The opinion of the individual as opposed to that of the majority is cited lest there be an hour of need, and they can rely upon it. The rabbis said: The opinion of the individual as opposed to that of the majority is cited so that when one says 'it is pure' and the other says 'it is impure,' this says 'it is impure in accordance with the view of R. Eliezer,' they reply to him, 'the ruling is in accordance with the tradition of R. Eliezer.'

The *Mishnah* rules that the minority view can be used by a more senior *beit din*, while the Tosefta says that it can be used to make changes in the law, when there is an hour of need.[1]

---

1. The *Mishnah* text has been the source of considerable discussion in recent times. See, e.g., Y. Blidstein, *Samhut u-Meri be-Hilchot ha-Rambam: Perush Nirhav le-Hilchot Mumrim* (chapter 1–4), Tel-Aviv, 2002, pp. 83–84; K. Albeck, *Mavo la-Mishnah*, Jerusalem, 1999, *Nezikin*, pp. 475–476; Y.M. Epstein, *Aruch ha-Shulhan be-Atid*, Jerusalem, 1969. Hilchot Mumrim 5:5; M. Fisch, "*Parshanut Dehukah ve-Textim Mehaivim: Ha-Okimta ha-Amorait ve-ha-Filosopfiah shel ha-Talmud*," apud *Iyyunim Hadashim be-Filosofiah shel ha-Halachah*, eds. A. Ravitzky, A. Rosenak, Jerusalem, 2008, p. 265; M. Rorth, *Orthodoxiah Humanit: Mahshevet ha-Halachah Shel ha-*

However, let us go back to the classical commentators to the *Mishnah*, such as R. Yisrael Lifschitz, who in his *Tiferet Yisrael* ad loc., explains:

> It should seem to me that he wishes to say that one can rely on the individual opinion at times of need, as it is stated, "R. Shimon is worthy to be relied upon in times of need,"[2] (*B. Gittin* 19a, *B. Berachot* 9a, *B. Shabbat* 45a, *B. Nidah* 6a, 9b).

Similarly, R. Shlomo ha-Adani, in his *Melechet Shlomo* ad loc., writes:

> For were it not for the opinion of the individual it would be impossible to annul the opinion of the majority, even in times of need . . . But if there

---

Rav Professor Eliezer Berkovitz, Tel-Aviv, 2013, pp. 41–54, referring to Berkovitz's *Ha-Halachah Kochah ve-Tafkidah*, Jerusalem, 1981, pass., and other of his writings.

2. On the question when can one rely on a single opinion (*data yahid*) in times of need (*shaat ha-dehak*), whether also in cases of biblical authority or merely in those of rabbinic authority, see the penetrating study of R. Yitzhak Shilat, entitled "*Semichah al Daat Yahid be-Shaat ha-Dehak* (*Le-Birur Mahloket ha-Rayah ve-ha-Hazon Ish*," apud *Birurim be-Hilchot ha-Rayah*, eds. M. Tzvi Neriah, A. Stern, N. Gotel, Jerusalem, 1992, pp. 451–476. The subject of his analysis is the conflict between the view of Rav Kook, in his *Shabbat ha-Aretz* (in *Tosefet Shabbat*), vol. 1, introduction, Jerusalem, 1903, chapter 10, pp. 140–144, and that of the Hazon Ish, in vol. *Zeraim*, Bnei Brak, 1873, Sheviit sect. 23, pp. 292–296 (*entitled Hanhagot Issur ve-Heter*) and in *Yoreh Deah*, sect. 150, 180a–181a. See also the most recent discussion by R. Micah Segalman, "The Status of Minority Opinions in Halacha," *Journal of Halacha and Contemporary Society* 71, 2016, pp. 60–81.

The basic source is the responsum of the Rashba no. 253, cited by R. Akiva Eiger, sect. 60; see also R. Ovadiah Yosef, *Halichot Olam*, vol. 5, p. 162.

The rationale behind this principle would seem to be that since the minority view may be correct, and according to some is probably correct, and the majority opinion merely a *humra*, in such circumstances one should take the lenient path. This indeed is the rationale for leniency in the case of *hefsed merubeh*, as we find in the Rema's introduction to his *Torat ha-Hata*, (see *Hilchot Olam*, vol. 6, p. 70, and ibid., vol. 7, p. 164).

And the Rema's explanation is also to be found in the *Pri Megadim, Klalim be-Horaah* 6, the *Aruch ha-Shulhan, Yoreh Deah* 242:66; *Ralbah, Klalim* at the end of his *Get Pashut* 6, etc.

Here it is worth citing what R. Moshe Feinstein wrote in his *Igrot Moshe, Yoreh Deah*, vol. 1, New York, 1960, no. 101, p. 186:

But one should not be haughty in making a decision, and refrain where possible. But in a case of great need or human suffering such as this case we (even we) are certainly obligated to give a ruling if we can find any means to be lenient, and it is prohibited for us to decide to be among the modest and so cause suffering to a daughter of Israel.

was a difference of opinion on a certain issue, then a different court, even of lesser status, can rely on the minojrity view . . .

He adds further proof for this assertion from a statement by R. Saadia Gaon to *B. Ketubot* 93a (cited in *Otzar ha-Geonim*, by B.M. Lewin, Jerusalem, 1939, p. 310, no. 721). There is a difference of opinion as to whether this methodology applies also to biblical laws or merely to rulings of rabbinic status, the Siftei Cohen, Shach (Shabtai ben Meir ha-Cohen, 1621–1661) (to *Yoreh Deah* 242 ad fin.) taking the former position, and the *Turei Zahav* by R. David ha-Levi Segal (1586–1667), (*Yoreh Deah* 293) the latter.

R. Menasheh of Ilya (Lithuania 1767–1831) clarified the *Eduyot* statement as follows:

> We thus learn that a court may rely on some individual and, at its discretion, change a law from the one that had bound their ancestors . . . (*Alfei Menasheh*, vol. 1, Jerusalem, 1979, p. 44).

This too is the view of the Raavad (as against that of the Rambam), and also of Tosafot to *Megilah* 5b, as explicated by R. Moshe Tzvi Neriah, in his article "*Yahid ve-Rabim*" *Or Hamizrach* VIII, 1961, (3/33), pp. 9–11.

Indeed, it could well be that both dissenting views are actually correct. So we read in *B. Eruvin* 13b and *B. Gittin* 6b that:

> R. Abba stated in the name of Samuel: For three years there was a dispute between Beit Shamai and Beit Hillel, with these claiming "the halachah is as we say," then a heavenly voice declaired, "These and these are the words of the living God, but the halachah follows the rulings of Beit Hillel . . ."

And see Ritba to *Eruvin* ibid. ed. M. Goldstein, Jerusalem, 1974, p. 107, who writes as follows:

> They asked the Rabbis of France, of blessed memory: "How is it possible that both [opinions] be the words of the Living God, when they forbid and they permit?" And they replied that when Moses went up to the heavens to receive the Torah, they [the angels] showed him for every

single detail forty-nine facets to forbid and forty-nine facets to permit. And he questioned the Holy One blessed be He concerning this. And He said that it would be given to the Sages of Israel in each generation [to make a determination], and that determination would be according to their ruling. And this is correct according to the homily, but in truth there is a secret [explanation], (i.e., an isoteric one).

(See Moshe Halbertal's analysis in *People of the Book: Canon, Meaning, and Authority*, Cambridge, Mass. and London, 1997, pp. 63–72, on what he calls "The Constitutive View".)

And compare *Midrash* Psalms 12:4, ed. Buber, pp. 107–108:

> Said R. Yannai: The Torah was not given "cut and dried" (*hatichin*), but for each word that God gave to Moses He gave forty-nine facets for [declaring] purity and forty-nine for impurity. Said Moses before Him, "Master of the Universe, how then will we be able to clarify the issues?" He replied to Him, "We follow the majority; if the majority declare impurity, it is impure, if purity, it is pure."

(This text derives itself from *Y. Sanhedrin* 4:2, 22a. See further *B. Eruvin* 6b. See further R. Hayyim Vital, *Shaar ha-Kavanot: Inyanei Tefilin, Derush* 6, 11a, ed. Yeshivat-ha-Mekubalim, Jerusalem n.d. but c. 2005, vol. 1, p. 199.)

And, perhaps similarly, we read in *B. Hagigah* 3b:

> "The masters of the assemblies" (Ecclesiastes 12:11) – these are the scholars who gather together in assemblies and study Torah, some ruling pure and other ruling impure, some prohibiting and others permitting, some rejecting and others accepting. Were one to say, "How, then, can I learn Torah from now on?" The Scripture says, "they are given from our Shepherd" (Ecclesiastes 12:11). "One God gave them, and Leader attends them."[3]

---

3. See the parallel in *Tosefta Sotah* 7:12, ed. S. Lieberman, New York, 1973, p. 195; idem, *Tosefta ki-feshutah*, vol. 8, New York, 1973, p. 681. There have been varying interpretations of this text as to how we should understand it, and what degree of pluralism it possibly reflects. See. S. Naeh, "*Aseh Libcha Hadrei Hadarin*" apud *Mehuyavut Ychudit Mehudeshet*, eds. A. Sagi and Tzvi Zohar, Tel-Aviv, 2001, pp. 851–878, questioning D. Hartman, *A Heart of Many Rooms: Celebrating the Many Voices of*

And R. Menahem Recanati, in his commentary on the verse "And God spoke all these words saying" (Exodus 20:1), writes as follows:

The rabbis said in *B. Hagigah* 3b: "[The words of the wise are as goads and as nails fastened] by the masters of the assemblies . . ." (Ecclesiastes 12:11) – these are the learned Sages; "assemblies assemblies," they who are studying Torah; these declare pure and these declare impure, these declare kosher and these declare not kosher, these permit and these forbid. Should a person say: How can I now learn [i.e., what is correct]? For this we learn "And God spoke all these words saying" (Exodus ibid.) – they all have one father, all were given by one Master, they were spoken by the Lord of all acts. And they said: R. Meir had one pupil who could prove the insect to be pure in forty-nine ways, (*B. Eruvin* 13b). [And, of course, insects, vermin, are impure.] And all this is because the words spoken [by God] were [in] "a great voice which did not end" (Deuteronomy 5:19) – [a voice] which had all the facets which change and turn over from impure to pure, to forbidding and permitting, to not kosher and to kosher. Because we cannot possibly believe that that voice lacks anything. And therefore in the greatness of the voice were things that could turn in all directions. And each of the Sages received his own ["voice"], for

---

Judaism, Woodstock, 1999. See most recently David Brezis, *Bein Kanaut le-Hesed: Megamot Anti-Karaiot be-Mahshevet Hazal*, Ramat-Gan, 2015, pp. 13–14, note 10.

See on this whole subject the comprehensive and penetrating analytical study of Avi Sagi, in his *The Open Canon: On the Meaning of Halakhic Discourse*, New York, 2007, pass.; Eliezer Berkovitz, *Not in Heaven: The Nature and Function of Halakha*, New York, 1983, pp. 50–53. See further Yitzhak Yosef, *Maarechet ha-Shulhan*, vol. 2, Jerusalem 2010, on the rationale for ruling according to a minority opinion where there is great loss (*hefsed merubeh*) or in special circumstances (*shaat ha-dehak*) and ibid., p. 642, as to whether the rulings in the *Shulhan Aruch* are final and certain or remain in the area of uncertainty – *mi-koah safek* (citing as examples, Hayyim David Hazan, *Responsa Nediv Lev*, Salonica-Jerusalem 1862–1866, *Hoshen Mishpat*, sect. 50, and his father Rephael Yosef Hazan, in his *Hikrei Lev* vol.3, Salonica, 1787, *Yoreh Deah*, sect. 127, and others). See further Hanina Ben Menahem, *Judicial Deviation in Talmudic Law: Governed by Men, not by Rules*, London Paris etc. 1991, pp. 158–165, on using minority views, and pp. 173–182, on *horaat shah*. This problematic notion was also discussed in depth by R. Arieh Leib Heller (1745-1812) in his magisterial *Ketzot ha-Hoshen*, first published in Lvov, 1888–1896, in the introduction. Likewise, R. Moshe Feinstein, in his *Igrot Moshe, Orah Hayyim*, vol. 1, in the introduction, grapples with this issue, distinguishing between "*ha-emet le-horaah*," truth as to adjudication and "*emet mamash*" or "*ha-emet klapei shemaia*" – "the real truth" or "the truth as it is in heaven." Here we cannot examine these views in detail.

not only the prophets received from Mount Sinai, but all Sages in every generation, each of them receives his own [message]. And this is what the verse (ibid.) tells us, "these words the Lord spoke unto *all your assembly* [in the mount out of the midst of the fire, of the cloud, and of the thick darkness." And in relation to this it is stated that "Both these and these are the words of the living God." For if one of them was mistaken, they would not have made this statement. And these are the seventy facets that the Torah has, which turn to all sides, for that "voice" split up into seventy branches, as we have explained in our commentary to Psalms. Our Sages, of blessed memory taught that God gives to a great host of exponents the "word" which splits up into seven times seven voices, i.e., seventy tongues. And R. Yehoshua ha Levi explained it, like a man who strikes the anvil and numerous sparks fly out in all directions. So too the great host of exponents. The hammer is but one single thing, and it splits up a stone [which it [smites] into many fragments. So too is "the voice" in which the Torah was given. And if you think about it, this clears up all the uncertainties. (My emphasis – D.S.)

R. Shlomo Luria, Maharshal, in his introduction to his *Yam Shel Shlomo*, formulates this notion as follows:

Everything that is found in the words of the Sages of the Torah, from the time of Moses up to the present day, these are the Sages concerning whom is it said, "The Words of the wise are as goads" (Ecclesiastes 12:11) – they were all given by one shepherd. (*B. Hagigah* 3b). And be not surprised by the various differences of opinion, which are so very distant one from the other, if these opinions are directed to heaven . . . But all are the words of the living God, as though each one of them received [his tradition] from God and from Moses, even though what came out of Moses' mouth could never be two opposite statements on one single issue. And the kabbalists explained that all souls were present at Sinai and received [the words] through forty-nine channels (*tzinorot*), seven times seven purified (cf. Psalms 12:7). These are the voices (or sounds) which they heard and saw. [cf. Exodus 20:18, "And all the people saw the thunderings and the lightenings . . ."] These are the opinions that were transferred through the channels (or conduits), each one seeing through his channel in according with his own understanding. So each one receives in accordance with the strength of his soul, . . . such that one reaches one conclusion, declaring impure, and the other another one, declaring pure . . . *and all are true.* And you may understand this. And for this reason the Torah was given to the Sages inserted in each and every generation, each according to the source of his understanding . . . and in accordance with that which is shown to them from the heavens. (My emphasis – D.S.)

This seems to express the view of continued revelation, and this indeed is the view of R. Moshe Alsheich in his commentary to Proverbs 21:17. There, he has an extended discussion on what clearly for him was a very vexing provocative question, as to how two conflicting views can both be correct. His solution is also based on his Kabbalistic views. (See below.) (See also Abraham J. Heschel, *Prophetic Inspiration of the Prophets: Maimonides and other Mediaeval Authorities*, Hoboken, N.J., 1996.)

And R. Moshe Feinstein, in his *Igrot Moshe, Yoreh Deah* 3:92, writes similarly:

Our Sages describe the opposing views of halachic debate as both being "the words of the living G-d." This means that Torah study of the diverse views of Sages inherently does not contain something which is not true. Thus the opposing views of Beit Shammai and Beit Hillel are both true. This rule applies also to the disputes of R. Eliezer and all the *Tannaim* and *Amoraim*. All of them were given from One Shepherd. Thus it was not untrue when the Heavenly *Bat Kol* announced that the halachah was in accord with R. Eliezer. His words were inherently true – even though in this world we decide practical halachah on the basis of majority decision. Because of the inherent truth of all views of our sages, we say the blessing "Who gave to us the Torah of truth" even if we are only learning the views that have been rejected from practical halachah such as those of Beit Shammai or minority opinions.

And ibid. introduction to *Orah Hayyim*:

It is correct and obligatory for the sages of the latter generations to decide halachah – even if they are not qualified according to the standards of the sages of the *Gemara*. Therefore there is definitely a concern that their halachic determinations are not in accord with the view of Heaven. However in truth we are guided by the principle that Torah is not in

Heaven. Rather it is determined according to what appears correct to the rabbi after proper study of the issue to clarify the halachah according to the Talmud, and the writings of *poskim*. He is to use his full abilities to seriously deliberate with fear of Heaven – in order to determine what appears to be the correct halachah. Such a *psak* is viewed as true and he is obligated to issue his conclusion. This obligation exists even if in fact his ruling is contrary to the halachah in Heaven. His ruling is also considered the "word of the living G-d" as long as he is convinced he is correct and it is internally consistent. He will receive reward for his rulings even if the truth is not in accord with his position. Proof for this is found in *B. Shabbat* 130a: A certain city in Israel that followed the halachah according to R. Eliezer – even though this was not the accepted halachah – received great reward in terms of long life . . . Thus, the ruling which a rabbi is obligated to teach and receive reward for it, is that which he decides after studying the issue with his full ability. This obligation and the receiving of reward exists even if the ruling is not in accord with the truth. This is the nature of all disputes of the *Rishonim* and *Ahronim* concerning what is permitted and what is prohibited. As long as a universal ruling has not been determined – each rabbi can make decisions for his followers according to that which he thinks is correct – even though the objective halachah is only in accordance with one of them. Both will also receive reward for their rulings. Because of this we find much dispute also in the most severe prohibitions – with variations between places that rule like the Rambam and *Beit Yosef* and those that rule like Tosafot and the Rema. Both of the opposing views are "the words of the living God, even though the actual truth as understood by Heaven, is only like one of them."

This almost mystical view is echoed in a statement by the *Shlah ha-Kadosh* (*Toldot ha-Adam: Beit Hochmah*, sect. 8):

How do we understand the concept that all the words of our sages are the words of the living God? We read in *Eruvin* 13b: For three and a half years Beit Shammai and Beit Hillel argued concerning whose views were actually halachah. A *Bat Kol* announced from Heaven that both views were the worlds of the living G-d but the halachah was in accord with Beit Hillel. The Ritba writes in the name of the rabbis of France that the halachah was given in 49 different ways of prohibition and 49 different ways of permission – it was left up to the rabbis of each generation to determine what was the correct halachah for their generation. There is a problem with this explanation. Only when both sides can be right is it reasonable to say, "both are the words of the living God." For example, in B. *Gittin* 6b, concerning the concubine of Givah, the views are not mutually exclusive and both could be correct. However in a dispute where one side says it is prohibited and the other side says it is permitted – then surely both cannot be correct! Therefore, if we chose one side, how can we say about the rejected view that it is "the word of the living G-d"? The rational mind is simply not satisfied with the words of the French rabbis. In fact, the resolution of this problem is dependent – as the Ritba alluded – upon kabbalistic reasoning and secrets . . . The explanation of this issue, in my humble opinion, is found in B. *Bava Metzia* 59b concerning the dispute between R. Eliezer and R. Yehoshua whether Heaven can decide the halachah. I already have explained that every single mitzvah has a source in Heaven. According to one's attachment in Heaven, that is how the mitzvah manifests itself in the physical world. The carrying out of the actual mitzvah is directly related to the nature of the attachment. However, not everyone has the same level of attachment. Therefore, each rabbi will decide the halachah based upon his personal attachment and consequently they will not necessarily agree. The final halachah is decided by the majority which indicates the most representative means of attachment to Heaven . . . This is so even though a particular individual might have a much higher type of attachment in Heaven. The halachah is determined by what is the most appropriate way that the mitzvah performed physically for the majority. Thus, we can see why two mutually opposing views can both be the "words of the living G-d." For example, in the dispute concerning *tefilin* between Rashi and Rabbenu Tam, each holds that the *tefilin* of the other is invalid. Would you think that one side never fulfilled the mitzvah of *tefilin* during his entire life?! The answer is that each side had a unique attachment to Heaven which determined their ruling about *tefilin*. However, the final halachah is determined by the majority . . .

Indeed, throughout the generations scholars struggled with the concept of multiple truths – *"eilu ve-eilu"*, seeking kabbalistic explanations, or finally admitting that such is beyond human comprehension. This R. Tzadok ha-Cohen of Lublin, in his *Dover Tzedek*, Pietrokov, 1911, p. 4, writes:

The expression *eilu ve-eilu* refers to the fact that . . . all the aspects and parts are in fact a unity, and they all are the words of the living G-d. However, this concept is truly beyond rational comprehension. How is it possible that complete opposites are both true. We know that it is impossible that truth is anything other than one. How can diverse and conflicting things all be a unity? . . . Therefore, this concept of *eilu ve-eilu* is beyond the material intellect of man. That is also why there is no absolutely clear halachah in the Oral Law that is beyond dispute – except for *halachah le-Moshe* which is not disputed, as the Rambam states . . .

And similarly in R. Abdallah Somech's *Zivhei Tzedek*, Bagdad, 1813– 1829, *Yoreah Deah*, sect. 26:

Question: How could the conflicting opinions of our sages – where one asserts that something is prohibited and another claims that it is permitted – all be given to Moshe on Mount Sinai? Answer: The answer to this question is extreme deep and we are not able to answer it properly. Even the *Rishonim* did not have a full response to it. . . .

He then quotes the Ritba (cited above), the Shlach, the Hida, etc. finally admitting that:

Even the Ritba indicated that the genuine answer is from the mysteries of *Kabbalah*. Therefore, the bottom line is that this question is beyond our ability to understand. We see the many answers that were to give a little comfort – especially to the masses. Thus, they will have to suffice because the real answer is found in Kabbalah which is not appropriate for either of us.

Each of these authorities seeks to explain how two contradictory views can, in a sense, both be correct. And we for our part can hardly know which is the "more correct." For us, then, we are left with a situation of continued uncertainty – *Safek*.

And moving into modern times R. Yitzhak Hutner, in his *Pahad Yitzhak: Quntras Ve-Zot Hanukah*, Brooklyn 5624 (1964), p. 18, wrote as follows:

Our perception of the power of *Torah she-be'al Peh* as revealed through disagreements is greater than when there is agreement. For within the principle that "these and those are the Word of the Living G-d" is included the essential principle that even the *shittah* that is rejected as practical halachah is nevertheless a Torah view, when it is expressed according to the norms of the discourse of *Torah she-be'al Peh*. This is because the Torah was given by the *da'at* of the Sages of the Torah (as enunciated by the Ramban). And if they then vote and decide according to the rejected view, the halachah then changes in a true sense (*aliba' de-emet*) . . . The result is that in disagreement the power of *Torah she-be'al Peh* is revealed to a greater extent than by [the Sages'] agreement. The "war of Torah" (*milhamtah shel Torah* – Torah debate) is thus not merely one mode of *divrei Torah* among others, but rather "the war of Torah" is a positive creation of new Torah values, whose like is not to be found in ordinary words of Torah [where there is no disagreement].

This is the opinion of R. Yaakov Hagiz (1620–1674) in his *Halachot Ketanot*, Jerusalem, 1974, part 1, no. 146 (p. 18), where he was asked if a controversy between the decisors is regarded as a *safek* (uncertainty), and he replies in the affirmative, (or in his formulation, "so it seems most likely").

Furthermore, it is a generally accepted view that even though we have accepted the rulings of Maran, R. Yosef Karo, this is not because we are certain that his views are correct (*ain zeh mi-torat vadai*), but only as a pragmatic means to get out of the area of uncertainty (*mi-torat safek*).So we learn from *Shut Nediv Lev*, by R. Hayyim David Hazan, Saloniki-Jerusalem, 1862–1866, vol. 2, sect. 63. Likewise in *Rav Poalim*, by R. Yosef Hayyim, Jerusalem, 1901–1913, vol. 4, *Yoreh Deah*, sect. 4 ad fin.; *Penei Yitzhak*, by R. Yitzhak Abulafia, Aram Tzovah, Livorno, Izmir, 1871–1888, vol. 1, *Yoreh Deah*, sect. 9, 13; vol. 2, 28c, vol. 5, 162d, etc. See R. Ovadiah Yosef, *Halichot Olam*, vol. 7, Jerusalem, 2002, p. 32, who cited additional sources.

And again, ibid., p. 259, R. Yosef writes:

> But it seems . . . that in a difference of opinions among the *poskim*, the [ruling] never leaves the area of uncertainty (*safek*) even though the Torah ruled to follow the majority, this is only in certain cases – here he

lists them – but this is not the case in a *mahloket poskim*, which always remains within the area of uncertainty . . .

See continuation when he brings numerous sources, early and late to prove his contention. R. Asher Weiss, in his *Minhat Asher*, vol. 2, Jerusalem, 2014, p. 171 expresses much the same opinion, namely that to follow the majority is not clearly a biblical injunction, (referring to B. *Eruvin* 46a).

We find a similar *sevarah* (reasoning) much earlier in the *Shitah Mekubetzet* to *Baba Metzia* 6b, in the name of Rosh that even the view of a majority remains a *safek*, but that the Torah ruled that we should follow such an opinion (cited by R. Shlomo Kluger, in his *U-Bacharta ba-Hayyim*, Budapest, 1934, sect. 12, and discussed by R. Ovadia Yosef in *Yabia Omer*, vol. 10, no. 60:3, p. 198; likewise by my sainted grandfather, R. David Sperber, in his *Afrakasta de-Anya*, vol. 1, Brooklyn, N.Y., 2002, no. 91, pp. 237–239). However, see *Pri Megadim* to *Yoreh Deah* 100, sect. 37, who calls this principle into doubt. And see, in brief, Moshe Avigdor Haikin, *Klalei ha-Poskim*, London, 1923, p. 70:10.[4]

---

4. Indeed, the whole notion of the majority, *rov*, is by no means clear and is exceeding by complex. See *Hazon Ish* to *Kilaim* 1:1.

Furthermore, see R. Yaakov Emden (called Yavetz), in his *Sheilat Yavetz*, vol. 1, Lemberg, 1884, no.157, 70a, who wrote as follows:

But one should ponder (i.e., question) the accepted view that the latter-day *poskim* accept to follow the majority of opinions, for who assembled together [all these people], and who counted them, to make sure that one was not absent, and who examined all the books of the *poskim* that should be considered too and who counted them, and who is he that can estimate and evaluate what constitutes the majority in number and structure (*minyan* and *binyan*), whose opinion is more weighty. These are the considerations that we find so difficult.

See further, *Sefer ha-Hinuch, Mitzvah* 78, ed. Ahavat Shalom, vol. 1, Jerusalem, 1998, pp. 126–127 (with the notes of R. David Pipano), and most recently, Yaakov Yosef Meischlas, *Meishiv ke-Halachah*, Brooklyn, 2008, pp. 100–101, note 48.

However, one should point out that here we are dealing with a statistical *rov* (*ruba de-leita kaman*). But a factual majority, *ruba de-ita kaman*, establishes a factual halachic presumption, halachic certainty. *Hazakah*, on the other hand, remains within the area of uncertainty, and from a pragmatic point of view establishes a continuation of a given status. (See R. Elhanan Wasserman *Kovetz Shiurim Ketubot* no. 74, ibid., vol. 2, *Kovetz Biurim* to *Shev Shemateta* no.4:5, 13.)

An interesting parallel is found in the discussion on the part of the *Aharonim* on the subject of testimony. The *Yad ha-Melech*, by R. Eliyahu Palomba, Salonica 1804, to the Rambam *Hilchot Yesodeh ha-Torah* 7:7 raises the very basic question: why do we believe the testimony of witnesses, even to the extent that we execute people of the

And the great early twentieth century authority, R. (Avraham Yitzhak ha-Cohen) Kook (1865–1935), in his *Shabbat ha-Aretz*, Jerusalem, 1985, p. 42, writes as follows:

> We find that even when a number of *Mishnayot* rule stringently and this was the practice for many generations, nonetheless, when [some rabbis] relied upon an individual view to rule leniently, [other] rabbis did not object ... Even when they had always ruled stringently in accordance with the view of the majority, when later, in times of need and necessity for the sake of the community, they ruled on a rejected view, the rabbis leveled no objections.

Indeed, there are times and situations when it is encumbent upon us to resort to minority opinions. When the gravity of the situation demands it great authorities made lenient decisions based on such minority positions. This is especially the situation in the case of the so-called "enchained woman" (*agunah*), a woman whose husband has vanished and is not known to be dead, so that she cannot be divorced, but neither can she remarry. This was well summed up in a passage by the great 16th century Rabbi, Avraham ha-Levi, who lived in Egypt, in his response *Ginat Veradim, Even ha-Ezer* Part 3, sect. 20 (Jerusalem, 1951) (cited above note 53).

> If we were to examine the opinions of the sages of ancient times – in order to fulfill what they obligate us to do and as we do in all other areas of law – and follow the majority rule so that there would never be any challenges to our decisions, then there would never be freedom for the *agunah* from any rabbinic teacher. And it is our fault that there are terrible situations which result in the daughters of our father Abraham remaining grass widows with living husbands. And there is none to be gracious or kind to them, and they are left starving and thirsty and desti-

---

basis of their statements? Surely it is clear that a certain percentage of individuals do not tell the truth? In other words how can we execute people when we cannot be sure of the honesty of the testimony? From which he concludes that the court's decision is not because the judges are convinced of the absolute truth of the evidence, but only because the Torah determined that the court accept the testimony and rule accordingly. Or to put it differently, the acceptance of the testimony is Torah-directed a pragmatic decision, rather than one based on certainty.

tute. And we shall also be concerned lest they follow paths of immorality: great poverty can lead one to such a path. Moreover, these women are young and virile (and will not be able to wait with restraint.) Yet, if we want to follow the lenient decisions, the seriousness of the issue holds us back. Therefore, we have no alternative but to follow the path that was firmly established by our earliest rabbis – to follow the path of straight thinking even if it is against the consensus of the *gedolim* from whose waters we drink, as it is written in the Talmud, "It is sufficient to rely on (the minority opinion) of Rabbi X, even though it is not the accepted halachah." And it has already been stated at the end of B. *Yevamot* 122a, "We allow a woman to marry on the authority of an echo," i.e., that they were lenient with her because of her *iggun* [enchainment].

Admittedly, this is a somewhat special halachic category; but we may learn from it that in cases of what may be regarded as a form of necessity, we do have recourse to minority opinions. Indeed, there are numerous examples in rabbinic literature of recourse to the use of minority opinions, such, for example, R. Moshe Feinstein, *Igrot Moshe, Orah Hayyim* 4, sect. 66, idem, *Orah Hayyim* 2, sect. 18.

In view of the above it becomes clear that one is permitted to take a minority position in *psak*. This is evident in the writings of the great Baghdadi *posek*, R. Yosef Hayyim (author of the famous *Ben Ish Hai*) in his introduction to his major responsa *Shut Rav Poalim*, vol. 1, Jerusalem, 2001. For there, when analyzing the different kinds of responsers (*meshivim*), he writes:

> There is he who is nimble and effective in knocking on the doors of the books of all the responsers, early and late ones, and even the latest, minor and major up to our times, even of authors who are still alive, and his intention is to search in order to see and understand the opinion of each and every scholar who was involved in the specific issue, and this is certainly an admirable approach. For one thing, because, if he finds an author who examined the issue in depth, and he agrees with his conclusion, then his ruling to the question posed before him and for which he has to give a practical solution, will not be his alone, but also on the basis of this other opinion, and he will not be a "lone judge" (referring to the first *Mishnah* in *Sanhedrin*, and cf. B. *Sanhedrin* 5a).

Clearly then, the *posek* who has examined numerous sources may legitimately rule in accordance with his own conclusions (see below Appendix 4 and see *Shut ha-Rashba*, vol. 1, no. 253, Jerusalem, 1997, p. 108), but it is preferable that he couples his adjudication with yet another opinion, even if this be a minority position.

In my extensive study of this issue, in *Darkah shel Halachah*, I brought a variety of additional sources to support this contention.[5] Furthermore, in my *Netivot Pesikah*, Jerusalem, 2008, pp. 32–35,[6] I discussed the status of sources discovered more recently which may have the effect of changing accepted halachic practice, and the degree of legitimacy to making use of them in order to bring about such change.[7]

---

5. And see also ibid., pp. 104–109. And here we may add the following references: R. Ovadiah Yosef, *Yabia Omer*, vol. 10, Jerusalem, 2004, *Yoreh Deah*, sect. 43; R. Meir Sigron, *Or Torah* 44/2 (532), 2012, pp. 153–156; Meiri to *Sanhedrin* 32b, p. 144, that one should always try to find compromise and rule mercifully, i.e., leniently; Y. Porat, in *Or ha-Mizrach* 12/1, 540, 1963, p. 6, 8, on R. Naftali Tzvi Berlin's (Netziv) position on relying on alternative positions which are more lenient, etc.

6. And see also my discussion in my *Legitimacy and Necessity: Scientific Disciplines and the Learning of Talmud*, Jerusalem, 2006, pp. 23–25, and also pp. 60–63. On the Rema's use of minority opinions, see Asher Ziv, *Rabbenu Moshe Isserles (Rema)*, New York, 1972, pp. 109–110.

7. Here I may add that the standard rule is that when there is a difference of opinion between an earlier and a later authority, we usually follow the later one, for even though he may be a lesser scholar, he is, as it were, a dwarf on the shoulders of a giant, who has a broader horizon. (On this phrase, see Shmuel Ashkenazi, *Alfa Beta Kadmaita de-Shmuel Zeira*, Jerusalem, 2000, pp. 322–327.) The Meiri was intimately acquainted with the Rambam's writings, but still took an independent position. (See on this principle of *Halachah ke-Batrai*, in my *Darkah shel Halachah*, Jerusalem, 2007, p. 9, and most recently the remarks of R. Yaakov Hayyim Sofer, in *Or Israel* 17/1 (63), 2011, pp. 240–242, where he also brings a variety of sources proving that one follows the later authority, even when he is single opinion against many. He also draws the parameters within which this rule may be applied.) See below pp. 306–307 note 4.

On the very important issue of how we act or react when discovering new sources (or readings) that were unknown to earlier *poskim* and might change the halachah, I wrote extensively in my *Legitimacy and Necessity: Scientific Disciplines and the Learning of Talmud*, Jerusalem, 2006, pp. 22–25, 58–63, and again in my *Netivot Pesikah*, Jerusalem, 2008, pp. 31–41. We showed there that the Hazon Ish believed that "new data" cannot change established halachah. (See S. Leiman, *Tradition* 19, 1981, pp. 301–310, for a full discussion of the Hazon Ish's view see further S.Z. Havlin, *Ha-Maayan* 8:2, 1968, pp. 35–37; M. Bleich, *Tradition* 27, 1993, pp. 22–55; Y. Tzvi Halevi Lehrer, *Tzefunot* 16, 1992, pp. 68–73; S. Spiegel, *Amudim be-Toldot ha-Sefer ha-Ivri: Hagahot u-Megihim* , Ramat-Gan, 1993, pp. 495, 508–513, and finally, Benjamin Brown, *Ha-Hazon Ish*, Jerusalem, 2001, pp. 392–395.)

To the above we should now add the following related issue, namely

---

In his opinion information that was not known to the *Beit Yosef*, for instance, such as that found in the Meiri, was hidden from him by divine providence, so that the halachah be crystallized as is was. The later discovery of the Meiri cannot change that crystallized halachah of the *Beit Yosef*.

A similar view is voiced by R. Aharon David Deitsch (cited in the introduction to Y.N. Stern's edition of *Hiddushei ha-Hatam Sofer al Sugyot ve-Perek Shevuat ha-Edut*, 1929) in the name of the Hatam Sofer as follows:

I heard from our good teacher the author of the Hatam Sofer *zt"l*, who said of himself that when a question comes before him, he reads the question before he examines it in depth, for he has to concentrate his thought so that he only wishes to respond to his questioner, [reading] the truth before Him that gives the Torah, be He blessed. And afterwards, that which occurs to him to reply, he regards as the truth. [And] even if later the questioner raises a difficulty from a *Gemara* or the *poskim*, one that had he remembered at the time of writing [his response], he would have changed his ruling, and would not have bothered to justify his [earlier] opinion and ruling; even so, *since the Holy One blessed be He in the first instance hid this [data] from him*, and he was certain of himself that he had searched for the truth, *he would put his mind to justifying his first opinion and legitimate it through a deep analysis.* (My emphasis – D.S.)

See Maoz Kahana's M.A. thesis, Hebrew University Jerusalem, 2004, p. 107, where he brings further evidence that this indeed was the Hatam Sofer's position, referring us to his responsum, *Even ha-Ezer* vol. 2, no. 102, from 1809 (which in turn refers to R. Yonatan Eibeschutz's *Urim ve-Tumim*, Jerusalem, 1977, sect. 125).

However, we showed that the Rema to *Hoshen Mishpat* 25:2, wrote:

But if at times there is a responsum of a Gaon which was not mentioned in the books, and we find them (later on) differing from him, we do not have to follow the later authorities, because it is possible that they did not know the view of the Gaon, and had they known it they would have withdrawn their view (*Maharik*, sect.94).

So too he writes in his responsum no. 19 (ed. A. Ziv, Jerusalem, 1971, p. 128) concerning *minhagim* (customs):

But in a place where something was innovated and this was unknown to the earlier authorities . . . it is certainly the case that it is permitted to enact new enactments . . . for we can presume that the early authorities would not have make their enactment in such a situation.

This is indeed also formulated by the *Shach* (in his *Kitzur be-Hanhagot Issur ve-Heteir*, sect. 8) who writes:

Everywhere where the words of the *Rishonim* are written in a book and [hence] well-known, and the later decisors disagree with them, we follow the *Aharonim*. However, if a responsum of a Gaon is discovered, which was not known before and did not appear in an [available] book. . . . one does not need to rule like the *Aharonim*, because it is possible that they were not aware of the words of the Gaon, and had they known [his opinion] they would most likely have recanted.

His formulation is based on that of the Maharik, R. Yosef Colon (died 1480). (Somewhat ironically, the Maharam Alschech [sect. 39,] who likewise held this position, as a result ruled in opposition to a certain ruling of the Maharik himself. See *Meorot ha-Daf-ha-Yomi* no. 829, to *Ketubot* 69–75, 2015, p. 1, where a passage from

B. *Ketubot* 69a is shown to support this view, and indeed the Maharik used this as a proof-text. However some of the references there need corrections.)

And, indeed, this is the majority view, see *Kenesset ha-Gedolah* to *Yoreh Deah* 37, *Beit Yosef*, no. 50, 149. See further on this matter, R. Yaakov Hayyim Sofer, *Beit Ya'akov* (Jerusalem, 1985), p. 19, n. 5, 52–53; and his *Tiferet Yitzhak* (Jerusalem, 1981), p. 46, 115, and his copious references in his *Hadar Yaakov*, vol. 6, Jerusalem, 2006, pp. 195–197, etc. Hence, discoveries of new early texts of *Geonim* and *Rishonim* should certainly be taken into account. A case in point is the Meiri, who was only recently fully discovered, and in whose writings we find numerous *psakim* of relevance to our day. (See *Beit Ya'akov*, p. 52, n. 17.) See eg. R. Ovadiah Yosef, *Yabia Omer*, vol. 4, *Orah Hayyim* 24:11, who writes that "had the *Aharonim*, who ruled stringently [on a certain issue] known the words of Meiri (to *Rosh ha-Shanah* 28b), who plainly holds the opposite view, they would certainly have abandoned their own conclusions in favor of his" (p. 103). And so too in vol. 4, *Orah Hayyim* 5:1, he writes, "and had the aforementioned *Aharonim* seen the responsum of R. Abraham son of the Rambam, they would surely not have differed from him" (p. 48). See further his introduction to his volume 5.

So too we read in Rav Kook's *Orah Mishpat*, Jerusalem, 1979, no. 112, p. 121:

And it is known that the *Or Zarua*, which we just some tens of years ago had the privilege [to be revealed to us] . . . [but] . . . was hitherto a hidden manuscript; and most assuredly if his words had been known, they would have been used, together with other names, to rule permissively, . . . as is well known from *Hoshen Mishpat* 25:2, in the Rema.

A further aspect of this issue may perhaps be seen in the frequently found argument that one does not have to follow a specific early authority because he did not yet know the *Zohar*, which was only revealed after his time. See, for example, Lewy, *Minhag Yisrael Torah*, vol. 1, 2nd ed., Brooklyn, 1991, pp. 107, 132, etc. See also, other outstanding halachic sources, such as the response of the Maharam (Rabbi Meir b. Barucsh) of Rothenberg (see, for example, R. Josef Katz, *She'erit Yosef*, ed. Ziv (New York, 1984), sec. 62, p. 149, etc). The argument is, of course, that had they had known the *Zohar*, they would have ruled in accordance with it. And the same argument is applied to the rulings of the *Ari*. Thus, for example, R. Yitzhak Barda (*Responsa Yitzhak Yeranen*, vol. 3, sec. 13) writes, "had the *Poskim* known what the Ari knew, they would have reversed their opinions." So too, the Hida writes (*Birkei Yosef, Orah Hayyim*, 421: 1, etc.), "We follow him (the Ari) often even when he rules contrary to Maran (R. Yosef Karo). For the rabbis maintained (*kim le-hu Rabanan*), that had Maran heard the words of the Ari, he would have changed his mind." (See M. Hallamish, *Kabbalah in Liturgy, Halakhah and Customs* [Ramat-Gan, 2000], chapter 5, pp. 117–145 [Hebrew].)

We could add many additional sources to bear out our contention, but let us suffice with just one more example, a responsum of the *Avnei Nezer*, of R. Avraham Bornstein of Sochotchov, *Orah Hayyim* 362:

And it is known that the second part of the letter was published in our time [Lvov 1860], and in the time of R. Meir of Lublin (16 cent.) and the *Magen Avraham* (17 cent.), it was not published, and (hence) his words gain no mention. And it is possible that had known of it they would have changed their opinion, since in an issue of rabbinic status (*mi-derabanan*) it is advisable to take the lenient position.

that the fact that the majority hold a given opinion does not necessarily means that that opinion is truly the correct one, as is evident from the *Mishnah* in *Eduyot* cited above.[8]

Thus some commentators ed loc., explain that the rejected opinion could become the correct halachic approach. We already noted that this is the opinion of R. Menashe of Ilya, which we cited above.

Indeed, it could well be that both dissenting views are actually correct, as we have already pointed out above, and so we learn from *B. Eruvin* 13b and *B. Gittin* 6b (cited above) that the views of Beit Shamai and Beit Hillel actually were both correct. And there are Kabbalistic statements that in the time of the Messiah the halachah will be according to Beit Shamai, and also that its dominant view on the form of the *tefilin* will be that of Rabbenu Tam.

To the above we may add the remarks of R. Yisrael Zeev Gustman, in his *Kuntresei Shiyurim to Kiddushin*, Brooklyn, 1970, 24/2, that only when there is an absolutely certain ruling in this binding, but where there is a difference of opinion between the authorities this is not an absolute ruling, and hence in a *safek de-Rabbanan*, in a point of uncertainty in an issue of rabbinic status, we rule leniently.[9]

Furthermore, see R. Ovadiah Yosef, *Halichot Olam*, vol. 6, Jerusalem, 2001, p. 226, where he argues that in a case where the *Beit Yosef* for some reason was unaware of a *Yerushalmi* text and a whole range of *Rishonim* ruled in accordance with that text, had the *Beit Yosef* been aware of all this material, he surely would have ruled differently. He brings a number of authorities who hold this position (the Hida in his *Shut Hayyim Shaal* vol. 1, sect. 56; idem, *Yosef Ometz* sect. 80 ad fin.; R. Yehuda Ayash, *Shut Benei Yehudah*, vol. 2, sect. 124, fol. 202.b, etc.).

I have been somewhat terse here, and even so have been overly extensive. For this subject requires a full examination in its own right.

8. See Yitzhak Namni and Tzvi Idles, *Samhuyot ha-Rov be-Halachah*, Kiryat Arba, 2002, p. 16, following on a statement by R. Shimon Shkop, *Shaarei Yosher, Shaar 3*, chapter 1. In fact, in many cases the Talmud does not adopt the majority view. See Paul Heger, *The Pluralistic Halakkah: Legal Innovations in the Late Second Temple and Rabbinic Periods*, New York, 2003, pp. 187–200, in a section entitled "Preference for Individual Opinion."

9. See most recently R. Elhanan Wasserman, *Kuntres Divrei Sofrim*, ed. Daat Sofrim, 2014, p. 78, note 85.

Here we should point out that there is a considerable body of contemporary legal discussion on the subject of what we might call "halachic pluralism." So, for example, Norman Lam and Aaron Kirschenbaum, "Freedom and constraint in the Jewish Judicial Process" *Cardozo Law Review* 1, 1979, pp. 99–133, in the section entitled "The Halakhic System: Monistic or Pluralistic"; Hanina Ben-Menahem, "Is there always One Uniquely Correct Answer to a Legal Question in the Talmud?"

And we may quote the very beautifully fommulated statement of Isidore Twersky, in his *Introduction to the Code of Maimonides (Mishneh Torah)*, New Haven and London, 1980, in a section entitled "The Impossibility of Absolute Finality" (p. 139):

> Many of these categories converge upon one overriding fact: Maimonides' realization that law has immanent uncertainties, that the legist regularly and unavoidably faces unimagined contingencies and new hesitations. Absolute finality is a utopian construct. Like the historical process or personal experience, law can never be purified of its mutations and individuality. A code is a rational construction which captures and freezes as much as possible of a fluid, unpredictable, sometimes recalcitrant reality, but there is always a fluctuating residuum which must be confronted openly and freshly. Maimonides was well aware of this and indicated it in various ways.

And on p. 142 he adds:

> All his desires for finality, objectivity, and universality notwithstanding, Maimonides was sophisticated and realistic, sensitized by the very Rabbinic tradition which he was codifying. He knew that despite his major contribution to condensation and consolidation the vitality and effervescence of halakhah could not be fully contained or compressed. The logic of law and the contingencies of life have always to be aligned. Halakhah and reality are both multifaceted realities.

To the above we may add the view that even the rulings of R. Yosef Karo in his *Shulḥan Aruch*, which are so widely accepted, at least in the Sefardi communities, are not accepted because they are "certainly

---

Jewish Law Annual 6, 1987, pp. 164–175, David Kremer, *The Mind of the Talmud: An Intellectual History of the Bavli*, New York, 1990, who argues that the rabbis of the Babylonian Talmud are engaged in the persuit of truth, but they hold that a single confident truth is ultimately indeterminable. See on this "Legal Truth, Right Answers and Bent Answers: Dworkin and the Rabbis," by Christine Hayes, in *Dinei Yisrael* 25, 2008, pp.74* – 80*. She herself has a different approach to the problem, see ibid., pp.73x–121x. Her position has been questioned by Richard Hidary, in his article "Right Answers Revisited: Monism and Pluralism in the Talmud," *Dinei Yisrael* 26–27, 2009–2010, pp. 229* – 255*, and Christine Hayes replies, ibid., pp. 257*– 307*, in an article entitled "Theoretical Pluralism." (See also below Appendix 6.)

correct," but out of a level of uncertainty, or as formulated by R. Yaakov Hayyim Sofer, in his article *"Hachraot u-Piskei ha-Gaon Erech ha-Shulhan,"* which appeared in *Zechor le-Avraham,* ed. A. Berger, 1993, p. 233:

דמה שקבלנו עלינו את הוראות מרן ז"ל לא היתה קבלה זו מתורת ודאי אלא רק מתורת ספק.

This is also the position of R. Yosef Hayyim, in his *Rav Poalim,* vol. 4, *Yoreh Deah,* sect. 5 ad fin; R. Ben Tziyyon Aba Shaul, *Or Tziyyon,* vol. 2, introduction sect. 1:2; R. Moshe ha-Levi, *Yosef Daat,* sect. 12:3; R. Hayyim David Hazan, *Nediv Lev,* vol. 2, *Hoshen Mishpat* sect.63; R. Raphael Yosef Hazan, *Hikrei Lev,* vol. 1, *Yoreh Deah* sect. 127; R. Meir Mazuz , in his introduction to the *Ben Ish Hai,* p. 12; perhaps also R. Ovadiah Yosef, *Yabia Omer,* vol. 9, no. 17:21, p. 193 , and no. 105, p. 225, sect. 3 ad fin., and many additional sources cited by R. Yaakov Hayyim Sofer, etc.[10]

Admittedly, this view is not universally accepted, and in the subject of considerable controversy, such that other authorities claim the *Shulhan Aruch*'s rulings are absolute, containing no elements of uncertainty, and they seek to refute the above authors' contentions. See, e.g., R. Neriah Gafni *Magen Yosef,* vol. 1, Jerusalem, 2011, pp. 117–132, and R. Yitzhak Yosef, *Ein Yitzhak,* vol. 3, Jerusalem, 2009, pp. 95–99, for extensive polemic discussions, turning upon the interpretation of a passage in his introduction to his *Beit Yosef.* Nonetheless the views of these great authorities cannot be summarily discarded.

Thus, in addition to all that has been stated above, there is an innate element of uncertainty in all aspects of halachah, and this element

---

10. It is for this reason that R. David Hazan, in his responsa *Nediv Lev,* Saloniki-Jerusalem, vol. 2, 1866, *Hoshen Mishpat,* sect. 63, was willing to use the principle of *sfek sfeika,* to rule leniently, even when one of the *sefeikot* is contrary to the view of R. Yosef Karo, since his rulings were only accepted *mi-torat safek,* i.e., remaining in the realm of uncertainty. He also claimed that this was the view of his father, the author of *Hikrei Lev* (by R. Refael Yosef Hazan).

The position of R. Ovadiah Yosef is more complex, since he appears to contradict himself in several responsa, e.g., vol. 9, *Yoreh Deah* 6:5, contra vol. 9, *Orah Hayyim* 108:5, and see vol. 10, *Yoreh Deah* 43:2. The apparent contradiction is explained in his son's *Ein Yitzhak,* vol. 3, Jerusalem, 2009, pp. 106–107. (I am endebted Amir Zuaretz, who discussed this issue in his doctorate on *Judicial Policy and Halachic Methods Used by Rabbi Ovadia Yosef to Reach Decisions on Family Law,* Ramat Gan, 2015, pp. 24–25.)

does not weaken it, but rather strengthens it by admitting of greater flexibility and hence resilience.[11]

Samuel Morell, in his *Studies in the Judicial Methodology of Rabbi David Ibn Abi Zimra*, New York and Oxford, 2004, pp. 177–209, discusses ben Zimra unique way of ruling according to the "middle way," and he summarizes his findings (ibid., p. 208) that:

> The message of the "middle way" is that there is no substantive preference for one opinion over another.

Is this not what R. Yitzhak Colon (died 1480) wrote in his responsum *Sheelot u-Teshuvot Maharik*, Warsaw, 1884, no. 163, p. 176:

> In my humble opinion it would appear that wherever the Talmud notes that so and so, the ruling is like this, the Talmudic authorities did not plumb the depths of each and every controversy, deciding that the halachah should be in accordance with him whom they stated to be the authoritative one, because it was not possible for the Talmudic Sages to examine in depth every single difference of opinion of the *Tannaim* and *Amoraim* and to determine according to whom is the halachah in detail. Rather they followed the majority view, [especially] when they saw that a certain Tanna was sharper or more accepted than his fellow Sages. And, so too, with the *Amoraim*. And they relied on this approach to determine that the halachah be in accordance with this opinion, except in certain exceptional cases where they knew that the halachah is in accordance with the dissenting view. And the Sages of the Talmud had the authority to determine the halachah as they saw fit, and [saw their ruling] as beyond doubt. And this was the case until the period of Rav Ashi and Ravina, who end the period of *horaah* – decision-making. And in this way they determined the laws. And I have many proofs that this is the case, but I have no time at the present to elaborate on this . . .

---

11. Compare R. Menasheh of Ilya's notion of "relativism in the Talmud" and "The Suppressed Minority" on which see Yitzhak Barzilay, *Manasseh of Ilya: Precursor of Modernity Among the Jews of Eastern Europe*, Jerusalem, 1999, pp. 98–113. Recently this issue was discussed in detail, albeit from a different starting point, by Adiel Schremer, in his *Towards Critical Halakhic Studies*, New York, 2010 (Tikva Working Paper 04/10), pass., but especially pp. 28–31.

So these rulings in accordance with the majority were for the most part pragmatic rather than minutely reasoned decisions.

On the other hand there maybe a considerable danger in consistently taking the stringent path, as we have already indicated above. See, for example, the very harsh statement of the Radbaz, R. David ben Zimra, in his responsa, part 4, no.1368:

> . . . But in any case if he wishes to take *upon himself* stringencies [he may do so], and he should close himself off in his own house, [but he should not do so for others], for [in so doing] he leads to conflicts, and to vain hatred, and the desecration of the Name, God forfend, and may the Good Lord pardon him, Amen. (My emphasis, D.S.)

Indeed, the superior status of leniency is a guiding principle in many of his rulings. So writes Israel M. Goldman, in his *The Life and Times of Rabbi David Ibn Abi ben Zimra*, New York, 1970, p. 23:

> To those scholars who would pile on stringency upon stringency, he expressed himself in terms such as follows: "Leave our people Israel alone! It is enough for them if they are careful about that which the Torah has forbidden, and about that which the rabbis have forbidden, and still you come along and add doubt upon doubt." [*Responsa of RDBZ* vol. 2, Venice 1749, no. 637]. Again, I do not deem it necessary to add such stringencies for Israel which the earlier authorities have not instituted. Would that Israel would observe that which has already been placed upon them, for if you grasp for too much you may grasp nothing, with the result that nothing is left in the hand, [ibid., vol. 1, no. 163]. And in an impatient tone to one writer: "You come to create new forbidden foods out of your own head!" [ibid., no. 145].

Goldman (ibid., pp. 23–24) continues to give some concrete examples of the Radbaz's approach. He writes:

> To illustrate: A Jew was sick and it was deemed necessary to violate the Sabbath on his behalf. But because of his piety he refused to allow them to violate the Sabbath on his account. R. David, maintaining the traditionally humane Jewish views in such matters, calls this man "A pious fool who will have to give account for his life to God. The Torah

taught 'You shall live by them' and not die by them [ibid., vol. 4, Livorno, 1652, 67]." Even in a case where the doctor does not think it necessary to make a medicine which would cause a violation of the Sabbath, but the patient feels that such a medicine will help him, R. David decides that the principle, "a man's own heart feels the bitterness of his soul the most," applies in such a case and the medicine should be procured, [ibid., 66]. Further, the great authorities differ on the point whether it is permitted to do anything for a sick person which would cause Sabbath violation if those things are not absolutely necessary. R. David clearly takes his stand with the words: "There is a difference of opinion on this among the legal authorities, but I am among the lenient interpreters" [ibid., 130]. In the same spirit, when a man was sick during the Passover week and he needed barley water as a medicine, R. David gives careful instructions how it can be prepared with the least possibility of leaven cereal being spread and adds: "I see fit to permit this for a sick man even if he is not in danger." Should a Jew who is in prison on the Sabbath and who has no food, be allowed to tell the jailer to buy and bring him food on the Sabbath? Or, shall he fast till the next day, since the prison is locked at night? R. David decides that it is permitted to send the jailer on the Sabbath day [ibid., vol. 3, Fürth, 1781, 576].[12]

Even more harsh and forceful against those "who put stringency upon stringency" are the words of R. Yaakov Emden (1697–1776) in his *Sheilat Yaavetz*, vol. 2, Lemberg, 1884, no. 150 (fol. 48), where he rails against the Ashkenaz *humrot*, which he says are kept to even more than biblical laws (*gufei Torah*), and which he claims leads to very serious errors is clearly prohibited laws, stating that he who prohibits the permitted in the end will permit the prohibited. He accuses them of blindness and having lost any sort of wisdom, making the insignificant essential, leading to great loss.

One could greatly multiply such statements, (see e.g., *Maharatz Chajes* to B. *Niddah* 34a, or responsa of the Mabit (R. Moshe Mi-Trani), vol. 3, sect. 68, Brooklyn, 1961, 13ab, who wrote: "Do not be

---

12. A more detailed analysis of Ben Zimra's halachic approach and his tendency to leniency (most especially in the case of *Agunot*, but not solely) may be found in Samuel Morell's *Studies in the Judicial Methodology of Rabbi David Ibn Abi Zimra*, New York and Oxford, 2004, pp. 58–75, 87–90, 170–171.

very pious (*hassidim harbei*) [for] it is sufficient for you [to accept] that which the Torah prohibited" (cf. *Y. Nedarim* 9:1), i.e., you need not add new prohibitions, but the above should suffice to underscore the dangers of excessive stringencies. (And cf. above note 126.)

Here I would like to recall a wonderful story (that I cited in my *On the Relationship of Mitzvot between Man and His Neigbor and Man and His Maker*, Jerusalem and New York, 2014, pp. 40–43) that R. Yehuda Leib Maimon records in his *Toldot ha-Gra* (Jerusalem: 1970, 7), concerning the rabbi of Frankfurt, R. Avraham-Abush, a contemporary of the Gaon of Vilna:

> They relate that once the *shochtim* (slaughterers) of Frankfurt came before him with a query concerning [the kashrut of] a lung, a matter on which the Rema and the rest of the Polish authorities ruled most stringently. The incident took place on the eve of a festival, and the matter was one which potentially involved a very considerable monetary loss for the impoverished slaughterer. The members of the *beit din* wished to rule stringently and declare the meat not kosher (in accordance with the view of the Rema), but R. Avraham-Abush began to search for ways of finding it kosher. The judges of the *beit din* insisted on their position that it is impossible to rule leniently against the view of the Rema and his colleagues, but R. Avraham-Abush argued with them, discussing the halachic issues involved, and finally ruled that the meat was kosher. The members of the *beit din* were astonished, asking him: How could one possibly rule leniently declaring it kosher against the ruling of the Rema and the great authorities of Poland who held the same opinion?!
>
> R. Avraham-Abush replied to them as follows: I prefer at the end of my days when I come [before the Heavenly Court] to argue my case with the Rema and his colleagues, rather than with this poor slaughterer. The slaughterer is a simple man, and it will be very difficult for my to argue my case with him before the Heavenly Court, if he brings me to court claiming that I declared his animal *tareif*, and that in doing so I caused him great monetary loss (הפסד מרובה),[13] and that I damaged his business

---

13. On this halachic concept, see what I wrote in *Darkah shel Halachah* (Jerusalem: 2007, 117–118, 140–141, 175–177); *Minhagei Yisrael*, vol. 3 (Jerusalem: 1994, 53–54); idem, vol. 8 (Jerusalem: 2007, 263); *Encyclopedia Talmudit*, vol. 10 (Jerusalem: 1961, 32–41).

Bension Cohen of New York (in an internet communication from Sept. 15, 2010)

on the eve of the festival. But I am sure that when I lay out my arguments
before the Rema and his colleagues, we will reach an agreement . . .

The logic in R. Avraham Abush's position is clarified in a similar tale
told by Yaakov Rimon and Yosef Zundel Wasserman in the book,
*Shmuel be-Doro: R. Shmuel Salant zt"l, Rabbah shel Yerushalayim
1841–1909, Hayyav u-Poalav*, Tel-Aviv: 1961, 122–126:

Once upon a time some learned rabbis were arguing with him (R. Shmuel
Salanter) on a case where he had ruled kosher, and needless to say he

---

would wish that there be here an amplified explanation of R. Avraham-Abush's ruling
so that it be more clearly understood. He would interpret it as follows:
. . . both the slaughterer and the Rabbi were caring for the poor, they were concerned about *Mitzvot she-Bein Adam le-Havero* as well as the *Mitzvot Bein Adam
la-Makom*. The lung is one of the least desirable organs for a butcher, generally sold
to the poor. The strict rendition of *treifa*, the slaughterer argued, would make all the
poor who rely on this meat not to have the ability to celebrate the holiday with a little
meat, making the poor unnecessary anguish, before *Yom Tov*. Therefore, . . . the Rabbi
who recognized the potential anguish, of the poor not having cheap meat for *Yom
Tov* as well as the greater monetary loss required of them to purchase clearer portions
of the meat, rendered a lenient *psak* predicated on the *shitah*. . . . There is a double
consideration of *Kevod ha-Kelal* and the recognition of the *Tzaar*. The explanation
presented . . . while very lofty presents an argument made by a true Gadol.

My thanks to Mr. Cohen for this insightful amplification, which is certainly much
clearer and more forceful than a mere reference to the concept of *hefsed merubeh*,
which might lead one to the erroneously simplistic conclusion that when it comes to
money the Rabbis are ready to be lenient, (as Cohen writes, warning us against such
an understanding). This is, indeed, partially true, but requires a detailed understanding
of the concept of *hefsed merubeh*, for which reason I gave some basic references.

Here we may add that there is a general misconception that it is easier to rule
stringently – *le-humra*, thus avoiding the dangers of permitting the forbidden. However,
the Rosh, in his response, *Klal Bet*, sect.17 ad fin., writes, "and he who rules forbidding
something (והאוסר) must bring clear and strong evidence, for the Torah was concerned
for the property of Israel (כי התורה חסה על ממונם של ישראל)." See above note 10. Further
details may be found in R. Yitzhak Yosef's *Ein Yitzhak*, vol. 3 (Jerusalem, 2009,
298–306, 596).

A different approach to a similar situation is told of R. Yosef Dov Soloveitchik.
It was his way to be extremely stringent in cases of *kashrut* for himself. But when it
came to others, he feared mistakenly to declare something not kosher, thus causing
damage and as it were stealing other people's property. On one occasion, he felt he
had no alternative but to declare some meat non-kosher, "even though according to
the Shach it is kosher, I may not cause you monetary loss and be considered a thief
according to the view of the Shach." There and then, on the spot he took from his purse
the value of the animal and gave it to the butcher (A. Tobolsky, *Hizaharu be-Mamon
Haverchem* [Bnei Brak: 1981] 249).

refuted their counter-arguments. One of them turned to him and said to him: "You have refuted our arguments, but what will happen when you come before the Heavenly Court and have to argue with the *Beit Yosef* and the Rema?" they asked. He replied as follows: "Surely you will agree with me that it will be better for me to argue my case with them, since I believe that I understood in depth their opinion, rather than having a claim against me on the part of the ox [i.e., on the part of the owner of the ox] that I incorrectly declared *tareif . . .*"[14]

Both these tales have a common denominator: namely, that if the rabbi ruled incorrectly, declaring *tareif* meat kosher, he has sinned against God, and Yom ha-Kippur will atone for this sin. But should he have ruled kosher meat as *tareif*, he will have caused damage, hurt and monetary loss to the slaughterer, and this is a sin against his fellow-man for which Yom ha-Kippur does not automatically atone; and hence he preferred to err on the side of leniency rather than risk erring on the side of stringency.[15]

Indeed, much the same concept is to be found in a responsum of R. Eliezer Fleckles, *Teshurah me-Ahavah*, vol. 1, Prague, 1806, no. 181. There we read:

---

14. See my *On the Relationship of Mitzvot between Man and His Neighbor and Man and His Maker*, Jerusalem and New York, 2014, pp. 41–43.

15. See my discussion in *Darkah Shel Torah*, 140-141. Here we may add the following story brought by Meir Tamari in his *Al Chet: Sins in the Marketplace* (Northvale, N.J. and London: 1996, 24):

A *shochet*, ritual slaughterer, once came to the Chafetz Chaim for advice, saying, "The laws of *shechitah* are so many and difficult I am afraid that I may sin and cause others to sin through an infringement of them. I think I will go into business." The Chafetz Chaim's reply was simple and direct: "If your major concern is the safety of your soul, you should remain a *shochet*. The laws of the marketplace and of money are far more numerous and onerous, while God, your partner, is an ever-present witness and judge to any deviations."

We find much the same idea reflected in the Netziv (R. Naftali Zvi Yehuda Berlin), in his *Haamek Davar* to Genesis 20:7 "[Now therefore restore the man his wife; for he is a prophet], and he shall pray for thee, and thou shalt live":

According to what we have explained . . . that the sin was that [Avimelech] caused grief to our forefather Abraham, surely he only needed to appease him, and there was no need for prayer. However, from here we may learn that one who sins against his neighbor also sins against God, and it is not sufficient to appease one's neighbor alone. One must also beg forgiveness from God. And for this reason he needed Abraham's prayer, in order to be completely expiated.

He was wont to say to his disciples, "Go and see who is more severely punished: he who is overly stringent (*she-loke-din*) or he who is overly lenient. And you will understand that he who is overly stringent is more severely punished. For he who is overly lenient sins a sin between man and his Maker, and he will be repentant and be forgiven (*ve-shav ve-ripa lo*). But he who is overly stringent must appease his neighbour." This is hinted at in the statement, "Your donkey (*hamorcha*) is gone, Tarfon" (*B. Sanhedrin* 33a) [a double word-play on *hamor* (donkey) and *humra* (stringency)][16] for that is a hint at one who rules with excessive stringency and declare everything as forbidden [i.e., to be eaten]. See Rashi and Tosafot to tractate *Beitzah* 2b, (*de-heteira*) on the (*koach de-heteira adif*).

We may also note the word-play on Tarfon and *tareif*.

Let us further take note of the very explicit instructions formulated by the *Shlah ha-Kadosh* (R. Yishaya Horowitz, author of *Shnei Luhot ha-Brit*, Amsterdam, 1698), and aimed at rabbinic decisors. And so he writes (ibid., 184b, in *Masechet Shevuot*, ed. M. Katz, vol. 2, Haifa, 2002, p. 266, nos. 89–91):

89: The goal of study is to study and to teach, to keep [the law] and carry it out. You, my children, may the Lord guard over you, if you are asked to give a ruling, and have the privilege to be decisors, take great care in your decisions, that you stumble not, God forfend . . . And before you give your judgement, make sure that the law is as clear as daylight in your heart, without any hint of uncertainty . . . And if there is any uncertainty, be not ashamed to discuss this with other students. Who was greater than Rav Huna, who when he had to rule in matters of *tereifot*

---

16. To understand this "hint" we must see it in its fuller context as recorded in *B. Sanhedrin* ibid. There we are told (on the basis of *M. Bechorot* 4:4) that:
. . . Once a cow whose uterus was missing [was brought before] R. Tarfon who fed it to dogs, (because he regarded it as not kosher). And the case was brought before the Sages at Yavneh and they declared it Kosher . . . Said R. Tarfon, "Your donkey has gone, Tarfon." Rashi explains: Namely, I must sell my donkey in order to repay the loss of the cow to its owners.
See continuation of the text, where R. Akiva confronts him that he does not have to pay for the "damage" he did. Cf. the formulation at the end of responsum 112, of R. Moshe Al-Ashkar, Jerusalem 1959, p. 282, cited also by R. Ovadiah Yosef, in his *Yabia Omer*, vol. 2, *Orah Hayyim* 23. See also Ariel Pikard, *Mishnato shel ha-Rav Ovadiah Yosef be-Idan shel Temurah*, Jerusalem, 2007, pp. 93–94.

(non-kosher foods), would gather others [to join in the decisions], so that "each would carry a chip off the beam" [i.e., share the responsibility] (*B. Sanhedrin* 7b). [Cf. the Shlah's son, R. Sheftel's instruction in *Hanhagot ha-Tzadikim*, vol. 1, Jerusalem, 1988, p. 109, no. 22.] And may the fear of God be in your hearts.

90: In any case, do not say, if that is the case, let us be stringent in most cases. For this is not called a [decision of a] decisor, to rule stringently for others not in accordance with the law, though he may do so for himself, should he so wish. And in *Massechet Berachot* in the first chapter (4a), it talks of the generation of King David, when their hands were soiled with foetus and placenta . . . in order to declare a wife pure to her husband. It does not say whether they wished to purify or declare impure; only that they toiled so much not to declare the pure to be completely certain impure, thus keeping them from the mitzvah of procreation. So the decisor is cautioned not to cause others err, God forfend, but we should learn of the power of leniency. And this is the law in all rulings, even one for himself [i.e., when the decisor decides for himself], that the measure of piety is that he be stringent for himself, if there is place for stringency; but if there is not, but he merely wishes to take upon himself a stringent position because of his lack of knowledge, had he studied and gone more deeply into clarifying the issue, he would see that there is no place for stringency, and if he nonetheless rules stringently, he is a pious fool (*hassid shoteh*).

91: . . . But greater is he who toils [in his learning of] Torah, and studies until it is clear to him that it is permitted . . . Then, praise be he in this world . . . and it will be good for him in the world to come that he steeped himself in Torah. . . .

And here I would like to add a further consideration: For there is a well-established rule in Jewish law, that we find formulated by the Shach [*Siftei Cohen*, by Shabtai Cohen, 1621–1663, he being a major commentator to a part of the *Shulhan Aruch*], in his *Kitzur Hanhagot Issur ve-Heter* 9, *Yoreh Deah* 245, thus,

> Just as it is forbidden to permit that which is forbidden, so it is forbidden to forbid that which is permitted.

This principle is already found reflected in the prayer of R. Nehunya ben ha-Kanah (flor. Palestine c. 80–110 C.E.), found in the Talmud (*B.*

Berachot 28b), where he expresses the hope that he will not err in his judgements:

> That I do not declare the impure pure, *neither the pure impure* . . . (My emphasis – D.S.)

And see the parallel in *Y. Terumot* 5 ad fin., a statement of the 3rd century C.E. Rabbi [E]liezer; *Y. Hagigah* 1:8; *Y. Sotah* 8:2, cited in mediaeval sources such as, *Semag Asin* 111, *Hagahot Maimoniyot*, *Mamrim* 1:5. And see also *Teshuvot Maimoniyot* to *Maachalot Asurot* 15, in the name of the *Yerushalmi*.

Cf. *B. Berachot* 28b, and *Rokeah* sect. 28 who wrote, "The sin of permitting things that are prohibited is just as the sin of prohibiting things that are permitted." And see further R. Ovadiah mi-Bertinoro to *Avot* 5:8, and Yitzhak Yosef, *Shulhan ha-Maarechet*, vol. 2, Jerusalem, 2010, pp. 409–411. We may further recall the words of R. Dimi in the name of R. Yitzhak in *Y. Nedarim* 9:1, that the judges exhort him who took upon himself a prohibitive oath, saying, "Is not sufficient for you that which the Torah prohibited, but that you wish to prohibit other things!"[17] Of course, this principle also has its parameters, and the rabbis frequently imposed prohibitions to distance and prevent people from sinning, *le-afrishei me-issura*. However, this subject is beyond the scope of our present study.

But see the note in my grandfather's *Afracasta de-Anya*, vol. 2, Brooklyn, 2002, and end of no. 139, p. 348, by his great grandson R. Asher Gedaliah Pollack.

This clearly places a great degree of responsibility upon the decisor, requiring him to examine most intensively any issue before declaring it prohibited. For it is always easier to say "No, it is forbidden," than to say "Yes, it is permitted," The easy way is not the way of halachah; rather, one must attempt to reach a clarification of the truth.[18]

There may be an exception to this rule in the case of a repentant who has to take upon himself additional stringencies in order to counteract his natural tendency to give in to his evil inclinations. For him, writes

---

17. See Baruch Halevi Epstein, *Baruch she-Amar* to *Avot*, 2nd edition, Tel Aviv, 1905, pp. 72–73.

18. See my *Netivot Pesikah*, Jerusalem, 2009, pp. 173–176.

R. Yona Girondi, in his commentary to *Avot* 3, 16, that the *baalei teshuvah* should distance themselves from that which is permissible in the area in which he sinned. Thus, if he was an adulterer, he should be abstinent from his wife. But this is a special situation. (See also his *Shaarei Teshuvah* 1:2, N. Rakover, *Takanat ha-Shavim*, Jerusalem, 2007, p. 676.) But these are the exceptions to the rule.

This principle is discussed in numerous rabbinic sources, and is the subject of an extensive responsum on the part of R. Menashe Klein, in his *Mishne Halachot*, vol. 5, Tel-Aviv, 1973, no. 104, pp. 150–153, and cf. idem, vol. 4, Brooklyn, 1977, no. 105, p. 172, etc., and the many additional references collected by Lior Silber, in his *Milei de-Hassiduta*, 2nd edition (c. 2014).

Furthermore, the *Pithei Teshuva* to *Yoreh Deah* 116:10, ad fin., cited the *Solet le-Minhah* (that is the *Solet le-Minhah ve-Shemen le-Minhah*, which is the 2nd edition of R. Yaakov Reischer's *Minhat Yaakov*, Dessau, 1696), *Klal* 76, *Din* 8, that "one who is stringent in those laws where there was no stringency mentioned among the Amoraim (such as 'annulment in sixty,' (*bitul be-Shishim*) or a 'secondary vessel,' (*kli sheni*) is, as it were, practicing *epikorsut*, herecy, and there is no benefit in his action only loss . . ."

We may add the observation of Tzvi Zohar, in his *Heiru Pnei ha-Mizrach: Halachah ve-Hagut etzel Hachmei Yisrael ba-Mizrah ha-Tichon*, Tel-Aviv, 2001, p. 343, that R. Ovadia Yosef stresses the preference for leniency in *pesak*, wherever it is possible. And (ibid., pp. 79–80, note 79) he notes that this principle is explicitly spelled out in R. Yosef's article "*Mishnato shel Yisa Berachah*" *Shevet Ve-Am*, second series 1/6, 1971, pp. 95–103. He further points out that in R. Yosef's volumes of responsa, *Yabia Omer* and *Yehaveh Daat*, the phrase *Kocha de-heteira* appears 118 times (!), giving a sampling of references.

The great burden of responsibility upon the decisor, that we mentioned above, is very revealingly reflected in a passage by Rav [Avraham Yitzhak ha-Cohen] Kook [1865–1935], which with singular clarity expresses his personal concern as to when to rule stringently and when leniently, and what are the implications of the two alternatives:

> For I know clearly the nature of the people of our generation, that it is just when they see that we permit all that is permissible according to the depth of the law, they will understand that whatever we do not permit

is because this is the true law of the Torah. Consequently the masses will follow the rulings of halachic decisors – which is not the case if it becomes evident that there are things which, from the point of view of the halachah, are permitted, and the rabbis, neglecting to taking note of the troubles and distresses of Israel, leave the situation as prohibited. For then, the result, God forbid, will be to bring about a great desecration of God's name, (*Orah Mishpat*, Jaffa, 1985, sect. 112, fol. 126b, and cf. *Mishpat Cohen* no. 76).[19]

It is precisely this kind of concern that posits the careful persuit of halachic clarification and determination.[20]

---

19. On which B. Gelman, in his article in *Milin Havivin* 3, 2007, p. 90, comments: Rabbi Kook realized that permissive rulings, when appropriate, increase the public's trust in rabbinic leadership, and with increased trust will come increased levels of observance from a trusting public. Conversely, needless, stringent rulings can lead to distrust, less observance, and a breakdown in rabbinic authority. While Rabbi Kook issued these warnings regarding Passover stringencies, his words can easily and appropriately be applied to other areas of halachah as well.

20. Finally, we should also take account of the statement in *Y. Berachot* 2 ad fin., and *Y. Shabbat* 1:1, that one who is exempt from something and nonetheless does it is an ignorant person (*hediot*). I discussed this principle at length in my *On the Relationship of Mitzvot between Man and His Neighbor and Man and His Maker*, Jerusalem and New York, 2014, chapter 10, pp. 69–78, which needs no repetition here. I would only add a reference to R. Yosef Zechariah Stern, *Zecher Yehosef*, vol. 1, Jerusalem, 2014, sect. 67, pp. 318–320, who, in his usual fashion, gives plentiful pertinent references to the discussion.

APPENDIX 3: ON THE LEGITIMACY
OF HALACHIC INNOVATION

O FTEN WHEN SEAKING TO FIND AN INNOVATIVE SOLUTION TO
a complex contemporary halachic challenge, one would appear to come
up against what seems to be an insurmountable barrier, namely the
ancient Talmudic ruling found on the first page of tractate *Megillah*,
that "a *beit din* cannot overrule (or annul) the ruling of another *beit
din* unless it is greater than the first in wisdom and number" (See also
M. Eduyot 1:5, *B. Moed Katan* 3b, *B. Gittin* 36b, *B. Avodah Zarah*
36b.) Without going into the question as to how to measure wisdom,
or what is the meaning of "number," we are well acquainted with the
Talmudic doctrine of "decline of the generations" (*yeridat ha-dorot*)
positing that each generation is of lesser wisdom and authority than
the preceding one. Hence, later authorities cannot overrule the rulings
of earlier authorities.[1] However, the question that raises itself is, is this

---

1. See *B. Shabbat* 102b, *B. Ta'anit* 24a, *Y. Demai* 1:3, *Y. Shekalim* 5 ad init., etc.,
for the classic formulation.
   If the early authorities (*Rishonim*) were the sons of kings, we are like sons of
[ordinary] people; and if the early authorities were [ordinary] people, we are like asses,
and not even like the ass of R. Pinhas ben Yair, but like other asses.
   See *Avot de R. Natan* I, chapter 8 ad fin, ed. Schechter, Vienna 1887, p. 38, on the
ass of R. Haninah ben Dosa.
   Against this background we may understand the division of the history of halachah
into distinct periods, where authorities of a later period have not the authority to
disagree or rule differently to those of an earlier period. Thus, *Amoraim* do not disagree
with *Tanaim*, *Geonim* with *Amoraim*, *Rishonim* with *Geonim*, and *Aharonim* with
Rishonim. (Of course, there are many exceptions to this generic rule.) See S.Z. Havlin's
chapter entitled "*Ha-Hatimah ha-Sifrutit: Mashmautah ve-Tafkidah*" in his *Masoret
ha-Torah she-Baal-Peh*, Jerusalem, 2012, pp. 345–406 which examines this notion of
"halachic periodization." And see, for instance, *Y. Yosef*, *Ein Yitzhak*, vol. 1, Jerusalem,
2009, pp. 240–241, on the relationship between *Amoraim* and *Tannaim*. See also Z.M.
Koren's article "*Tannaim Amoraim Geonim ve-Rishonim: Samhut ha-Rishonim Klapei*

the case even when the original ruling was accompanied by an explicitly stated reason, and that reason is no longer applicable or relevant? In such a case does the earlier ruling still remain authoritative, or can it now be annulled, since the reason for its institution is no longer relevant? If the former be the case, then we are destined to be shackled to archaic inapposite institutions. If the latter, we are granted a measure of flexibility to suggest innovative changes.

Now this is actually a well known controversy between the Rambam and the Raavad, the Rambam ruling that even if the reason for a decree is no longer relevant it is in no way loses its authority, while the Raavad disagrees.[2] R. Yehoshua Boaz, author of the *Shiltei Gibborim*, in his *Sefer ha-Machlokot* (ed. Shmuel David ha-Cohen Friedman, Bnei Brak, 2012, vol. 3, pp. 14–16.), shows that the view of the Raavad was shared

---

ha-Aharonim," apud *Birurim be-Hilchot ha-Rayah*, eds. M. Tzvi Neriah, A. Stern, N. Gotel, Jerusalem, 1992, pp. 423–450.

This is too broad a subject to deal with here. We shall just note that my late father, R. Shmuel Sperber, in a chapter entitled "'*Hemshech ha-Dorot*' *be-Mishnato shel ha-Rav Kook*" in his *Maamarot*, Jerusalem, 1978, pp. 301–310, shows that Rav Kook had quite a different view on this subject.

An impressive array of citations to the effect that subsequent generations are on in lesser level than their predecessors is to be found in Michael David Bush's *Kevod Hachamim*, Kiryat Sefer, 2006, pp. 166–188. However, many of those citations require individual analysis, since they would appear to represent the deep respect of a disciple for his master rather than the overall view of the decline of the generations.

Cf. above p. 19 note 3, p. 26 note 8, pp. 233–234 notes 43, 44.

2. Rambam, *Hilchot Mumrim* 2:2, and Raavad, ibid.; Rambam, *Responsa Peer ha-Dor* no.148, ed. David Yosef, Jerusalem, 1984, p. 291, and editor's notes ibid. See in detail Israel Schepansky, *Ha-Takkanot be-Yisrael*, Jerusalem and New York, 1991, vol. 1, pp. 8–9 notes 37–41, 78–80, 84–87. In point of fact, the issue is far more complex. Since the Beraita's statement is a negative one, we may regard it – if not as advice – as a *gezerah* rather than a *takanah*. (On the definition of a *gezerah* as a negative enactment, see *Entziklopedia Talmudit*, vol. 5, Jerusalem, 1963, 529–530.) Schepansky, p. 8, who points out that according to the Rosh, though one may not cancel a *takanah* the reason for which is no longer relevant, a *gezerah* whose reason is no longer valid may be annulled. (*Teshuvot ha-Rosh*, *Klal Beit*, sect.8 ad fin., cited in the *Beit Yosef* to *Orah Hayyim* 9, and *Magen Avraham*, ibid., sect.7, *Mahtzit ha-Shekel*, ibid.) Schepansky (ibid., note 38) discusses the view of the *Mahtzit ha-Shekel*, and concludes decisively that the Rosh made this clear distinction between a *gezerah* and a *takanah*. See also *Entziklopedia Talmudic*, ibid., 539, on the limitations of a *gezerah* when there is no "*hashash*." See also Menachem Elon, *Ha-Mishpat ha-Ivri: Toldotav, Mekorotav, Ekronotav*, Jerusalem, 1973, p. 445, and especially note 201. See also R. Yehoshua Boaz, the author of *Shiltei Giborim*, *Sefer ha-Mahlokot*, *Even ha-Ezer*, ed. S.D. ha-Cohen Friedman, vol. 3, Bnei Brak, 2012, pp. 14–16.

by the *Hagahot ha-Rosh* to *B. Ketubot* 3b while the Rambam seems to be following the positions of Rashi to *B. Beitzah* 5a, and likewise the Rosh to *Beitzah* sect. 3, and also the Semag (*Sefer Mitzvot Gaddol*).

It is true that in controversies between the Rambam and the Raavad, we normally follow the Rambam; however, it is equally true that it is not *certain* that the Rambam's view is really the correct one. Perhaps the Raavad's position is more correct. In other words, there still exists an element of uncertaintly, a *safek*, as to whose view is the right one. It is only that in accordance with certain pragmatic rules of halachic adjudications (*kelalei ha-psak*) that we follow the rulings of the Rambam. (See Appendix 2 for details.)

An additional point to be taken in consideration is that it is not always altogether clear whether a ruling cited in the Talmud is to be understood as constituting a definitive decree, or whether it was merely an indication of rabbinic advice. Elsewhere I have given several examples of such a *safek*.[3] Hence at times there may even be an additional element of uncertainty to be considered.

Moreover, R. Joseph Messas added yet a further consideration, arguing (with regard to *setam yeinam*, non-Jewish wine or milk milked by a non-Jew) that even according to the view of Rambam (and the Rivash, no. 255) this principle only applies where there is a fear that the original reason could be relevant in the future. But in a case where there is little or no reason to think that the reason will resurface, the original prohibions may be disregarded (*Otzar Michtavim* 1, 454; cf. Marc B. Shapiro, *Conversations* 7, 2010, p. 101).

Now, even if one could not be sure that R. Messas' interpretation is necessarily correct, and one could not be absolutely certain of his ruling, that in itself would imply that there exists yet another *safek*, i.e., namely whether to rule like Rambam or the Raavad, and even if one follows Rambam, should we accept R. Messas' interpretation thereof.

Furthermore, the Rambam himself did away with the *takana* that the *shaliah tzibbur* repeat the *Amidah* prayer (at *Shaharit, Musaf,* and *Minhah*) for the benefit of those who had not said it or could not do so. See his son Abraham's response at the beginning of *Maaseh*

---

3. See my chapter on *Kevod ha-Tzibbur* etc., in my essay entitled "Congregational Dignity and Human Dignity," apud *Women and Men in Communal Prayer: Halachic Perspectives*, ed. C. Trachtman, Jersey City, N.J., 2010, pp. 39–49.

Rokeah (and in the Freimann edition of Rambam's responsa nos. 35 and 36, Blau ed. 256, 258, cited by David Yosef ibid., note 13; see also the additional references he cites ibid.). David Yosef explains that this does not contradict his basic position of not annulling *takanot*, because he too would agree to such annulment when the *takanah* itself has negative effects, referring us to *Hilchot Mumrim* 2:4, and to yet another of his responsa, in ed. Freimann no. 38, ed. Blau 291. (Even if it is thought that there be a contradiction, there is an opinion that when there is a contradiction between the Rambam's rulings in *Mishneh Torah* and those in his responsa, we follow the responsa.[4]) Furthermore, R. Ovadiah Yosef, in his *Yehaveh Daat*, vol. 5, no. 12, Jerusalem, 1983, ruled to annul the Rambam's *takanah* and to reestablish the *hazarat ha-shatz*, again explaining that the times and circumstances had changed! And see further Rav Kook's responsum in his *Orah Mishpat* to *Orah Hayyim* no. 58, on the ability to change or annul a *takanah* under certain circumstances. He formulates his argument as follows:

> Nonetheless, in order to annul a *takanah*, it is sufficient if there is another reason, according to which it would not have been worthwhile establishing the *takanah* [in the first place].

For an explanation of this reasoning, see Amiram Domovitz, *Ha-Halachah ve-ha-Olam ha-Moderni*, Gush Etzion (n.d.), p. 153.

We should further add that the Radbaz, on the Rambam, ibid., is even more lenient than the Raavad, for he states that "if the *takanah* was clearly stated to have been enacted for a given reason, and that reason no longer obtains, then the *takanah* is annulled." And the Rosh (*Responsa, Klal* 2:8) goes even so far as to rule that even if the reason for the *takanah* was not expressly stated to be its determining factor, if nonetheless the reason was known and is no longer relevant, the *takanah* is annulled.

But in point of fact, although R. Messas' ruling may appear to be very innovative, i.e., a great *hiddush*, it is actually well attested in a number of different halachic contexts. Above in note 89, we brought one such example regarding "uncovered water." We shall not repeat it

---

4. See Yitzhak Yosef, *Ein Yitzhak*, vol. 1, Jerusalem, 2009, pp. 407–408. However, this seems to be a minority view, ibid., pp. 206–208.

here, but conclude that there we showed conclusively that despite the fact that the rabbis instituted a prohibitional regulation (*gezerah*), when (and where) the reason for its enactment was no longer applicable, the prohibition was ignored or rejected with the consent of the rabbis. Indeed, there are many other such examples of halachic regulations enacted because of the fear of some sort of danger – *mi-shum sakanah* (or *mi-shum hashasha*) – that subsequently became regarded as irrelevant and fell into desuetude, again with the approbation of the rabbis. Or in the words of Schepansky (ibid., p. 86):

> That which [the rabbis] forbade *mi-shum hashasha*, out of fear or apprehension (of some kind), even if they enacted it *be-minyan*, i.e., through the agency of a court of law (*beit din*), if that fear is now allayed, one does not require a court of law to permit it.

He then gives the example we have cited above, adding that nowadays we do not observe strictly the practice of *mayyim aharonim* (rinsing the hands at the end of the meal) required by the Talmud (*B. Hulin* 106a), because we no longer use *melech sedomit*, a kind of salt which if left on one's hands, which may afterward touch one's eyes, might blind them (*Tosafot Berachot* 53b).[5]

Indeed, there are numerous additional examples of decrees and early regulations that were annulled, whether because the original decree was not universally accepted (*lo pashat issuro be-chol Yisrael*, see *B. Avodah Zarah* 71b), or because the annulment would have a positive effect, (see *Shulhan Aruch, Orah Hayyim* 9:6), or because of changed circumstances. Thus, for instance, though Ezra instituted the scriptural text translated during the Torah reading by a *Turgeman*, nowadays this has been abolished in most communities (Rambam, *Hilchot Sanhedrin* 12:10), because nowadays no one understands the Armaic translation (*Beit Yosef, Orah Hayyim* 145:3). Likewise, in *Tosafot Beitzah* 6a we read that nowadays that there are no Magi (*havrei*) who may carry out all funerary requirements on the second day of *Yom Tov*. So too, the *Mordechai* to *Avodah Zarah*, chapter 1 rules that one may carry out

---

5. See the additional example cited by Schepansky, ibid., p. 87, note 22, and *Entziklopedia Talmudit* vol. 26, Jerusalem, 2004, 669, on looking in a mirror.

business-transactions on days of pagan festivals (*yom eidam*), because the gentiles no longer are idolatrous, etc.[6]

In an article published in *Yeshurun* 31, 2014, pp. 100–106, entitled "*Kol Davar She-be-Minyan Tzarich Minyan Aher le-Hatiro*," R. Asher Weiss brings five cases where the *Tosafot* permitted what the rabbis of the Talmud had forbidden, arguing that the reason for the *takanah* was no longer relevant. He brings additional examples of this phenomenon, seeking to clarify the parameters for such permission.

We see, then, that in many a case there are several areas of uncertainty, and we may make use of the principle of *sfek sfeika*, double (or even triple) uncertainties as a means to attaining a more lenient judgement (*sfek speika* le-heteira).[7]

---

6. See R. Tzvi Hirsch Chajes, *Kol Kitvei Maharatz Hayes*, vol. 1, Jerusalem 1958, *Darkei ha-Horaah*, chapter 5, pp. 229–233, for additional examples. However see his extended discussion, pp. 226-235, where he circumscribes this notion to specific cases, and especially his summary, ibid., p. 235. See also *Pri Hadash* to *Yoreh Deah* 116.

7. Here we shall not go into all the complexities of *sfek sfeika*. See, for instance Shach, *Dinei Sfek Sfeika Yoreh Deah* 110, Yitzhak Yosef, *Ein Yitzhak*, vol. 2, Jerusalem, 2009, pp. 281–352, and especially, 301–307, section 15–17, and also page 287, where a triple *safek* is always a path to leniency, and vol. 3, pp. 309–311. See further Reuven David Nawi, *Yehi Reuven*, Jerusalem, 1983, p. 83, no. 16, who argues that we may use a *sfek sfeka* to contradict a clear ruling of the *Shulhan Aruch*. See also Rambam, *Hilchot Mumrim* 2:1, that "a *beit din* that derived a ruling through one of the hermeneutical rules according to their understanding, and another *beit din* saw a way to refute that argument, they may rule otherwise, as it is said, 'to that judge that will be in those days'(*Deuteronomy* 17:9). You only have to go to the *beit din* of your generation." Again, this is too involved an issue to be comprehensively dealt with here.

APPENDIX 4: ON THE NECESSITY
OF A RABBI HAVING AN
INDEPENDENT STANCE

O N THE PRIMARY IMPORTANCE OF INDEPENDENT THINKING, which I touched upon above in the section entitled "An Independent Stance,"and see what I wrote in the introduction to *Darkah shel Halachah*, Jerusalem, 2007, pp. 7–9 (and also in my study "*Congregational Dignity and Human Dignity*." which appeared in *Women and Men in Communal Prayer: Halakhic Perspectives*, ed. C. Trachtman, Jersey City, N.J., 2010, pp. 31–34). I began by quoting that R. Tzvi Hersch Chajes, when he published his *Torat ha-Neviim*, Zolkiew 1836, expressed his fears that critics would scrutinize his work to find in it faults. The Hatam Sofer, R. Moshe Sofer, responded to him in a letter (in his responsa, *Orah Hayyim*, sect. 208), praising his book, and teaching him, and indeed all of us, a lesson in approbation and criticism. He explained as follows:

> In *B. Beitzah* 38ab, it is told of R. Aba, that before he came to Eretz Yisrael he prayed, "May it be Thy will that I will make statements that will be accepted." Rashi ad loc. adds: Accepted – "by the local Sages, so that I be not shamed." However, when he came to the academy of R. Yohanan in Eretz Yisrael, the students made fun of him when he offered an argument to support what they were studying that day.

On the other hand, points out the Hatam Sofer, in *B. Berachot* 28b, we learn of R. Nehunya ben ha-Kanah's prayer when entering the *beit midrash*, namely, "May it be your will . . . that no [halachic] mishap came about because of me, and I err not in matters of halachah, and that my colleagues rejoice in me . . ."

What, then, is the difference between these two prayers, asks the Hatam Sofer, that one was accepted and the other not?

The answer he offers is that R. Aba requested that he find favor and agreement among his colleagues, and therefore his request was not successful. For, "what difference does it make to me if they accept my opinion or not? Say your words in honesty and in your duty to Heaven!" Hence, his request was rejected. But R. Nehunya ben ha-Kanah prayed that his thinking be aimed toward the truth of the Torah, and he was little concerened with what his colleagues might say, nor did he seek their approval.

Or as the Hatam Sofer put it:

> May the discussion take place in a manner such that my opinion and line of reasoning is well-grounded according to my intellect. Thus, when my colleague argues against me, I shall examine in my mind to determine if his words are correct; and if his words do not seem right to me, I will insist upon my own opinion. What difference is it to me whether he agrees or not, seeing that it is not my purpose to turn his opinion toward mine?

Hence, R. Nehunya merited that his views were accepted. The Hatam Sofer concludes:

> A person who knows in himself that his intention is entirely for the sake of the Almighty, may He be praised, and to magnify and make great the Torah, but he withholds sustenance [i.e., what he knows to be true Torah] because of those who seek faults and mock and insult the angels of God – such a person commits a sin. And just as he would be punished for preaching [i.e., incorrectly], so too will he be punished for refraining [i.e., from teaching true Torah].

Rema (*Shulhan Arukh, Yoreh Deah* 242:2, 3) notes that it is even permissible for a student to dissent from his rabbi's ruling, if he has proofs and arguments to uphold his opinion. Rabbi Hayyim Palache, the great halachic authority of 19th century Izmir, wrote that:

> The Torah gave permission to each person to express his opinion according to his understanding . . . It is not good for a sage to withhold his words out of deference to the sages who preceded him if he finds

in their words a clear contradiction . . . A sage who wishes to write his proofs against the kings and giants of Torah should not withhold his words nor suppress his prophecy, but should give his analysis as he has been guided by Heaven.

(See Raphael Hayyim Yosef Hazan, *Hikekei Lev*, Saloniki, 1853, *Orah Hayyim* 6; and *Yoreh Deah* 42.)

It is interesting to note that the Hida, in his *Shem ha-Gedolim* (*Maarechet Gedolim, alef* 11) explains that though the Raavad sometimes criticized the Rambam in very sharp tones, he apologized to him (in his *Hasagot* to *Hilchot Kilaim* 6:2) and admitted to the greatness and the grandeur of his achievement in amassing the vast material called from the *Bavli, Yerushalmi, Tosefta* etc.:

And the reason that he disagreed with him in so sharp and forceful a manner was so that future generations should not rely totally upon him believing that one may not stray from his words, especially since he called his work *Mishneh Torah* ("repetition of the Torah"), [as if] after the written Law (Torah) the Rambam's work [also has, as it were, the status] of the written law, as [it is] a repetition of it.

So too, R. Ovadiah Yosef in *Yabia Omer*, vol. 4, in his introduction cited the Sheilat Yaavetz (vol. 1, sect. 4 ad fin.):

Certainly the disciple is permitted to disagree with his mentor on the basis of proofs and evidence, be they in writing or oral. And those who are truly wise are in no way offended by those who dissent from them. Quite the contrary, they are grateful to them that they saved them from falling into the net of error.

Similarly, the *Noda bi-Yehudah* (*Tinyana, Orah Hayyim*, sect. 101 and init.) writes:

The many justifications that you wrote in your letter to pacify me that I should not be angered that you disagree with me, were all unnecessary. For surely it is my prayer, and I wrote this in the introduction to my book, that anything [I wrote] that is incorrect should not be accepted.

On the contrary, I am deeply thankful to you for [your comments on my position] . . . and let the truth emerge . . .

Likewise in *Kama, Orah Hayyim*, sect.35, he wrote:

> Even though in the Responsa of the *Havat Yair* he ruled otherwise, would you say that in every case we find a responsum of one of the *Aharonim* we should decide in accordance [with that responsum]! The palate will taste and eat (based on Job 34:3), i.e., we will examine the situation anew, and in accordance with our understanding (our "taste"), we will decide.

And the *Havat Yair* himself, in the introduction to his *Makor Hayyim* (printed at the end of *Havat Yair*) wrote:

> An author in that world (i.e., the World to Come) is pleased when someone comes after him, and removes the dross from his works.

And perhaps even more remarkable are the words of R. Hayyim Volozin (in his *Ruah Hayyim*, chapter 1 of *Avot*), quoting his mentor the Gaon of Vilna, that there may be no favoring in the area of halachah. In this way he explained that which we find in *Avot* 1:4, "Let your house be a meeting-house for Sages and sit amidst the dust (*hevei mitabek*) of their feet and drink their words with thirst," *mitabek* is like that which we read in Genesis 32:25, "[And Jacob was left alone.] And there wrestled (*va-yeavek*) a man with him until the breaking of the day." This means that one must wrestle in conflict [in learning], for this is a mitzvah conflict (*milhemet mitzvah*). But one must take care not to be arrogant and think one has reached the level of one's master. To which R. Hayyim himself added (*Shut Hut ha-Meshulash*, sect. 9):

> Even though I served my Master the High-Priest (i.e., the Gaon of Vilna) and I must honor him and fear him as the fear of Heaven, I, nonetheless, follow what the Sages said (in *B. Baba Kama* 130b), "When a halachic ruling comes before you and you see in it a point of refutation, do not follow it, for a judge only has that which his eyes see." And I have already been warned by my Master, the Gaon of Vilna, not to favor anyone when it comes to adjudication.

Most of the above sources draw their authority from a responsum of the Rashba, (vol. 1, no. 253, Jerusalem, 1997, p. 108), who wrote as follows:

> And in this way all who followed the practices of one of the great authorities, such as in a place where all followed the practices of Rav Alfasi, or those places where they always followed the Rambam, so too their leaders followed their masters. However, if there is someone who is wise and fitted to give rulings, and he saw reason to forbid that which they had permitted, then they should follow the prohibition, because they (i.e., the earlier authorities) were not really their masters, so that if they dissent from their opinions they are not dishonouring them. . . .

R. Yosef Karo himself in his *Avkat Rochel* (sect. 154) wrote:

> Even though the Ritba and the Rivash were more knowledgeable than us in explaining the words of the *Rishonim*, this is only in the case of a statement without its rationale. But when there is a rationale, and we can question it, we may do so, for we too are not simpletons (literally: one who cuts down reeds in the marshes, cf. *B. Sanhedrin* 87b).

We may also recall the words of R. Yeshayah di-Trani (in *Shut ha-Rid* no. 62) that:

> This is my way, that anything that does not seem to me to be correct, even if Joshua bin Nun himself had said it, I do not harken to him, and I do not hesitate to say what seems right to me, according to my limited understanding, "and I will speak of thy testimonies also before (*neged*, also meaning against) kings" (Psalms 119:46).

So one must be willing to express one's own opinions, even if they be critical of authorities greater than you ("kings").

Similarly, R. Yissochar Eilenberg rejected his master's ruling on the "Vienna Get," in his *Tzedah la-Derech*, Prague, 1623, *Emor*, prefacing his argument with the request for "a thousand pardons" from his master. (See on this *Shut Maharam mi-Lublin*, sect. 123.)

We could add numerous additional references, but these should suffice. (For more, see Neriah Jeffrey, *Magen Yosef*, Jerusalem, 2011, pp. 5–11.)

This further touches upon the very basic question which Moshe Halbertal, in his *People of the Book: Canon, Meaning, and Authority*, Cambridge, Mass. and London, 1997, p. 72 et seq., calls "From a Flexible Canon to a Closed Code." In that contex he quotes a passage, very pertinent to our discussion (p. 78), attributed to R. Yaakov Pollack and R. Shalom Shachne:

> I know [that if I write a code] rabbis would rule only according to me because [in case of a disagreement between an earlier and later authority] the Halachah follows the later and I do not want "the world" to rely upon me. For example, when there is a disagreement between rabbinic authorities, a rabbi should decide or entertain his own opinion since "the judge should only follow that which he sees with his own eyes" (see *B.Baba Batra* 131a, *B. Sanhedrin* 6b). "Everyone, therefore, should rule according to the needs of the hour as his heart decrees." (*Responsa Rema*, Jerusalem, 1971, no. 25).

(See further Asher Ziv, *Rabbenu Moshe Isserles (Rema)*, New York, 1972, pp. 363–364.)

R. Hayyim mi-Velozin wrote to R. Noah Hayyim Tzvi, the Rabbi of Hamburg, as follows:

> I had already been warned in this matter from the mouth of my master and teacher, R. Eliyahu of Vilna, not to show preference (*la-seit panim*) when ruling, even to the decisions of our rabbis, the authors of the *Shulḥan Aruch*.

(*Aliyot Eliyahu*, p. 36; Ziv, ibid., p. 368, and see his note 24, ibid., that the end of this statement was omitted in some versions, which instead of "the authors of the *Shulḥan Aruch*" have "*ve-chu*," etc.)

I would like to add what R. Ovadiah Yosef wrote in his introduction to *Halichot Olam*, vol. 1, Jerusalem, 1998, p. 5, a book which comments, often argumentatively, on R. Yosef Hayyim's *Ben Ish Hai*. He was severly criticized for voicing disagreement with some of the Ben Ish Hai rulings, to which he responds:

And even if some of the people from Babylonia [in Bagdhad, where the Ben Ish Hai flourished] grumble resentfully against me, in that I [sometimes] rule against the Ben Ish Hai, my master, the Gaon R. Ezra Atiah *zt"l* strengthened and encouraged me to rule according to my own understanding and not to take note of the [criticisms] of this multitude, who do not know and do not understand . . .

And on p. 9 he writes in a letter to one of his denigrators:

And I know that all your fight [against me] is in order to put fear upon me so that I will not publish my notes [on the Ben Ish Hai]. But our teachers have already taught us that one should fear no man (*lo taguro mi-pnei ish*, Deuteronomy 1:17), do not contain, i.e., suppress (*taagor*), your words because of anyone.

(This is based on B. *Sanhedrin* 7b; and cf. responsa of Rosh, *Klal* 52:29.)

In the introduction to the third volume of *Halichot Olam*, Jerusalem, 2000, he softened his style omitting the last phrase about not taking note of the multitude, etc. There (p. 11) he quotes R. Hayyim Palache, in his responsa *Hikrei Hayyim, Yoreh Deah*, sect. 42, as teaching us that one must not suppress one's prophecy (i.e., understanding) when ruling halachah, and one is duty-bound to reveal one's personal opinion and publicize it in a book, for there can be no partiality in this matter. He brings additional citations to bolster this position.

Perhaps we may also remind ourselves of what R. Menahem Azariah di-Lonzano (c. 1550-1623) wrote in the introduction to his *Derech Hayyim*, Constantinople 1575:

Do not think that scholars will be angry with me because I say they erred in some issue. God forbid it for them. [For] the scholars who love the truth and admit it will not hate me for this. On the contrary they will love me and be delighted [at my corrections]. For "He also shall be my salvation: for an hypocrite shall not come before him" (Job 13:16).

R. Meshulam Roth in his "*Hearot le-Sifrei ha-Tosafot Yom-Tov*," in *Li-Chvod Yom Tov*, Jerusalem, 1956, p. 93 in a note quotes R. Menachem di-Lonzano in order to justify his voicing a criticism of the *Tosafot Yom Tov* in one case.

The great 20th century sage, Rabbi Haim David Halevy, ruled:

> Not only does a judge have the right to rule against his rabbis; *he also*
> *has an obligation to do so* [if he believes their decision to be incorrect
> and he has strong proofs to support his own position]. If the decision of
> those greater than he does not seem right to him, and he is not comfort-
> able following it, and yet he follows that decision [in deference to their
> authority], then it is almost certain that he has rendered a false judgment.

(*Aseh Lecha Rav*, Tel-Aviv, 1978, vol. 2, no. 61, p. 220.)
And ibid. nos. 36–39, p. 146, he writes:

> . . . and there was never a halakhic decision of any great sage in Israel
> after the completion of the Talmud that is binding, and permission is
> given to every person to disagree even with his teachers with correct and
> straightforward proofs . . . and even Maimonides and Maran (Rabbi
> Yosef Karo) of blessed memory, both their contemporaries and those
> who came after them disagreed with them, and in many matters, we do
> not follow them.

Rabbi Moshe Feinstein, in rejecting an opinion of Rabbi Shelomo
Kluger, wrote that "one must love truth more than anything." (*Igrot*
Moshe, Yoreh Deah, 3:88). See also M. Elon, *Ha-Mishpat ha-Ivri*, 2nd
edition, Jerusalem, 1988, p. 902–904, 1013–1017.

R. Moshe himself wrote in his *Igrot Moshe, Yoreh Deah*, vol. 1, New
York. 1960, no. 101, p. 186 (cited above in sections on "Dynamism in
Halachah"):

> . . . . Anyone who is capable of deciding any question that comes before
> him by thorough investigation in the Talmud and poskim with common
> sense and accurate proofs is obliged to do so even if it is a new issue
> which was not discussed in books. Even on a question which is found in
> books the rabbi must understand the issue and be able to decide it in his
> own mind and be able to rule on in, and not merely decide according to
> what is found (in a book). . . .
> Even if his decision contradicts that of some distinguished *Aharonim*
> – so what? We are authorized to disagree with the *Aharonim*, and some-
> times even with *Rishonim*, when there are good proofs, and especially

with straightforward reasoning. It is in reference to this type of situation that they said "The judge can act only on what is before their eyes"....
... since (the decision) does not contradict the views of famous poskim such as the authors of the *Shulhan Aruch* which have been accepted in all our communities....

I conclude as follows:

My grandfather of blessed memory, R. David Sperber *zt"l*, was among those who followed the approach of the Hatam Sofer. In his introduction to my grandfather's book, *Michtam le-David 'al ha-Torah* (Part I, Jerusalem, 1965), my father, of blessed memory, Rabbi Samuel Sperber *zt"l*, writes the following regarding my grandfather's character or personality:

> He had the quality of a Torah scholar and could be hard as steel when necessary. He was an expert judge on both public issues and monetary matters. He was invited to sit on rabbinical courts as a selected member of the tribunal or as its head on complex communal or individual matters. These discussions were at times stormy, and there were those who tried through various means to influence him or to reject his decision. I remember once after he issued a ruling in a matter that involved a very large loss of money to one of the litigants, they tried to attack him in a variety of ways. He said: "Why did they apparently choose me to head this tribunal? If because of my Torah knowledge, there are certainly others who are greater than me in Torah. If because of wisdom based on life experience, there are others who are wiser than me. There is, however, one quality that I have in my soul – 'You shall not recognize faces in judgment' (Deuteronomy 1:17), i.e., you should not be influenced by the litigants' status."[1]

---

1. The full verse is "Ye shall not respect persons in judgement; but ye shall hear the small as well as the great; ye shall fear no man; for the judgement is God's; and the cause that is too hard for you, bring it unto me, and I will hear it." See the opening words of Simhah Friedman, *Emunat Hachamim*, Jerusalem: Hakibbutz Hadati-Ne'emanei Torah va-Avodah, 1982, p. 4, who begins his essay with this responsum of the Hatam Sofer. He also added that one should always take heed of the verse, "You shall not recognize faces in judgement" (Deuteronomy 1:17), that is to say, never be influenced by the status of one's litigants.

In a similar vein, my mother, of blessed memory, Rebbetzin Miriam Sperber, wrote in her book *Mi-Sippurei ha-Savtah* (Jerusalem, 1986), in a chapter entitled, "The Story of the Butcher," pp. 70–71:

> Once a rock was thrown through the window at the home of my father-in-law, R. David Sperber, after he had ruled that a certain butcher shop was no longer to be considered kosher, and a baby who slept near the window was almost injured. My husband, R. Shmuel Sperber *zt"l*, asked him, "Is it worth being a rabbi, devoting years to a community, and then getting a rock thrown through your window?" My father-in-law replied: "Certainly it is worthwhile! You should know, my son, that a rabbi who is not involved in disputes, who is not subject to pressure, is not a rabbi; and a rabbi who submits to pressure is not a *mensch* (a decent human being)."[2]

Indeed, this was the way of the great masters. See, for example, the statement of R. David Mi-Trani (responsa *Ri"d*, sect. 62)[3]

> However, this is my way: Anything that is not right in my eyes – even if Yoshua the Son of Nun were to say it, I would not be obedient to him, and I do not refrain from expressing my opinion [critically] in accordance with what seemed to me to be correct according to my own limited understanding . . .

He continues to justify the legitimacy of disagreeing with earlier authorities. So he writes:

> Rather, I applied to myself the parable of the philosophers: . . . If a midget sits upon the shoulders of a giant, who sees further? Surely the midget, whose eyes are now higher than those of the giant. Similarly, we are midgets riding upon the shoulders of giants . . . In those places where we

---

2. See *B. Ketubot* 27b, the story of Rav Hisda, and my grandfather's *Afrakasta de Anya*, Brooklyn New York, 2002, vol. 1, sect. 197, pp. 438–439, on the slaughterer (*shochet*) who was suspended from his job.

3. Cf. ibid. sect.1; and in the introduction of *Shibolei ha-Leket*, and *Megilat Esther* on *Sefer ha-Mitzvot*, and most recently in the important article by R. Eliyahu Soloveitchik, "*Hirhurim al Mahapechat ha-Sifrut ha-Toranit ha-Hadashah*," *Ha-Maayan* 43/2, 2002, p. 78.

see that this one disagrees with that one, this one prohibits and that one says it is permitted, on whom shall we rely? . . . We can only examine their words, for "these and these are the words of the living G-d," and analyze and delve deeply into their words and attempt to see toward which side the law tends to incline. For this was done by the Sages of the *Mishnah* and the Talmud. And the later ones never refrained from speaking [critically] about the earlier ones, nor from deciding between them nor from refuting their words.[4]

But perhaps we should go back in time to the Rambam. For in *Hilchot Sanhedrin* 24:1, he writes of the judge – and here I find a parallelism, if not a full equivalence, between the judge (*dayan*) and the *posek*:

The judge when he judges in monetary matters must rule in accordance with those things that his understanding inclines him [to regard] as the truth, and it is firm in his heart that this is the case, even if there is no clear

---

4. Much has been written concerning the parable of the midget sitting on the shouders of the giant. See above pp. 232 note 42. Samuel Morell, *Studies in the Judicial Methodology of Rabbi David Ibn Abi Zimra*, New York and Oxford, 2004, 291–302, in a section entitled "The Law is in Accordance with the Later Authorities."

However, it should also be pointed out that the principle of *hilcheta ke-batrai* does not always apply. Thus the majority position among the *poskim* is that the principle of *hilkheta ke-batrai* (we follow the latest opinion) does not apply if the later authority was unaware of the opinions of earlier authorities. And when this is the case, we assume that had this earlier opinion been known, he would have judged accordingly. Hence, we follow the earlier opinion, especially if it is that of a *Rishon*. See, for example, Rema, *Hoshen Mishpat* 25:2: "But if at times there is a responsum of a Gaon which was not mentioned in the books, and we find them (later on) differing from him, we do not have to follow the later authorities, because it is possible that they did not know the view of the Gaon, and had they known they would have withdrawn their view (*Maharik*, sec. 94)."

This, as mentioned above, is the majority view. See *Kenesset ha-Gedola* to *Yoreh Deah* 37, *Beit Yosef*, no. 50, 149. See above pp. 273–276 note 7.

I discussed this matter at length in my book *Legitimacy and Necessity: Scientific Disciplines and the Learning of Talmud*, Jerusalem, 2006, pp. 60–61, and again in my *Darkah shel Halachah*, Jerusalem, 2007, pp. 9–10, 123–124. We may now add: Menasheh ha-Katan (Klein), *Mishneh Halachot*, vol. 3, Brooklyn, N.Y., 1960, 3b–4a, who quotes the Shach to *Hoshen Mishpat* 25, referred to above, and to the responsum of R. Moshe Alsheich no. 39, etc. There he asserts vigorously that the above principle does not apply in a case where the early authority was not known to the latter-day ones. In my *Legitimacy and Necessity: Scientific Disciplines and the Learning of Talmud* I also discussed the view of the Hazon Ish. However, that is too broad an issue to be discussed here.

evidence for it, and needless to say if he is certain that this is so, for he judges according to his knowledge . . . for the matter is only given to the heart of the judge according to what appears to him to be the true law . . .

This clearly goes back to the Talmudic dictum: "The judge has only what his eyes see," (*B. Shabbat* 10a, *B. Sanhedrin* 6b, ibid., 7a). (See the detailed analysis of the Rambam's position in S. Hefetz, *Reayot Nesibatiot ba-Mishpat ha-Ivri*, Hebrew University doctorate, 1974, p. 50 et seq.; Yaakov Blidstein "*Ha-Emet shel ha-Dayan ke-chli Pesikah*" *Dinei Yisrael* 24, 2007, p. 120 et seq.) This is very clear formulation of the duty of the judge to hold an independent position.

But together with this firmly independent stance,[5] and always with deep respect for great authorities of the generation, as well as contemporary ones, we should always be deeply cognizant of R. Nehunya ben ha-Kanah's prayer, mentioned above: "May no mishap happen because of me, and may I not stumble in matters of halachah."

5. See Marc. C. Angel, *Loving Truth & Peace: The Grand Religious Worldview of Rabbi Benzion Uziel*, Northvale N.J. and Jerusalem, 1999, pp. 87–88, who describes R. Uziel understanding of rabbinic leadership thus:

A posek surely had to be respectful of the sages of earlier generations. Yet, this respectfulness was not to quash the posek's independence. Rabbi Uziel noted that the posek was not bound to rule like his predecessors, even though he certainly had to be aware of their arguments and decisions (*Michmanei Uziel*, Tel Aviv 5699, p. 376). Even in antiquity, when the Great Court functioned in Jerusalem as the authoritative body of Jewish law for the entire nation, the decisions of each Great Court could be overturned by a later Great Court (Maimonides, *Mishneh Torah, Hilkhot Mumrim* 2:2). The rabbis of each generation had the freedom and responsibility to come to their own decisions as long as these decisions were firmly based in halachic sources and supported by valid arguments.

Israel M. Goldman, in his *The Life and Times of Rabbi David Ibn Abi Zimra* [=*RDBZ*], New York 1970, p. 22, points out that the *RDBZ* would not be intimidated by those wishing to object to his rulings, referring us to his responsa vol. 4, Livorno, 1652, no. 101, where he writes in a certain context:

I feared not his words, for I was not closing this for my glory nor for the honour of my father's house, but in order that dissensions shall not be multiplied in Israel, and in order that our Torah shall not be made into two Torahs.

APPENDIX 5: AN EXAMPLE OF COMPASSION
WITHOUT COMPROMISE

Rabbi Chaim Rapoport, the strictly Orthodox spiritual leader of the Ilford Synagogue in London, published an article in the *Jewish Chronicle* in February, 2000, on the sensitive issue of "Homosexuality and Judaism." He received a number of reactions to which he responded to in his classic volume *Judaism and Homosexuality: An Authentic Orthodox View*, London and Portland, Oregon, 2004. I cite here a reaction and his response on pp. 119–120, which, I believe, is an excellent example of a sensitive compassionate halachic attitude to a complex and deeply troubling subject:

Is there Room for Empathy?
Question: *I was quite horrified by your article in the Jewish Chronicle. I thought that as an Orthodox Rabbi, you would know better than to single out homosexuals, who violate prohibitions for which one must sacrifice one's life (rather than violate) for special 'understanding' and 'empathy.' It appears to me that you have been brainwashed by the forces of political correctness into distorting, even if slightly, the Torah view. Sodomy is not just another sin like eating a cheeseburger in Mc Donalds. Sodomy is non-negotiable.*

Answer: It is precisely because I am an Orthodox Rabbi that I take the view expressed in my article in the *Jewish Chronicle*. Or perhaps, I should say that it is because I espouse the compassionate attitude delineated in my article, that I am able, with God's help, to serve as an Orthodox Rabbi to a community that consists of members across the spectrum of religious observance, or the lack of it. The Jewish people to whom I minister vary in their backgrounds, social position, faith, and observance of Jewish

Law. I have had occasion to attend to the needs of Jewish prisoners, guilty of minor or major offences; people brought up in Orthodox homes and in irreligious homes; healthy family environments' and unhealthy ones. Naturally, it is part of the awesome responsibility of a rabbi to reprove people for their shortcomings and inspire sinners to repent. Yet surely a pre-requisite to all the above is the ability to be compassionate and understanding. If a rabbi cannot adopt such an attitude, he would be better off avoiding the pastoral ministry. Any counsel, or rebuke for that matter, can usually only have a positive effect if it is administered in a compassionate and understanding manner.

I take it that as an Orthodox Rabbi, you have probably had occasion to counsel young couples about the observance of *taharat ha-mishpachah*. You are surely aware that sexual intercourse with a *niddah* is a most severe infraction. It is likewise a sin for which one is obliged to forfeit one's life, rather than violate it. It is also 'not just another sin like eating a cheeseburger in McDonalds.' Intercourse with a *niddah* (whether within or without the bonds of marriage) is 'non-negotiable.' When you seek to inspire observance of *taharat ha-mishpachah* of those of your members who totally disregard these laws, do you succeed with fire and brimstone alone? Or do you try and appreciate their backgrounds, circumstances, and trials? I, for one, have found that the only way to communicate Torah ideals to the uninitiated is by adopting an extremely sensitive and sympathetic approach.

The reason that I singled out homosexuals for 'special' understanding is stated explicitly in my article. As I wrote, 'the bachelor, the spinster, the homosexual or a person trapped in a sexless marriage' may face untold loneliness, misery and sexual frustration. Is that not a good enough reason to advocate 'special' consideration for people who may face such a predicament through no fault of their own? Do you not think that a homosexual who does not have any legitimate sexually emotional outlet, and who may be compelled constantly to face temptation, is a subject worthy of compassion? At any rate, the challenges of a homosexual must be inconceivably greater than those of a married couple who have to abstain from relationships during the days of the wife's ritual impurity. It is for this reason that I maintain that, if we can be kind and understanding to all other people, irrespective of their religious or moral shortcomings, then *a fortiori*, we must adopt the same attitude towards those who face the challenges, say, of an exclusive homosexual orientation.

If I were not an Orthodox Rabbi, but, say, a Reform or Liberal thinker, I may be 'justified' in taking a more harsh attitude towards homosexuals. For those who are not bound by the Laws of the Torah, and who mould their Judaism in accordance with their personal conscience – which is naturally affected by personal and social prejudices and biases – may indeed take the liberty of projecting their personal bigotry onto the Torah. It is, as I said, precisely because I am an Orthodox Rabbi that I cannot allow my personal aversion for homosexual intercourse and discomfort with the whole concept to corrupt the correct attitude to brothers and sisters of homosexual orientation. As you wrote, 'Sodomy is non-negotiable' – but for that matter, neither is *ahavat Yisrael* ('Love Thy Neighbour'), at least in the school I come from.

Rabbi Rapoport's humanity expresses itself throughout the remarkable piece of rabbinic scholarship. As a single, but representative example I refer the reader to the summary at the end of a very long, involved, and detailed footnote (no. 11) on p. 142. It deals with the issue of masturbation on the part of homosexuals. He writes as follows:

> However, notwithstanding any qualms that may be raised with regard to the above-mentioned thesis, the ruling of the *Chelkat Mechokek* and the *Bet Shmuel* [*Chelkat Mehokek*, of R. Moshe b. Yitzchak Yehuda Lerna, c. 1605–1658; *Beit Shemuel* by R. Shmuel ben Shraga Feivush, c. 1640–c. 1700, to *Even ha-Ezer* 23:1, basing themselves on *Sefer Hasidim* no.176.] whatever its rationale may be – may provide rabbis and counselors with useful guidelines when instructing homosexuals. In what almost inevitably amounts to commitment to lifelong celibacy, there are bound to be situations in which some homosexuals will find themselves on the verge of violating the biblical prohibition of male-to-male intercourse or the rabbinic extensions of that prohibition. Also, in the event of practicing homosexuals attempting to return to the ways of the Torah and abstain from all forbidden acts, it may be nearly impossible for them to change their *modus vivendi* from one extreme to another. In all such situations, it is possible that the mentor may be justified in taking recourse to the views expounded by the above-mentioned authorities when forming their advice to their charges.

Finallly, I could have cited many other examples, but I chose this one because of its clear transparent articulation.

Very recently someone brought to my attention a very interesting article by R. Ysoscher Katz, Chair of the Talmud department at Yeshivat Chovevei Torah Rabbinical School, and Director of the Lindenbaum Center on Halakhic Studies. He writes as follows:

> The Orthodox conversation over the Supreme Court's gay marriage decision reminds me why I am Modern Chassidish and not Modern Orthodox.
>
> There are many differences between these two streams, but the defining distinction is this: their views differ greatly over the role of Halacha (Jewish law) in religious life. The Modern Orthodox Jew experiences the world exclusively through the prism of Halacha, while the Modern Chassid's view is broader and more encompassing. Halacha is what informs and inspires the Modern Orthodox observer. It is also the exclusive barometer that he or she uses to determine the validity of one's life and legitimacy of one's choices.
>
> On the other hand, for the Modern Chassid, Halacha is merely a framework, a way of life that creates an infrastructure in which the religious persona grows and flourishes. The Chassid's purview encompasses much more than the observance of commandments. He allows for a broader mix of theological considerations to inform his religious stances and attitude towards others.
>
> So far, the Orthodox leadership's reaction to the Supreme Court's decision has been exclusively, narrowly halachistic (legalistic) – very much in line with how the Vilna Gaon would have reacted. The response of Chassidic rebbes who follow the Ba'al Shem Tov would have been very different, in tenor and content. That is the voice sorely missing in our community. While we are blessed with plenty of rabbis opining about the decision and its consequences, we are desperately missing the voice of a rebbe.
>
> The plight of gay people presents a huge challenge to the Orthodox believer. The rabbi and rebbe have very different clerical roles to play in this religious conundrum. The rabbi's role is to judge, the rebbe's is to provide pastoral care. The rabbi, guided by the Talmud and codes, opines and adjudicates, while the rebbe, whose halachic thinking is augmented

by a spiritualist orientation, shuns judgment in favor of spiritual care.

While the Chassidic theologian draws on many traditional sources, there are two that stand out as distinctly potent. One is an insightful lesson taught by the wife of Rabbi Meir in the Talmud. Advocating a nuanced approach towards sin, she admonished her husband, who mistakenly conflated sin with the sinner. Her understanding of the pastoral task was that the devout can separate the person from his or her behavior, looking past their misdeeds to see the humanity inherent in every human being.

Along these lines there is a Talmudic statement that lauds the criminal who pleads for divine support before committing a crime. This provocative teaching intimates that there can be spiritual significance even in those moments when an individual's life is not in consonance with Halacha's religious prescripts.

While the halachists explore the minutiae of Jewish law to see if Orthodoxy can make room for the gay people in their midst, the rebbes have a different role to play. The rebbes need to be these people's spiritual chaperones, walking alongside them on the arduous journey of reconciliation between their religious convictions and their inherent sexual predisposition, in the process helping them sanctify this torturous journey.

There's a story I like about Rabbi Levi Yitzchak of Berdichev. When walking down the street one day he noticed a follower saying his daily prayers while oiling the wheels of his carriage. Instead of reacting with opprobrium, he set aside his legalistic discomfort, turned towards the heavens, and said: "God, look at your wonderful people! They love praying so much that even while they are oiling the wheels they still turn to you in prayer and supplication." As a Chassid he allowed his pastoral sensitivity to trump his judicial sensibilities. Instead of scolding the Chassid for his legalistic shortcomings, he chose to sanctify that very sin, believing that such a stance will lead to greater spiritual growth.

The legalistic voice has dominated the Orthodox public sphere – but our gay brothers and sisters deserve to have the harshness of moral certitude dulled by the tenderness of spiritually infused pastoral care. History will determine how the journey of Orthodox homosexuality will turn out. The modern Chasid's role is to ensure that this journey, which will hopefully lead people towards greater religious observance, is as sacred as it can be. I hope that the important voice of the rebbe will soon be added to the cacophony of religious voices on this issue. Our gay brethren deserve and desperately need it . . . [For it is here that we encounter the divinity embedded in every human being, regardless of deed, creed, or sexual orientation.]

Although R. Katz does not deal with the halachic issues here, he does express, in his own way, the urgent need for a compassionate approach to the phenomenon.

Finally, we may recall the words of the Rambam, in *Hilchot Sanhedrin* 2:3 (based on *B. Sanhedrin* 36b):

> One does not appoint to the Sanhedrin either a very elderly person or a eunuch, because they have a certain degree of cruelty. Neither do we appoint someone who has no children, *to ensure that [the judge] will be compassionate.* (My emphasis – D.S.)

APPENDIX 6: "ITS WAYS ARE THE WAYS OF PLEASANTNESS" AND "CHARITABLE INTERPRETATION"

THIS PRINCIPLE RUNS AS A BASIC RECURRENT THEME THROUGH-
out this study. We shall therefore look into it a little more closely.

Above in the section entitled, "Its Ways Are the Ways of Pleasantness," we explained how the rabbis identified the four species of the
lulav, rejecting those that are thorny, "as it is inconceivable that the
Torah would require us to take species that would prick and scratch
one's hands, since 'its ways are ways of pleasantness and all its paths
are peace'" (Proverbs 3:17; *B. Sukkah* 32a). What this means is that the
rabbis determined the nature and details of a biblical commandment
(*mi-de-Oraita*) as the basis of an "external" moral value. This would
seem to be the explanation of how they are, at times, interpreted biblical
verses not according to their single straightforward meaning (*pshat*).
Thus despite the fact that the famous verse in Exodus 21:24 which
addresses the question of damages, stating that "payment" be an "eye
for eye, tooth for tooth, hand for hand, foot for foot" etc., (*lex talionis*),
and so too in Leviticus 24:20 and Deuteronomy 19:21, nevertheless, the
rabbis interpreted these texts as positing monetary payment (*B. Baba
Kama* 83b–84a; *Mechilta, Masechet Nezikin* 8, ed. Horowitz-Rabin,
2nd edition, Jerusalem, 1960. p. 277, etc.). Needless to say the rabbis
found both hermeneutic and logical reasons justifying the interpretation
(see references above). But that this is not the *pshat* of the verse is
clear, and indeed there is a solitary opinion of R. Eliezer (ibid.) that the
verses be interpreted literally.[1] The Rambam justifies this "non-literal"
interpretation by stating in *Hilchot Hovel u-Mazik* 1:2:

---

1. But see M.M. Kasher, *Torah Shelemah*, vol. 17, New York, 1956, p. 261. In-

"Eye for eye" – from tradition (*mi-pi ha-shemuah*) they learned that [the verse] is speaking that "for" (*tahat*) denotes payment in money.

In other words, he posits an oral tradition (*mi-pi ha-Shemua*) directing the manner in which to interpret this verse (or these verses). Cf. Rambam ibid. 2:11; *Shulhan Aruch, Hoshen Mishpat* 420:17; Maharal mi-Prague, *Gur Aryeh* to *Leviticus* ibid.; and Yehudah ha-Levi, *Kuzari* 3:47. (See for a detailed analysis of this issue, M.M. Kasher, *Torah Shelemah*, ibid., pp. 258–270; and see Copperman, ibid., p. 68.)

Similarly we find that R. Avraham ben ha-Rambam (S. Eppenstein, *Likkutim*, apud *Le-David Tzvi, Sefer ha-Yovel le-R. D. Tzvi Hoffmann*, Berlin, 1914, Kasher, ibid., p. 259) writes quite explicitly:

---

deed, this was the view of the *Baitosim*, as recorded in *Megilat Ta'anit* chapter 4, Kasher, ibid., p. 128, sect. 448, with his discussion on p. 260, where he cites Azria de Rossi's *Meor Enayim* who says that this is also Philo's position. (See Philo, *Spec.* 3:181–183; Erwin R. Goodenough, *An Introduction to Philo Judaeus*, New York, 1963, pp. 128–129, cf. idem, *The Jurisprudence of the Jewish Courts in Egypt*, New Haven, Conn., 1929, pp. 135–142. See also Adolf Berger, *Encyclopedic Dictionary of Roman Law*, Philadelphia, 1953, n. 730 s.v. Talis.) See also David Weiss Halivni, *Peshat and Derash*, New York and Oxford, 1991, pp. 85–88; Yehuda Copperman, *Li-Fshuto shel Mikra*, Jerusalem, 1974, for a full examination of the concept of *pshat*; Y. Maori, "The Approach of Classical Jewish Exegetes to *Peshat* and *Derash* and its Implications for Teaching Bible Today," *Tradition* 21/3, 1984, pp. 40–53; M. Arend, "*Peshuto Shel Mikra* and Halachic Probability: Remarks on Y. Copperman's Essay," *HaMaayan* 15/1, 1975, pp. 59–63.

See further S. Atlas, *Netivot ba-Mishpat ha-Ivri*, New York, 1978, pp. 83–129. A listing of articles on the subject of *lex talionis* is to be found in N. Rakover, *Otzar ha-Mishpat*, vol. 2, Jerusalem, 1990, no. 4338, 4346, 4352, 4364, etc. See also Aaron Kirschenbaum, *Equity in Jewish Law. Vol. 15: Formalism and Flexibility in Jewish Civil Law*. Hoboken N.J. and New York, 1991, pp. 28–32. In his examination of this issue he writes: (p. 29)

... equitable interpretations of statute are not regarded as intrusions or "reinterpretations" of the text based upon extrinsic considerations. On the contrary, many equitable interpretations are products of the interpreters search for "true," original, and authentic meanings of the passage ...

And on p. 32 he writes:

To the rabbis of the Talmud and to Maimonides, a literal interpretation of *An eye for an eye* represents bad law, and is totally foreign to sacred scripture.

Copperman's formulation is slightly different. He states that the *pshat* tells us what "ought to be" (*ha-raui*), i.e., that really a person deserves to have his eye taken out; but the halachah rules what is "desirable" in the eyes of the law (*ratzui*), namely that monetary compensation be given. (See ibid. p. 70 et seq.) Cf. Quine-Dworkin's principle below. Finally, see David Daube's extensive study entitled "Lex Talionis," Studies in Biblical Law, Cambridge, 1947, pp. 102–153.

THE IMPORTANCE OF THE COMMUNITY RABBI

"An eye for an eye" – the plain meaning of the text (*pshuto shel mikra*) is of itself self-evident. But rabbinic tradition explains that the intent of the verse is monetary compensation for the eye or the tooth, etc. And there is support for the rabbinic tradition from evidence taken from [other] biblical texts and analogy (*hekeish*) [which] R. Saadia Gaon wrote in his commentary . . . (referring to Exodus 21:15–19). (My emphasis – D.S.)[2]

So too, in a long passage that Ibn Ezra brings in his commentary to Exodus 21:24, ed. Asher Weiser, vol. 2, Jerusalem, 1977, p. 152, which records a polemic discussion on this same issue between R. Saadia Gaon and the Karaite Ben Zuta, where we read that R. Saadia states clearly that:

> . . . in principle we cannot interpret the mitzvot of the Torah in a complete manner if we do not rely upon the words of the Sages, for just as we received the [written] Torah from our forefathers, so too we received the Oral Torah, and there is no difference between them.[3]

And the Rambam wrote "it is known from rabbinic tradition (*be-kabbalot rabboteinu*) that it is money." This is explained more expansively in the Seforno ad loc. (See Yehudah Copperman, *Kedushat Pshuto Shel Mikra*, Jerusalem, 2009, pp. 161–164, with further analysis.)

We find a similar phenomenon in the interpretation of the verse in Deuteronomy 25:11–12:

> 11. And when men strive together one with another, and the wife of the one draweth near for to deliver her husband out of the hand of him that smiteth him, and putteth forth her hand, and taketh him by the secrets.

---

2. See Yehudah Ratzahbi, *Perushei Rav Saadia Gaon le-Sefer Shemot*, Jerusalem, 1998, p. 116.

3. See further Kasher, ibid., citing *Kuzari* 3:46–47; Ralbag ad loc. Indeed, this polemic continues into the time of the *Rishonim* in their responses to the "*minim*." See *Tosafot ha-Shalem: Otzar Perushei Baalei ha-Tosafot al Torah, Neviim u-Ketuvim*, ed. Yaakov Gelis, vol. 8, Jerusalem, 1990, pp. 223–224, nos. 1, 3. The founder of Karaism, Anan, appears to have taken the verse literally, but argues that since one can no longer inflict corporal punishment one must distance oneself from the criminal. See Leon Nemoy, *Karaite Anthology*, New Haven and London, 1952, pp. 13–14. As to Philo's position on this issue, see Loeb ed., transl. F.H. Colson, vol. 7, "The Special Laws" 3:171–198. pp. 582–599, and above note 235.

12. Then thou shalt cut of her hand, thine eye shall not pity her.

The plain and straightforward meaning of verse 12 is not in doubt, and is even strengthened by the summation "thine eye shall not pity her." Nonetheless, here too the rabbis interpreted it as meaning monetary payment (*mammon*) (R. Yehudah, *Sifrei Deuteronomy*, sect. 293, ed. Finkelstein Horowitz, Berlin, 1940, p. 312 with references). Here, too, we find a hermeneutical justification by reference to Deuteronomy 19:21, which we have seen above to have been interpreted as reference to monetary compensation. But is this not circular reasoning?[4]

Again, I believe the rabbis – or at least the majority of them – could not entertain accepting the literal meaning of these texts, since it went against all they understood to be moral values that underlie the halachah. Hence, they were forced to hermeneutically interpret them differently, in accordance with the principle that "its ways are the ways of pleasantness," and not those which they viewed as barbaric.

I believe we may see a continuation of policy of such "charitable interpretation" in the way the *Rishonim* interpret Talmudic texts. Thus in the first *Mishnah* of the second chapter of *Niddah*, we read that a man who continuously examines his penis (to see whether he had a seminal emission), "let it be cut off." The Talmud then inquires (*B. Nidah* 13b), whether the *Mishnah* meant this as a curse (*letuta*), or to be taken literally as the law (*dina*). The Talmud then brings a proof that this is meant to be taken literally from a statement in *B. Sanhedrin* 58b, where we are told that Rav Huna ruled that someone "who raised his hand against his neighbor," even if he did not actually hit him, should have his hand cut off, referring to the verse in Job 38:15, ". . . and the high arm is broken." Despite the fairly clear meaning of both sources, the Meiri to *Niddah* (ed. A. Sofer, New York, 1949, p. 50) writes:

> And they explained [i.e., the *Mishnah*] in the *Gemara* (ibid., 13b) that that which they said "let it be cut off" is not intended to be the law (*dina*) but to be understood as a curse (*letuta*).

---

4. See R. Baruch Halevi Epstein, *Torah Temimah* to Deuteronomy, ibid., p. 405, note 12, who seeks to justify this "non-literal" interpretation.

Likewise in *Sanhedrin*, ibid., the Meiri wrote with regard to cutting off the hand of one who raised his hand against his neighbor that: There are those who explain it as meaning he punished him demanding monetary compensation to the value of a hand. However, as the editor (ibid., note 3) rightly noted there is no clear conclusion in the Talmudic *sugya* that this is the case, and that the text should *not* be taken literally. The Meiri takes the position of the Ritva ad loc (as the editor noted, ibid.) despite the fact that R. Tarfon seems to take the *Mishnah* literally (*B. Niddah* ibid. and *Y. Niddah* 1:2). However, the *Yerushalmi* cites *havraiah* (members of the academy) who relate that R. Tarfon would curse one who carries on thus, hence, not taking the *Mishnah* literally that he would have his genitals excised, but finding a case sufficient. And Rashi to *Sanhedrin* ibid. explicitly interprets Rav Huna as having demanded a fine, while Tosafot ad loc. explains Rav Huna's action as a unique case, since the man was a continuous batterer.[5]

---

5. Cf. *Tosefta Niddah* 218, and R. David Pardo, *Hasdei David* ad loc., Jerusalem, 1971, pp. 195–196, and Y. Tamar, *Alei Tamar* to *Y. Niddah*, ibid., 1983, 325. Cf. *B. Sanhedrin* 46a that at times the rabbi would punish very severely, "not because the person was really culpable, but the circumstances required it (*ela she-ha-shaah tzericha le-chach.*)" See responsa of the Rivash, R. Yitzhak ben Sheshet (1326–1407), ed. David Metzger, vol. 1, Jerusalem, 1993, no. 251, pp. 320–322, on the authority of the courts to give extraordinary punishments. He takes the Rav Huna story literally.

We should further point out that it seems most unlikely that the rabbis would inflict serious corporal punishment basing themselves on a midrashic deviration from a verse in Job – *divrei kabbalah* (see *B. Hagigah* 10b, *B. Niddah* 23a; however, cf. *B. Baba Kama* 2b). It is also known that the Sages of the Talmud often exaggerated punishments in order to keep people away for transgression, but did not mean to be taken literally (Rivash, responses no. 171; Yitzhak Yosef, *Ein Yitzhak*, vol. 1, Jerusalem, 2009, no. 80, pp. 151–155, with numerous examples, though this one is not cited).

On the other hand we do have evidence of such an extreme form of punishment, derived from the same verse in Job. Thus, in *Sefer Hasidim*, ed. R. Margaliot, Jerusalem, 1957, no. 49, pp. 108–109, we read:

And he said to him that did the wrong, "Wherefore smiteth thou thy fellow?" (Exodus 2:13). He did not actually hit him, but merely raised his hand against him, and therefore was called a *rasha* (wicked one, one who "did the wrong"). And the rabbis said: "Anyone who punches his neighbour in the jaw, it is as though he has punched the *Shechinah*, (*B. Sanhedrin* 58b; *Zohar Genesis* 57a; *Zohar Hadash Ruth* 79b). This means: anyone who slaps a fellow Jew's cheek, it is as though he "put a knife to thy throat" (Proverbs 23:2), i.e., it is as though he hits the *Shechinah*. And he has no means of amendment other than cutting off his hand, as it is said, "And the high arm shall be broken" (Job 38:15) . . .

So too, ruled R. Meir of Rothenberg in his responsa, ed. Prague no.81, namely that one who beats his wife "should be excommunicated, whipped, and punished in all

So too, the Rambam in *Hilchot Issurei Biya* 21:23 does not mention a punishment of cutting off a man's hand for caressing his penis.
Rabbenu Hananel already explained Rav Huna's action as monetary
punishment (R. Reuven Margaliot, *Margaliot ha-Yam* to *Sanhedrin*, vol.

---

kinds of suppression, and have his hand or his leg cut off." See A. Grossman, *He Shall
Rule Over You: Medieval Jewish Sages on Women*, Jerusalem, 2011, pp. 198–199, 201,
[Hebrew], who suspects that this was more a threat than actual cutting off of a hand,
ibid., pp. 194, note 86. He also points out (p. 198) that it is not clear that this is part
of the original *Sefer Hasidim*. Nevertheless, he cites another passage in the Wistinetzki
ed. of *Sefer Hasidim*, Frankfurt a Main 1924, no. 631, p. 169, where we are told that
a certain R. Mordechai broke his own arm by closing the door on it, because he had
punched a Jew, citing the verses in Job 31:21–22, "If I have lifted up my hand against
the fatherless . . . let my arm fall from mine shoulder-blade [and mine arm be broken
from the bone]." But this is an extreme case of *teshuvat ha-mishkal*, which cannot
be discussed here. There is considerable literature on this subject; see, for instance,
Yitzhak Baer, *Ha-Megamah ha-Datit-Hevratit shel "Sefer Hasidim,"* Jerusalem, 1938,
pp. 18–20.
    However, see the responsa *Zichron Yehudah*, by R. Yehudah the son of the Rosh,
ed. A.Y. Havatzelet, Jerusalem, 2005, no. 79, p. 73, on cutting off the hands of one who
attacked a judge, (and cf. responsa of Rosh, *Klal* 18, *Siman* 13, and *Shulhan Aruch
Even ha-Ezer* 177:5, on mutilation as a punishment).
    See also responsa of Rosh, *Klal* 17, *Siman* 8 (in the addition in ed. Venice 1607)
concerning one who blasphemed God's name in Arabic before two witnesses that his
tongue be cut out. (See Z.W. Zicherman, *Otzar Plaot ha-Torah*, *Leviticus*, New York,
2016, p. 1134, who notes that this part of the responsum was omitted in later editions.
It is found in the latest edition, ed. Y.S. Yudlov, Jerusalem, 1994, p. 83.)
    Perhaps in this way we can understand the views expressed by a number of *Ris-
honim* to explain the verse in Genesis 38:24, where we are told that Judah, when he
found out that Tamar was pregnant ruled that she should be "taken out and burned."
(For reference, see *supra* p. 69.) For R. Yehudah ha-Hasid, cited in *Paneah Raza* ad
loc. stated:
    God forfend that she be taken out to be burned . . . "And let her be burned" is to
be interpreted that they brand her cheeks as a sign that she was a prostitute, as was
the custom in their times.
    So too, in the name of R. Yitzhak of Vienna. However, Mahri Katz in his comments
to *Paneah Raza* writes:
    Heaven forbid that such words came out of the holy mouth [of R. Yehudah ha-
Hasid] . . .
    See M.M. Kasher, *Torah Shelemah* ad loc., vol. 6 (tome 7), Jerusalem, 1938, note
96, who cites all these sources, concluding that those witnesses give clear testimony
that this was, indeed, the opinion of R. Yehudah ha-Hasid. Perhaps, he too wished to
soften the severity of the punishment through "charitable interpretation," even though
branding itself is very cruel, but still less than burning to death. Branding was used in
medieval Europe for heretics and prostitutes (see, e.g., Henry Charles Lea, *A History
of the Inquisition*, vol. 2, New York, 1955, p. 182; George P. Howard, *A History of
Matrimonial Institution*, London, c. 1923, pp. 169–178, etc.).

2, Jerusalem, 1958, p. 14, citing a fragment published by S. Assaf, apud *Ish ha-Torah ve-ha-Maaseh, Sefer Yovel le-chvod ha-Rav Ostrovsky,* Jerusalem, 1946, p. 71).

Furthermore, on the verse in Numbers 31:7, "And they [the Israelites] warned against the Midianites as the Lord commanded Moses . . .", the *Sifrei* ad loc., ed. Horowitz, 2nd edition, Jerusalem, 1966 (first ed. Leipzig 1917). p. 210, writes:

> They surrounded it from [all] four sides. R. Natan says: He gave them one fourth side [open] so that they could escape.

So too in *Midrash Tannaim*, ed. David Tzvi Hoffmann, Berlin, 1908– 1909, to Deuteronomy 20:12:

> "[And if it will make no peace with thee (after being warned), but will make war against thee], then thou shalt besiege it." – Surround them on [all] four sides. R. Nathan says: One gives them a way to escape.

R. Natan's view is also to be found in Targum Yonatan ad loc.: ". . . and they surrounded them on three sides" (see J. Lewy, *Chaldäisches Wörterbuch über die Targumim,* Leipzig, 1881, p. 318).

Now, normally, when there is an anonymous statement followed by an attributed one, the assumption is that the anonymous one is the majority opinion, and the attributed one a sole opinion. Consequently the halachah should follow the anonymous majority view. Yet the Rambam in *Hilchot Melachim* 6:7 rules:

> When one attacks a city to capture it, one does not surround it on [all] four sides, but [only] three, and one leaves a place to escape for whoever wishes to save his life, as it is written, "And they warred against the Midianites as the Lord commanded them" (Numbers ibid.). From our tradition [*mi-pi ha-shemuah*] we have learned that this is what they were commanded.

The Ramban, in his notes to Rambam *Sefer ha-Mitzvot*, forgotten positive commandments no. 5 (ed. Jerusalem, 1969, sect. 2, p. 42) writes as follows:

> We were commanded that when we besiege a city, we should leave one of the sides un-besieged, so that if they wish to escape they should have a way to do so. And from this we learn to behave with compassion even with our enemies during wartime, and it is also strategically advisable that we leave them a way of escape so that they will not strengthen their resolve against us, as it is written, "And they warned against the Midianites as the Lord commanded them . . ." In the *Sifrei* they interpreted [the verse]: They surrounded them on three sides. R. Natan says: Give them a fourth way to escape. And this was not only a mitzvah for the hour [they fought against] Midian, but is a commandment for all generations in all elective wars (*milhamot reshut*). And so wrote the Rav [Rambam] in his great compilation in *Hilchot Melachim u-Milhamotehem*.

The Ramban here is not quoting the *Sifrei* but paraphrasing it, and it is not clear what was the original reading he had before him.

The Semag, *Sefer Mitzvot Gadol*, by the Tosafist R. Moshe of Coucy, (part 2, positive commandment no.18 ad fin., Brooklyn, 1959, fol. 117b) also rules thus, basing himself on the same verse in Numbers, quoting no source (as is usual with him). Likewise, *Sefer ha-Hinuch*, *Mitzvah* 527, ed. Ahavat Shalom, vol. 2, Jerusalem, 1998, p. 258 (and see editor's note 3, ibid).

We shall not follow up with later sources, such as *Midrash ha-Gadol*, *Midrash Meor ha-Afelah*, etc., for what we have already shown suffices to demonstrate how all our halachic sources rule compassionately in accordance with what appears to be the minority view of R. Natan.

It has been suggested (*Sifrei Numbers* ibid. editor's note to line 13) that perhaps these authorities had a different reading in the *Sifrei*, where this constituted the majority opinion. But this is most unlikely since the *Sifrei* text is borne out by *Midrash Tannaim* referred to above, and R. Natan is explicitly mentioned in the Ramban.

That there is no real indication that the actual verse directing us to R. Natan's view is distinctly evident from the fact that the Rambam had to add that we learn this *mi-pi ha-shmuah*. Once again, then, we have an example of how "charitable interpretation" – for that must be the basis of the rabbinic "tradition" – sought to add an element of morality and compassion into the practical application of warfare, which is, of necessity, cruel, as the Rambam's added comment very clearly expresses.

We might perhaps add, as a possible homiletic source for R. Nata's view, that the verse ends "as the Lord commanded Moses." This phrase is basically superfluous since the chapter begins with, "And the Lord spoke to Moses saying . . . and Moses passed God's words on to the people." In the subsequent verses which describe how God's orders are carried out, there is no explicit mention that their actions were in accordance with God's command to Moses. What then does this phrase add? Perhaps R. Natan (or his earlier source) understood it as teaching that such military actions must include the element of compassion, for since God is merciful, so must we be merciful, i.e., *imitatio dei* (see Exodus 34:6, B. *Shabbat* 133b, Y. *Peah* 1 ad init, and in a different formulation in Targum Bendo Yonatan to Leviticus 22:28), and it is this that is hinted at by this additional phrase.[6]

---

6. Here we have employed a very common method used in rabbinic exegesis of biblical verses. See, for example, Rashbam's commentary to the opening of Genesis (as cited by Maori ibid. p. 47), and see his note 37, ibid., p. 52:

Most of the *halachot* derive from superfluities in the text or the changes from the language in which the simple sense of Scripture can be written to language from which the main point of a *derashah* can be derived; e.g., "These are the generations of heaven and earth in their being created [*bhbr'm*]" (Genesis 2:4), and the Sages interpreted by *derash* – through Abraham [*b'brhm*] from the lengthiness of the expression, since there was no need to say "*bhbr'm*."

He further writes in his commentary to Genesis 37:2 (Maori ibid.):

The essence of Torah is to teach and inform us, through the hints of *peshat*, *haggadot*, *halachot* and *dinim*, by means of extended phraseology, and with the aid of the thirty-two principles of R. Eliezer the son of R. Yose the Galilean and of the thirteen principles of R. Yishmael.

R. Baruch Halevi Epstein, who also frequently uses this methodology, in his *Torah Temimah* to Leviticus 31:7, p. 374, note 9, also discusses this same question. I quote him in full:

It is not clear why the Rambam ruled in accordance with R. Natan, in opposition to the Sages. It is also not well clarified what he meant saying that it was derived *mi-pi-ha-shmuah*, "from the mouth of tradition," for where is such a thing hinted at? And from where did R. Natan derive his *novum* (*hiddush*)?

Perhaps we may suggest a possible source from that which we find in Y. *Sheviit* 6:1, that Joshua sent three explicit warnings before entering into the land [of Canaan], the first: who wishes to run away may do so, . . . etc. And, behold, it is in no way clear how did Joshua knew to act thus. And we are forced to assume that he learned to do so from Moses, who acted thus in the wars he directed. So clearly, this is in accordance with R. Natan's view that he left a place through which the enemy could escape. And on this *beraita* [in Y. *Sheviit*] did R. Natan base his ruling, and since that [*Sheviit*] *beraita* is anonymous and is in accordance with R. Natan's view – circular reasoning?! – for this reason Rambam ruled accordingly. And this is what he meant by *mi-pi-ha-shmuah*, namely from Joshua's actions they learned that this was how Moses acted.

Recently, Adiel Schremer, in his thought-provoking essay *Towards Critical Halakhic Studies*, New York, 2010 (Tikvah Working Paper 0410), pp. 36–37, gave yet another example of this phenomenon:

> In a famous baraita, found in the Tannaitic midrash on Leviticus, the *Sifra*, and in both Talmudim, the Babylonian Talmud and the Palestinian Talmud, Rabbi Aqiva rejects the traditional accepted and authoritative interpretation of Lev. 15:33, according to which the words והדוה בנדתה are understood to mean that during her menstrual period a woman must actively take measures to be filthy and repulsive in her husband's eyes. That accepted interpretation was held by "The Early Sages" (זקנים הראשונים), a technical term in classical rabbinic texts which indicates the antiquity of the tradition. In contrast to the opinion of these Early Sages, Rabbi Aquiva reasoned that, "If so, she will be considered unfitting by her husband, and he might be inclined to divorce her." As such a result was considered undesirable by Rabbi Aquiva, he re-interpreted the words of the Torah so as to mean that a woman must adorn herself during her menstrual period.[7]
>
> Now, consider Rabbi Aqiva's argument. He does not base himself on any Scriptural text. Neither does he claim that the manner by which the Early Sages understood the words of the Torah is simply wrong. Rather, he claims that such an understanding as held by the Early Sages, that is, accepted by the tradition up to his own days, might yield undesirable results. He is then putting forward a new understanding of the Torah, which is based on, and motivated by, his understanding of the institution of marriage and his value judgment concerning divorce. By no means are these considerations presented by the midrash as stemming from the Torah! Rather, they reflect Rabbi Aquiva's perceptions of that which is good and right, and these perceptions shape, in turn, his halachic stance.

And the reason that the fourth side is left open is because they would not do so leaving no ways for escape, the enemy out of despair would fight to the end of their strength making the task of overcoming them more difficult, and this would not be the case if they were left with a chance of escape.

(Compare what we cited above from the Rambam. And on *Y. Sheviit* 6:1, see Y. Tamar, *Alei Tamar* vol. 2, Givataim, 1980, p. 83.)

7. See Moshe Halbertal, *Interpretative Revolutions in the Making*, Jerusalem, 1994, pp. 16–17.

And though we have by no means exhausted the sources,[8] I believe we have clearly demonstrated the continuing policy of "charitable" non-literal interpretation of Talmud, i.e., canonic, texts to mitigate the cruelty that they would appear to record, and thus encourage a more humane approach.

We shall now turn our attention to a very important study by Moshe Halbertal, in his *People of the Book: Canon, Meaning, and Authority*, Cambridge, Mass. and London, 1977, where on p. 27 et seq. he writes on "Canon and the Principle of Charity." There he explains what Williard Quine has called "the principle of charity," being that "interpretive method that would yield an optimally successful text." (See W.V.O. Quine, *World and Object*, Cambridge Mass., 1960, pp. 58–59.) He continues (p. 28):

> Ronald Dworkin[9] extends Quine's principle of charity in interpretation to the second level. Dworkin claims that the choice between competing interpretations is governed by the criterion of which interpretation shows the work in the best light. In legal interpretation the standard for the best possible interpretation is not aesthetic *but moral. We will select the interpretation that makes the best moral case of the legal material.* According to Dworkin, even those who claim that we must discover the original intention of the legislator base their opinion on the belief that this is the best possible way of reading a legal text. The writer's intention

---

8. Additional sources may be found in Kasher ibid., pp. 263–266, 270. One of the examples he cites is how the rabbis interpreted the verse in Exodus 21:6, which states that the Jewish slave who has his ear bored with an aul shall serve his master for ever (*ve-avado le-olam*). The rabbis interpreted *le-Olam* (forever) as meaning "until the Jubilee year," (*B. Kiddushin* 15a; see Kasher, ibid., pp. 41–42, nos. 139–142, and his notes 139–142). The Rashbam agrees that the *pshat* of the verse means "throughout all his life," and so too the Gaon of Vilna in his *Aderet Eliyahu*. Nonetheless, the Rabbis interpreted *le-olam* as "up to the Jubilee year," which could actually be the following year. Thus, the rabbis shortened the period of slavery even of one who wished to remain under his master's domination. And see Kasher's continuing discussion of the Rambam's view on this issue that when there is no Jubilee the word *olam* is taken in its literal sense, and the slave remain in servitude till his dying day. But subsequent dissenting opinions argued that when there is no Jubilee year, there can be no voluntary continuance of slavery (*Shaagat Aryeh ha-Hadashot*, sect.15, on the basis of *B. Eruvin* 33 and *B. Kiddushin* 15a, Kasher ibid.).

9. See Christine Hayes, "Legal Truth, Right Answers and Bad Answers: Dworkin and the Rabbis" *Dinei Yisrael* 25, 2008, p. 73x – 121xx. And see also above, Appendix 2, pp. 276–277 note 9 for additional bibliographic references.

does not provide an independent criterion for establishing the meaning of the text; Dworkin rejects that standard and argues that those who adopt it do so for political reasons. In their view, this is the only way that the legal system can achieve stability and be freed from the arbitrariness of the interpreter – the judge. Their prime guiding principle of interpretation is a value judgment concerning the optimal interpretative strategy, not an objective standard for interpretation. Moreover, according to Dworkin, in reconstructing the writer's intention we attempt to present it in the best possible light. Interpretation is thus closely linked to evaluation, and value serves as the ultimate standard for interpretation.

(See R. Dworkin, *Law's Empire*, Cambridge, Mass., 1985, pp. 58–63.) He then goes on (p. 29) as follows:

> In the case of a sacred text the speaker is God and it is thus by definition perfect; not only can no contradictions exist but the text is the best possible. Such an assumption naturally influences the way the text is read in relation to other sources that seem less perfect in comparison. Reading a holy text requires using the principle of charity as generously as possible in interpreting it, since it is inconceivable that such a text could err. We apply the principle of charity in our reading of a holy text not only to ensure its meaningfulness when literal interpretation creates an impression of meaninglessness, *but also to ensure that it corresponds to the highest criteria of perfection. In the case of the Scriptures, there is an a priori interpretative commitment to show the text in the best possible light.* Conversely, the loss of this sense of obligation to the text is an undeniable sign that it is no longer perceived as holy. Making use of the principle of charity, the following principle can be stipulated: the degree of canonicity of a text corresponds to the amount of charity it receives in its interpretation. The more canonical a text, the more generous its treatment. (My emphasis – D.S.)
>
> A conscious expression of the principle of pure charity in reading of Scripture is found in Maimonides' declaration in the *Guide to the Perplexed*:
>
> Know that our shunning the affirmation of the eternity of the world is not due to a text figuring in the Torah according to which the world has been produced in time. For the texts indicating that the world has been produced in time are not more numerous than those indicating that the

deity is a body. Nor are the gates of figurative interpretation shut in our faces or impossible of access to us regarding the subject of the creation of the world in time. For we could interpret them as figurative, as we have done when denying His corporeality (II, 25).

Halbertal (pp. 30–32), then shows that there is an opposing view, one in which:

> ... the reader must suspend his moral judgment facing the sacred text. The reader is not required to redefine his moral principles completely, but is forbidden to accommodate the text to these principles in the face of a contradictory commandment of God. It is the text that must determine the interpeter's concept of charity. He cannot postulate a conception of justice or truth that he formulated before his encounter with the text and still interpret the text in the best possible light. The holiness and authority of the text is so all-encompassing that it alone determines the concepts of good and evil, tuth and falsity; no other criterion exists by which it can be interpreted.

This would appear to be R. Eliezer's position, referred to above. Hence argues Halbertal:

> Interpretation of Scripture is thus divided into two opposing attitudes toward the principle of charity in interpretation. One claims that its nature as a sacred text demands absolute abstention from the principle of charity, since the text alone determines what is charity ...
>
>   These two contrary positions on reading Scripture "with charity" share one assumption: what is written in Scripture is truth. The dispute between [them] resides in their respective solutions to problems of apparent contradiction between Scripture and truth. In these cases, should Scripture be accommodated to the readers' beliefs about truth, or should those beliefs be accommodated to the meaning of Scripture?

I believe that in the areas of halachah at any rate – but not necessarily in the area of philosophy also discussed by Halbertal – the overarching position is the use of the Quine-Dworkin "principle of charity" in order to reach the best possible *moral* interpretation. And if this be the tendency of the overwhelming majority of early rabbinic Sages, and subsequent authorities throughout the following generations,[10] this should constitute the metaphorical "guidepost" orienting our direction in *psikat halachah*, towards one, in which "its ways are the ways of pleasantness."[11]

Finally, I would like to explain my understanding of the theological rationale for the reinterpretation of biblical texts. For if we truly believe that our Torah is a divine formulation, and that in the words of the Maimonidean inspired piyyut, *Yigdal,* "God will not change His law for any for all eternity", then we must also accept that it was intended to be understood/interpreted for all generations in accordance with their contemporary situations: that is to say, encoded or encapsulated within it are all true past, present and future understandings.

To use a simile: a given scene, let us say of inanimate objects, alters its appearance throughout the day or with the various seasons, with the changing light. A reel of photographic film will accurately and faithfully record these appearances, though each frame will be different.

And not only changes in time alter appearances and perspectives , but also variations of angles, differation of lenses etc. "Reality", then, in itself is new and can never be seen by the same person at two different moments (- a theme made chillingly evident in the film *Rashomon,* and

---

10. David Weiss Halivni, in his *Peshat and Derash: Plain and Applied Meaning in Rabbinic Exegesis,* New York and London, 1991, pass., has a somewhat different explanation as to rabbinic deviation from literal understanding of the Biblical text, which I find somewhat problematic. Nonetheless, my suggestions do not necessarily contradict his approach, but merely supplement it.

11. Returning to the "eye for an eye" issue, we may also comment that lopping off a person's limb might constitute a punishment that would warn off others from acting in this fashion, but it hardly helps the injured party. Monetary compensation is, therefore, not only a means of repentence (*teshuvah*) and expiation (*kappara*), but also serves as a form of social amelioration (*tikun olam*), and is therefore a more satisfactory and ethical way of "interpreting" the biblical text.

Indeed, this is also the rationale behind *takanot ha-shavim* discussed above in the section "Encouraging Repentence." For the rabbis were clearly aware that most people would not take apart the roof of their apartment in order to return a stolen bean. So, despite the fact that this is what biblical law really requires, the rabbis saw no point in trying to keep to this law as it is biblically, since the thief will neither be repentant, nor will the original owner of the bean have any sort of satisfaction, monetary or otherwise. It is far better to permit or obligate the thief to make a monetary compensation, enabling him to rectify and compensate the person from whom he stolen. Indeed, this is obviously at the basis of all the cases of damages, namely that punishment should also be compensatory to the damaged.

also in Durrell" *Alexandria quartet*).[12] So by analogy, coevally a variety of interpretations of a single text may be both truthful and legitimate. That, I believe, is what the Rabbis intimated when they said that there are multiple facets to the Torah,[13] like sparks flying off the hammered anvil, the anvil being the Torah, and the glittering sparks, those manifold comprehensions, at a bewildering variety of levels, that brilliantly illuminate the single anvil-text.[14]

What, however constitutes "truthful and legitimate" interpretation, as opposed to a false one, is a very challenging question. We can only hope, that by following the classical homiletic parameters with true intellectual integrity, and with *siyyata de-shemaya*, we will not be "severing the shoots" (cf. *B. Hagigah* 15a) but remain firmly rooted in our sources, allowing a healthy growth of those "shoots". For our Torah is like a deeply enplanted "tree of life to them that hold fast unto her (*Proverbs* 3:18).

---

12. Durrell's tetralogy of novels, published between 1958 and 1960, offer the same sequence of events through several points of view, allowing individual perspectives of a single set of events, as the author explains in the Preface to the second volume of the quartet, *Balthazar*, (1958). It is, therefore, an explanation of relativity and the notions of continuum and subject-object relation.

13. Midrash Psalms 12:7, *B. Shabbat* 88b, *B. Sanhedrin* 34a, etc.

14. That is why, for instance, R. Yitzhak bar Yossi Mehozaah could every day say *milin hadetin be-Oraita*, literally "new words," i.e., explanations, interpretations, in the Torah (*Zohar* 1, 63b), etc.

SUBJECT INDEX

adjudication: Gaon of Vilna and, 307; *"ha-emet le-horaah"* and, 273n3; halachic, 45–54, 300; legitimacy of new, 34n7; lenient, 266; *posek* and, 281; rabbinic, 26, 266; sin of indolence in, 200–203

aggadah, 95n47, 184; halachah versus, 150, 150–155n96, 169n6

agunah (agunot), 11, 36, 133–134, 133n84, 279, 289n12. *See also* women

Aharonim, 32, 60, 93n45, 125, 138n88, 171n6, 256n8, 282n7, 283n7, 298n1, 307, 311–312; on testimony, 278–279n4

ain aniyut bi-mekom ashirut, principle of, 45n2, 46n2. *See also* ha-Torah Hasah al Mamonam shel Yisrael

ain anu muzharim kol kach, 48n3

am (amei) Ha-aretz, 126, 273, 287, 298n1

amidah. *See* prayer

Amoraim, 201, 273, 287, 298n1

anaf etz avot, 54

artificial insemination, 102

asmachta, 40, 40n1

atarah, 72. *See also* tallit

Av (month), 51n5, 52n5, 98n50, 207, 207n22. *See also* Tisha b'Av

Av beit din, 242

baal keri (seminal emission), 98, 251–252

baalot (*baal, baalei*) *teshuvah*, 146, 159, 296

ba'al tashhit, principle of, 44n2, 45n2

bat kol (heavenly voice), 33, 115, 273, 274

beit din (court of law), 72, 115, 164n107, 267, 290, 302, 303n7; conversion and, 104; divorce and, 142n89 overruling another, 298; women not called to, 63

benevolence, 114; expressed in a number of ways, 192; quality of, 193, 197. *See also* charity, *hesed*

birkat erusin, 84. *See also* wedding

birkat-Kohanim, 90

bi-mekom tza'ar lo gazru rabbanan, principle of, 100

birth control, 36, 57n9, 60

The Blind (story), 253–260

blind eye, casting a, 12, 141–149, 227n36, 230n36, 231n36

blind people, 251n2, 253–260, 265n14, 289

branding, 170n6, 327n5

brit milah. *See* circumcision

Charcoal and Distress (*B. Berachot 28a*) (story), 186–188

charity, 113, 114, 197, 205, 211, 211n29, 332; feeding a guest, 92n44; giving at night time, 209, 209n24; giving to the poor, 204n18, 204–205, 209; Maimonides and, 333–334; mitzvot relating to, 204n18; non-observant communities and, 229n36; Quine-Dworkin principle of, 332–333, 334; R. Hanina bar Papa and, 209; R. Hayyim's, 135n86; R. Kook's ruling on, 229n36; R. Yonah

337

NAME INDEX

Aba ha-Cohen bar Papa, 73
Aba Oshaiah of Turia, 119
Abba (R.), 75, 269
Abbaye, 73, 256n8
Abele, Avraham (R.), 226n36
Abraham (son of Rambam), R.,
    283n7, 300–301
Abraham, 78, 88, 134, 210,
    248n54, 279, 292n15, 330n6
Abuhatzeira, Yosef Hayyim Masud
    (R.), 124
Adani, Shlomo ha- (R.), 268
Aha bar Rav Hanina (R.), 173
Alfandari, Eliyahu (R.), 245n49
Alfasi, Yitzhak (Rif) (R.), 70n18,
    164n107, 308
Alsheich, Moshe (R.), 273, 314n4
Altaretz, Yehudah (R.), 177n10
Alter, Yitzhak Meir (Rebbe of Ger),
    43n2, 219Amar, Zohar, 49n3,
    50n3
Ami (R.), 186n18, 231n36. See
    also R. Imi
Amital, Yehuda (R.), 34n8, 39n1,
    74n21, 132n82
Ammi (R.), 172
Ammon, 128
Amram Gaon (R.), 174n10
Amsterdam, Naftali (R.), 221
Anan ben David, 324n3
Angel, Marc C., 58, 94, 136
Annenberg, Walter, 35
Arauro, Yitzhar (R.), 187n18
Ariel, Yaakov (R.), 92
Asa, 241n43
Asher ben Jehiel (Rosh) (R.), 26,
    51n5, 55n7, 70n18, 93, 107n63,
    109n66, 162n107, 164n107,
    170n6, 195n5, 216, 231n36,
    250, 251, 278, 291n13, 299n2,
    300, 301, 310, 327n5

Ashi (R.), 111n66, 177, 231n36,
    287
Ashkenazi, Shmuel (R.), 281n7
Ashkenazi, Yosef (R.), 179n11
Asi (R.), 186n18
Auerbach, Shlomo Zalman (R.),
    90, 106n82, 258n9, 263–264
Avimelech, 292n15
Avraham, Avraham-Sofer, 250n1,
    257n8, 258n9, 261n10
Avraham ben ha-Rambam (R.),
    323
Avraham ben Shlomo (R.), 251
Avraham-Abush (R.), 290–291,
    291n13
Ayash, Yehuda (R.), 81–82
Azria de Rossi, 323n1

Baal ha-Itur, 156
Ba'al ha-Tanya, 171n6
Baal ha-Turim, Yaakov, 170n6
Baal Shem Tov, 80, 226n36
Bachrach, Yair Hayyim (R.), 96,
    126
Bahya, Rabbenu, 41, 55n7,
    248n53, 248n54
Bar Bei Rav, 178n11
Barda, Yitzhak (R.), 283n7
Bar-Ilan, Meir (R.), 222
Bar-Ilan, Naftali Tzvi Yehuda,
    212n29
Bar-Kappara, 155n96
Bar-Zakkai, Yisrael, 199n12
Barzilai, Moshe (R.), 250
Beer Haiteiv, 203, 208, 231n36
Beer, Moshe, 165n2, 168n6,
    169n6, 186n18
Belial, 147
Belzer Rebbe, 181n11
Ben Azzai, 183
Ben Zuta, 324

350

SOURCE INDEX

OLD TESTAMENT

MISHNAH

BAVLI AND COMMENTARIES

MIDRESHEI HALACHAH VE-AGGADAH

RAMBAM AND COMMENTARIES

OTHER HALACHIC WORKS BY THE RAMBAM

TUR AND SHULCHAN ARUCH AND COMMENTARIES

ABOUT THE AUTHORS

Rabbi Professor DANIEL SPERBER is a leading scholar of Jewish law, customs, and ethics. He taught in the Talmud Department of Bar-Ilan University, where he also served as dean of the Faculty of Jewish Studies and president of the Jesselson Institute for Advanced Torah Studies. In 1992, he was awarded the Israel Prize for Jewish Studies. Prof. Sperber currently serves as rabbi of the Menachem Zion Synagogue in the Old City of Jerusalem.

The descendant of a line of distinguished Orthodox rabbis, Prof. Sperber was born in 1940 in a castle in Ruthin, Wales, and studied in the Yeshivot of Kol Torah and Hevron in Jerusalem. He earned a BA in art history at the Courtauld Institute of Art and received a PhD in classics, ancient history, and Hebrew studies from University College, London.

Prof. Sperber has published more than thirty books and four hundred articles on the subjects of Talmudic and Jewish socio-economic history, law and customs, classical philology, and Jewish art. Among his major works is a well-known, eight-volume series, *Minhagei Yisrael*, on the history of Jewish customs. More recently, he has written books on halachic methodology and rabbinic decision-making in confrontation with modernity, and has established an independent *beit din* dealing with *agunah* issues. He is the author of *On Changes in Jewish Liturgy: Options and Limitations*; *On the Relationship of Mitzvot Between Man and His Neighbor and Man and His Maker*; and *Rabba, Maharat, Rabbanit, Rebbetzin: Women with Leadership Authority According to Halachah*, all published by Urim Publications.

Rabbi DOV LINZER is the President and Rosh HaYeshiva of Yeshivat Chovevei Torah Rabbinical School, and is the primary architect of its groundbreaking curriculum. Rabbi Linzer has been a leading rabbinic voice in the Modern Orthodox community for over 20 years. He hosts a number of highly popular podcasts, including "Joy of Text," "*Iggros Moshe* A to Z," and his *"Daf Yomi"* podcast, covering all of *shas*. Rabbi Linzer has published many Torah articles, writes a widely-read weekly parsha sheet, and authors *teshuvot* on a wide range of contemporary halachic topics. He teaches regular classes in advanced Talmud, advanced halachah and the thought of Modern Orthodoxy, and serves as a religious guide to the yeshiva's current rabbinical students and over 125 rabbis serving in the field.

CHAIM TRACHTMAN is chief of pediatric nephrology at NYU Langone Medical Center. He is on the board of Yeshivat Maharat and is editor of the book *Women and Men in Communal Prayer: Halakhic Perspectives* (Ktav, 2010).